P9-DBL-583

GREAT FOOD
Fast & Easy!

Every family cook with a busy schedule needs menu ideas that are tasty, inventive, easy to assemble and appealing to young and old alike. Sound impossible? Not with this year's QUICK COOKING ANNUAL RECIPES!

This 14th edition in our ever-popular *Quick Cooking Annual Recipes* series features every single dish that appeared in *Simple & Delicious* magazine during 2011. Plus, you get dozens of helpful hints. It all adds up to more than 600 recipes and tips!

With hundreds of beautiful, full-color photos showing the delicious recipes already prepared, this collection of go-to dishes will make it easier than ever for you to serve up scrumptious, homemade meals on a regular basis.

Here's what else you'll find inside:

■ QUICK—TASTY—SATISFYING ■

20 CONVENIENT CHAPTERS

If you turn to the Table of Contents on page 3, you'll find the chapters, which start with "Readers' Favorite Fast Meals" and end with "Easy Odds & Ends."

One glance and it will be obvious that there's a chapter for all your recipe needs. Want to eat healthier? See "Lightened-Up Delights," which is full of calorie-conscious recipes with Nutrition Facts. Looking for treats for your next gathering? Turn to "Appetizers & Beverages," "Holiday & Seasonal Pleasers" or "Effortless Entertaining."

All of these recipes are fast, but the "30 Minutes to Mealtime," "Finished in 15 Minutes" and "Give Me 5 or Fewer" chapters might be exactly what you need when looking for super-quick dishes!

SIX-WEEK MENU PLANNER

The experts in our Test Kitchen put their best recipes together to create the "Shop Once...Eat All Week" chapter, which offers six weeks worth of shopping lists and recipes. The order of the meals throughout the week is up to you, so you can personalize them according to your own schedule.

CONTEST-WINNING DISHES

Turn to page 4 to see which recipes earned honors in the six national recipe contests held last year. You'll also find the Grand Prize winners. Each winning recipe includes the page number, so you can easily locate it in the book.

TIPS & SECRETS FOR SIMPLE COOKING

You'll find helpful tip boxes full of kitchen and shopping wisdom scattered throughout the book. And two chapters, "Test Kitchen Secrets" and "Easy Odds & Ends," focus on cooking techniques, such as making omelets, budget cooking, grilling and from-scratch condiments, so curious cooks can improve their kitchen skills and recipe repertoire.

TWO HANDY INDEXES

See the General Recipe Index on page 314 to locate any recipe by category and/or major ingredient...or check the Alphabetical Index on page 331 when you're looking for a specific dish by name. In both indexes, you'll find a red checkmark (✓) next to recipes that include Nutrition Facts.

Our Test Kitchen experts selected every rapid recipe in this collection with on-the-go cooks like you in mind. So no matter how hectic your schedule may be, you and your family can enjoy this essential cookbook for years to come.

taste of home 2012 quick COOKING ANNUAL RECIPES

p. 99

p. 118

p. 240

EDITOR IN CHIEF: Catherine Cassidy
VICE PRESIDENT, EXECUTIVE EDITOR/BOOKS: Heidi Reuter Lloyd
CREATIVE DIRECTOR: Howard Greenberg
FOOD DIRECTOR: Diane Werner, RD
SENIOR EDITOR/BOOKS: Mark Hagen
EDITORS: Krista Lanphier, Michelle Rozumalski
ASSOCIATE CREATIVE DIRECTOR: Edwin Robles, Jr.
ART DIRECTOR: Gretchen Trautman
FOOD EDITOR: Amy Welk-Thieding, RD
CONTENT PRODUCTION MANAGER: Julie Wagner
DESIGN LAYOUT ARTIST: Nancy Novak
COPY CHIEF: Deb Warlaumont Mulvey
PROJECT COPY EDITOR: Barbara Schuetz
RECIPE ASSET SYSTEM MANAGER: Coleen Martin
RECIPE TESTING AND EDITING: Taste of Home Test Kitchen
FOOD PHOTOGRAPHY: Taste of Home Photo Studio
ADMINISTRATIVE ASSISTANT: Barb Czysz
COVER PHOTOGRAPHER: Rob Hagen
COVER FOOD STYLIST: Alynna Molson
COVER SET STYLIST: Dee Dee Jacq

NORTH AMERICAN CHIEF MARKETING OFFICER: Lisa Karpinski
VICE PRESIDENT/BOOK MARKETING: Dan Fink
CREATIVE DIRECTOR/CREATIVE MARKETING: Jim Palmen

THE READER'S DIGEST ASSOCIATION, INC.
PRESIDENT AND CHIEF EXECUTIVE OFFICER: Robert E. Guth
EXECUTIVE VICE PRESIDENT, RDA AND PRESIDENT, NORTH AMERICA: Dan Lagani

INTERNATIONAL STANDARD BOOK NUMBER (10): 0-89821-975-2
INTERNATIONAL STANDARD BOOK NUMBER (13): 978-0-89821-975-3
INTERNATIONAL SERIAL NUMBER: 1522-6603

Printed in U.S.A.
1 3 5 7 9 10 8 6 4 2

PICTURED ON FRONT COVER:
Make-Ahead Lasagna (p. 245), Chive and Cheese Breadsticks (p. 81), Italian Spinach Salad (p. 104) and Chocolate Frosted Peanut Butter Cupcakes (p. 80).

PICTURED ON BACK COVER:
Unstuffed Jalapeno Popper Burgers (p. 124), Chipotle-Black Bean Chili (p. 190), Polenta Rounds with Sausage Ragout (p. 14), Slow-Cooker Bread Pudding (p. 172), Apple-Sage Roasted Turkey (p. 35) and Potato & Bacon Frittata (p. 296).

Contents

RECIPE CONTESTS YIELD QUICK WINNERS....4
See a list of all of the contest-winning recipes from the past year, including the Grand Prize winners.

READER'S FAVORITE FAST MEALS....6
Busy cooks who are big fans of *Simple & Delicious* magazine share dinners they rely on regularly.

HOLIDAY & SEASONAL PLEASERS....20
Your special celebrations will go smoothly with these festive meals and delectable sweets.

30 MINUTES TO MEALTIME....44
Every meal in this chapter can be prepared in half an hour or less.

COOKING FOR KIDS....70
Kids will love these delightful recipes, from whimsical snacks to wholesome dinners.

GIVE ME 5 OR FEWER....82
These recipes require just five ingredients or less for streamlined dishes that don't skimp on taste.

FINISHED IN 15 MINUTES....96
When you need food on the table quick, you can find delicious yet super-fast fare here.

SHOP ONCE...EAT ALL WEEK....108
Enjoy six weeks of dinners planned out for you along with complete shopping lists.

SPEEDY SIDES & SALADS....128
It's easy to find speedy main course accompaniments with the delicious ideas in this chapter.

EFFORTLESS ENTERTAINING....140
These wonderful recipes will help to make your party planning a breeze.

SLOW-COOKED SENSATIONS....154
After preparing these dishes, which come together easily, the slow cooker does the work for you.

BREAKFAST & BRUNCH FAVORITES....174
Your family won't be able to resist this incredible variety of yummy morning fare.

QUICK SOUPS & SANDWICHES....186
This classic pairing makes a perfect lunch or light dinner any day of the week.

EXPRESS ENTREES....198
It takes only half an hour or less to get each of these delicious main courses on the table.

DELECTABLE DESSERTS....216
These recipes prove that decadent dinner finales do not have to take all day to make!

MAKE-AHEAD MARVELS....238
By making double dishes now, you reap the rewards later when supper takes hardly any time to prepare.

CASSEROLES & OVEN SUPPERS....250
Bubbling casseroles and hot dishes fresh from the oven are guaranteed family pleasers.

LIGHTENED-UP DELIGHTS....266
If you're trying to eat healthier by reducing fat, sugar or salt from your diet, then these dishes are for you.

APPETIZERS & BEVERAGES....278
These tasty, easy-to-make snack and drink recipes will tide everyone over until mealtime.

TEST KITCHEN SECRETS....290
Our Test Kitchen shares clever hints and techniques to speed up your cooking.

EASY ODDS & ENDS....302
This chapter features easy stovetop suppers, delicious grilled entrees and homemade condiments.

GENERAL RECIPE INDEX....314
Every recipe in this book is listed according to food category, major ingredient and/or cooking method.

ALPHABETICAL RECIPE INDEX....331
Every recipe in this book is listed alphabetically by the recipe name.

A YEAR OF RECIPE CONTEST WINNERS

LET'S DO BRUNCH

During the season of giving, Pamela Shank offers family and friends in Parkersburg, West Virginia, gifts money just can't buy. "I feel like cooking and baking are such a part of me, a special gift that I inherited from my mother, and a way to show people how much I care about them," says this grand-prize winner in our brunch contest.

Her winning Southwest Breakfast Tart is a delicious example. It blew our judges away with its easy prep and hearty flavors. She developed the recipe herself and prepares it at least once a month for company.

GRAND PRIZE
Southwest Breakfast Tart .... p. 180

2ND PLACE
Tiramisu Crepes .... p. 178

3RD PLACE
Breakfast Tortas .... p. 182

4TH PLACE
Gingerbread Scones with Lemon Butter .... p. 181

RUNNERS-UP
Apricot & White Chocolate Coffee Cake .... p. 29
Baked Fruit Compote .... p. 182
Brie and Sausage Brunch Bake .... p. 176
Cinnamon Roll Coffee Cake .... p. 185
Crab Quiche .... p. 176
Cranberry Orange Pancakes .... p. 177
Crustless Quiche Bake .... p. 179
Hash Brown Pancetta Casserole .... p. 184

SENSATIONAL CITRUS

A little lemon goes a long way. Just ask Geneva Garrison of Jacksonville, Florida, winner of our citrus contest. Or perhaps ask her husband. "The lemon in my chicken recipe comes from my husband, who can't stay out of the kitchen when I'm cooking. He likes to go to the fridge, grab some lemons and squeeze them all over the chicken," she explains. "So I added the lemon sauce for even more lemon flavor. Now it's a family favorite."

GRAND PRIZE
Roasted Chicken with Lemon Sauce .... p. 265

2ND PLACE
Best Lime Tart .... p. 222

3RD PLACE
Halibut with Orange Salsa .... p. 263

4TH PLACE
Sunshine Cobbler .... p. 237

RUNNERS-UP
Caramelized Grapefruit Salad .... p. 137
Chicken Skewers with Sweet & Spicy Marmalade .... p. 280
Coconut Citrus Bars .... p. 233
Key Lime Bites .... p. 236
Orange Chicken Wraps .... p. 197
Salsa Roja .... p. 106
Tangerine Tabouleh .... p. 136
Zesty Lemon Broccoli .... p. 107

MAKE-AHEAD MARVELS

Erin Chilcoat's colorful Blue Cheese Walnut Tart earned the Grand Prize. With its rich flavors and hint of heat, this tasty tart was an instant hit with our judges. But what really won them over was its convenience and freezer-friendly preparation that lets you heat and eat when time's tight.

Erin, from Smithtown, New York, and her husband love this elegant dish for special meals. "Whenever we entertain, I prefer to serve a number of smaller portions. I often turn to this recipe for such occasions because it's not only a cinch to put together, but it can be made in advance. Leftovers are perfect for lunch the next day."

GRAND PRIZE
Blue Cheese Walnut Tart .... p. 247

2ND PLACE
Italian Brunch Bake .... p. 246

3RD PLACE
Moist Turkey Breast with White Wine Gravy .... p. 169

4TH PLACE
Three-Cheese & Pepper Penne .... p. 249

RUNNERS-UP
Burrito Pie .... p. 245
Chipotle-Black Bean Chili .... p. 190
Company Lasagna .... p. 242
Country Chicken Casserole .... p. 244
Family-Favorite Beef Roast .... p. 166
Spring Morning Casserole .... p. 241
Tater Tot Casseroles .... p. 242
Tex-Mex Chicken with Black Beans & Rice .... p. 171

FAST AND FRESH-PICKED

Inspired by shows and chefs like Julia Child, Wolfgang Puck and Jacques Pepin, Jodie Gharbi of Shreveport, Louisiana, started cooking for her family at the age of 10. "I watched cooking shows, made a list of ingredients, and my mother took me shopping to get what I needed for the week," she says. "I learned baking skills from my mother, and my dad was great on the grill. I later learned classical French techniques by earning my degree at Le Cordon Bleu College of Culinary Arts in Austin, Texas, and worked in a few local restaurants and bakeries."

Now married and working as a French teacher at a local high school, Jodie makes sit-down meals for her husband, John (a radar navigator in the Air Force), and herself five nights a week. "We follow a very healthy diet, so we eat veggies and fruits from our garden, whole grains, and lean organic meats and seafood." So it's no wonder that her beautiful Fresh Tomato & Cucumber Salad is filled with garden-picked flavors. "I created the recipe for a dinner party at a friend's house. I'm so excited to share the recipe," she says. "I hope you all enjoy it!"

GRAND PRIZE
Fresh Tomato & Cucumber Salad.................................. p. 134

2ND PLACE
BBQ Shrimp Quesadillas .... p. 307

3RD PLACE
Strawberry Ginger Tart .... p. 228

4TH PLACE
Maple-Glazed Green Beans.. p. 134

RUNNERS-UP
Cilantro-Pepita Pesto .... p. 312
Greek Grilled Chicken Pitas.. p. 243
Lemonade Fruit Salad .... p. 133
Melon-Mango Salsa... p. 284
Prosciutto-Wrapped Asparagus with Raspberry Sauce .... p. 86
Roasted Grape Tomatoes .... p. 283
Tropical Guacamole... p. 285
Watermelon Spritzer.. p. 243

DUDE FOOD

Dan Mayer is one lucky dude. His wife Shanon invented a recipe that our contest judges considered so awe-inspiring, so absolutely mouthwatering and so wrong, that it's right—so they had to award it the grand prize in our "Dude Food" contest. "Meat-atarian Subs are truly my husband's favorite meal," says Shanon, a working mom of two from Mountain View, Wyoming.

Shanon's sub was made by accident. "I didn't have enough butter to make garlic bread, so I added a little mayo instead. I love Italian sandwiches, and I just put the two together," she says. Though her husband would love to eat these winning subs every night, Shanon prefers to plan weekly or monthly menus with a healthy balance of great-tasting foods.

GRAND PRIZE
Meat-atarian Sub... p. 189

2ND PLACE
Chili-Cheese Egg Rolls.. p. 285

3RD PLACE
Chipotle-Honey Grilled T-Bones .... p. 309

4TH PLACE
Chocolate Frosted Peanut Butter Cupcakes................... p. 80

RUNNERS-UP
Big Daddy's BBQ Ribs .... p. 260
Bourbon Brat Skewers.. p. 308
Breakfast Biscuit Cups .... p. 183
Mexican-Seasoned Grilled Chicken .... p. 309
Pepperoni Pizza Chili .... p. 195
Pulled Pork Taters .... p. 170
Steak House Burgers .... p. 194
Touchdown Brat Sliders .... p. 195

OUT-OF-THE-BOX DESSERTS

Inspired by snickerdoodles, Maiah Albi made magic with a box of white cake mix. Cinnamon & Sugar Cake, her translation from cookie to cake, won the grand prize. "I was trying to develop something different," she recalls. "Snickerdoodle flavor is good in cookies, so I thought, why not translate it to a cake?"

The Carlsbad, California, cook learned to bake in her mom's kitchen. "When my twin sister and I were young, Mom had us help make chocolate chip cookies or carrot cake. She also taught us how to make zucchini bread. Eventually I taught myself how to bake. With this cake, don't be afraid to use your favorite flavors."

GRAND PRIZE
Cinnamon & Sugar Cake .... p. 219

2ND PLACE
Chocolate Cannoli Cake Roll... p. 224

3RD PLACE
German Chocolate Thumbprint Cookies........................ p. 230

4TH PLACE
Pumpkin Streusel Cupcakes .... p. 232

RUNNERS-UP
Caramel-Pecan Dream Bars.. p. 225
Chocolate-Peanut Cheesecake Bars............................... p. 231
Cranberry-Pear Crisp.. p. 221
Fluted Tiramisu Cake.. p. 219
Lemon Cream Cake .... p. 230
Salted Peanut Bars .... p. 78
Pumpkin Walnut Squares .... p. 233
Triple-Chocolate Cake with Raspberry Sauce................. p. 228

CHAPTER 1

Readers' Favorite Fast Meals

Every busy cook should have go-to recipes for those days when time is particularly short. These no-fuss meals are just the ticket, because each takes only 30 minutes or less to prepare!

Mouthwatering menus, such as savory Cashew Chicken with Noodles, Almond & Mandarin Orange Salad and, for dessert, Grilled Pineapple Sundaes make food preparation easy, while still providing a delicious dinner for your family!

Why bother with expensive takeout when you can serve quick-to-fix food spreads such as Ginger Pork Stir-Fry, Teriyaki Egg Rolls and Lemon Spiced Tea? This chapter takes the dread out of dinner decisions! ■

FAST AND FABULOUS. Polenta Rounds with Sausage Ragout and Balsamic Arugula Salad (p. 14).

SMALL STEPS TO HUGE FLAVOR

A very special person inspired Jeannie Klugh of Lancaster, Pennsylvania, to cook. "I was brought up like my grandmother, who loved to cook and was great at making something wonderful out of very little," Jeannie says. "She taught me that the most important ingredient in any recipe is passion," a trait Jeannie has plenty of.

Whether she's spending Sunday trying new dishes for the week ahead or playing around in the kitchen with one (or three) of her 11 grandchildren, Jeannie says she loves creating new meals for her family.

She's doing her best to pass that joy down to her grandkids, age 3 to 16, who are a constant source of entertainment. "I love having them around," she says. "I often give them a project and turn them loose. This introduces creativity, which I think is important for young minds. It's fun showing them that it doesn't take much to give menus a lot of flavor."

For exactly $5 per plate (for salmon!), the dinner Jeannie shares here takes that philosophy to the next level. Maple Glazed Salmon wonderfully balances sweet and savory in just four delicious ingredients, while Lemon-Pepper Broccoli is a versatile, stellar go-to with any entree. "Try it with cauliflower or other vegetables," she suggests. But Jeannie's favorite is her Dill Potato Wedges. "I've served them for years." We think you will, too. ■

Tasty Maple-Glazed Salmon

Prep/Total Time: 20 min.

- **2 tablespoons hoisin sauce**
- **2 tablespoons maple syrup**
- **2 teaspoons prepared mustard**
- **4 salmon fillets (6 ounces *each*)**

In a small bowl, combine the hoisin sauce, syrup and mustard; set aside. Place salmon, skin side down, on a greased broiler pan.

Broil 4-6 in. from the heat for 5 minutes. Brush half of the sauce over salmon. Broil 7-10 minutes longer or until fish flakes easily with a fork, brushing occasionally with remaining sauce. **Yield:** 4 servings.

HOISIN SAUCE

A common soy-based ingredient in Chinese cuisine, this sauce is described as sweet, salty and spicy. Used to flavor sauces for stir-fry dishes or as a condiment for Moo Shoo Pork and Peking Duck, hoisin sauce is found in the ethnic section of the grocery store.

Dill Potato Wedges

Prep/Total Time: 15 min.

- **1 package (20 ounces) refrigerated red potato wedges**
- **1/2 teaspoon salt**
- **1/2 teaspoon pepper**
- **1 tablespoon olive oil**
- **2 tablespoons grated Parmesan cheese**
- **1 teaspoon snipped fresh dill *or* 1/4 teaspoon dill weed**

In a large skillet, cook potato wedges, salt and pepper in oil over medium heat for 10-15 minutes or until golden brown, stirring occasionally. Remove from the heat; stir in cheese and dill. **Yield:** 4 servings.

Lemon-Pepper Broccoli

Prep/Total Time: 15 min.

- **5 cups frozen broccoli florets**
- **2 tablespoons water**
- **1 tablespoon butter**
- **1/2 teaspoon lemon-pepper seasoning**
- **1/4 teaspoon salt**
- **1/4 teaspoon pepper**

Place broccoli and water in a microwave-safe bowl. Cover and microwave on high for 6-8 minutes or until broccoli is tender; drain. Add the remaining ingredients; toss to coat. **Yield:** 4 servings.

Editor's Note: This recipe was tested in a 1,100-watt microwave.

TAKE A TRIP TO THE FAR EAST

When it comes to serving good food in a hurry, Adeline Russell of Hartford, Wisconsin, is an old pro. "Like most moms, between work and the kids, I don't have lots of time to cook. Unfortunately, my husband Riley travels a lot for his job, and we don't get to spend as much quality time together as we'd like," Adeline explains. "When he's home, I'd rather be with him instead of in the kitchen, so it's important to me to have good, quick recipes I can count on."

Adeline is also busy with her two children, Joe, 8, and Elizabeth, 6, who are very involved in after-school activities. "They both play soccer, and my daughter goes to dance and gymnastics classes a few nights a week as well," she says. "Between all of our commitments, there's hardly any time to focus on cooking and good food. Some nights, I just want to go home and crash."

When crashing isn't an option, Adeline knows just what to do. "I like to get the kids involved as much as possible with dinner preparation. They love mixing together the stir-fry sauce. I leave out the pepper flakes if the kids are eating with us, but otherwise, it's a true family favorite," she says. ■

Ginger Pork Stir-Fry

Prep/Total Time: 20 min.

2 tablespoons cornstarch
1 cup beef broth
3 tablespoons soy sauce
1 tablespoon sugar
1-1/2 teaspoons ground ginger
1/2 teaspoon garlic powder
1/2 teaspoon crushed red pepper flakes
1 pork tenderloin (1 pound), cut into 2-inch strips
2 tablespoons canola oil, *divided*
1 package (16 ounces) frozen sugar snap stir-fry vegetable blend, thawed
Hot cooked rice
Minced fresh cilantro, optional

In a small bowl, combine the cornstarch and broth until smooth. Stir in soy sauce, sugar, ginger, garlic powder and pepper flakes; set aside.

In a wok or large skillet, stir-fry pork in 1 tablespoon oil until juices run clear. Remove and keep warm. In the same pan, stir-fry vegetables in remaining oil until crisp-tender.

Stir broth mixture and add to the vegetables. Bring to a boil; cook and stir for 1 minute or until thickened. Return pork to the pan; heat through. Serve with rice and sprinkle with cilantro if desired. **Yield:** 4 servings.

Lemon Spiced Tea

Prep/Total Time: 10 min.

4 cups boiling water
7 lemon-flavored tea bags
3 cinnamon sticks (3 inches)
1/4 cup honey
1/4 to 1/2 teaspoon lemon extract, optional
Lemon slices and additional cinnamon sticks

In a large saucepan, bring water to a boil. Remove from the heat; add tea bags and cinnamon sticks. Cover and steep for 6 minutes.

Discard tea bags and cinnamon sticks. Stir in honey and extract if desired. Serve warm in mugs. Garnish with lemon slices and cinnamon sticks. **Yield:** 4 servings.

Teriyaki Egg Rolls

Prep/Total Time: 20 min.

3-1/2 cups coleslaw mix
1 tablespoon canola oil
3 tablespoons teriyaki sauce
4 egg roll wrappers
Oil for deep-fat frying
Sweet-and-sour sauce

In a large skillet, saute coleslaw mix in oil until crisp-tender. Stir in teriyaki sauce; remove from the heat.

Position one egg roll wrapper with a corner facing you. (Keep remaining wrappers covered with a damp paper towel until ready to use.) Using a slotted spoon, spoon about 1/3 cup coleslaw mixture on bottom third of wrapper. Fold bottom corner over filling; fold sides over filling toward center. Moisten the top corner with water; roll up tightly to seal. Repeat with remaining wrappers and filling.

In an electric skillet, heat 1 in. of oil to 375°. Fry egg rolls for 1-2 minutes on each side or until golden brown. Drain on paper towels. Serve with sweet-and-sour sauce. **Yield:** 4 egg rolls.

SEAFOOD MAKES A SPEEDY SUPPER

Quick meals are a busy cook's best friend. In fact, readers have told us that they love speedy suppers so much, we made 30-minute menus the subject of a contest in *Simple & Delicious* magazine, featuring some of the biggest prizes awarded! After testing and tasting the top meals submitted by cooks from across the country, Jennifer Reid of Farmington, Maine, was chosen as the Grand Prize Winner!

A college professor with two grown daughters, Jennifer says cooking is her main hobby. "I learned the basics from my mother, who was a dynamite cook," she says. "From there, it has been trial and error as I've incorporated new cuisines and foods into my daily repertoire."

To simplify meals, Jennifer eats fast breakfasts and lunches during the week and turns to recipes she knows best, such as her delicious winning menu, at dinnertime. "I make these recipes often, as do my family members," she says. "We frequently borrow successful dishes from one another.

"The fish tacos are an adaptation of a dish I was served in Bermuda. They're quick because there's so little prep work involved." For a speedy side, Jennifer serves an avocado salad. "My mother came up with this when she had too many ripe avocados and tomatoes on hand."

Dressed-up strawberries give the meal an elegant finish. With brown sugar and a hint of lime, they're sweet, tangy and so tasty, you'll want more! ■

Southwest Fish Tacos

Prep/Total Time: 20 min.

1-1/2 pounds sole fillets, cut into 1-inch strips
1 tablespoon taco seasoning
1/4 cup butter, cubed
1 package (10 ounces) angel hair coleslaw mix
1/2 cup minced fresh cilantro
1/2 cup reduced-fat mayonnaise
1 tablespoon lime juice
1 teaspoon sugar
1/4 teaspoon salt
1/4 teaspoon pepper
8 taco shells, warmed
8 lime wedges

SUPER CILANTRO

With its slightly sharp flavor, cilantro, also known as Chinese parsley, gives a distinctive taste to Mexican, Latin American and Asian dishes. Like all other fresh herbs, cilantro should be used as soon as possible.

Sprinkle the sole fillets with the taco seasoning. In a large skillet over medium heat, cook the fish in butter for 3-4 minutes on each side or until fish flakes easily with a fork.

Meanwhile, in a small bowl, combine the coleslaw mix, minced cilantro, mayonnaise, lime juice, sugar, salt and pepper.

Place fish in taco shells. Top with coleslaw mixture; serve with lime wedges. **Yield:** 4 servings.

Avocado-Tomato Salad

Prep/Total Time: 10 min.

2 medium ripe avocados, peeled and cubed
2 cups grape tomatoes
1/4 cup thinly sliced red onion
1/4 cup reduced-fat Italian salad dressing
1 tablespoon lime juice
1 teaspoon sugar
1/2 teaspoon chili powder
1/4 teaspoon salt
1/4 teaspoon pepper

In a large bowl, combine the avocados, tomatoes and onion. In a small bowl, whisk the remaining ingredients. Pour over avocado mixture; toss gently to coat. **Yield:** 4 servings.

Dunked Strawberries

Prep/Total Time: 5 min.

1/2 cup sour cream
1/2 teaspoon grated lime peel
1/2 cup packed brown sugar
12 fresh strawberries

In a small bowl, combine sour cream and lime peel. Place brown sugar in another small bowl. Dip strawberries in sour cream mixture; then coat with brown sugar. Serve immediately. **Yield:** 4 servings.

RUSTIC & RAPID ITALIAN FEAST

Kudos go to Lisa Speer of Palm Beach, Florida. Her modern take on Polenta Rounds with Sausage Ragout, Balsamic Arugula Salad and Pistachio Meringue Sundaes won second place in our "Best 30-Minute Menus" contest.

"My primary hobby and passion is creating food," Lisa tells us. "Cooking, baking, grilling—I love it all!"

It's no wonder—cooking is in her blood. "I started cooking and baking with my grandmothers and mother when I was a young girl. I'm grateful to them for teaching me so much."

These days, Lisa prepares meals every day for her husband, mother or friends and also bakes several days a week for a local senior citizens center. Over the years, she has developed her own method for cutting kitchen time.

"I believe the fastest, most satisfying way to cook is to start with the best ingredients and incorporate high-quality premade convenience items when appropriate," she says. "Simple is usually best!"

For her winning meal, ready-made polenta and canned tomatoes make short work of the entree. "It looks and tastes like you've slaved for hours, but it's ready in a flash!" Lisa promises.

Prewashed arugula and prepared meringue shells help the side and dessert come together fast.

"It's the ideal go-to menu—quick, easy, versatile and delicious," she says. We couldn't agree more. ■

Pistachio Meringue Sundaes

Prep/Total Time: 5 min.

- **2 cups pistachio gelato *or* pistachio ice cream**
- **4 miniature meringue cookies *or* vanilla wafers**
- **4 teaspoons chocolate syrup**
- **1/4 cup finely chopped pistachios**

Scoop gelato into four dessert dishes. Top each with a cookie and drizzle with chocolate syrup. Sprinkle with pistachios. **Yield:** 4 servings.

Balsamic Arugula Salad

Prep/Total Time: 5 min.

- **6 cups fresh arugula *or* baby spinach**
- **1/2 cup cherry tomatoes, halved**
- **1/4 cup grated Parmesan cheese**
- **1/4 cup balsamic vinaigrette**

In a large bowl, combine the arugula, tomatoes and cheese. Drizzle with vinaigrette; toss to coat. Serve immediately. **Yield:** 4 servings.

Polenta Rounds with Sausage Ragout

Prep/Total Time: 25 min.

- **1 pound bulk Italian sausage**
- **1 garlic clove, minced**
- **2 cans (14-1/2 ounces *each*) diced tomatoes with basil, oregano and garlic, drained**
- **1/8 teaspoon pepper**
- **1/4 cup minced fresh basil**
- **1 tube (1 pound) polenta, cut into 1/2-inch slices**
- **1/4 cup olive oil**
- **1/2 cup grated Parmesan cheese**

In a large skillet, cook the sausage and garlic over medium heat until sausage is no longer pink; drain. Stir in tomatoes and pepper. Cook and stir for 4-5 minutes or until heated through. Remove from the heat; stir in the basil.

In another skillet, cook polenta slices in oil over medium-high heat for 3-4 minutes on each side or until lightly browned. Serve with sausage mixture; sprinkle with cheese. **Yield:** 4 servings.

PLENTIFUL POLENTA

Polenta is an Italian-style mush that's prepared from cornmeal and water, often flavored with Parmesan or Gorgonzola cheese. It is cooked until thickened and smooth, and served as a side dish much like rice or mashed potatoes. It's an ideal accompaniment to main dishes with sauce or gravy. Premade polenta comes in tubes and can be purchased either in the pasta or produce aisles at the supermarket.

MORNING TREATS MADE EASY

With a hungry husband and toddler to feed, Elisabeth Larsen of Ammon, Idaho, has a few smart, time-saving strategies for getting meals on the table quickly. Her winning 30-minute menu, Cornmeal-Wheat Pancakes, Ham and Avocado Scramble, and Berry Breakfast Smoothies, is a perfect example.

"The whole meal comes together quickly because you can prepare the eggs and pancakes at the same time," says Elisabeth. "We enjoy having special breakfasts, and this meal is one of our favorites."

To speed up the egg dish, "I either buy pre-diced ham or dice leftover ham I've saved," she says. "It really cuts time."

If she's missing an ingredient, she doesn't worry. Elisabeth just substitutes something else her family will like. "You can easily change the fruits or yogurt flavors in the smoothie to fit your family's tastes, too," she says.

While this menu was inspired by memories of her father's weekly pancake breakfasts, it was baking cookies with her mom that sparked a culinary interest when she was young.

"She encouraged me to try recipes and practice cooking in my teenage years," Elisabeth recalls. Even now she likes to try a few new dishes every week, but she especially loves playing around with a recipe and figuring out a twist. As she says, "It makes everyday cooking fun and rewarding!" ■

Ham and Avocado Scramble

Prep/Total Time: 15 min.

8 eggs
1/4 cup 2% milk
1 teaspoon garlic powder
1/4 teaspoon pepper
1 cup cubed fully cooked ham
1 tablespoon butter
1 medium ripe avocado, peeled and cubed
1 cup (4 ounces) shredded Colby-Monterey Jack cheese

In a large bowl, whisk the eggs, milk, garlic powder and pepper; stir in ham. In a large skillet, melt butter over medium-high heat. Add egg mixture; cook and stir until almost set. Stir in avocado and cheese. Cook and stir until completely set. **Yield:** 4 servings.

AVOCADO PREPARATION

Wash avocado, then halve lengthwise, cutting around the seed. Twist halves in opposite directions to separate. Slip a spoon under the seed and remove it. With a large spoon, scoop out the flesh from the skin.

Cornmeal-Wheat Pancakes

Prep: 15 min. **Cook:** 5 min./batch

3/4 cup all-purpose flour
1/2 cup whole wheat flour
1/4 cup cornmeal
2 teaspoons sugar
1 teaspoon salt
1 teaspoon baking powder
3/4 teaspoon baking soda
2 eggs
1-1/2 cups buttermilk
1/4 cup canola oil
HONEY BUTTER:
1/4 cup butter, softened
1/4 cup honey
1 teaspoon ground cinnamon

In a large bowl, combine the first seven ingredients. Combine eggs, buttermilk and oil; add to dry ingredients just until moistened.

Pour batter by 1/4 cupfuls onto a greased hot griddle; turn when bubbles form on top. Cook until the second side is golden brown.

In a small bowl, combine butter, honey and cinnamon. Serve with the pancakes. **Yield:** 12 pancakes (1/2 cup honey butter).

Berry Breakfast Smoothies

Prep/Total Time: 5 min.

2 cups cranberry juice
2 containers (6 ounces *each*) raspberry yogurt
1 cup frozen unsweetened raspberries
1 cup frozen unsweetened blueberries
8 ice cubes

In a blender, combine all ingredients; cover and process for 30-45 seconds or until blended. Pour into chilled glasses; serve immediately. **Yield:** 5 servings.

TASTIER THAN TAKEOUT

Fast can be fabulous, reader Anita Beachy of Bealeton, Virginia, believes, and we couldn't agree more. Her restaurant-quality meal of Almond & Mandarin Orange Salad, Cashew Chicken with Noodles and Grilled Pineapple Sundaes captivated our taste buds, earning her one of three runner-up spots in our Best 30-Minute Menus contest.

"I love recipes that are quick and simple, yet adventurous enough to keep cooking fun," Anita says. Her menu is a mix of family favorites and recipes that evoke "Doesn't this sound amazing!" tidbits from friends.

The single administrative assistant loves to find new recipes and often caters large events at her job. "I'm all about time-saving tips that help me pull off group events, and I try to have a plan that keeps me from cooking for myself every day," she says.

The fourth in a family of six, Anita became a great cook mostly by default, choosing a hobby that older siblings hadn't already taken. "After high school, I took an interest in cooking, so Mom let me take over," she recalls. "Now I don't call my mom with food and cooking questions, she calls me!"

To cut kitchen time, Anita doubles the preparation of meals so she can freeze the extra portion, and strives to do as much as possible ahead of time. And she keeps two goals in mind: Meals have to be simple and balanced. "One, have a plan, and two, be healthy. If you can keep these things in mind, and also keep the meal basic, it's very doable." ■

Cashew Chicken with Noodles

Prep/Total Time: 20 min.

8 ounces uncooked thick rice noodles
1/4 cup soy sauce
2 tablespoons cornstarch
3 garlic cloves, minced
1 pound boneless skinless chicken breasts, cubed
1 tablespoon peanut oil
1 tablespoon sesame oil
6 green onions, cut into 2-inch pieces
1 cup unsalted cashews
2 tablespoons sweet chili sauce

Cook the rice noodles according to package directions. Meanwhile, in a small bowl, combine the soy sauce, cornstarch and minced garlic. Add the chicken. In a large skillet, saute the chicken mixture in the peanut and sesame oils until no longer pink. Add the onions and cook 1 minute longer.

Drain the noodles; stir into skillet. Add cashews and chili sauce and heat through. **Yield:** 4 servings.

Almond & Mandarin Orange Salad

Prep/Total Time: 15 min.

1 package (5 ounces) spring mix salad greens
1 can (11 ounces) mandarin oranges, drained
6 green onions, sliced
3/4 cup slivered almonds
1/2 cup crumbled cooked bacon

VINAIGRETTE:

2 tablespoons olive oil
1 tablespoon plus 1-1/2 teaspoons honey
1 tablespoon white wine vinegar
1/4 teaspoon celery salt
1/4 teaspoon ground mustard
1/4 teaspoon paprika

In a large bowl, combine the first five ingredients. In a small bowl, whisk the vinaigrette ingredients; pour over salad and toss to coat. **Yield:** 6 servings.

Grilled Pineapple Sundaes

Prep/Total Time: 10 min.

4 fresh pineapple slices (about 1/2-inch slices)
4 scoops coconut *or* vanilla ice cream
1 cup whipped topping
1/2 cup hot caramel ice cream topping, warmed
1/4 cup flaked coconut, toasted

Cook pineapple slices on an indoor grill for 2-3 minutes or until heated through. Transfer to individual serving plates. Top each with a scoop of ice cream and whipped topping. Drizzle with ice cream topping; sprinkle with coconut. **Yield:** 4 servings.

CHAPTER 2

Holiday & Seasonal Pleasers

Special occasions are a joyous time full of laughter and good food. These holiday menus will help ensure that the festivities with your family and friends are seamless, by providing straightforward recipes for New Year's all the way through to next Christmas!

For instance, check out the amazing lineup for Easter, which includes Baked Ham with Honey-Chipotle Glaze, Potato and Mushroom Gratin, Green Beans with Tomatoes & Basil, and Makeover Chocolate Truffle Dessert. Wow!

You'll also find fabulous feasts for Mardi Gras, Father's Day, Fourth of July, Halloween and Thanksgiving, with simple-to-follow recipes guaranteed to make your celebrations turn out merry and bright! ■

BOUNTIFUL TABLE. Apple-Sage Roasted Turkey (p. 35).

NEW YEAR'S COUNTDOWN

Ring in the New Year with delectable dishes that are sure to please. Easily impress your guests with the wonderful flavor of these tongue-tingling appetizers. Even better, making Party Vegetable Dip, Sensational Stuffed Mushrooms and Pecan Cheese Logs won't stress you out! For something sweet, what better way to celebrate with friends than with yummy Mocha Dessert Fondue? You and your guests will have a blast kicking off the year with these tasty treats! ■

Party Vegetable Dip

(Pictured below)

Prep: 10 min. + chilling

This is an excellent dip for holiday parties when it's difficult to find time to cook. I've had many compliments on this because it's fast to make, great-tasting and truly enjoyable! —*Amy Engle, Geneva, Nebraska*

2 cups mayonnaise
1-1/2 cups (12 ounces) 4% cottage cheese
1 cup (8 ounces) sour cream
1 envelope (1 ounce) ranch salad dressing mix
1 tablespoon dried minced onion
1/2 teaspoon garlic powder
Assorted fresh vegetables

In a food processor, combine the first six ingredients; cover and process until blended. Transfer to a serving bowl. Cover and refrigerate for 1 hour or until chilled. Serve with vegetables. **Yield:** 4 cups.

Sensational Stuffed Mushrooms

(Pictured at right)

Sometimes I use fewer mushrooms than this recipe calls for and really pile up the stuffing. —*Sandy Harz, Grand Haven, Michigan*

30 large fresh mushrooms
1/2 pound bulk pork sausage
1 package (8 ounces) cream cheese, softened
1 cup dried tart cherries, chopped
2 green onions, chopped

Remove stems from mushrooms (discard stems or save for another use); set caps aside.

In a large skillet, cook sausage over medium heat until no longer pink; drain. Remove from the heat. Stir in the cream cheese, cherries and onions. Stuff into mushroom caps.

Place stuffed mushrooms on greased baking sheets. Bake at 425° for 8-10 minutes or until mushrooms are tender. **Yield:** 2-1/2 dozen.

Mocha Dessert Fondue

(Pictured at right)

Prep/Total Time: 15 min.

I love to entertain, but with a full-time job, a 2-year-old and another one on the way, I don't have a lot of time. This is one of my favorite quick ways to have a memorable night with others. There's nothing like catching up with friends as we gather around a fondue pot!
—Tonya Vowels, Vine Grove, Kentucky

8 ounces semisweet chocolate, chopped
1 can (14 ounces) sweetened condensed milk
1/3 cup strong brewed coffee
Assorted fresh fruit

In a heavy saucepan, melt chocolate with milk over low heat, stirring constantly. Stir coffee into chocolate mixture; keep warm. Serve with assorted fruit. **Yield:** 2-1/2 cups.

Pecan Cheese Logs

Prep: 25 min. + chilling

Monterey Jack, Colby and cream cheese come together with various seasonings to create these logs that everyone truly enjoys. Roll them in toasty pecans for the perfect finishing touch. *—Melissa Goff, Burkburnett, Texas*

1 package (8 ounces) cream cheese, softened
2 cups (8 ounces) shredded Colby cheese
2 cups (8 ounces) shredded Monterey Jack cheese
1/4 cup mayonnaise
1 teaspoon garlic powder
1 teaspoon onion powder
1/4 teaspoon Worcestershire sauce
2 cups chopped pecans, toasted
Butter-flavored crackers

In a large bowl, beat cream cheese until smooth. Stir in the shredded cheeses, mayonnaise, garlic powder, onion powder and Worcestershire sauce. Shape mixture into two logs, about 6 in. long. Roll in pecans, pressing down gently.

Wrap each in plastic wrap; refrigerate for at least 2 hours or overnight. Serve with crackers. **Yield:** 2 logs (12 servings each).

MEAL FOR MARDI GRAS

In French, "Mardi Gras" means Fat Tuesday, the celebration that takes place before Lent, where revelers fill up on ultra-rich food and sweets. Everything a host needs to hold a successful party is here: festive, colorfully decorated Mardi Gras Cupcakes; aromatic New Orleans Gumbo; bite-size Brunch Beignets; and, of course, hearty Captain Russell's Jambalaya. ■

Mardi Gras Cupcakes

(Pictured below)

Prep: 25 min. **Bake:** 20 min. + cooling

Our Test Kitchen staff created these simple gems for Mardi Gras. Take them to a get-together and watch them disappear. Kids love helping decorate them.

1 package (18-1/4 ounces) white cake mix
1 cup (8 ounces) sour cream
2/3 cup canola oil
1/3 cup sugar
4 eggs
3 tablespoons *each* lemon, lime and grape gelatin powder
1 can (16 ounces) cream cheese frosting
Purple, green and yellow sprinkles

In a large bowl, combine the cake mix, sour cream, oil, sugar and eggs; beat on low speed for 30 seconds. Beat on medium for 2 minutes. Divide evenly among three bowls.

Stir one flavor of gelatin powder into each bowl until blended. Fill paper-lined muffin cups with 2 tablespoons of each flavored batter.

Bake at 350° for 18-22 minutes or until a toothpick inserted near the center comes out clean. Cool for 10 minutes before removing from pans to wire racks to cool completely. Frost with cream cheese frosting. Decorate with sprinkles. **Yield:** 2 dozen.

New Orleans Gumbo

(Pictured above)

Prep: 25 min. **Cook:** 20 min.

I'm originally from New Orleans, and I've been making this gumbo for about 30 years. It's a nice taste of the Vieux Carre (French Quarter). Everyone who tries my gumbo wants the recipe; my family requests it often.
—Dolores Bridges, Danville, Kentucky

2 cups chicken broth
1 cup uncooked converted rice
2 celery ribs, chopped
1 medium onion, chopped
2 garlic cloves, minced
1 can (28 ounces) diced tomatoes, undrained
1 pound boneless skinless chicken breasts, cut into 1/2-inch cubes
1/2 pound smoked kielbasa *or* Polish sausage, cut into 1/2-inch slices
1 teaspoon dried thyme
1 teaspoon pepper
2 bay leaves
1/4 teaspoon cayenne pepper
3 tablespoons all-purpose flour
1/4 cup cold water
1 pound uncooked medium shrimp, peeled and deveined
1 large green pepper, chopped
1/4 cup minced fresh parsley

In a large saucepan, bring broth to a boil. Stir in the rice, celery, onion and garlic. Reduce heat; cover and simmer for 20 minutes.

Meanwhile, in a Dutch oven, combine the tomatoes, chicken, kielbasa, thyme, pepper, bay leaves and cayenne. Bring to a boil. Reduce heat; cover and simmer for 10 minutes.

Combine flour and water until smooth; gradually stir into chicken mixture. Stir in shrimp and green pepper. Cook, uncovered, over medium heat for 4-6 minutes or until shrimp turn pink and gumbo is thickened. Discard the bay leaves.

Remove rice from the heat and let stand for 5 minutes; stir in parsley. Serve with gumbo. **Yield:** 8 servings.

Brunch Beignets

(Pictured below)

Prep: 20 min. **Cook:** 5 min./batch

Enjoy breakfast the New Orleans way with these warm, crispy bites. Topped with powdered sugar, they are a delight! —*Lois Rutherford, Elkton, Florida*

2 eggs, *separated*
1 cup all-purpose flour
1 teaspoon baking powder
1/8 teaspoon salt
1/2 cup sugar
1/4 cup water
1 tablespoon butter, melted
2 teaspoons grated lemon peel
1 teaspoon vanilla extract
1 teaspoon brandy, optional
Oil for deep-fat frying
Confectioners' sugar

Place egg whites in a small bowl; let stand at room temperature for 30 minutes.

Meanwhile, in a large bowl, combine the flour, baking powder and salt. Combine the egg yolks, sugar, water, butter, lemon peel, vanilla and brandy if desired; stir into dry ingredients just until combined. Beat the egg whites on medium speed until soft peaks form; fold into the batter.

In an electric skillet or deep-fat fryer, heat oil to 375°. Drop batter by teaspoonfuls, a few at a time, into hot oil. Fry until golden brown, about 1-1/2 minutes on each side. Drain on paper towels. Dust with confectioners' sugar. Serve warm. **Yield:** about 2 dozen.

Captain Russell's Jambalaya

(Pictured above)

Prep: 15 min. **Bake:** 40 min.

A tour guide in New Orleans gave me this recipe. It's so easy to prepare. The deliciously authentic Cajun flavors make it one of my favorite recipes.
—*Donna Lamano, Olathe, Kansas*

1 can (10-1/2 ounces) condensed French onion soup
1-1/4 cups reduced-sodium beef broth
1 can (8 ounces) tomato sauce
1/2 cup butter, cubed
1 small green pepper, chopped
1 small onion, chopped
1-1/2 teaspoons Creole seasoning
1 teaspoon hot pepper sauce
1 pound uncooked medium shrimp, peeled and deveined
1/2 pound fully cooked andouille sausage links, halved lengthwise and cut into 1/2-inch slices
2 cups uncooked long grain rice

In a large saucepan, combine the first eight ingredients. Bring to a boil. Remove from the heat; stir in the shrimp, sausage and rice. Transfer to a greased 13-in. x 9-in. baking dish.

Cover and bake at 375° for 30 minutes. Remove foil and stir; cover and bake 10-15 minutes longer or until rice is tender. **Yield:** 6 servings.

Editor's Note: The following spices may be substituted for 1 teaspoon Creole seasoning: 1/4 teaspoon ***each*** salt, garlic powder and paprika; and a pinch ***each*** of dried thyme, ground cumin and cayenne pepper.

EASTER SUNDAY SPECIALTIES

There are a few holidays that stand out as extra important when it comes to spending time with your family and friends...and Easter is one of those special occasions. For a beautiful meal that will make lasting memories, you've come to the right place!

The Baked Ham with Honey-Chipotle Glaze is sure to dazzle guests with its irresistible flavor, and the two side dishes, Green Beans with Tomatoes & Basil, and Potato and Mushroom Gratin, are real people-pleasers. The dinner finale, Makeover Chocolate Truffle Dessert, will silence everyone—because they'll be too busy indulging! ■

Baked Ham with Honey-Chipotle Glaze

(Pictured below)

Prep: 10 min. **Bake:** 2 hours + standing

Your Easter celebration will be simple to orchestrate with this sweet, smoky ham recipe. Created by our Test Kitchen, it feeds a crowd and tastes fantastic.

1 fully cooked bone-in ham (8 to 10 pounds)
2-1/4 cups ginger ale
1 cup packed brown sugar
3 tablespoons honey
4-1/2 teaspoons cider vinegar
4 chipotle peppers in adobo sauce, minced
2 garlic cloves, minced
1-1/2 teaspoons Dijon mustard
3/4 teaspoon ground cinnamon
3/4 teaspoon ground cumin

Place ham on a rack in a shallow roasting pan. Score the surface of the ham, making diamond shapes 1/2 in. deep. Bake, uncovered, at 325° for 1-1/2 hours.

Meanwhile, in a small saucepan, combine the ginger ale, brown sugar, honey and vinegar. Bring to a boil; cook until glaze is reduced by half, about 15 minutes. Reduce heat. Stir in the remaining ingredients; cook 5 minutes longer. Remove from the heat. Set aside 1 cup for sauce.

Baste the ham with some of the remaining glaze. Bake 30 minutes longer or until a meat thermometer reads 140°, basting twice with additional glaze. Let stand for 10 minutes before slicing. Serve with reserved sauce. **Yield:** 16 servings.

Green Beans with Tomatoes & Basil

Prep/Total Time: 30 min.

Our busy Test Kitchen found this fast and easy way to dress up fresh green beans. Basil adds bright flavor, while lemon juice and garlic bring spring to mind.

1-1/2 pounds fresh green beans, trimmed
1 shallot, halved and sliced
1/4 cup butter, cubed
3 garlic cloves, minced
1 tablespoon sugar
1 tablespoon lemon juice
3/4 teaspoon salt
1/2 teaspoon dried parsley flakes
1/4 teaspoon pepper
2 cups cherry tomatoes, halved
2 tablespoons minced fresh basil

Place green beans in a steamer basket; place in a large saucepan over 1 in. of water. Bring to a boil; cover and steam for 8-10 minutes or until crisp-tender.

Meanwhile, in a large skillet, saute shallot in butter until tender. Add the garlic, sugar, lemon juice, salt, parsley and pepper; cook 2 minutes longer. Stir in beans and tomatoes; heat through. Sprinkle with basil. **Yield:** 9 servings.

Potato and Mushroom Gratin

(Pictured above right)

Prep: 20 min. **Bake:** 55 min.

Rich, decadent and indulgent, this creamy recipe is laced with wine and makes a perfect take-along side dish for potlucks or open houses. It has an impressive appearance and is always a huge hit!

—Laurie LaClair, North Richland Hills, Texas

2 jars (4-1/2 ounces *each*) sliced mushrooms, drained
3 shallots, finely chopped
1 tablespoon olive oil

2 tablespoons marsala wine
3 large potatoes (about 1-1/2 pounds), peeled and thinly sliced
1 cup (4 ounces) shredded Swiss cheese
1/2 cup shredded Parmesan cheese
2 tablespoons minced fresh basil *or* 2 teaspoons dried basil
1-1/2 cups heavy whipping cream
1 tablespoon butter, cubed
1/8 teaspoon salt
1/8 teaspoon pepper

In a large skillet, saute mushrooms and shallots in oil until tender. Add wine; cook and stir for 2 minutes.

Arrange a third of the potatoes in a greased 10-in. round shallow baking dish. Layer with half of the mushroom mixture, cheeses, basil and another third of potatoes. Repeat layers. Pour cream over top. Dot with butter; sprinkle with salt and pepper.

Bake, uncovered, at 350° for 55-65 minutes or until potatoes are tender. **Yield:** 8 servings.

Makeover Chocolate Truffle Dessert

(Pictured at right)

Prep: 30 min. **Bake:** 25 min. + chilling

This over-the-top truffle cake created by the Test Kitchen tastes like it took all day to make, but we trimmed the steps to give you scrumptious results in less time.

1 box fudge brownie mix (8-inch square pan size)
3 cups (18 ounces) semisweet chocolate chips
2 cups heavy whipping cream, *divided*
6 tablespoons butter, cubed
1 tablespoon instant coffee granules
3 tablespoons vanilla extract
14 to 16 Pirouette cookies, cut into 1-1/2-inch pieces

Prepare brownie batter according to package directions. Spread into a greased 9-in. springform pan. Place on a baking sheet. Bake at 350° for 25-30 minutes or until a toothpick inserted near the center comes out clean. Cool on a wire rack.

Place chocolate chips in a food processor; cover and process until finely chopped. In a small microwave-safe bowl, combine 1 cup cream, butter and coffee granules. Microwave, uncovered, on high for 1 to 1-1/2 minutes or until butter is melted; stir until smooth. With food processor running, add cream mixture to chocolate chips in a slow, steady stream. Add vanilla; cover and process until smooth.

Cut a small hole in the corner of a pastry or plastic bag. Fill with 1/4 cup chocolate mixture; set aside for garnish. Transfer the remaining chocolate mixture to a large bowl.

Remove sides of springform pan. Spread half of the chocolate mixture over brownie layer, spreading evenly over top and sides. In a small bowl, beat remaining cream until soft peaks form; fold into the remaining chocolate mixture. Spread over chocolate layer. Gently press cookies into sides of dessert.

Pipe the reserved chocolate mixture on top of dessert. Cover and refrigerate for at least 4 hours or overnight. Remove from the refrigerator 5 minutes before cutting. **Yield:** 16 servings.

Editor's Note: The amount of vanilla called for in the recipe is correct.

FATHER'S DAY BREAKFAST

When Pop's special day rolls around, have this cache of awesome dad-centric recipes to create a meal he'll always remember. The dishes come together quickly, and this hearty version of bacon, eggs and pancakes will be sure to win accolades from the number one father in your life! ■

Breaded Brunch Bacon

(Pictured below)

Prep: 15 min. **Bake:** 30 min.

This recipe earned a permanent spot in my tried-and-true collection after one bite! Guests can't resist it.

—Rebecca Novakovich, Dallas, Texas

2 eggs
2 tablespoons white vinegar
1 teaspoon prepared mustard
1/2 teaspoon cayenne pepper
1-1/2 cups finely crushed reduced-sodium saltines (about 45 crackers)
10 thick-sliced bacon strips, halved widthwise

In a shallow dish, whisk the eggs, vinegar, mustard and cayenne. Place cracker crumbs in another shallow dish. Dip bacon in egg mixture, then roll in crumbs.

Arrange in a single layer on two foil-lined 15-in. x 10-in. x 1-in. baking pans. Bake at 350° for 15 minutes; turn. Bake 15-20 minutes longer or until golden brown. Remove to paper towels to drain. Serve warm. **Yield:** 10 servings.

Scrambled Eggs with the Works

(Pictured below left)

Prep/Total Time: 25 min.

Loaded with fantastic flavors, this colorful, savory egg dish is perfect for hungry appetites. It's loaded with pork sausage plus tons of vegetables, including mushrooms, green pepper and onion, for a hearty breakfast.
—Susan Zientara, Decatur, Illinois

- **1/4 pound bulk sage pork sausage**
- **1-1/4 cups sliced fresh mushrooms**
- **1 medium green pepper, chopped**
- **1 small onion, chopped**
- **10 eggs**
- **2/3 cup shredded cheddar cheese**
- **1/4 cup water**
- **1/4 teaspoon salt**
- **1/4 teaspoon pepper**
- **1 plum tomato, chopped**

In a large skillet, cook the pork sausage, mushrooms, chopped green pepper and onion over medium heat until the meat is no longer pink; drain.

In a large bowl, whisk the eggs, cheese, water, salt and pepper; add to skillet. Cook and stir over medium heat until the eggs are set. Stir in the chopped tomato. **Yield:** 5 servings.

Cinnamon Flapjacks

(Pictured at left)

Prep: 15 min. **Cook:** 5 min./batch

Kids will love helping to create our fun breakfast treat for Dad—the Test Kitchen had fun making the pancakes and syrup! It's delightful, easy and a great way to tell your father how much you love him!

- **2 cups complete buttermilk pancake mix**
- **1-1/2 cups water**
- **1 tablespoon maple syrup**
- **1 tablespoon butter, melted**
- **1/2 teaspoon ground cinnamon**

SYRUP:

- **1 cup packed brown sugar**
- **1/4 cup water**
- **1 tablespoon butter**
- **1/2 teaspoon vanilla extract**

In a small bowl, combine the pancake mix, water, syrup, butter and cinnamon. Pour the batter into a plastic squirt bottle. Squeeze the batter into desired letters and shapes onto a greased hot griddle. When the underside is browned, turn pancakes and cook until second side is golden brown.

Meanwhile, in small saucepan, combine the brown sugar, water and butter. Bring to a boil. Reduce the heat and simmer, uncovered, for 4-5 minutes or until the brown sugar is dissolved. Remove from the heat; stir in the vanilla extract. Serve with flapjacks. **Yield:** 4 servings 3/4 cup syrup).

Apricot & White Chocolate Coffee Cake

(Pictured above)

Prep: 15 min. **Bake:** 20 min.

Here's a luscious make-and-take recipe for those holiday brunches you're invited to. It couldn't be simpler or quicker to prepare, and you can vary the preserves to any flavor you have on hand.
—Holly Bauer, West Bend, Wisconsin

- **2 cups biscuit/baking mix**
- **2 tablespoons sugar**
- **1 egg**
- **2/3 cup 2% milk**
- **2 tablespoons canola oil**
- **1/2 cup white baking chips**
- **1/2 cup apricot preserves**

TOPPING:

- **1/3 cup biscuit/baking mix**
- **1/3 cup sugar**
- **2 tablespoons cold butter**

In a large bowl, combine the biscuit mix and sugar. Whisk the egg, milk and oil; stir into dry ingredients just until moistened. Fold in chips. Pour into a greased 9-in. round baking pan.

Drop the preserves by teaspoonfuls over batter. Cut through batter with a knife to swirl the preserves.

For topping, combine biscuit mix and sugar in small bowl; cut in butter until crumbly. Sprinkle over batter.

Bake at 400° for 20-25 minutes or until golden brown. Serve warm. **Yield:** 12 servings.

FOURTH OF JULY COOKOUT

On sunny and relaxed summer holidays, outdoor cookouts are what life is all about. There's no need to put all of your time in creating a July 4th menu, because we've streamlined fabulous dishes for you. The tasty recipes here include pork ribs made quick with use of the microwave, potato salad, corn on the cob and an impressive yet easy-to-make Summer Fruit Pizza that is patriotic and delicious! ■

Cherry-Barbecue Pork Ribs

(Pictured below)

Prep: 25 min. **Grill:** 10 min.

This goof-proof recipe for lip-smacking ribs from our Test Kitchen features microwave ease and smoky grilled flavor. You'll love the jazzed-up barbecue sauce.

4 pounds bone-in country-style pork ribs
1/2 cup orange juice
2 teaspoons Liquid Smoke, optional
1 teaspoon garlic powder
1/4 teaspoon pepper
2/3 cup barbecue sauce
1/3 cup cherry preserves
1 tablespoon molasses

Place ribs in a 3-qt. microwave-safe dish. In a small bowl, combine orange juice, Liquid Smoke if desired, garlic powder and pepper; pour over ribs. Cover and microwave on high for 15-20 minutes or until meat is tender.

Meanwhile, in a small saucepan, combine the barbecue sauce, preserves and molasses. Bring to a boil. Reduce heat; simmer, uncovered for 2 minutes, stirring occasionally.

Drain ribs. Moisten a paper towel with cooking oil; using long-handled tongs, lightly coat the grill rack. Grill the ribs, covered, over medium heat for 8-10 minutes or until browned, basting with the sauce and turning occasionally. **Yield:** 8 servings.

Editor's Note: This recipe was tested in a 1,100-watt microwave.

Bacon & Egg Potato Salad

(Pictured below left)

Prep: 15 min. **Cook:** 25 min. + chilling

Vinegar and lemon juice add a slightly tangy taste to this creamy potato salad. It's wonderful with baked beans and barbecue. —Melissa Davies, Clermont, Florida

6 cups cubed red potatoes (about 2-1/2 pounds)
4 hard-cooked eggs, sliced
1 small onion, chopped
4 bacon strips, cooked and crumbled
1 tablespoon minced fresh parsley
1 cup mayonnaise
2 tablespoons dill pickle relish
3 to 5 teaspoons prepared mustard
1 tablespoon white vinegar
1 tablespoon lemon juice
1/2 teaspoon salt
1/2 teaspoon celery seed
1/2 teaspoon dill weed
1/2 teaspoon pepper

Place potatoes in a Dutch oven; cover with water. Bring to a boil. Reduce heat; cover and cook for 10-15 minutes or until tender. Drain and cool.

Place potatoes in a large bowl. Add the eggs, onion, bacon and parsley. In a small bowl, combine the mayonnaise, relish, mustard, vinegar, lemon juice and seasonings. Pour over potato mixture and toss gently to coat. Refrigerate until chilled. **Yield:** 8 servings.

Sweet Corn with Parmesan and Cilantro

(Pictured at far left)

Prep/Total Time: 25 min.

A little tart and a touch of sass, this fun way to fix corn will be a hit. Just a few minutes of pan frying gives it a delightful golden color. —Faye Sloan, Las Vegas, Nevada

4 large ears sweet corn, husks removed
1/3 cup grated Parmesan cheese
6 tablespoons olive oil, *divided*
1 tablespoon lime juice
1 garlic clove, minced
1 teaspoon ground cumin
1/2 teaspoon hot pepper sauce
1/4 teaspoon salt
1/4 teaspoon pepper
1/4 cup minced fresh cilantro

Place corn in a stockpot; cover with water. Bring to a boil; cover and cook for 3-5 minutes or until tender. Drain.

In a small bowl, combine the cheese, 5 tablespoons oil, lime juice, garlic, cumin, pepper sauce, salt and pepper. Brush 1 tablespoon over each ear of corn.

In a large skillet, cook corn in remaining oil over medium heat for 4-6 minutes or until lightly browned, turning occasionally. Stir cilantro into remaining cheese mixture; brush over corn. **Yield:** 4 servings.

Summer Fruit Pizza

(Pictured above)

Prep: 35 min. **Bake:** 15 min. + cooling

I first made this eye-pleasing treat for a church social. Not only were people impressed with the flavor, but it was one of the most beautiful desserts there. —Krista Collins, Concord, North Carolina

1 package (8 ounces) cream cheese, softened
1/2 cup sour cream
1/4 cup confectioners' sugar
2 tablespoons 2% milk
1 tube (16-1/2 ounces) refrigerated sugar cookie dough, softened
2 cups fresh blueberries
2 cups fresh raspberries
8 fresh strawberries, sliced
3/4 cup apricot preserves

In a large bowl, beat cream cheese and sour cream until smooth. Beat in confectioners' sugar and milk. Chill.

Meanwhile, press cookie dough onto an ungreased 14-in. pizza pan. Bake at 350° for 15-18 minutes or until deep golden brown. Cool completely on a wire rack.

Spread cream cheese mixture over crust to within 1/2 in. of edges. Arrange fruit over top.

In a small microwave-safe dish, microwave preserves, uncovered, on high for 45-60 seconds or until melted. Drizzle over fruit. Chill until serving. Refrigerate leftovers. **Yield:** 16 servings.

HALLOWEEN BLOCK PARTY

When the ghouls and goblins come out on All Hallow's Eve, there's no need to go hungry! Let these frightfully flavorful fixin's be the hit of your next Halloween party. We've got delicious cornmeal muffins, robust turkey chili, festive quesadillas that are perfect for kids, and irresistible brownies topped with gooey caramel, candy and nuts! ■

Confetti Cornmeal Muffins

(Pictured at right)

Prep: 20 min. **Bake:** 20 min.

Pretty flecks of green and red pepper give these moist muffins a colorful look that friends will be drawn to. After one bite of what one person described as "the best corn muffins I've ever had," they'll be hooked.

—Priscilla Gilbert, Indian Harbour Beach, Florida

3/4 cup chopped green pepper
3/4 cup chopped sweet red pepper
1/2 cup chopped onion
1/2 cup butter, *divided*
1-1/2 cups cornmeal
1-1/4 cups all-purpose flour
1/3 cup sugar
3 tablespoons cornstarch
2-1/2 teaspoons baking powder
1/4 teaspoon salt
2 eggs
1 cup 2% milk
1 cup (4 ounces) shredded Mexican cheese blend

CILANTRO BUTTER:

1/2 cup butter, softened
1 tablespoon minced fresh cilantro
1/4 teaspoon grated lime peel

In a large skillet, saute peppers and onion in 2 tablespoons butter for 3-4 minutes or until tender. In a large bowl, combine the cornmeal, flour, sugar, cornstarch, baking powder and salt. Melt the remaining butter. Whisk in the eggs and milk until combined. Stir into the dry ingredients just until moistened. Fold in the pepper mixture and cheese.

Fill greased or paper-lined muffin cups three-fourths full. Bake at 400° for 18-20 minutes or until a toothpick comes out clean. Meanwhile, in a small bowl, combine spread ingredients. Cool muffins for 5 minutes before removing from pan to a wire rack. Serve warm with butter. **Yield:** 1 dozen.

CORNMEAL COLORS

Cornmeal can be white, yellow or blue. White is popular in the South, and yellow is preferred in the North. Blue can be found in specialty stores. All three types can be used interchangeably in recipes.

Turkey Chili with Pasta

(Pictured at far right)

Prep: 10 min. **Cook:** 30 min.

Some may call it witches' stew, but we think this hearty chili is the ultimate comfort food. It's a perfect warmer on chilly autumn nights.

—Pat Schmeling, Germantown, Wisconsin

1 package (20 ounces) lean ground turkey
3 celery ribs with leaves, chopped
1 large green pepper, chopped
1 large onion, chopped
2 garlic cloves, minced
1 can (46 ounces) tomato juice
1 can (11-1/2 ounces) V8 juice
2 cans (8 ounces *each*) tomato sauce
2 tablespoons brown sugar
2 tablespoons chili powder
1/2 teaspoon salt
1/2 teaspoon ground cumin
1/4 teaspoon pepper
1 bay leaf
1 cup uncooked elbow macaroni
2 cans (16 ounces *each*) kidney beans, rinsed and drained
Optional toppings: sour cream, shredded cheddar cheese, thinly sliced green onions and ripe olives

In a Dutch oven, cook the turkey, celery, green pepper, onion and garlic over medium heat until meat is no longer pink. Add the juices, tomato sauce, brown sugar, seasonings and bay leaf. Bring to a boil. Reduce heat; simmer, uncovered, for 20 minutes.

Meanwhile, cook macaroni according to package directions; drain. Add beans and macaroni to turkey mixture; heat through. Discard bay leaf before serving. Garnish servings with toppings of your choice. **Yield:** 10 servings (4 quarts).

“Candy Corn” Quesadillas

(Pictured below)

Prep: 25 min. **Cook:** 10 min.

This Test Kitchen creation lends a savory touch to your celebration. The "candy corn" triangles will be a smash with kids, and the flavor will win over adults. Let kids join in the fun by filling a bag with the nacho tortilla chips to crush with a rolling pin while you do the rest.

1 rotisserie chicken, cut up
1 jar (16 ounces) salsa
1 cup frozen corn, thawed
1/4 cup barbecue sauce
1/2 teaspoon ground cumin
1/2 cup butter, melted
8 flour tortillas (10 inches)
1 jar (15-1/2 ounces) salsa con queso dip, warmed
4 cups (16 ounces *each*) shredded Mexican cheese blend
2-2/3 cups crushed nacho tortilla chips
1/2 cup sour cream

In a large sauce pan, combine the first five ingredients; heat through.

Brush butter over one side of each tortilla. Place one tortilla, buttered side down, in a large skillet. Spread with 1 cup chicken mixture; top with another tortilla, buttered side up. Cook over medium heat for 1-2 minutes or until bottom is lightly browned. Flip.

Spread 1/2 cup queso dip over top of quesadilla. Sprinkle cheese around outside edge. Cover and cook for 1-2 minutes or until cheese begins to melt. Remove to a cutting board. Sprinkle chips over middle of quesadilla. Spoon a dollop of sour cream into the center. Cut into six wedges. Repeat with remaining ingredients. **Yield:** 2 dozen.

Spooktacular Brownies

(Pictured above)

Prep: 20 min. **Bake:** 25 min. + cooling

Ghosts and goblins of all ages won't be able to stop reaching for these mouthwatering goodies. They're ooey-gooey and fudgy. —*Sandy Krohn, Albion, Nebraska*

1 package fudge brownie mix (13-inch x 9-inch pan size)
15 caramels
3 tablespoons milk
1/2 cup semisweet chocolate chips
1/2 cup chopped walnuts
1/2 cup orange, red, yellow and brown milk chocolate M&M's

Prepare and bake brownies according to package directions. Place on a wire rack.

In a small saucepan, melt caramels with milk over low heat; stir until blended. Top warm brownies with chocolate chips, walnuts, caramel and M&M's. Cool before cutting. **Yield:** 3 dozen.

THANKSGIVING PLENTY

There's a good reason that Thanksgiving is such a popular holiday—the food! The classic, comforting dishes make this day extra special, and we've got all the savory recipes you need for an impressive feast. Your family and friends will be delighted with roast turkey, traditional side dishes, such as cranberry sauce and green bean casserole, and more! ■

Tarragon Mashed Potato Casserole

(Pictured below)

Prep: 35 min. + chilling **Cook:** 15 min.

You can prepare this casserole the night before and refrigerate it. Then simply reheat it in the microwave for a quick and easy side. —*Kris Campion, Marshall, Minnesota*

10 medium potatoes, peeled and quartered
1 package (8 ounces) cream cheese, softened
1 cup (8 ounces) sour cream
1/4 cup butter, cubed
1 teaspoon pepper
3/4 teaspoon salt
1/2 teaspoon garlic powder
1/2 teaspoon dried tarragon
1/4 teaspoon paprika, optional

Place the potatoes in a large saucepan and cover with water. Bring to a boil. Reduce heat; cover and simmer for 15-20 minutes or until tender. Drain.

In a large bowl, beat cream cheese and sour cream until smooth. Add potatoes; beat until light and fluffy. Beat in the butter, pepper, salt, garlic powder, tarragon and paprika if desired. Spoon into a greased 2-qt. microwave-safe dish. Cover and refrigerate overnight.

Remove from the refrigerator 30 minutes before microwaving. Microwave, uncovered, on high for 10 minutes, stirring once. Microwave 4-6 minutes longer or until heated through. **Yield:** 9 servings.

Editor's Note: This recipe was tested in a 1,100-watt microwave.

Autumn Tossed Salad

(Pictured at left)

Prep/Total Time: 10 min.

For a company-special dish, whip up this simple homemade dressing the night before and toss it with the salad just before serving. —*Greta Igl, Menomonee Falls, Wisconsin*

1 package (6 ounces) fresh baby spinach
1 medium pear, sliced
1 celery rib, chopped
1/4 cup dried cranberries
1/4 cup chopped pecans, toasted
VINAIGRETTE:
1/4 cup canola oil
2 tablespoons sugar
2 tablespoons cider vinegar
1 tablespoon minced fresh parsley *or* 1 teaspoon dried parsley flakes
1/4 teaspoon salt
Dash hot pepper sauce

In a large bowl, combine the first five ingredients. In a small bowl, whisk the vinaigrette ingredients. Pour over salad; toss to coat. **Yield:** 6 servings.

WHAT IS BABY SPINACH?

Baby spinach is a variety of spinach with a small, flat leaf that is tender in texture. Found in grocery stores in bulk or in several different-sized cellophane bags already cleaned, it can be eaten cooked or raw.

Apple-Sage Roasted Turkey

(Pictured above)

Prep: 20 min. **Bake:** 3-1/2 hours + standing

Apple flavor gives this classic recipe a new spin that will appeal to even your pickiest eaters. The lovely aroma as this moist and beautiful turkey cooked in the kitchen had everyone talking. —Suzy Horvath, Milwaukie, Oregon

1/2 cup apple cider *or* juice
1/2 cup apple jelly
1/3 cup butter, cubed

TURKEY:

1/3 cup minced fresh sage
1/4 cup butter, softened
1 turkey (14 to 16 pounds)
2 tablespoons apple cider *or* juice
1-1/2 teaspoons salt
1-1/2 teaspoons pepper
2 large apples, cut into wedges
1 large onion, cut into wedges
8 fresh sage leaves

In a small saucepan, combine the apple cider or juice, apple jelly and butter. Cook and stir until the butter is melted. Remove the saucepan from the heat and set aside. Reserve 2 tablespoons of cider mixture for finishing after the turkey is cooked.

In a small bowl, combine the minced sage and softened butter. With your fingers, carefully loosen the skin from the turkey breast; rub the butter mixture under the skin. Brush the turkey with the apple cider or juice. Sprinkle the salt and pepper over the turkey and inside the cavity.

Place the apples, onion and whole sage leaves inside the cavity. Tuck the wings under the turkey and tie the drumsticks together. Place the turkey breast side up on a rack in a roasting pan.

Bake the turkey, uncovered, at 325° for 3-1/2 to 4 hours or until a meat thermometer reads 180°, basting occasionally with the apple cider mixture. Cover the turkey loosely with foil if it browns too quickly. Brush with the reserved apple cider mixture. Cover to keep warm and let stand for 20 minutes before slicing. **Yield:** 14 servings.

Apple-Almond Stuffing

(Pictured above)

Prep: 30 min. **Bake:** 30 min.

One Thanksgiving, I lost the recipe I planned to use, so I threw this together. My cousin Sandy, a die-hard traditional stuffing fan, said this was the best stuffing she'd ever tasted! Talk about a compliment!
—Beverly Norris, Evanston, Wyoming

3/4 pound bulk Italian sausage
2 celery ribs, finely chopped
1 small onion, finely chopped
6 garlic cloves, minced
1 can (14-1/2 ounces) chicken broth
1/2 cup butter, cubed
1 package (12 ounces) seasoned stuffing cubes
1-1/2 cups chopped apples
1 cup dried cranberries
1/2 cup slivered almonds
1-1/2 teaspoons dried sage leaves
1-1/2 teaspoons dried thyme
1/8 teaspoon pepper
Dash salt
1 to 1-1/2 cups apple cider *or* juice

In a Dutch oven, cook the sausage, celery, onion and garlic over medium heat until the sausage is no longer pink; drain. Add broth, stirring to loosen browned bits from pan. Add butter; cook and stir until butter is melted. Remove from the heat.

Stir in the stuffing cubes, apples, cranberries, almonds, sage, thyme, pepper, salt and enough cider to reach desired moistness.Transfer to a greased 13-in. x 9-in. baking dish.

Cover and bake at 350° for 25 minutes. Uncover; bake 5-10 minutes longer or until lightly browned. **Yield:** 12 servings.

Maple-Dijon Sprout Medley

(Pictured below)

Prep/Total Time: 25 min.

Maple syrup pairs perfectly with Dijon mustard in this party-perfect veggie dish from our Test Kitchen.

1-1/2 pounds fresh brussels sprouts, halved
2 cups frozen pearl onions
1 cup fresh baby carrots, halved lengthwise
1/4 cup butter, cubed
1/3 cup maple syrup
4 teaspoons Dijon mustard
1/2 teaspoon dried thyme
1/4 teaspoon salt
1/4 teaspoon pepper
1 cup walnut halves, toasted

Place the brussels sprouts, onions and carrots in a steamer basket; place in Dutch oven over 1 in. of water. Bring to a boil; cover and steam for 8-10 minutes or until crisp-tender. Transfer to a large bowl.

In a microwave, melt butter and syrup; stir until smooth. Stir in the mustard, thyme, salt and pepper. Pour over vegetables and toss to coat. Sprinkle with walnuts. **Yield:** 9 servings.

Lemon Cranberry Sauce

(Pictured below)

Prep/Total Time: 25 min.

Tangy and refreshing, this quick-fix stovetop sauce will please both guests and the cook!
—Robyn Badtke, Green Lake, Wisconsin

1 package (12 ounces) fresh *or* frozen cranberries, thawed
1 cup sugar
1 cup water
1/4 cup Triple Sec *or* orange juice
3 tablespoons lemon juice
1-1/2 teaspoons grated lemon peel

In a large saucepan, combine the cranberries, sugar, water, Triple Sec and lemon juice. Cook over medium heat until berries pop, about 15 minutes.

Remove from the heat; stir in lemon peel. Transfer to a small bowl. Chill until serving. **Yield:** 2 cups.

Jazzed-Up Green Bean Casserole

(Pictured above)

Prep: 20 min. **Cook:** 5-1/2 hours

This is not your mama's green bean casserole, but she'll still be raving about it! After trying many variations, I decided to give this old standby extra kick. The crunchy texture, cheesy goodness and bacon make it a hit.
—Scott Rugh, Portland, Oregon

2 packages (16 ounces *each*) frozen cut green beans, thawed
2 cans (10-3/4 ounces *each*) condensed cream of mushroom soup, undiluted
1 can (8 ounces) sliced water chestnuts, drained
1 cup 2% milk
6 bacon strips, cooked and crumbled
1 teaspoon pepper
1/8 teaspoon paprika
4 ounces process cheese (Velveeta), cubed
1 can (2.8 ounces) French-fried onions

In a 4-qt. slow cooker, combine the green beans, soup, water chestnuts, milk, bacon, pepper and paprika. Cover and cook on low for 5-6 hours or until the beans are tender; stir in the cheese. Cover and cook for 30 minutes or until the cheese is melted. Sprinkle with onions. **Yield:** 10 servings.

Tarragon Butter

(Pictured below)

Prep/Total Time: 5 min.

This seasoned butter is a delicious way to add great herb flavor and a hint of color to your favorite breads, rolls and vegetables.
—Connie Moore, Medway, Ohio

1 cup butter, softened
2 tablespoons minced fresh tarragon *or* 2 teaspoons dried tarragon
2 tablespoons minced fresh parsley
1 teaspoon minced chives
1 garlic clove, minced
Dash pepper

In a large bowl, combine all the ingredients. Store in the refrigerator. **Yield:** 1 cup.

Editor's Note: Spread butter on French bread before toasting in the oven, season cooked vegetables with it or use when cooking fish.

A PINCH HERE, A DASH THERE

Traditionally, a pinch is thought to be the amount of a dry ingredient that can be held between your thumb and forefinger. A dash is a very small amount of seasoning added with a quick downward stroke of the hand. If, when cooking, you use a pinch or a dash of an ingredient, then you're using somewhere between 1/16 and a scant 1/8 teaspoon. With long-held family recipes, you might have to experiment with amounts to get the same delicious results.

MERRY GIFTS OF GOOD TASTE

During the Christmas holiday season, giving an edible offering to someone you care about feels extra special because it's a gift from the heart. Whether you treat your coworkers to Heavenly Hot Chocolate Mix, give friends decorated jars of Cranberry BBQ Sauce or send boxes of Drizzled Peppermint Cookies to family members, goodies that were prepared in your own kitchen are a personal way to show someone just how much they mean to you. ■

Marshmallow Snowmen

(Pictured at left)

Prep: 20 min. + standing

Kids will love making these as much as teachers enjoy receiving them. These cute snowmen from our Test Kitchen are sure to bring smiles all around. And the best part? They melt beautifully in hot chocolate.

5 ounces milk chocolate candy coating, melted
18 large marshmallows
6 small wooden skewers
Orange and black decorating icing

For hats, spoon six 1/2-teaspoon rounds of candy coating onto waxed paper. Dip six marshmallows in remaining coating and place in the center of each round; let stand until set.

On each skewer, thread two plain marshmallows and one hat. Use decorating icing to draw faces and arms. **Yield:** 6 snowmen.

Heavenly Hot Chocolate Mix

(Pictured at left)

Prep/Total Time: 10 min.

At Christmastime, I make up several batches of this mix to give away. I package it in clean, empty instant coffee jars and add a festive label. People frequently return the jars for refills! —Sara Tatham, Plymouth, New Hampshire

5 cups nonfat dry milk powder
2 cups confectioners' sugar

2 cups instant chocolate drink mix
1 cup powdered nondairy creamer
1 cup malted milk powder
1 cup chocolate malted milk powder
1/2 cup baking cocoa

In a large airtight container, combine all ingredients. Store in a cool dry place for up to 2 months (mixture will settle).

To prepare hot chocolate: Place 1/3 cup mix in a mug; add 3/4 cup hot water and stir until blended. **Yield:** 30 servings (10 cups mix).

Drizzled Peppermint Cookies

(Pictured above left)

Prep: 35 min. + standing

My daughters made these super-simple cookies for their teachers and friends, and they were a big hit.
—Carla Salard, Robeline, Louisiana

20 ounces white candy coating, coarsely chopped
1 package (16.6 ounces) cream-filled chocolate sandwich cookies
5 peppermint candy canes, crushed

In a microwave-safe bowl, melt candy coating; stir until smooth. Drizzle coating over each cookie. Place on waxed paper. Sprinkle with crushed candies; let stand until set. **Yield:** 45 cookies.

Cranberry BBQ Sauce

(Pictured above)

Prep/Total Time: 15 min.

Packed alongside cheese and crackers, this homemade barbecue sauce is a delightful, savory gift option.
—Darla Andrews, Lewisville, Texas

1 can (14 ounces) whole-berry cranberry sauce
1-1/2 cups barbecue sauce
1 teaspoon ground cinnamon
1 teaspoon chili powder
1 teaspoon ground cumin
1 teaspoon pepper
1/2 teaspoon salt
Gouda cheese and assorted crackers

In a small saucepan, combine the first seven ingredients; heat through. Store in an airtight container in the refrigerator for up to 1 month. To serve, reheat sauce and serve with cheese and crackers. **Yield:** 2-2/3 cups.

EASY CHRISTMAS COOKIES

Cookie swaps are a great way to take a break from the busy and stressful Christmas season, because it's time spent having fun and catching up with friends. The beautiful and yummy cookies featured here either start out with a convenience product or are based on a simple, homemade cookie mix. There's a cookie for every personality! ■

Holiday Pinwheel Cookies

(Pictured at right)

Prep: 20 min. + chilling **Bake:** 10 min./batch

Little helpers will have a blast helping to create these adorable pinwheels. They're an absolute cinch to make!
—Karen Moore, Jacksonville, Florida

1 tube (16-1/2 ounces) refrigerated sugar cookie dough
1/2 cup all-purpose flour
3 tablespoons red colored sugar
3 tablespoons green colored sugar

Let cookie dough stand at room temperature for 5-10 minutes to soften. In a small bowl, beat cookie dough and flour until combined. Divide dough in half.

On a lightly floured surface, roll one portion into a 12-in. x 7-in. rectangle. Sprinkle with red sugar. Tightly roll up jelly-roll style, starting with a short side; wrap in plastic wrap. Repeat with remaining dough and green sugar. Refrigerate for 2 hours or until firm.

Unwrap and cut into 1/2-in. slices. Place 2 in. apart on ungreased baking sheets. Bake at 350° for 8-10 minutes or until edges begin to brown. Cool for 1 minute before removing from pans to wire racks. Store in an airtight container. **Yield:** 2-1/4 dozen.

White Chocolate-Macadamia Snowball Cookies

(Pictured at right)

Prep: 30 min. **Bake:** 10 min./batch + cooling

Just like snowflakes, these fluffy cookies from our Test Kitchen will melt in your mouth and disappear before they touch the cookie tray.

1 tube (16-1/2 ounces) refrigerated sugar cookie dough
1/2 cup all-purpose flour
1/2 teaspoon vanilla extract
1/2 cup finely chopped macadamia nuts
28 Hershey's Bliss white chocolate meltaways
GLAZE:
1 cup confectioners' sugar
2 tablespoons 2% milk
1/4 teaspoon lemon extract
1 cup flaked coconut

Let cookie dough stand at room temperature for 5-10 minutes to soften. In a large bowl, beat the cookie dough, flour and vanilla until combined. Stir in nuts. Shape 1 tablespoonful of dough around each chocolate.

Place 2 in. apart on parchment paper-lined baking sheets. Bake at 350° for 10-12 minutes or until edges are golden brown. Remove to wire racks to cool completely.

In a small bowl, combine the confectioners' sugar, milk and extract. Place coconut in a shallow bowl. Dip cookies in glaze; coat with coconut. Let stand until set. **Yield:** 28 cookies.

Glazed Ornament Cookies

(Pictured at right)

Prep: 30 min. **Bake:** 10 min./batch + cooling

A few ingredients and a tube of cookie dough make these luscious treats, created by our Test Kitchen, a breeze to whip up. The beautiful swirled colors will look gorgeous on your holiday cookie tray!

1 tube (16-1/2 ounces) refrigerated sugar cookie dough
1/2 cup all-purpose flour
1/2 teaspoon lemon extract
GLAZE:
1 cup confectioners' sugar
2 tablespoons 2% milk
1/4 teaspoon lemon extract
Food coloring of your choice

Let cookie dough stand at room temperature for 5-10 minutes to soften. In a large bowl, beat the cookie dough, flour and extract until combined.

On a lightly floured surface, roll dough to 1/8-in. thickness. Cut with floured 2-in. ornament-shaped cookie cutters. Place 2 in. apart on ungreased baking sheets.

Bake at 350° for 9-11 minutes or until the edges are lightly browned. Remove to wire racks to cool completely.

Combine the confectioners' sugar, milk and extract. Spread over cookies. Immediately place a drop of food coloring on top of each cookie and swirl with a toothpick. Let stand until set. **Yield:** 2 dozen.

Italian Spumoni Cookies

(Pictured at right)

Prep: 30 min. + chilling **Bake:** 10 min./batch

Our Test Kitchen wanted these festive cookies to look and taste like they're made from scratch. But refrigerated cookie dough makes them a cinch to create. We'll never reveal your secret!

2 tubes (16-1/2 ounces *each*) refrigerated sugar cookie dough
1 cup all-purpose flour, *divided*
1/4 cup chopped maraschino cherries
4 to 6 drops red food coloring, optional
2 tablespoons baking cocoa
2 teaspoons hazelnut liqueur
1/3 cup chopped pistachios
4 to 6 drops green food coloring, optional

Let cookie dough stand at room temperature for 5-10 minutes to soften. In a large bowl, beat cookie dough and 3/4 cup flour until combined. Divide dough into three portions.

Add the cherries, red food coloring if desired and remaining flour to one portion. Add cocoa and liqueur to the second portion. Add pistachios and green food coloring to the remaining portion.

Roll each portion between two pieces of waxed paper into an 8-in. x 6-in. rectangle. Remove waxed paper. Place cherry rectangle on a piece of plastic wrap. Layer with chocolate and pistachio rectangles; press together lightly. Wrap with the plastic wrap and refrigerate overnight.

Cut chilled dough in half widthwise. Return one rectangle to the refrigerator. Cut remaining rectangle into 1/4-in. slices. Place 1 in. apart on ungreased baking sheets. Repeat with remaining dough.

Bake at 375° for 8-10 minutes or until set. Cool for 2 minutes before removing to wire racks. Store in an airtight container. **Yield:** 4 dozen.

Quick Cookie Mix

Prep: 10 min.

This fast mix is the foundation for all of the cookie recipes I share on these pages. I found this recipe in a bag of flour some 30 years ago and have used it ever since!
—Jeanette Meidal, Savage, Minnesota

1-1/2 cups butter, softened
3 teaspoons salt
2 teaspoons baking powder
6 cups all-purpose flour

In a large bowl, beat the butter, salt and baking powder until blended. Gradually add flour and mix just until crumbly. Store in an airtight container in the refrigerator for up to 1 month.

Quick Cookie Mix may be used to prepare the following recipes: Apricot Thumbprints, Butter Almond Cookies, Peanut Butter Blossoms and Toffee Triangles. **Yield:** 8 cups.

Joyful Cutout Cookies

(Pictured above)

Prep: 30 min. **Bake:** 10 min./batch + cooling

Spell out season's greetings with a flurry of these simple but elegant cookies created by our Test Kitchen.

1 package (17-1/2 ounces) sugar cookie mix
1 tablespoon all-purpose flour
3/4 teaspoon ground cinnamon
1/4 teaspoon ground nutmeg
Dash ground cloves
1/3 cup butter, softened
1 egg

ICING:
4 cups confectioners' sugar
6 tablespoons 2% milk
1/4 teaspoon almond extract
Food coloring of your choice
Snowflake sprinkles, edible glitter and shaved *or* shredded coconut

In a large bowl, combine the cookie mix, flour, cinnamon, nutmeg and cloves. Add butter and egg; mix well.

On a lightly floured surface, roll dough to 1/4-in. thickness. Cut with floured 3-in. stocking-, wreath- and angel-shaped cookie cutters.

Place 1 in. apart on ungreased baking sheets. Bake at 375° for 7-9 minutes or until lightly browned. Remove to wire racks to cool completely.

In a large bowl, whisk the confectioners' sugar, milk and extract. Tint as desired with food coloring; spread over cookies. Decorate as desired with sprinkles, glitter and coconut. Let stand until set. Store in an airtight container. **Yield:** 1-1/2 dozen.

Editor's Note: Snowflake sprinkles and edible glitter are available from Wilton Industries. Call 1-800-794-5866 or visit *www.wilton.com.*

Toffee Triangles

(Pictured at far right)

Prep: 20 min. **Bake:** 15 min. + cooling

Add a touch of elegance to cookie trays with these easy nutty bars. They're perfect with coffee, cocoa or tea.
—Jeanette Meidal, Savage, Minnesota

2 cups Quick Cookie Mix
1 cup packed brown sugar
1/3 cup butter, softened

1 teaspoon vanilla extract
1 egg
1 cup (6 ounces) semisweet chocolate chips
1/2 cup mixed nuts, chopped

In a large bowl, beat cookie mix, brown sugar, butter and vanilla until mixture resembles coarse crumbs. Add egg and mix well.

Spread into a greased 13-in. x 9-in. baking pan. Bake at 350° for 12-15 minutes or until lightly browned.

Sprinkle with chocolate chips; let stand for 5 minutes. Spread the chocolate over bars. Sprinkle with nuts. Let stand until chocolate is set. Cut into squares, then cut in half to form triangles. Store in an airtight container. **Yield:** 5 dozen.

Peanut Butter Blossoms

(Pictured below right)

Prep: 20 min. **Bake:** 10 min./batch

Better watch out! These peanut butter cookies topped with dark chocolate candies could be gone before Christmas.
—Jeanette Meidal, Savage, Minnesota

1 cup packed brown sugar
1/2 cup peanut butter
1/3 cup shortening
1 egg
1/2 teaspoon vanilla extract
2 cups Quick Cookie Mix
Red and green colored sugar
36 dark chocolate kisses

In a small bowl, cream the brown sugar, peanut butter and shortening until light and fluffy. Beat in egg and vanilla. Gradually add cookie mix and mix well.

Roll dough into 1-in. balls. Roll in colored sugar.

Place 2 in. apart on ungreased baking sheets. Bake at 375° for 8-10 minutes or until surface cracks. Immediately press a chocolate kiss into the center of each cookie. Cool for 5 minutes before removing from pans to wire racks. Store in an airtight container. **Yield:** 3 dozen.

Apricot Thumbprints

(Pictured at right)

Prep: 20 min. **Bake:** 10 min./batch

Each dimpled delight holds a dab of apricot preserves.
—Jeanette Meidal, Savage, Minnesota

2 tablespoons butter, softened
1/2 cup packed brown sugar
1 egg
1 teaspoon vanilla extract
2 cups Quick Cookie Mix
1 egg white, lightly beaten
3/4 cup finely chopped cashews
1/3 cup apricot preserves

In a small bowl, cream butter and brown sugar until crumbly. Beat in egg and vanilla. Gradually add cookie mix and mix well.

Place egg white and cashews in separate shallow bowls. Shape dough into 1-in. balls. Dip in egg white, then roll in cashews.

Place 1 in. apart on ungreased baking sheets. Using the end of a wooden spoon handle, make an indentation in the center of each cookie. Fill with preserves. Bake at 350° for 10-12 minutes or until set. Remove to wire racks to cool. Store in an airtight container. **Yield:** 3 dozen.

Butter Almond Cookies

(Pictured below)

Prep: 20 min. **Bake:** 20 min. + cooling

Tender and toasty, these buttery almond bites are a winner with taste testers.
—Jeanette Meidal, Savage, Minnesota

2 packages (3 ounces *each*) cream cheese, softened
6 tablespoons butter, softened, *divided*
1 egg, *separated*
2 cups Quick Cookie Mix
3/4 cup sugar
2 teaspoons almond extract
1/4 cup sliced almonds

In a large bowl, beat the cream cheese, 5 tablespoons butter and egg yolk until smooth. Add cookie mix and mix well.

Turn dough onto a lightly floured surface; knead 15-20 times or until smooth. Roll into a 12-in. square. Spread remaining butter to within 1/2 in. of edges.

Combine sugar and extract; sprinkle over half of the dough. Fold dough over sugar mixture; pinch edges to seal. Brush top with egg white; sprinkle with almonds.

Place on a greased baking sheet. Bake at 375° for 20-25 minutes or until lightly browned. Remove to a wire rack to cool.

Transfer to a cutting board. Cut widthwise with a serrated knife into 1/2-in. slices; cut each slice in half lengthwise. Store in an airtight container. **Yield:** 4 dozen.

CHAPTER 3

30 Minutes to Mealtime

If you consider how little half an hour is compared to an entire day, it's clear how speedy supper preparation can be. We've compiled 24 two-recipe meals that can each be made from start to finish in just 30 minutes—that's enough meals for almost a whole month!

Each menu includes an entree plus a side or dessert, providing hearty, wholesome food for your entire family. There's a variety of food to choose from, including beef, pork, chicken, fish and even meatless entrees.

Try the Shrimp Linguine with Parmesan Cream Sauce and the Sauteed Spinach. Or go for Steaks with Molasses-Glazed Onions with a side of Herbed Potato Fans. With these family classics, saving time and money has never been easier! ■

SOUTHERN SUPPER. Creamy Sweet Corn with Okra and Cajun Pecan Catfish (p. 66).

FAMILY-PLEASING COUNTRY MEAL

In less than 30 minutes, you can put this dressed-up meal on the table. Orange-Glazed Ham Steaks, from Bonnie Hawkins of Elkhorn, Wisconsin, combine orange marmalade and maple syrup for a terrific taste that goes beyond dinner. Bonnie likes to serve leftovers at brunch. "Men love it with fruit and scrambled eggs," she says. We paired it with Marie Rizzio's Brown Rice Pilaf. "It's one of my favorite sides," says Marie, of Interlochen, Michigan. ■

Orange-Glazed Ham Steaks

Prep/Total Time: 20 min.

- **1/2 cup orange marmalade**
- **2 tablespoons maple syrup**
- **4-1/2 teaspoons orange juice**
- **1-1/2 teaspoons chili powder**
- **4 boneless fully cooked ham steaks (5 ounces *each*)**

In a small bowl, combine the marmalade, syrup, orange juice and chili powder.

Grill ham steaks, covered, over medium heat or broil 4 in. from the heat for 3-4 minutes on each side or until heated through, brushing occasionally with marmalade mixture. **Yield:** 4 servings.

Brown Rice Pilaf

Prep/Total Time: 20 min.

- **1/4 cup chopped green onions**
- **2 teaspoons butter**
- **1-1/3 cups instant brown rice**
- **1/3 cup chopped walnuts**
- **1-1/3 cups water**
- **1/3 cup dried apricots, thinly sliced**
- **1/4 teaspoon salt**
- **1/8 teaspoon pepper**

In a small saucepan, saute green onions in butter until tender. Add rice and walnuts; cook and stir for 1-2 minutes or until walnuts are toasted. Add the water, apricots, salt and pepper.

Bring to a boil. Reduce heat; cover and simmer for 5 minutes or until liquid is absorbed. Let stand for 5 minutes. Fluff with a fork. **Yield:** 4 servings.

DOWN-HOME AND DELICIOUS

Simple, satisfying and speedy, here's a meat-and-potatoes meal no one will want to miss. Carrots with Lemon Butter, shared by Agnes Ward of Stratford, Ontario, are quickly microwaved and taste lovely with a splash of citrus. They make a fresh, colorful side for Hamburger Steaks with Mushroom Gravy, a hearty main dish the whole family will cozy up to, from Denise Wheeler of Newaygo, Michigan. ■

Hamburger Steaks With Mushroom Gravy

Prep/Total Time: 25 min.

1 egg
1/2 cup dry bread crumbs
1 envelope onion soup mix, *divided*
Dash pepper
1 pound ground beef
3 tablespoons all-purpose flour
1-3/4 cups cold water
1 teaspoon Worcestershire sauce
1 jar (4-1/2 ounces) whole mushrooms, drained
Hot cooked mashed potatoes

In a large bowl, combine the egg, bread crumbs, 2 tablespoons soup mix and pepper. Crumble beef over mixture and mix well. Shape into four patties.

In a large skillet, cook patties over medium heat for 4-5 minutes on each side or until a thermometer reads 160° and juices run clear. Set aside and keep warm.

Combine the flour, water, Worcestershire sauce and remaining soup mix until blended; stir into skillet. Add mushrooms. Bring to a boil; cook and stir for 5 minutes or until thickened. Serve with patties and mashed potatoes. **Yield:** 4 servings.

Carrots with Lemon Butter

Prep/Total Time: 10 min.

1 pound fresh baby carrots
2 tablespoons water
2 tablespoons butter
1 tablespoon lemon juice
1 teaspoon grated lemon peel
1/4 teaspoon salt
1/8 teaspoon pepper

Place carrots and water in a microwave-safe bowl. Cover and microwave on high for 4-6 minutes or until crisp-tender; drain and keep warm.

In another microwave-safe bowl, combine the remaining ingredients; cook on high for 30-45 seconds or until butter is melted. Pour over carrots and toss to coat. **Yield:** 4 servings.

Editor's Note: This recipe was tested in a 1,100-watt microwave.

WEEKNIGHTS TURNED SPECIAL

Turkey isn't just for holidays. This entree from Lisa Varner is just right any night of the week. Ready in 25 minutes, her Pecan-Crusted Turkey Cutlets are moist and tender. "Pecans make this dish extra-crisp and delightful," says Lisa, of Charleston, South Carolina. Paired with thyme-flavored Green Bean & Corn Medley, from Kimberly Stine of Milford, Pennsylvania, this tasty meal is a keeper. ■

Green Bean & Corn Medley

Prep/Total Time: 15 min.

3 cups frozen cut green beans, thawed
1 package (10 ounces) frozen corn, thawed
2 tablespoons butter
1 teaspoon canola oil
1-1/2 teaspoons dried thyme
1/4 teaspoon salt
Dash pepper

In a large skillet, saute beans and corn in butter and oil until tender. Stir in the thyme, salt and pepper. **Yield:** 4 servings.

Pecan-Crusted Turkey Cutlets

Prep/Total Time: 25 min.

1/3 cup all-purpose flour
2 egg whites
1 egg
3 tablespoons honey Dijon mustard
1/2 teaspoon cayenne pepper
1/4 teaspoon salt
2/3 cup dry bread crumbs
2/3 cup ground pecans
1 package (17.6 ounces) turkey breast cutlets
1/4 cup canola oil

Place flour in a shallow bowl. In another shallow bowl, whisk the egg whites, egg, mustard, cayenne and salt. In another shallow bowl, combine bread crumbs and pecans. Coat cutlets with flour, then dip in egg mixture and coat with bread crumb mixture.

In a large skillet, cook turkey in oil in batches over medium heat for 2-3 minutes on each side or until juices run clear. **Yield:** 4 servings.

DRY BREAD CRUMBS

Dry bread crumbs may be purchased or made from very dry bread or crackers. Place bread or crackers in a large resealable plastic bag and crush with a rolling pin. Or, pulse and process the dry bread or crackers in a food processor.

COMFORTING MAINSTAY

This spicy Pepper Jack Mac is a favorite of Sarah Gilbert from Beaverton, Oregon, who tops it with Parmesan bread crumbs and bakes, uncovered, in a casserole dish at 375° for 30 minutes. Pair it with Romaine and Walnut Salad from Beverly Nichols of Midland, Texas, for a satisfying meal. ■

Pepper Jack Mac

Prep/Total Time: 25 min.

1 cup uncooked elbow macaroni
2 bacon strips, chopped
1/4 cup chopped onion
1/4 cup sliced fresh mushrooms
1-1/2 teaspoons butter
1 tablespoon all-purpose flour
1/4 cup plus 2 tablespoons chicken broth
1/4 cup plus 2 tablespoons 2% milk
3/4 cup shredded pepper Jack cheese
1/4 teaspoon Italian seasoning
Dash salt and pepper

Cook the macaroni according to package directions. Meanwhile, in a small skillet, cook bacon over medium heat until crisp. Remove to paper towels with a slotted spoon; drain, reserving 3/4 teaspoon drippings.

In the same skillet, saute onion and mushrooms in drippings and butter until tender. Stir in flour until blended; gradually stir in broth and milk. Bring to a boil; cook and stir for 1-2 minutes or until thickened. Stir in the cheese, Italian seasoning, salt and pepper. Cook and stir over medium heat until cheese is melted.

Drain macaroni; stir macaroni and bacon into sauce mixture. **Yield:** 2 servings.

Romaine and Walnut Salad

Prep/Total Time: 10 min.

2 cups hearts of romaine salad mix
1 plum tomato, sliced
1/4 cup sliced fresh mushrooms
3 tablespoons chopped walnuts
2 tablespoons red wine vinegar
4-1/2 teaspoons canola oil
1 tablespoon honey
1/8 teaspoon ground mustard

In a small bowl, combine the romaine, tomato, mushrooms and walnuts. In another bowl, whisk the remaining ingredients. Pour over salad; toss to coat. **Yield:** 3 servings.

RESTAURANT-QUALITY ENTREE WITH "WOW"

Tonight, invite a few friends over for wine, good conversation and an incredible Italian meal that is as simple as it is delicious. Flavorful Chicken Marsala, from Cher Schwartz of Ellisville, Missouri, and our Test Kitchen's fast and easy Herbed Asparagus offer a no-fuss way to make any weeknight *delizioso*! ■

Chicken Marsala

Prep/Total Time: 30 min.

4 boneless skinless chicken breast halves (4 ounces *each*)
2 tablespoons all-purpose flour
2 tablespoons olive oil
2 cups sliced fresh mushrooms
2 tablespoons butter
3/4 cup marsala wine *or* chicken broth
2 tablespoons minced fresh parsley
1/4 teaspoon dried rosemary, crushed
2 tablespoons grated Parmesan cheese, optional

Flatten chicken to 1/4-in. thickness. Place flour in a large resealable plastic bag. Add chicken, two pieces at a time, and shake to coat.

In a large skillet over medium heat, cook chicken in oil for 3-5 minutes on each side or until a thermometer reads 170°. Remove and keep warm.

In the same skillet, saute mushrooms in butter until tender. Add the wine, parsley and rosemary. Bring to a boil; cook until liquid is reduced by half. Serve with chicken; sprinkle with Parmesan cheese if desired. **Yield:** 4 servings.

Herbed Asparagus

Prep/Total Time: 15 min.

1 pound fresh asparagus, trimmed
2 garlic cloves, minced
1/2 teaspoon dried basil
1/4 teaspoon dried rosemary, crushed
1/4 teaspoon dried thyme
1/8 teaspoon salt
1/8 teaspoon pepper
2 teaspoons olive oil
1/4 cup roasted sweet red peppers, drained and chopped
2 tablespoons chopped walnuts

In a large skillet, bring 1/2 in. of water to a boil. Add asparagus; cover and boil for 3-5 minutes or until crisp-tender. Drain and keep warm.

In the same skillet, saute garlic and seasonings in oil until tender. Add asparagus, red peppers and walnuts; heat through. **Yield:** 4 servings.

AMERICAN MASTERPIECE

If you have a steak lover at home, then Steaks with Molasses-Glazed Onions, from Marie Rizzio of Interlochen, Michigan, is bound to be a hit. She says, "I wanted something different, and this brings smiles to all who try it." Pair with tasty Herbed Potato Fans from our Test Kitchen for a memorable meal. ■

Steaks with Molasses-Glazed Onions

Prep/Total Time: 25 min.

- **2 bacon strips, diced**
- **2 beef top sirloin steaks (6 ounces *each*)**
- **1/2 teaspoon salt, *divided***
- **1/2 teaspoon pepper, *divided***
- **1 large sweet onion, thinly sliced**
- **1-1/2 teaspoons balsamic vinegar**
- **1/2 teaspoon molasses**

In a large skillet, cook bacon over medium heat until crisp. Remove to paper towels with a slotted spoon; drain, reserving 1-1/2 teaspoons drippings in the skillet and 1-1/2 teaspoons drippings in a small bowl. Set bowl aside.

Sprinkle the steaks with 1/4 teaspoon salt and 1/4 teaspoon pepper. In the skillet, cook steaks over medium heat for 4-6 minutes on each side or until meat reaches desired doneness (for medium-rare, a meat thermometer should read 145°; medium, 160°; well-done, 170°). Remove and keep warm.

Add onion and reserved drippings to the skillet; saute until tender. Add the vinegar, molasses and remaining salt and pepper; heat through. Serve onion mixture with steaks; sprinkle with bacon. **Yield:** 2 servings.

Herbed Potato Fans

Prep/Total Time: 20 minutes

- **2 medium baking potatoes**
- **2 tablespoons olive oil**
- **1 teaspoon white wine *or* chicken broth**
- **1/4 teaspoon salt**
- **1/8 teaspoon *each* dried parsley flakes, thyme and rosemary, crushed**
- **1/8 teaspoon pepper**
- **Green onions and sour cream, optional**

With a sharp knife, cut each potato into 1/2-in. slices, leaving slices attached at the bottom. Place on a microwave-safe plate.

Combine the oil, wine and seasonings; drizzle over potatoes. Microwave, uncovered, on high for 8-12 minutes or until tender, turning once. Garnish with onions and sour cream if desired. **Yield:** 2 servings.

STRESS-FREE MEDITERRANEAN PASTA & SALMON

A boatload of toppings gives this seafood dinner a burst of flavor in every bite. Mediterranean Roasted Salmon from Wolfgang Hanau of West Palm Beach, Florida is topped with chopped veggies and a homemade vinaigrette that's mouthwatering! Serve it over delicious Lemon-Feta Angel Hair, shared by Melissa Just of Minneapolis, Minnesota, and you've got a Mediterranean menu that's truly a catch! ■

Lemon-Feta Angel Hair

Prep/Total Time: 20 min.

8 ounces uncooked angel hair pasta
2 garlic cloves, minced
2 tablespoons olive oil
1 package (4 ounces) crumbled feta cheese
2 teaspoons grated lemon peel
1/2 teaspoon dried oregano
1/2 teaspoon salt
1/2 teaspoon pepper

Cook pasta according to package directions.

In a large skillet, saute garlic in oil for 1 minute. Drain pasta; stir into skillet. Add the remaining ingredients; toss to coat. **Yield:** 4 servings.

Mediterranean Roasted Salmon

Prep/Total Time: 30 min.

4 salmon fillets (6 ounces *each*)
1/2 teaspoon salt, *divided*
1/2 cup olive oil
2 tablespoons balsamic vinegar
2 teaspoons honey
1 teaspoon Dijon mustard
3 plum tomatoes, chopped
1/4 cup chopped red onion
1/4 cup chopped green pepper
2 tablespoons chopped pitted green olives
2 tablespoons chopped ripe olives

Place salmon in a greased 15-in. x 10-in. x 1-in. baking pan; sprinkle with 1/4 teaspoon salt. In a small bowl, whisk the olive oil, balsamic vinegar, honey, mustard and remaining salt. Spoon 1 tablespoon over each salmon fillet.

In a large bowl, combine the tomatoes, onion, green pepper, chopped olives and remaining oil mixture. Spoon over fillets.

Bake at 425° for 12-15 minutes or until fish flakes easily with a fork. **Yield:** 4 servings.

A TWIST ON THE SOUTHWEST

If you love tacos, but are tired of the regular variety, why not give Three-Chili Turkey Tacos, from Cathy Tang of Redmond, Washington, a try? Complete the menu with fresh Zucchini & Corn with Cilantro, from Jeannie Klugh of Lancaster, Pennsylvania. ■

Zucchini & Corn with Cilantro

Prep/Total Time: 20 min.

3 medium zucchini, quartered and sliced
2 cups frozen corn
1 teaspoon olive oil
4 teaspoons minced fresh cilantro
2 teaspoons lime juice
1/2 teaspoon lemon-pepper seasoning
1/4 teaspoon salt

In a large skillet, cook zucchini and corn in oil over medium heat for 6-8 minutes or until tender. Remove from heat. Stir in remaining ingredients. **Yield:** 6 servings.

Three-Chili Turkey Tacos

Prep/Total Time: 30 min.

1 pound ground turkey
1 small onion, chopped
1/3 cup chopped sweet red pepper
1/3 cup beer *or* nonalcoholic beer
1/3 cup chili sauce
1 can (4 ounces) chopped green chilies
3-1/4 teaspoons chili powder
1-1/2 teaspoons Worcestershire sauce
1 garlic clove, minced
1/4 teaspoon salt
1/8 teaspoon pepper
10 taco shells, warmed
1-1/4 cups shredded lettuce
2/3 cup shredded cheddar cheese

In a large skillet, cook the ground turkey, onion and sweet red pepper over medium heat until the meat is no longer pink; drain.

Stir in the beer, chili sauce, green chilies, chili powder, Worcestershire sauce, minced garlic, salt and pepper. Bring to a boil. Reduce the heat; simmer, uncovered, for 5-7 minutes or until heated through.

Spoon the turkey mixture into the warmed taco shells; top with shredded lettuce and cheddar cheese. **Yield:** 5 servings.

SENSATIONAL STIR-FRY

Peanut butter, soy sauce and Catalina dressing make the yummy base to Asian Beef with Noodles shared by Denise Patterson of Bainbridge, Ohio. For a sweet finale, try Orange Marmalade Cake Sauce from Denise DuBois of Coral Springs, Florida. ■

Orange Marmalade Cake Sauce

Prep/Total Time: 10 min.

3/4 cup orange marmalade
2 tablespoons butter
1/4 teaspoon ground ginger
4 slices angel food cake *or* pound cake

In a small saucepan, combine the marmalade, butter and ginger. Cook and stir until butter is melted and mixture is blended. Serve with cake. **Yield:** 4 servings (1 cup sauce).

Asian Beef With Noodles

Prep/Total Time: 25 min.

8 ounces uncooked spaghetti, broken in half
3 cups fresh sugar snap peas
1 cup julienned sweet red pepper
1/2 cup Catalina salad dressing
1 pound beef top sirloin steak, cut into thin strips
2 tablespoons creamy peanut butter
2 tablespoons soy sauce
1/2 cup thinly sliced green onions
1/2 cup dry roasted peanuts

In a large saucepan, cook spaghetti according to package directions, adding the snap peas and pepper during the last 2 minutes of cooking; drain.

Meanwhile, in a large skillet, heat salad dressing over medium-high heat. Add beef; cook for 8-10 minutes or until meat reaches desired doneness. Add peanut butter and soy sauce; cook for 2 minutes or until thickened. Stir in spaghetti mixture and onions; sprinkle with peanuts. **Yield:** 6 servings.

FAST, EASY & FLAVORFUL FIESTA

Crispy outside and cheesy inside, Black Bean-Chicken Quesadillas, from Christy Bounds of Canton, Mississippi, will bring your family running to the table. Serve the sassy wedges with Red Pepper Corn from Kasia Rachfall of Langley, British Columbia. ■

Red Pepper Corn

Prep/Total Time: 15 min.

- **3 cups fresh *or* frozen corn**
- **1/3 cup finely chopped sweet red pepper**
- **2 tablespoons water**
- **2 tablespoons maple syrup**
- **3/4 teaspoon salt**
- **3/4 teaspoon chili powder**

Place corn, red pepper and water in a 2-qt. microwave-safe bowl. Cover and microwave on high for 8-10 minutes or until corn is tender; drain. Add the remaining ingredients; toss to coat. **Yield:** 4 servings.

Editor's Note: This recipe was tested in a 1,100-watt microwave.

Black Bean-Chicken Quesadillas

Prep/Total Time: 25 min.

- **1 can (15 ounces) Southwestern black beans, drained**
- **1 can (10 ounces) diced tomatoes and green chilies, undrained**
- **1 package (6 ounces) ready-to-use Southwestern chicken strips**
- **1 tablespoon onion powder**
- **1 cup (4 ounces) shredded cheddar cheese**
- **1/2 cup shredded part-skim mozzarella cheese**
- **8 flour tortillas (8 inches)**
- **2 tablespoons canola oil**

Sour cream, salsa and guacamole, optional

In a large skillet, combine the beans, tomatoes, chicken and onion powder. Bring to a boil. Reduce heat; simmer, uncovered, for 5-8 minutes or until thickened.

In a small bowl, combine the cheeses. Sprinkle half of the cheese mixture over four tortillas. Layer with chicken mixture and the remaining cheese mixture. Top with remaining tortillas.

In a large skillet over medium heat, cook quesadillas in 1 tablespoon oil for 1-2 minutes on each side or until cheese is melted, using additional oil as needed. Cut into wedges. Serve with sour cream, salsa and guacamole if desired. **Yield:** 4 servings.

QUICK AND COZY CLASSIC COMBO

On a hectic day, it's tempting to head to a cafe for a quick bite. But with recipes this easy and tasty on the menu, you'll look forward to eating at home! Frozen broccoli speeds preparation of satisfying Cheddar Broccoli Soup from Louise Beatty of Amherst, New York. Paired with Italian Roast Beef Sandwiches, from Tyler Sherman of Williamsburg Virginia, it makes an energizing meal that'll lift spirits in no time! ■

Italian Roast Beef Sandwiches

Prep/Total Time: 15 min.

1/2 cup grated Parmesan cheese
1/2 cup Italian salad dressing
1/2 teaspoon pepper
4 cups spring mix salad greens
4 ciabatta rolls, split
1/2 pound sliced deli roast beef
1 medium tomato, sliced
8 cucumber slices
1/4 cup sliced ripe olives, drained

In a large bowl, combine the cheese, salad dressing and pepper. Add salad greens; toss to coat.

Place salad green mixture over roll bottoms. Layer with roast beef, tomato, cucumber and olives; replace tops. Serve immediately. **Yield:** 4 servings.

Cheddar Broccoli Soup

Prep/Total Time: 30 min.

1 small onion, chopped
2 garlic cloves, minced
2 tablespoons butter
2 tablespoons all-purpose flour
1 can (14 -1/2 ounces) beef broth
1-1/2 cups 2% milk
1 package (10 ounces) frozen chopped broccoli
1 teaspoon ground mustard
1 teaspoon Worcestershire sauce
1/4 teaspoon ground nutmeg
1 cup (4 ounces) shredded cheddar cheese

In a large saucepan, saute onion and garlic in butter until tender. Stir in flour until blended. Gradually stir in broth; bring to a boil. Cook and stir for 2 minutes.

Stir in milk, broccoli, mustard, Worcestershire sauce and nutmeg. Bring to a boil. Reduce heat; simmer, uncovered, for 6-8 minutes or until heated through. Stir in cheese until melted. **Yield:** 4 servings.

ELEGANCE ON THE FLY

With the right ingredients, it's easy to make meals shine. Amy Wenger of Severance, Colorado, tops turkey breast cutlets with a rich marsala wine sauce for restaurant-quality Tangy Turkey Saute. We paired it with our Test Kitchen's hassle-free Nutty Broccoli for an effortless menu your family will love! ■

Tangy Turkey Saute

Prep/Total Time: 30 min.

1/4 cup all-purpose flour
8 turkey breast cutlets (2 ounces *each*)
3 tablespoons olive oil, *divided*
2 cups sliced fresh mushrooms
1/2 cup thinly sliced green onions
1 garlic clove, minced
1/2 cup chicken broth
1 cup marsala wine *or* additional chicken broth
1/2 teaspoon salt
1/4 teaspoon dried thyme
1 tablespoon minced fresh parsley

Place flour in a large resealable plastic bag. Add turkey, a few pieces at a time, and shake to coat. In a large skillet, saute turkey in 2 tablespoons oil in batches for 2 minutes on each side or until no longer pink; drain. Remove and keep warm.

In the same skillet, saute mushrooms and onions in remaining oil for 3 minutes or until crisp-tender. Add garlic; cook 1 minute longer. Stir in the broth, wine, salt and thyme. Bring to a boil; cook and stir for 3 minutes or until slightly thickened. Stir in parsley. Serve with turkey. **Yield:** 4 servings.

Nutty Broccoli

Prep/Total Time: 10 min.

1 package (16 ounces) frozen chopped broccoli, thawed
1/2 cup shredded Swiss cheese
1/2 cup chopped pecans
1/4 cup butter, melted
1/4 teaspoon garlic salt
1/4 teaspoon pepper

Place broccoli in a large microwave-safe bowl. Combine the remaining ingredients; pour over broccoli. Cover and microwave on high for 3-4 minutes or until tender. **Yield:** 4 servings.

Editor's Note: This recipe was tested in a 1,100-watt microwave.

KID-FRIENDLY FAVORITES

Barb Templin of Norwood, Minnesota, created Chipotle Chili Dogs for the 125th anniversary of her hometown. "People of all ages love them," she says. Crispy Ranch Fries, from Phyllis Schmalz of Kansas City, Kansas, comes with a not-so-secret sauce. ■

Crispy Ranch Fries

Prep/Total Time: 20 min.

1 package (26 ounces) frozen French-fried potatoes
1 envelope ranch dip mix, *divided*
1/2 cup mayonnaise
1/2 cup ketchup

Arrange french fries in a single layer in a greased 15-in. x 10-in. x 1-in. baking pan. Sprinkle with 2 tablespoons dip mix; toss lightly to coat. Bake at 450° for 15-20 minutes or until lightly browned.

Meanwhile, in a small bowl, combine the mayonnaise, ketchup and remaining dip mix. Serve with fries. **Yield:** 6 servings.

Chipotle Chili Dogs

Prep/Total Time: 25 min.

6 hot dogs
1/2 pound ground beef
1/4 cup chopped onion
1 garlic clove, minced
1 can (8 ounces) tomato sauce
2-1/2 teaspoons minced chipotle peppers in adobo sauce
3/4 teaspoon chili powder
1/4 teaspoon salt
1/8 teaspoon pepper
6 hot dog buns, split
3 tablespoons sour cream
3 tablespoons salsa
3/4 cup shredded cheddar cheese
2 green onions, chopped

Cook the hot dogs according to package directions. Meanwhile, in a large skillet, cook beef, onion and garlic over medium heat until meat is no longer pink; drain. Stir in the tomato sauce, chipotle peppers, chili powder, salt and pepper. Bring to a boil. Reduce heat; simmer, uncovered, 4-5 minutes or until flavors are blended.

Place hot dogs in buns. Spoon chili over hot dogs. In a small bowl, combine sour cream and salsa; spoon over tops. Sprinkle with cheese and green onions. **Yield:** 6 servings.

MARKET FRESH AND EFFORTLESS

Marie Rizzio of Interlochen, Michigan shows us how to enjoy the flavors of the season with her Farmers Market Squash Saute that uses squash, grape tomatoes and basil. Our Test Kitchen partnered this summertime side with Simply Seasoned Chicken for a no-fuss, weeknight meal. Now that's a breath of fresh air. ■

Simply Seasoned Chicken

Prep/Total Time: 30 min.

2 boneless skinless chicken breast halves (5 ounces *each*)
2 tablespoons Dijon mustard
1 tablespoon honey
1/3 cup dry bread crumbs
1/2 teaspoon garlic powder
1/2 teaspoon seasoned salt
1/2 teaspoon dried oregano
1/2 teaspoon dried thyme
1/2 teaspoon paprika
1 tablespoon canola oil
1 tablespoon butter

Flatten chicken to 1/4-in. thickness. In a shallow bowl, combine mustard and honey. In another shallow bowl, combine the bread crumbs and seasonings. Dip chicken in mustard mixture, then coat with crumb mixture.

In a large skillet over medium heat, cook chicken in oil and butter for 5-6 minutes on each side or until a meat thermometer reads 170°. **Yield:** 2 servings.

Farmer's Market Squash Saute

Prep/Total Time: 15 min.

1 medium yellow summer squash, cut into 1/4-inch slices
1 medium zucchini, cut into 1/4-inch slices
1-1/2 teaspoons olive oil
1/4 cup grape tomatoes
1 garlic clove, minced
1/4 cup shredded part-skim mozzarella cheese
1 tablespoon minced fresh basil *or* 1 teaspoon dried basil
Dash salt
1 tablespoon grated Parmesan cheese

In a large skillet, saute squash and zucchini in oil until crisp-tender. Add tomatoes and garlic; cook 1 minute longer. Remove from the heat. Stir in the mozzarella, basil and salt. Sprinkle with Parmesan cheese. **Yield:** 3 servings.

TASTY AND LIP-LICKIN' GOOD

Savory, fork-tender Flavorful Pork Chops, from Patti Leonard of Valrico, Florida, are smothered in a scrumptious sauce that will make your family say mmm! Coupled with our Test Kitchen's own Classy Carrots, topped with crunchy, toasted pecans, it makes a fast and colorful meal that's guaranteed to please even the most persnickety palates. ■

Flavorful Pork Chops

Prep/Total Time: 30 min.

4 bone-in pork loin chops (8 ounces *each*)
1/2 teaspoon salt
1/4 teaspoon pepper
1 tablespoon olive oil
1/4 cup sliced onion
2 garlic cloves, minced
1/2 cup Worcestershire sauce
3 tablespoons honey
1 tablespoon Dijon mustard

Sprinkle pork chops with salt and pepper. In a large skillet, brown chops in oil. Remove and keep warm.

In the same skillet, saute onion until tender. Add the garlic; cook 1 minute longer. Add the Worcestershire sauce, honey and mustard to the skillet; stirring to loosen browned bits from pan. Bring to a boil. Return chops to the pan. Reduce heat; cover and simmer for 15-20 minutes or until tender. **Yield:** 4 servings.

Classy Carrots

Prep/Total Time: 15 min.

1 package (16 ounces) frozen sliced carrots
2 tablespoons water
2 green onions, thinly sliced
2 tablespoons butter, cubed
1/2 teaspoon dried oregano
1/4 teaspoon garlic salt
1/4 teaspoon pepper
2 tablespoons chopped pecans, toasted

Place carrots and water in a large microwave-safe bowl. Cover and microwave on high for 5 minutes. Stir in the onions, butter, oregano, garlic salt and pepper. Cover and cook 2-3 minutes longer or until carrots are crisp-tender. Sprinkle with pecans. **Yield:** 4 servings.

Editor's Note: This recipe was tested in a 1,100-watt microwave.

TAKE A CRUISE TO GREECE

Vacation on a plate is the only way to describe Lemon-Caper Baked Cod from Carolyn Schmeling of Brookfield, Wisconsin. To pair with this buttery, flaky filet, our Test Kitchen developed Greek Green Bean Medley for a duo that takes your family's taste buds on a flavorful voyage. ■

Lemon-Caper Baked Cod

Prep/Total Time: 20 min.

1/4 cup butter, cubed
2 tablespoons lemon juice
1/4 teaspoon garlic pepper blend
1/4 teaspoon grated lemon peel
2 tablespoons capers, drained
4 cod *or* haddock fillets (6 ounces *each*)
1/2 teaspoon seafood seasoning
1 tablespoon crumbled feta cheese

In a small microwave-safe bowl, combine the butter, lemon juice, garlic pepper and lemon peel. Microwave, uncovered, on high for 45-60 seconds or until butter is melted. Stir in capers.

Place cod in an ungreased 13-in. x 9-in. baking dish; sprinkle with seafood seasoning. Spoon butter mixture over fillets. Sprinkle with cheese. Bake, uncovered, at 425° for 10-15 minutes or until fish flakes easily with a fork. **Yield:** 4 servings.

Greek Green Bean Medley

Prep/Total Time: 20 min.

3/4 pound fresh green beans, trimmed
1 medium red onion, halved and thinly sliced
1/3 cup chopped sweet orange pepper
1 tablespoon olive oil
2 garlic cloves, minced
1/2 teaspoon Greek seasoning
1/4 teaspoon dried oregano
1/8 teaspoon salt
1/8 teaspoon pepper

Place beans in a steamer basket; place in a large saucepan over 1 in. of water. Bring to a boil; cover and steam for 8-10 minutes or until crisp-tender.

Meanwhile, in a large skillet, saute the onion and orange pepper in oil until crisp-tender. Stir in the garlic and seasonings; cook 1 minute longer. Add green beans; toss to coat. **Yield:** 4 servings.

FRESH AND DELICIOUS LUNCH

Summer lunches needn't be bland and boring just because you're short on time! In 30 minutes, you can fix this fresh, fun meal. Crunchy jicama complements smooth avocado, while cilantro and lime juice add a bit of zest to Avocado Chicken Salad from Patricia Collins of Imbler, Oregon. Paired with delectable Garlic-Cheese Flat Bread, shared by Suzanne Zick of Maide, North Carolina, this breezy midday meal is a delicious break from the summer heat. ■

Avocado Chicken Salad

Prep/Total Time: 20 min.

3 cups cubed cooked chicken
2 medium ripe avocados, peeled and cubed
1/4 cup cubed peeled jicama
1/4 cup pimientos, diced
1/2 cup sour cream
1/4 cup mayonnaise
2 tablespoons minced fresh cilantro
2 tablespoons lime juice
1/4 teaspoon salt
1/4 teaspoon pepper
1/2 cup chopped green onions
5 romaine leaves

In a large bowl, combine the chicken, avocados, jicama and pimientos. In a small bowl, combine the sour cream, mayonnaise, cilantro, lime juice, salt and pepper. Drizzle over chicken mixture; toss to coat. Top with onions. Serve on lettuce leaves. **Yield:** 5 servings.

Garlic-Cheese Flat Bread

Prep/Total Time: 25 min.

1 tube (11 ounces) refrigerated thin pizza crust
2 tablespoons butter, melted
1 tablespoon minced fresh basil
4 garlic cloves, minced
3/4 cup shredded cheddar cheese
1/2 cup grated Romano cheese
1/4 cup grated Parmesan cheese

Unroll the dough into a greased 15-in. x 10-in. x 1-in. baking pan; flatten the dough to 13 in. x 9 in. and build up edges slightly.

Drizzle with butter. Sprinkle with the minced basil, garlic and cheeses.

Bake at 425° for 11-14 minutes or until crisp. Cut into squares; serve warm. **Yield:** 12 servings.

PARMESAN CHEESE

If you decide to buy a chunk of Parmesan cheese and grate your own, use the finest section on your grating tool. You can also use a blender or food processor. Cut the cheese into 1-inch cubes and process 1 cup of cubes at a time on high until finely grated.

A FAMILIAR FAVORITE REVISED

Get ready to dish up seconds when you serve this family-friendly meal. "Sloppy Pizza Joes were invented on my way home," recalls Charlene Easter of Milan, Illinois. "One of our children wanted loose meat sandwiches; the other, pizza. This is what we came up with." Even picky eaters won't be able to stop munching on Broccoli-Apple Salad, a tasty medley of fruit and veggies from our Test Kitchen. ■

Broccoli-Apple Salad

Prep/Total Time: 15 min.

1/2 cup mayonnaise
1 tablespoon sugar
1 tablespoon cider vinegar
1-1/2 cups fresh broccoli florets
1-1/2 cups fresh cauliflowerets
1/2 cup seedless red grapes
1/4 cup golden raisins
1/4 cup chopped apple
1/4 cup shredded cheddar cheese
1 tablespoon bacon bits

In a small bowl, whisk mayonnaise, sugar and vinegar; set aside. In a serving bowl, combine the remaining ingredients. Drizzle with dressing; toss to coat. Chill until serving. **Yield:** 5 servings.

Sloppy Pizza Joes

Prep/Total Time: 25 min.

1 pound lean ground beef (90% lean)
1 jar (14 ounces) pizza sauce
3/4 teaspoon garlic powder
3/4 teaspoon dried rosemary, crushed
3/4 teaspoon dried oregano
3/4 teaspoon dried basil
1/4 teaspoon onion powder
1/4 teaspoon pepper
4 hamburger buns, split
4 slices part-skim mozzarella cheese

In a large skillet, cook beef over medium heat until no longer pink; drain. Stir in the pizza sauce and seasonings. Cook and stir until heated through. Serve on buns with cheese. **Yield:** 4 servings.

SAUTE, SIMMER AND SERVE

Holly Neuhart of Mesa, Arizona, gives a supper staple some zing with Spicy Tomato Pork Chops. "I like to add garlic powder to the chops before browning or Cajun seasoning for more kick." Orzo Pilaf with Mushrooms, from Renee Zimmer of Gig Harbor, Washington, is a lovely, flavorful partner. ■

Orzo Pilaf with Mushrooms

Prep/Total Time: 25 min.

1/2 pound sliced fresh mushrooms
1 small onion, finely chopped
2 tablespoons olive oil
2 garlic cloves, minced
1 can (14-1/2 ounces) chicken broth
1 cup uncooked orzo pasta
1/4 teaspoon salt
1/4 teaspoon pepper
2 tablespoons minced fresh parsley

In a large saucepan, saute mushrooms and onion in oil until tender. Add garlic; cook and stir 1 minute longer.

Add the broth, orzo, salt and pepper. Bring to a boil. Reduce heat; cover and simmer for 10-14 minutes or until pasta is tender. Stir in parsley. **Yield:** 4 servings.

Spicy Tomato Pork Chops

Prep/Total Time: 30 min.

4 boneless pork loin chops (5 ounces *each*)
1 tablespoon olive oil
1 large onion, chopped
1 can (8 ounces) tomato sauce
1/4 cup water
2 teaspoons chili powder
1 teaspoon dried oregano
1 teaspoon Worcestershire sauce
1/2 teaspoon sugar
1/2 teaspoon crushed red pepper flakes

In a large skillet, brown pork chops in oil. Remove and keep warm. In the same skillet, saute onion until tender. Stir in the tomato sauce, water, chili powder, oregano, Worcestershire sauce, sugar and pepper flakes.

Return chops to the skillet. Bring to a boil. Reduce heat; cover and simmer for 15-20 minutes or until pork chops are tender. **Yield:** 4 servings.

DECADENT NOODLE DINNER

Dress up dinner tonight with in-a-snap Shrimp Linguine with Parmesan Cream Sauce, from Athena Russell of Florence, South Carolina. Easy and elegant, this creamy pasta dish with a hint of heat makes a weeknight meal seem like a special affair. Round it out with colorful Sauteed Spinach, shared by Terra Fondriest of St. Joe, Arkansas. "My dad has grown spinach for years, and this makes a perfect side." ■

Shrimp Linguine with Parmesan Cream Sauce

Prep/Total Time: 25 min.

6 ounces uncooked linguine
1/3 cup chopped onion
1/3 cup sliced fresh mushrooms
2 garlic cloves, minced
1/4 cup butter, cubed
2 tablespoons olive oil
1/4 cup heavy whipping cream
2 tablespoons grated Parmesan cheese
1/4 teaspoon crushed red pepper flakes
15 uncooked medium shrimp, peeled and deveined
1/8 teaspoon salt
1/8 teaspoon pepper

Cook the linguine according to package directions. Meanwhile, in a large skillet, saute the onion, mushrooms and garlic in butter and oil for 2-3 minutes or until the vegetables are tender. Stir in cream and cheese; sprinkle with pepper flakes.

Drain linguine. Add shrimp and linguine to skillet; cook over medium-low heat, for 5-7 minutes or until shrimp are no longer pink. Sprinkle with salt and pepper. **Yield:** 3 servings.

Sauteed Spinach

Prep/Total Time: 15 min.

3 garlic cloves, minced
2 tablespoons olive oil
2 tablespoons white wine *or* chicken broth
2 packages (9 ounces *each*) fresh baby spinach
3/4 teaspoon salt

In a large skillet, saute garlic in oil for 1 minute. Add wine. Bring to a boil; cook until liquid is reduced by half.

Add spinach and salt; cook and stir for 2 minutes or just until spinach is wilted. Serve with a slotted spoon. **Yield:** 4 servings.

SOUL FISH FROM THE SOUTH

Hey, y'all, it's dinnertime! Jan Wilkins of Blytheville, Arkansas, shares one of her favorite recipes for fast Cajun Pecan Catfish—also a Christmas Eve tradition in her household. Adding to the Louisiana-style charm, our Test Kitchen whipped up Creamy Sweet Corn with Okra as a soulful side dish. A bit of half-and-half and a few crumbles of bacon lightly coat these veggies the whole family will love. ■

Cajun Pecan Catfish

Prep/Total Time: 25 min.

- **2 tablespoons olive oil**
- **2 teaspoons lemon juice**
- **1 teaspoon Cajun seasoning**
- **1/2 teaspoon dried thyme**
- **1/3 cup finely chopped pecans**
- **2 tablespoons grated Parmesan cheese**
- **1 tablespoon dry bread crumbs**
- **1 tablespoon dried parsley flakes**
- **4 catfish fillets (6 ounces *each*)**

In a small bowl, combine the oil, lemon juice, Cajun seasoning and thyme. In a small bowl, combine the pecans, cheese, bread crumbs, parsley and 1 tablespoon oil mixture.

Place the catfish on a greased 15-in. x 10-in. x 1-in. baking pan. Brush with remaining oil mixture. Spread pecan mixture over fillets. Bake at 425° for 10-15 minutes or until fish flakes easily with a fork. **Yield:** 4 servings.

Creamy Sweet Corn With Okra

Prep/Total Time: 20 min.

- **1 small onion, chopped**
- **2 tablespoons butter**
- **1 garlic clove, minced**
- **3 cups frozen corn, thawed**
- **1 cup frozen sliced okra, thawed**
- **1/4 cup half-and-half cream**
- **2 slices ready-to-serve fully cooked bacon, chopped**
- **1 tablespoon sugar**
- **1/2 teaspoon salt**
- **1/4 teaspoon pepper**

In a large skillet, saute onion in butter until tender. Add garlic; cook 1 minute longer. Stir in the remaining ingredients; heat through. **Yield:** 4 servings.

SPICY-SWEET ISLAND ESCAPE

"An island vacation in a bowl" might be the best way to describe Jamaican Ham and Bean Soup, shared by Mary Lou Timpson of Colorado City, Arizona. A splash of lime juice and a hint of jerk seasoning add tropical taste. The subtle sweetness of our Test Kitchen's Caribbean Chips with Apricot Salsa is a yummy counterpoint to the soup's flavors. The speedy island duo will be a welcome change for your family's taste buds. ■

Jamaican Ham and Bean Soup

Prep/Total Time: 30 min.

1 small onion, chopped
1 tablespoon canola oil
3 cups cubed fully cooked ham
2 cans (16 ounces *each*) vegetarian refried beans
1 can (14-1/2 ounces) chicken broth
1 can (11 ounces) Mexicorn, drained
1 can (7 ounces) white *or* shoepeg corn, drained
1 can (4 ounces) chopped green chilies
1/2 cup salsa
1 teaspoon Caribbean jerk seasoning
1 can (2-1/4 ounces) sliced ripe olives, drained
1/3 cup lime juice
Sour cream and lime slices

In a Dutch oven, saute onion in oil for 3-4 minutes or until tender. Stir in the ham, refried beans, broth, corn, chilies, salsa and jerk seasoning; bring to a boil. Reduce the heat; simmer, uncovered, for 5 minutes, stirring occasionally.

Stir in the olives and lime juice; heat through. Garnish servings with the sour cream and lime slices. **Yield:** 7 servings (2-3/4 quarts).

Caribbean Chips With Apricot Salsa

Prep/Total Time: 15 min.

2 teaspoons Caribbean jerk seasoning
1/4 teaspoon brown sugar
1/4 teaspoon dried thyme
1/8 teaspoon salt
1/8 teaspoon garlic powder
1/8 teaspoon ground allspice
4 flour tortillas (8 inches)
Cooking spray
1/2 cup salsa
1/2 cup apricot preserves

In a small bowl, combine the first six ingredients. Coat both sides of each tortilla with cooking spray; sprinkle with seasoning mixture.

Cut each tortilla into eight wedges. Transfer to an ungreased baking sheet. Bake at 400° for 5-7 minutes or until golden brown.

Meanwhile, in a small bowl, combine salsa and preserves. Serve with chips. **Yield:** 4 servings.

SHOEPEG CORN

The term "shoepeg corn" dates back to before the American Civil War. The corn was named for its peg-like shape. Shoepeg has smaller kernels and is sweeter than yellow corn. If you can't find it at your grocery store, use white or yellow corn in your recipes.

PASTA PERFECT AND DELIZIOSO

It's not every day that a cost-conscious menu pleases both the eye and the stomach, but Stovetop Italian Macaroni from Laila Zvejnieks of Stoney Creek, Ontario, does exactly that. Our Test Kitchen paired her hearty one-skillet wonder with tangy Italian Dressed Broccoli for a complete meal. ■

Stovetop Italian Macaroni

Prep/Total Time: 25 min.

1 pound ground beef
1 can (28 ounces) diced tomatoes, undrained
2 cups water
1 envelope onion soup mix
1 teaspoon Italian seasoning
1/4 teaspoon crushed red pepper flakes, optional
2 cups uncooked elbow macaroni
1/2 cup grated Parmesan cheese
1 cup (4 ounces) shredded part-skim mozzarella cheese

In a Dutch oven, cook beef over medium heat until no longer pink; drain. Add the tomatoes, water, soup mix, Italian seasoning and pepper flakes if desired. Bring to a boil. Stir in macaroni. Reduce heat; cover and simmer for 8-9 minutes or until macaroni is tender.

Remove from heat; stir in Parmesan cheese. Sprinkle with the mozzarella cheese. Cover and let stand for 2 minutes or until cheese is melted. **Yield:** 5 servings.

Italian Dressed Broccoli

Prep/Total Time: 20 min.

4 cups fresh broccoli florets
1 medium onion, halved and sliced
2/3 cup water
1/3 cup Italian salad dressing
1 tablespoon butter
1/2 teaspoon dried oregano
1/4 teaspoon garlic powder
1/4 teaspoon dried parsley flakes
1/4 teaspoon salt

Place the broccoli, onion and water in a large skillet. Bring to a boil. Reduce heat; cover and simmer for 3 minutes. Add the remaining ingredients. Cook and stir over medium heat for 2-4 minutes or until vegetables are tender and liquid is reduced. **Yield:** 5 servings.

SIMMER SENSE

To "simmer" means to cook liquids, or a combination of ingredients with liquid, just under the boiling point (180° to 200°). The surface of the liquid will have some movement and there may be small bubbles around the side of the pan.

A CASUAL MEAL, NO KNIFE NEEDED

Priscilla Yee from Concord, California, proves that the best things come in small packages with Sausage Sliders with Cran-Apple Slaw. Our Test Kitchen created the tasty side Spiced Sweet Potato Fries. ■

Spiced Sweet Potato Fries

Prep/Total Time: 25 min.

1 package (19 ounces) frozen French-fried sweet potatoes
1/2 teaspoon garlic powder
1/2 teaspoon curry powder
1/2 teaspoon pepper
1/4 teaspoon chili powder
1/8 teaspoon ground cinnamon
1/8 teaspoon salt

Bake fries according to package directions. Meanwhile, in a small bowl, combine the remaining ingredients. Sprinkle over fries; toss to coat. **Yield:** 6 servings.

Sausage Sliders with Cran-Apple Slaw

Prep/Total Time: 25 min.

2/3 cup coleslaw mix *or* shredded cabbage
1/3 cup chopped apple
3 tablespoons dried cranberries
3 tablespoons chopped pecans, toasted
4 teaspoons mayonnaise
4 teaspoons barbecue sauce

SLIDERS:

1 pound bulk pork sausage
4 slices sharp cheddar cheese, halved
8 dinner rolls, halved and toasted
3 tablespoons spicy brown mustard
8 lettuce leaves

In a large bowl, combine the first six ingredients. Chill until serving.

Shape sausage into eight patties. In a large skillet, cook patties over medium heat for 3-4 minutes on each side or until a thermometer reads 160° and juices run clear, adding cheese slices during the last 1-2 minutes of cooking time.

Spread rolls with mustard; top each with a sausage patty, lettuce and 2 tablespoons coleslaw mixture. Replace roll tops. **Yield:** 4 servings.

CHAPTER 4

Cooking for Kids

Kid-friendly recipes are a dream for rushed parents who want to put yummy food on the table for their children. You'll find popular dinner dishes, such as pizza and beefy pasta, that'll fill up hungry tummies in a jiffy.

We also have a handful of cool and colorful treats and snacks that are just the thing young ones crave on summer days. Kids will go crazy over Tropical Strawberry Pops, Blueberry Fizz Pops and Crazy-Colored Fruit Pops. And they'll love whimsical treats, such as Green Sherbet Froggie and Onion Rings (they're actually licorice twists covered with graham cracker crumbs!).

Busy moms and dads will love putting smiles on the faces of their children with these delightful recipes! ■

CHILDREN LOVE WAFFLES. Strawberry Breakfast Shortcakes (p. 79).

Pepperoni Pizza

(Pictured above)

Prep: 25 min. **Bake:** 30 min.

My husband worked in Chicago-area pizza restaurants throughout high school and college. He says pizza is a work of art, and his are beautiful. Our girls prefer Daddy's pizza to ordering out! —*Julie Host, Polk City, Iowa*

1 cup plus 2 tablespoons water (70° to 80°)
2 tablespoons grated Parmesan cheese
2 tablespoons olive oil
1-1/2 teaspoons Italian seasoning
1 teaspoon sugar
1 teaspoon salt
3 cups all-purpose flour
2-1/2 teaspoons active dry yeast
1 tablespoon cornmeal

TOPPINGS:

1 cup meatless spaghetti sauce
1 to 3 teaspoons sugar, optional
1 package (8 ounces) sliced pepperoni
2 medium tomatoes, chopped
1/2 cup chopped onion
4 cups (16 ounces) shredded part-skim mozzarella cheese
1/2 cup grated Parmesan cheese
1-1/2 teaspoons Italian seasoning

In bread machine pan, place the first eight ingredients in order suggested by manufacturer. Select dough setting (check dough after 5 minutes of mixing; add 1 to 2 tablespoons of water or flour if needed).

When cycle is completed, turn dough onto a lightly floured surface. Roll into a 14-in. circle. Sprinkle a greased 14-in. pizza pan with cornmeal. Transfer dough to prepared pan.

Combine spaghetti sauce and sugar if desired; spread over dough. Top with the pepperoni, tomatoes, onion, cheeses and Italian seasoning.

Bake at 400° for 30-35 minutes or until crust is lightly browned. Let stand for 10 minutes before cutting. **Yield:** 8 slices.

Onion Rings

Prep: 20 min. + standing

Fool even the most seasoned foodie with this basket of "onion" rings created by the Test Kitchen. Graham cracker crumbs cleverly coat Twizzlers to create the illusion of deep-fried goodness.

10 licorice pastels
10 pieces Twizzlers Rainbow Twists
5 ounces white candy coating, melted
3/4 cup graham cracker crumbs

Place a pastel in the end of a twist. Attach the other end of twist to pastel, forming a ring. Repeat with remaining pastels and twists.

Place melted coating and cracker crumbs in separate shallow bowls. Dip rings in coating allowing excess to drip off, then roll in crumbs. Place on waxed paper; let stand until set. **Yield:** 10 servings.

Tropical Strawberry Pops

(Pictured at right)

Prep: 10 min. + freezing

Our Test Kitchen combines banana and pineapple to bring a taste of the tropics to these icy treats bursting with sweet strawberry flavor.

2 cups strawberry-banana V8 juice blend
1 can (8 ounces) unsweetened crushed pineapple, undrained
1 cup frozen unsweetened strawberries, thawed
1 medium banana
18 Popsicle molds *or* paper cups (3 ounces *each*) and Popsicle sticks

Place the juice, pineapple, strawberries and banana in a blender; cover and process until pureed. Fill each mold or cup with 1/4 cup strawberry mixture; top with holders or insert sticks into cups. Freeze. **Yield:** 1-1/2 dozen.

Orange-Peach Thirst Quencher

(Pictured at right)

Prep/Total Time: 10 min.

Peaches are mixed with an already tasty OJ blend for a simple, tasty treat that's perfect for breakfast or brunch.
—Sherry Thompson, Seneca, South Carolina

2 cups orange-tangerine juice, chilled
1 cup carbonated water, chilled
1 tablespoon honey
1-1/2 teaspoons lemon juice
1 can (14-1/2 ounces) no-sugar-added sliced peaches, drained

In a blender, combine all of the ingredients; cover and process until smooth. Pour into chilled glasses. **Yield:** 4 servings.

Cinnamon Berry Cider

(Pictured below center)

Prep/Total Time: 10 min.

When the weather is gray and cold, put a warm mug of this drink into mittened hands and watch little faces thaw into smiles. Made in the Test Kitchen, one tester noted, "it tastes like the holidays with a twist."

2 cups berry juice blend
1 cup water
1 cup unsweetened apple juice
8 orange slices
3 cinnamon sticks (3 inches)
Dash ground nutmeg

In a large saucepan, combine all ingredients. Bring to a boil over medium heat. Reduce heat; simmer, uncovered, for 5 minutes. Discard cinnamon sticks. Ladle into mugs. **Yield:** 4 servings.

DRESS UP YOUR DRINK

A festive garnish can add pizzazz to any beverage. Skewer berries, grapes, cherries, melon chunks and/or pineapple, then perch fruit kabobs across the top of the glass. Or, accent beverages with festive candy-cane swizzle sticks or cinnamon sticks.

Ground Beef Macaroni Casserole

(Pictured below)

Prep: 20 min. **Bake:** 25 min. + standing

My mom often made this casserole when I was growing up, and it was one of my favorite meals. It tastes terrific served with a salad and rolls.

—Judy Hluchy, Mt. Prospect, Illinois

1 package (7 ounces) elbow macaroni
1 pound ground beef
1 medium onion, chopped
1 can (15 ounces) Italian tomato sauce
1 egg
1 can (10-3/4 ounces) condensed cream of chicken soup, undiluted
1-1/2 cups 2% milk
2 tablespoons butter, melted
1 tablespoon minced fresh parsley
1 cup (4 ounces) shredded cheddar cheese

Cook the macaroni according to package directions. Meanwhile, in a large skillet, cook beef and onion over medium heat until meat is no longer pink; drain. Stir in tomato sauce; heat through.

Drain macaroni; transfer to a greased 13-in. x 9-in. baking dish. In a small bowl, combine the egg, soup, milk, butter and parsley; pour over macaroni. Spoon beef mixture over top; sprinkle with cheese.

Bake, uncovered, at 350° for 25-30 minutes or until bubbly. Let stand for 10 minutes before serving. **Yield:** 8 servings.

Fruit-Filled Cupcakes

(Pictured above)

Prep: 30 min. **Bake:** 25 min. + cooling

Kids really love the fruity surprise tucked inside my sweet and tender cupcakes.

—Margaret Wilson, Sun City, California

1 package (18-1/4 ounces) strawberry cake mix
2 cups (16 ounces) sour cream
2 eggs
1/3 cup strawberry preserves
1 can (16 ounces) vanilla frosting, *divided*
Red food coloring
Red nonpareils and pink jimmies

In a large bowl, combine the cake mix, sour cream and eggs. Beat on low speed for 30 seconds; beat on medium for 2 minutes.

Place 27 paper or foil liners in heart-shaped or standard muffin tins. (If using standard tins, tuck a 1/2-in. foil ball or marble between the liner and cup to form a heart shape.) Fill cups half full with batter. Using the end of a wooden spoon handle, make an indentation in the center of each; fill with 1/2 teaspoon preserves. Top with remaining batter.

Bake at 350° for 22-27 minutes or until a toothpick inserted in the cake portion comes out clean. Cool for 10 minutes before removing from pans to wire racks to cool completely.

Place a third of the frosting in a small bowl; tint pink with red food coloring. Frost cupcakes with white frosting; pipe edges with pink frosting. Decorate with nonpareils and jimmies. **Yield:** about 2 dozen.

Meatball Sub

(Pictured below)

Prep: 20 min. + freezing

Do you have a fun-loving family that appreciates pranks? Give 'em a real gotcha this year they'll never forget. This "sub" features a pound cake "bun" and ice cream "meatballs." Our Test Kitchen had fun making it, and your kids will have fun eating it, too!

1/2 cup Cocoa Krispies, coarsely crushed
3 small scoops chocolate ice cream
1/2 cup plus 1 teaspoon seedless strawberry jam, *divided*
1/4 teaspoon hot fudge ice cream topping
1 loaf (10-3/4 ounces) frozen pound cake, thawed
1/3 cup marshmallow creme
2 teaspoons flaked coconut, toasted
1 tablespoon unsalted sunflower kernels

Place cereal in a shallow bowl. Roll ice cream scoops in cereal to coat. Cover and freeze for 1 hour or until firm.

Meanwhile, in a small microwave-safe bowl combine 1/2 cup jam and ice cream topping. Microwave on high for 10-20 seconds or until warmed. Cut pound cake in half horizontally. Place bottom half on a serving plate. Spoon half of the jam mixture over cake; top with ice cream scoops, remaining jam mixture, marshmallow creme and coconut. Replace cake top.

In another microwave-safe bowl, melt remaining jam. Brush over top of cake; sprinkle with sunflower kernels. Serve immediately. **Yield:** 6 servings.

Game-Night Nacho Pizza

(Pictured above)

Prep/Total Time: 20 min.

Some like it hot with jalapenos; others like it cool with a dollop of sour cream. But one thing's for sure: This is "nacho" ordinary pizza night.

—Jamie Jones, Madison, Georgia

1 prebaked 12-inch pizza crust
1 tablespoon olive oil
1 cup refried beans
1 cup refrigerated fully cooked barbecued shredded beef
1/2 cup chopped seeded tomatoes
1/2 cup pickled jalapeno slices
1 cup (4 ounces) shredded Colby-Monterey Jack cheese
Shredded lettuce, sour cream and salsa, optional

Place crust on an ungreased pizza pan. Brush with oil. Spread the beans over crust. Top with beef, tomatoes, jalapenos and cheese.

Bake at 450° for 10-15 minutes or until cheese is melted. Serve with lettuce, sour cream and salsa if desired. **Yield:** 6 slices.

BAKING TWO PIZZAS

Two pizzas that bake at the same temperature can be put in the oven at the same time. Each pizza should be on its own shelf. Halfway through the baking time, rotate the pizzas, moving the pizza from the higher rack to the lower, and vice versa. You may need to add 5 to 10 minutes to the baking time.

Cool Watermelon Pops

(Pictured at right)

Prep: 20 min. + freezing

Kids will flip for the miniature chocolate chips in these picture-perfect pops made in our Test Kitchen. They're almost too cute to eat (but you'll be glad you did).

- **2 cups boiling water**
- **1 cup sugar**
- **1 package (3 ounces) watermelon gelatin**
- **1 envelope unsweetened watermelon cherry Kool-Aid mix**
- **2 cups refrigerated watermelon juice blend**
- **1/3 cup miniature semisweet chocolate chips**
- **2 cups prepared limeade**
- **2 to 3 teaspoons green food coloring, optional**
- **28 Popsicle molds *or* paper cups (3 ounces *each*) and Popsicle sticks**

In a large bowl, combine the water, sugar, gelatin and Kool-Aid mix; stir until sugar is dissolved. Add watermelon juice. Fill each mold or cup with 3 tablespoons of the watermelon mixture. Freeze until almost slushy, about 1 hour. Sprinkle with chocolate chips. Top with holders or insert sticks into cups. Freeze.

In a small bowl, combine limeade and food coloring if desired. If using Popsicle molds, remove holders. Pour limeade mixture over tops. Return holders. Freeze completely. **Yield:** 28 pops.

Crazy-Colored Fruit Pops

(Pictured at right)

Prep: 20 min. + freezing

Orange, pear, banana, raspberry, grape—the gang's all here! See if your poolside pals can guess the flavors in one of these summery rainbow pops.

—Vikki Spengler, Ocala, Florida

- **1 cup orange-tangerine juice**
- **2 cans (15 ounces *each*) reduced-sugar sliced pears, drained and *divided***
- **1 medium banana, sliced and *divided***
- **2 to 3 drops yellow food coloring, optional**
- **4 drops red food coloring, optional, *divided***
- **1 cup red raspberry juice**
- **1 cup grape juice**
- **19 Popsicle molds *or* paper cups (3 ounces *each*) and Popsicle sticks**

In a blender, combine the orange-tangerine juice, 3/4 cup pears, a third of the banana slices, yellow food coloring and 1 drop red food coloring if desired; cover and process until smooth. Fill each mold or cup with 1 tablespoon mixture; top with holders or insert sticks into cups. Freeze for 30 minutes or until firm.

In a blender, combine the raspberry juice, 3/4 cup pears, a third of the banana slices and red food coloring if desired; cover and process until smooth. If using Popsicle molds, remove holders. Pour raspberry mixture over orange layer. Return holders. Freeze for 30 minutes or until firm.

In a blender, combine the grape juice, remaining pears and remaining banana slices; cover and process until smooth. If using Popsicle molds, remove holders. Pour grape mixture over tops; return holders. Freeze for 30 minutes or until firm. **Yield:** 19 pops.

Blueberry Fizz Pops

(Pictured at right)

Prep: 20 min. + freezing

The whole family will go bananas when they taste this fizzy concoction of frozen berries and grape juice. Let's see those smiling purple lips!

—Margie Haen, Menomonee Falls, Wisconsin

- **2 cups white grape juice**
- **2 Kool-Aid Gigglin' Grape Fun Fizz drops**
- **2 cups fresh *or* frozen blueberries**
- **1 medium ripe banana**
- **3 to 4 drops neon purple food coloring, optional**
- **16 Popsicle molds *or* paper cups (3 ounces *each*) and Popsicle sticks**

Place grape juice and Fizz drops in a blender; cover and process until drops are dissolved. Add the blueberries, banana and food coloring if desired; cover and process until blended.

Fill each mold or cup with 1/4 cup blueberry mixture; top with holders or insert sticks into cups. Freeze. **Yield:** 16 pops.

Berry Blue Pops

(Pictured at right)

Prep: 25 min. + freezing

Our Test Kitchen staff had a blast bopping around the kitchen and swirling together the colorful mixes in these berrylicious pops. They were sorry to be finished in less than 30 minutes!

- **6 tablespoons berry blue gelatin**
- **1 cup sugar, *divided***
- **2 cups boiling water, *divided***
- **2 cups cold water, *divided***
- **6 tablespoons strawberry gelatin**
- **18 Popsicle molds *or* paper cups (3 ounces *each*) and Popsicle sticks**

In a small bowl, dissolve berry blue gelatin powder and 1/2 cup sugar in 1 cup boiling water. Stir in 1 cup cold water. In another bowl, dissolve strawberry gelatin powder and remaining sugar in remaining boiling water. Stir in remaining cold water.

In a small bowl, combine half of the berry blue gelatin mixture and half of the strawberry gelatin mixture. Place all in freezer for 1-3/4 to 2 hours or until slushy. In a large bowl, swirl the three colors as desired. Fill each mold or cup with 1/4 cup gelatin mixture; top with holders or insert sticks into cups. Freeze. **Yield:** 18 pops.

Salted Peanut Bars

(Pictured below)

Prep: 20 min. **Bake:** 15 min. + chilling

You'll never look at Rice Krispies Treats the same way again after sampling my nutty three-tiered cookie, marshmallow and cereal bars.
—Denise Kirsch, McLeansboro, Illinois

- **1 package (17-1/2 ounces) peanut butter cookie mix**
- **3 tablespoons canola oil**
- **1 tablespoon water**
- **1 egg**
- **1 package (10 ounces) peanut butter chips**
- **2/3 cup corn syrup**
- **1/4 cup butter, cubed**
- **2 cups Rice Krispies**
- **2 cups salted peanuts**
- **2 teaspoons vanilla extract**
- **3 cups miniature marshmallows**

In a large bowl, combine cookie mix, oil, water and egg. Press onto the bottom of a greased 13-in. x 9-in. pan.

Bake at 350° for 12-15 minutes or until set. Meanwhile, in a large saucepan, combine the chips, corn syrup and butter. Cook and stir over medium-low heat until smooth. Remove from the heat. Stir in the Rice Krispies, peanuts and vanilla.

Sprinkle marshmallows over crust. Bake 1-2 minutes longer or until marshmallows begin to puff. Spread cereal mixture over top. Cool completely on a wire rack. Refrigerate until firm. Cut into bars. **Yield:** 2 dozen.

Peanut Butter Blondies

(Pictured above)

Prep: 10 min. **Bake:** 25 min. + cooling

The Test Kitchen came up with these easy after-school treats that moms and dads will love. Don't want the kids to see you with your hands in the cookie jar? Be sure to wash down the evidence with a cold glass of milk.

- **2 eggs**
- **3/4 cup packed brown sugar**
- **1/2 cup creamy peanut butter**
- **1/4 cup butter, melted and cooled**
- **3 tablespoons 2% milk**
- **1 cup all-purpose flour**
- **1 teaspoon baking powder**
- **1/8 teaspoon salt**
- **4 peanut butter cups, chopped**

In a large bowl, beat the eggs and brown sugar for 3 minutes. Add the peanut butter, butter and milk; mix well. Combine the flour, baking powder and salt; gradually add to the sugar mixture, beating just until blended. Stir in the peanut butter cups.

Spread into a greased 8-in. square baking dish. Bake at 350° for 23-25 minutes or until a toothpick inserted near the center comes out clean. Cool on a wire rack. Cut into bars. **Yield:** about 1 dozen.

SOFTENING BROWN SUGAR

To soften brown sugar, place a slice of bread with the brown sugar in a covered container for a few days. Or microwave on high for 20-30 seconds, but watch carefully because the sugar will begin to melt. Always store brown sugar in an airtight container.

Hearty Mac & Cheese

Prep: 25 min. **Cook:** 10 min.

Whether a cold winter night or rainy summer day, this is quick-and-easy comfort food at its very best! And it's a great way to jazz up boxed macaroni mix.
—Carol Wohlgemuth, Riding Mountain, Manitoba

1 package (7-1/4 ounces) macaroni and cheese dinner mix
1 pound ground beef
3 tablespoons chopped onion
2 tablespoons chopped green pepper
1 can (10-3/4 ounces) condensed tomato soup, undiluted
2 tablespoons water
2 tablespoons ketchup
2 teaspoons prepared mustard
1 teaspoon seasoned salt
1 teaspoon chili powder
1/2 teaspoon dried oregano
1/4 teaspoon ground cumin
1/4 teaspoon pepper
1 cup frozen corn, thawed
1 cup (4 ounces) shredded cheddar cheese
1/4 cup butter, cubed
1/4 cup 2% milk

Cook the macaroni according to package directions; set cheese packet aside. Meanwhile, in a large skillet, cook the beef, onion and green pepper over medium heat until meat is no longer pink and vegetables are tender; drain.

Add soup, water, ketchup, mustard and seasonings. Bring to a boil. Reduce heat; simmer, uncovered, for 4 minutes.

Drain macaroni; add to the beef mixture. Stir in the corn, cheese, contents of reserved cheese packet, butter and milk. Cook over medium heat until heated through. **Yield:** 6 servings.

Green Sherbet Froggie

(Pictured above)

Prep/Total Time: 10 min.

Don't kiss summer goodbye until you've puckered up to this sublime dessert in disguise from our Test Kitchen. This one's so easy, kids could make it themselves!

1 scoop lime sherbet
3 green grapes (2 small and 1 large), halved
2 fresh blueberries
Green decorating gel *or* icing

Just before serving, place a rounded scoop of sherbet on an individual serving dish. Position small grape halves for legs.

For eyes, insert large grape halves into sherbet; add blueberries for eyeballs. Draw a smile with decorating gel. Serve immediately. **Yield:** 1 serving.

Strawberry Breakfast Shortcakes

(Pictured at left)

Prep/Total Time: 10 min.

Being short on time is no excuse for an unhealthy breakfast. Protein, fruit, dairy and whole grains come together in a flash for a delicious start to the day.
—Paula Wharton, El Paso, Texas

4 frozen low-fat multigrain waffles
1 cup fresh strawberries, sliced
1/2 cup plain Greek yogurt
Maple syrup

Prepare waffles according to package directions. Divide among two serving plates. Top with strawberries and yogurt. Serve with syrup. **Yield:** 2 servings.

Editor's Note: If Greek yogurt is not available in your area, line a strainer with a coffee filter and place over a bowl. Place 1 cup plain yogurt in prepared strainer; refrigerate overnight. Discard liquid from bowl; proceed as directed.

Wagon Wheel Casserole

(Pictured above)

Prep: 20 min. **Bake:** 40 min. + standing

This comforting casserole with ground beef, wagon wheel pasta and spaghetti sauce is guaranteed to earn thumbs up from all ages. —Barbara Hopkins, Lusby, Maryland

1 pound lean ground beef (90% lean)
1 pound sliced fresh mushrooms
1 large onion, chopped
8 ounces wagon wheel pasta, cooked and drained
1/3 cup grated Parmesan cheese
1 large green pepper, thinly sliced
1 jar (26 ounces) meatless spaghetti sauce
1 cup (4 ounces) shredded part-skim mozzarella cheese

In a large nonstick skillet, cook the beef, mushrooms and onion over medium heat until meat is no longer pink; drain. In a shallow 3-qt. baking dish coated with cooking spray, layer the pasta, Parmesan cheese, green pepper, beef mixture and spaghetti sauce.

Cover and bake at 350° for 30 minutes. Uncover; sprinkle with mozzarella cheese. Bake 10 minutes longer or until cheese is melted. Let stand for 10 minutes before serving. **Yield:** 8 servings.

Chocolate Frosted Peanut Butter Cupcakes

(Pictured below)

Prep: 30 min. **Bake:** 20 min. + cooling

Cupcakes aren't just for girls! My dad and brothers love peanut butter cups, so they love these.
—Alisa Christensen, Rancho Santa Margarita, California

1 package (18-1/4 ounces) yellow cake mix
3/4 cup creamy peanut butter
3 eggs
1-1/4 cups water
1/4 cup canola oil
FROSTING:
1-2/3 cups semisweet chocolate chips
1/2 cup heavy whipping cream
1/2 cup butter, softened
1 cup confectioners' sugar

In a large bowl, combine the cake mix, peanut butter, eggs, water and oil; beat on low speed for 30 seconds. Beat on medium for 2 minutes.

Fill paper-lined muffin cups two-thirds full. Bake at 350° for 18-22 minutes or until a toothpick inserted near the center comes out clean. Cool for 10 minutes before removing from pans to wire racks to cool completely.

Place the chocolate chips in a large bowl. In a small saucepan, bring cream just to a boil. Pour over chocolate; whisk until smooth. Cool, stirring occasionally, to room temperature. Add butter and confectioners' sugar; beat until smooth. Frost cupcakes. **Yield:** 2 dozen.

Editor's Note: Reduced-fat or generic brands of peanut butter are not recommended for this recipe.

Chive and Cheese Breadsticks

(Pictured above)

Prep: 15 min. + rising **Bake:** 15 min.

No Italian supper would be complete without bread. With two types of cheese, garlic and minced chives, these tasty twists go above and beyond.
—Rebekah Beyer, Sabetha, Kansas

1 loaf (1 pound) frozen bread dough, thawed
1/3 cup butter, softened
2 tablespoons minced chives
1 garlic clove, minced
3/4 cup shredded part-skim mozzarella cheese
1/2 cup shredded Parmesan cheese, *divided*

On a lightly floured surface, roll dough into a 12-in. square. In a small bowl, combine the butter, chives and garlic; spread over dough. Sprinkle with mozzarella cheese and 1/4 cup Parmesan cheese.

Fold dough in half. Cut into sixteen 3/4-in.-wide strips. Twist each strip 2-3 times; pinch ends to seal.

Place 2 in. apart in a greased 15-in. x 10-in. x 1-in. baking pan. Cover and let rise until nearly doubled, about 40 minutes.

Sprinkle with remaining Parmesan cheese. Bake at 375° for 13-15 minutes or until golden brown. **Yield:** 16 breadsticks.

Chicken Tetrazzini

(Pictured below)

Prep: 30 min. **Bake:** 30 min.

This creamy tetrazzini has been one of my favorite recipes for over 20 years. I always hear, "Yum. Is there any more?" Even overnight guests ask for leftovers the next day! *—Amanda Hertz-Crisel, Eagle Point, Oregon*

12 ounces uncooked spaghetti
1 small onion, chopped
1 celery rib, chopped
1/4 cup butter, cubed
1 can (14 ounces) chicken broth
1-1/2 cups half-and-half cream
1 package (8 ounces) cream cheese, cubed
2 cups cubed cooked chicken
1 can (4 ounces) mushroom stems and pieces, drained
2 to 4 tablespoons sliced pimientos
1/2 teaspoon salt
1/4 teaspoon pepper
1/2 cup sliced almonds, toasted
1/4 cup grated Parmesan cheese
1/4 cup crushed potato chips

Cook the spaghetti according to package directions. Meanwhile, in a large skillet, saute onion and celery in butter until tender. Stir in the broth, cream and cream cheese. Cook and stir just until cheese is melted. Remove from the heat.

Stir in the chicken, mushrooms, pimientos, salt and pepper. Drain spaghetti; add to chicken mixture and toss to coat. Transfer to a greased 13-in. x 9-in. baking dish.

Bake, uncovered, at 350° for 20 minutes. Sprinkle with almonds, Parmesan cheese and chips. Bake 10-15 minutes longer or until heated through and topping is golden brown. **Yield:** 6 servings.

CHAPTER 5

Give Me 5 or Fewer

Whether you have a hectic schedule, you've run out of time or need streamlined, no-stress recipes, these fast-to-fix dishes prove that cooking does not have to be a chore. From appetizers to cookies, every recipe here uses only five ingredients or fewer!

For a delicious starter, try the Foolproof Mushrooms. These bite-size stuffed mushrooms pack a lot of flavor, but the recipe uses four ingredients!

For a speedy, mouthwatering main course, try the Quick Sweet-and-Sour Chicken, which uses convenience products to create a better-than-takeout meal in only 25 minutes!

And for a divine dessert, take a look at the Chocolate Caramel Cookies that start with a rich, chocolaty cake mix. ■

LESS THAN FIVE INGREDIENTS. Brie Phyllo Cups (p.95).

Quick Sweet-and-Sour Chicken

(Pictured above)

Prep/Total Time: 25 min.

On a really busy night, this fast main dish that uses convenient, frozen stir-fry mix and chicken nuggets will hit the spot in no time.
—Mary Tallman, Arbor Vitae, Wisconsin

1 package (13.2 ounces) breaded chicken nuggets
1 package (21 ounces) frozen sweet-and-sour stir-fry mix
1 package (8.8 ounces) ready-to-serve whole grain brown rice
3 tablespoons salted cashews

Cook chicken nuggets according to package directions. Meanwhile, in a large skillet, cook the stir-fry mix, covered, over medium heat for 6-8 minutes or until heated through. Stir in chicken nuggets.

Microwave rice according to package directions. Serve with stir-fry mixture; sprinkle with cashews. **Yield:** 3 servings.

Editor's Note: This recipe was tested in a 1,100-watt microwave.

WHAT IS BROWN RICE?

It's rice that has had the husk removed but not the bran layer. The bran layer retains more vitamin, mineral and fiber content than white rice. When cooked, grains are separate with a chewy texture.

Monterey Ranch Bread

(Pictured below)

Prep/Total Time: 25 min.

This rich, cheesy loaf is a quick and easy addition to any meal. —Shirley Privratsky, Dickinson, North Dakota

2 cups (8 ounces) shredded Monterey Jack cheese
3/4 cup ranch salad dressing with bacon
1 loaf (1 pound) unsliced French bread
2 tablespoons butter, melted
Minced fresh parsley

In a small bowl, combine cheese and salad dressing; set aside. Cut bread in half lengthwise; brush with butter. Place on baking sheets. Broil 4 in. from the heat until golden brown. Spread with cheese mixture. Bake at 350° for 10-15 minutes or until cheese is melted. Sprinkle with parsley. **Yield:** 8 servings.

Fresh Peach Lemonade

(Pictured right)

Prep/Total Time: 20 min.

Looking for a new twist on lemonade? Fresh peaches lend a fruity flavor to this summertime must-have.
—Joan Hallford, North Richland Hills, Texas

4 cups water, *divided*
2 medium peaches, chopped
1 cup sugar
3/4 cup lemon juice
1 medium lemon, sliced
Mint sprigs, optional

In a small saucepan, bring 2 cups water, peaches and sugar to a boil. Reduce heat; cover and simmer for 5-7 minutes or until peaches are tender. Remove from the heat. Cool. Strain, discarding peach skins.

In a large pitcher, combine the peach mixture, lemon juice and remaining water. Add lemon slices and mint if desired. Serve over ice. **Yield:** 5 servings.

Prosciutto-Wrapped Asparagus With Raspberry Sauce

(Pictured above)

Prep/Total Time: 30 min.

What a delightful way to kick off a summer party! This upscale appetizer will make guests feel like you fussed. With only four ingredients, it's incredibly easy and oh, so yummy. —*Noelle Myers, Grand Forks, North Dakota*

1/3 pound thinly sliced prosciutto *or* deli ham
16 fresh asparagus spears, trimmed
1/2 cup seedless raspberry jam
2 tablespoons balsamic vinegar

Cut the prosciutto slices in half. Wrap a prosciutto piece around each asparagus spear; secure the ends with toothpicks. Moisten a paper towel with cooking oil; using long-handled tongs, lightly coat the grill rack.

Grill asparagus, covered, over medium heat for 6-8 minutes or until prosciutto is crisp, turning once. Discard toothpicks.

In a small microwave-safe bowl, microwave jam and vinegar on high for 15-20 seconds or until jam is melted. Serve with asparagus. **Yield:** 16 appetizers.

Garlic Butter Shrimp

Prep/Total Time: 25 min.

Garlic and lemon lend a pleasant flavor to these speedy sauteed shrimp. I like to serve them over wild rice mix from a box. —*Sheryll Hughes-Smith, Brandon, Mississippi*

1 pound uncooked medium shrimp, peeled and deveined
2 to 3 garlic cloves, minced
1/4 cup butter
3 tablespoons lemon juice
Hot cooked rice

In a large skillet, saute the shrimp and garlic in butter for 5 minutes or until shrimp turn pink. Add the lemon juice; heat through. Serve with rice. **Yield:** 4 servings.

Chocolate Caramel Cookies

(Pictured below)

Prep: 25 min. **Bake:** 10 min.

Kids will look forward to going back to school with a few of these in their lunch box. Each scrumptious chocolate cookie has a fun caramel surprise in the middle. —*Melanie Steele, Plano, Texas*

1 package (18-1/4 ounces) devil's food cake mix
2 eggs
1/2 cup canola oil
42 Rolo candies
Chopped hazelnuts

In a large bowl, combine the cake mix, eggs and oil. Roll tablespoonfuls of dough into balls. Press a candy into each; reshape balls. Dip tops in hazelnuts.

Place 2-in. apart on ungreased baking sheets. Bake at 350° for 8-10 minutes or until tops are cracked. Cool for 2 minutes before removing from pans to wire racks. Store in an airtight container. **Yield:** 3-1/2 dozen.

Editor's Note: If the dough is sticky, spray hands lightly with nonstick cooking spray before rolling into balls.

Easy Hummus

(Pictured above)

Prep/Total Time: 5 min.

Using sun-dried tomato salad dressing instead of tahini adds a new dimension of flavor to this nutritious predinner snack. —*Jeannette Jeremias, Kitchener, Ontario*

- **1 can (15 ounces) garbanzo beans *or* chickpeas, rinsed and drained**
- **1/2 cup sun-dried tomato salad dressing**
- **2 garlic cloves, minced**
- **Baked pita chips *or* assorted fresh vegetables**

In a food processor, combine the beans, salad dressing and garlic. Cover and process for 30 seconds or until smooth. Serve with chips. **Yield:** 1-1/2 cups.

Marmalade-Glazed Steaks

Prep/Total Time: 20 min.

Marmalade and mustard? They may sound like strange bedfellows, but this tasty main course proves that they're a match made in heaven.
—*Mike Tchou, Pepper Pike, Ohio*

- **1/2 cup orange marmalade**
- **2 tablespoons spicy brown mustard**
- **2 tablespoons cold butter**
- **1 beef top sirloin steak (1-1/4 pounds), cut into four steaks**
- **2 green onions, chopped**

In a small saucepan, heat marmalade and mustard over low heat. Whisk in butter until melted. Set aside 1/4 cup glaze for serving.

Broil steaks 4 in. from the heat for 5-7 minutes on each side or until meat reaches desired doneness (for medium-rare, a thermometer should read 145°; medium, 160°; well-done, 170°), basting occasionally with the remaining glaze.

Spoon reserved glaze over steaks; sprinkle with the onions. **Yield:** 4 servings.

Garlic Chicken Breasts

(Pictured below)

Prep/Total Time: 25 min.

Everyone loves the great flavor of this moist chicken dish. Cook up a little extra for a delicious salad topping or tasty sandwich. Either way, you're going to like it!
—*LaDonna Reed, Ponca City, Oklahoma*

- **1/2 cup grated Parmesan cheese**
- **1 envelope garlic and herb *or* Italian salad dressing mix**
- **2 boneless skinless chicken breast halves (6 ounces *each*)**

In a large resealable plastic bag, combine cheese and dressing mix; add chicken. Seal bag and shake to coat.

Place chicken in a greased 8-in. square baking dish. Bake, uncovered, at 400° for 20-25 minutes or until a meat thermometer reads 170°. **Yield:** 2 servings.

HANDLING POULTRY

To avoid contamination with other foods, always wash your hands and anything that has come in contact with the uncooked poultry (such as knives, cutting boards, countertops) with hot soapy water.

Frozen Macaroon Dessert

(Pictured at left)

Prep: 25 min. + freezing

Put summer on freeze and enjoy a slice of sweet bliss. With all the flavors of paradise, this pie whisks you away to a tropical staycation. —Mavis Gannello, Oak Park, Illinois

- **3 cups crumbled soft macaroon cookies**
- **1 can (20 ounces) crushed pineapple**
- **1/2 gallon butter pecan ice cream, softened**
- **1/2 cup chopped macadamia nuts**
- **1 carton (8 ounces) frozen whipped topping, thawed**

Sprinkle cookie crumbs onto an ungreased baking sheet. Bake at 350° for 8-10 minutes or until golden brown. Cool completely. Drain pineapple, reserving 1/4 cup juice; set pineapple aside.

In a small bowl, combine the cookie crumbs and reserved juice until crumbly; set aside and refrigerate 3 tablespoons for topping. Press remaining crumb mixture onto the bottom and 1 in. up the sides of an ungreased 9-in. springform pan.

Bake at 400° for 8-10 minutes or until lightly browned. Cool for 10 minutes. In a large bowl, combine the ice cream, pineapple and nuts; spread over crust. Cover and freeze until firm.

Carefully run a knife around edge of pan to loosen. Remove sides of pan. Spread whipped topping over top. Sprinkle with reserved crumb mixture. Let stand at room temperature for 15 minutes before serving. **Yield:** 12 servings.

Pesto Halibut

Prep/Total Time: 20 min.

In this entree, the mildness of halibut contrasts perfectly with the deep flavor of pesto. It literally takes minutes to get the fillets ready for the oven, so you can quickly start on your side dishes. Nearly anything goes well with this delightful fish. —April Showalter, Indianapolis, Indiana

- **2 tablespoons olive oil**
- **1 envelope pesto sauce mix**
- **1 tablespoon lemon juice**
- **6 halibut fillets (4 ounces *each*)**

In a small bowl, combine the oil, sauce mix and lemon juice; brush over both sides of fillets. Place in a greased 13-in. x 9-in. baking dish.

Bake, uncovered, at 450° for 12-15 minutes or until fish flakes easily with a fork. **Yield:** 6 servings.

Strawberry Pies

(Pictured at left)

Prep: 10 min. + chilling

How do you remember how to spell dessert correctly? In this case, double the "S" for double the deliciousness in these fluffy, fruity pies. —Peggy Key, Grant, Alabama

- **1 can (14 ounces) sweetened condensed milk**
- **1/4 cup lemon juice**
- **1 carton (12 ounces) frozen whipped topping, thawed**
- **1 quart fresh strawberries, sliced, *divided***
- **2 graham cracker crusts (9 inches *each*)**

In a large bowl, combine milk and lemon juice. Fold in whipped topping. Set aside 1/3 cup strawberries for garnish; stir remaining strawberries into filling. Spoon into crusts. Refrigerate for at least 4 hours before serving. Garnish with the reserved strawberries. **Yield:** 2 pies (8 servings each).

Creamy Lemon Cake Bars

(Pictured below)

Prep: 20 min. **Bake:** 35 min. + cooling

These refreshing delicacies caused a stir when our Test Kitchen was creating them. Are they cakes or bars? You'll just have to try them and let us know what you think!

- **1 package (18-1/4 ounces) lemon cake mix**
- **1/2 cup butter, softened**
- **1 egg**

FILLING:

- **1 can (16 ounces) lemon frosting**
- **1 package (8 ounces) cream cheese, softened**
- **2 eggs**

In a large bowl, beat the cake mix, butter and egg until crumbly. Press onto the bottom of a greased 13-in. x 9-in. baking pan.

In another bowl, beat the frosting and cream cheese until smooth. Set aside 1/2 cup for topping. Add eggs to the remaining mixture; beat on low speed just until combined. Spread over crust.

Bake at 350° for 35-40 minutes or until filling is set. Cool on a wire rack for 1 hour. Spread reserved frosting mixture over top. Refrigerate for at least 2 hours. Cut into bars. Store in the refrigerator. **Yield:** 16 servings.

Pork & Tomato Pasta Sauce

(Pictured above)

Prep/Total Time: 30 min.

This main dish is a favorite with my husband and two small children. Even my neighbors make it now. Simple ingredients, simple preparation, no fuss.
—Jackie Hughes, Baltimore, Maryland

1 pound bulk pork sausage
2 cups heavy whipping cream
1 can (14-1/2 ounces) diced tomatoes with basil, oregano and garlic, undrained
1/2 cup julienned oil-packed sun-dried tomatoes
Hot cooked fettuccine

In a large skillet, cook sausage over medium heat until no longer pink; drain.

Stir in cream and tomatoes. Bring to a boil. Reduce heat; simmer, uncovered, for 15-20 minutes or until liquid is reduced by half. Serve with fettuccine. **Yield:** 5 servings.

Pesto Dip with Parmesan Toast

Prep/Total Time: 20 min.

We created this recipe at my office when we had leftover mayonnaise and pesto, and weren't sure what to do with them. We figured it out and love this no-fuss dip.
—Laurel Churchman, Waco, Texas

1 French bread baguette (10-1/2 ounces), cut into 1/4-inch slices
1 cup grated Parmesan cheese, *divided*
2 cups mayonnaise
1 jar (8.1 ounces) prepared pesto
1 teaspoon garlic powder

Place baguette slices on greased baking sheets. Broil 4-6 in. from the heat for 1-2 minutes or until toasted. Turn slices over; sprinkle with 1/2 cup cheese. Broil 1 to 1-1/2 minutes longer or until lightly browned.

In a small bowl, combine the mayonnaise, pesto, garlic powder and remaining cheese. Serve with toast slices. **Yield:** 20 servings (2-1/2 cups dip).

Mozzarella Sticks

Prep/Total Time: 20 min.

You won't believe something this easy could taste so fantastic! Crunchy on the outside, gooey cheese on the inside...this is a treat all ages will love. Kids can help out by wrapping them, too.

—Shirley Warren, Thiensville, Wisconsin

12 pieces string cheese
12 egg roll wrappers
Oil for deep-fat frying
Marinara *or* spaghetti sauce

Place a piece of string cheese near the bottom corner of one egg roll wrapper (keep remaining wrappers covered with a damp paper towel until ready to use). Fold the bottom corner over cheese. Roll up halfway; fold sides toward center over cheese. Moisten remaining corner with water; roll up tightly to seal. Repeat with remaining wrappers and cheese.

In an electric skillet, heat 1/2 in. of oil to 375°. Fry sticks, a few at a time, for 30-60 seconds on each side or until golden brown. Drain on paper towels. Serve with marinara sauce. **Yield:** 1 dozen.

Scalloped Shrimp and Potatoes

(Pictured below)

Prep/Total Time: 20 min.

Shrimp and spinach take scalloped potatoes up a notch in this flavoful Test Kitchen-created entree. It really couldn't be easier to fix.

1 package (4.9 ounces) scalloped potatoes
2-1/4 cups water
1/3 cup 2% milk
1 pound peeled and deveined cooked medium shrimp

3 cups fresh baby spinach, coarsely chopped
1 cup (4 ounces) shredded Colby-Monterey Jack cheese

In a large skillet, combine the potatoes, contents of sauce mix, water and milk. Bring to a boil. Reduce heat; cover and simmer for 8-10 minutes or until potatoes are tender, stirring occasionally.

Add shrimp and spinach. Cook and stir until spinach is wilted. Stir in cheese until melted. **Yield:** 4 servings.

Snickers Cookies

(Pictured above)

Prep/Total Time: 30 min.

A sweet surprise is inside these two-ingredient cookies. It's a great way to dress up refrigerated cookie dough.

—Kari Pease, Conconully, Washington

1 tube refrigerated chocolate chip cookie dough
28 miniature Snickers candy bars

Cut dough into 1/4-in.-thick slices. Place a candy bar on each slice and wrap dough around it. Place 2 in. apart on ungreased baking sheets. Bake at 350° for 8-10 minutes or until lightly browned. Remove to wire racks to cool. **Yield:** about 2 dozen.

Editor's Note: 2 cups of any chocolate chip cookie dough can be substituted for the refrigerated dough. Use 1 tablespoon of dough for each cookie.

WARM COOKIES

To freshen homemade cookies, pop a few of them at a time in the microwave for 20-30 seconds. You'll have warm cookies that taste like they just came out of the oven!

Curried Chicken Salad

Prep: 15 min. + chilling

I turned last night's cooked chicken into a delightful salad that's perfect for lunch.
—Linda Bevill, Monticello, Arkansas

4 cups cubed cooked chicken
1 can (20 ounces) pineapple tidbits, drained
1 cup halved seedless grapes
1/2 cup mayonnaise
1/2 teaspoon curry powder

In a large bowl, combine the chicken, pineapple and grapes. In a small bowl, combine mayonnaise and curry; pour over the chicken mixture; toss to coat. Cover and refrigerate until serving. **Yield:** 6 servings.

Caesar Shrimp and Pasta

(Pictured below)

Prep/Total Time: 20 min.

Here's an easy entree that's ready in a dash. Creamy Caesar salad dressing beautifully coats pasta, shrimp and broccoli for a flavorful meal.
—Jo Ann Boyer, Bloomingdale, Ohio

3 cups uncooked bow tie pasta
3 cups fresh broccoli florets
1 pound peeled and deveined cooked medium shrimp
2 tablespoons plus 1/2 cup reduced-fat creamy Caesar salad dressing, *divided*
1/3 cup grated Parmesan cheese

In a large saucepan, cook pasta according to package directions, adding the broccoli during the last 4 minutes of cooking.

Meanwhile, in a large skillet, cook the shrimp in 2 tablespoons dressing over medium heat for 3-4 minutes or until heated through.

Drain pasta mixture; transfer to a large bowl. Add the shrimp, cheese and remaining dressing; toss to coat. Serve immediately. **Yield:** 4 servings.

Peanut Butter Clusters

(Pictured above)

Prep: 20 min. + chilling

Four ingredients and 20 minutes—could a fabulous last-minute gift idea be any easier? This yummy chocolate-coated crunch also freezes well, so keep some on hand for unexpected company. *—Pat Maxwell, Taft, California*

2 cups peanut butter chips
1 cup milk chocolate chips
1-1/2 cups dry roasted peanuts
1 cup crushed ridged potato chips

In a microwave-safe bowl, melt peanut butter chips and chocolate chips; stir until smooth. Stir in peanuts and potato chips. Drop by level tablespoonfuls onto waxed paper-lined baking sheets. Refrigerate until firm. Store in an airtight container. **Yield:** about 3-1/2 dozen.

Editor's Note: This recipe was tested in a 1,100-watt microwave.

Foolproof Mushrooms

(Pictured at right)

Prep/Total Time: 25 min.

These savory bites pack a lot of zingy flavor. Add some chopped artichoke hearts for an extra-special touch.
—Gail Lucas, Olive Branch, Mississippi

1 package (5.2 ounces) garlic-herb cheese spread
3 tablespoons grated Parmesan cheese, *divided*
30 small fresh mushrooms, stems removed
Thinly sliced fresh basil, optional

In a small bowl, combine cheese spread and 2 tablespoons Parmesan cheese; spoon into mushroom caps.

Transfer to a foil-lined baking sheet; sprinkle with remaining Parmesan cheese. Bake at 400° for 10-12 minutes or until lightly browned. Garnish with basil if desired. **Yield:** 2-1/2 dozen.

Brie Phyllo Cups

(Pictured at left)

Prep/Total Time: 20 min.

Mini phyllo shells from the freezer section hurry along these elegant cups. They look fancy and taste delicious but are a snap to put together for a special occasion.
—Brenda Little, Boise, Idaho

1 package (1.9 ounces) frozen miniature phyllo tart shells
3 tablespoons crushed gingersnaps
6 ounces Brie cheese, rind removed, cubed
1/4 cup spreadable fruit of your choice

Place the tart shells on an ungreased baking sheet. Sprinkle about 1/2 teaspoon gingersnap crumbs into each shell; top with Brie and spreadable fruit.

Bake at 325° for 5 minutes or until cheese is melted. **Yield:** 15 appetizers.

Slow Cooker Cheese Dip

Prep: 15 min. **Cook:** 4 hours

I brought this slightly spicy cheese dip to a gathering with friends, where it was a huge hit. To make things easier, you can also make it ahead of time.
—Marion Bartone, Conneaut, Ohio

1 pound ground beef
1/2 pound bulk spicy pork sausage
2 pounds process cheese (Velveeta), cubed
2 cans (10 ounces *each*) diced tomatoes and green chilies
Tortilla chips

In a large skillet, cook beef and sausage over medium heat until no longer pink; drain. Transfer to a 5-qt. slow cooker. Stir in cheese and tomatoes.

Cover and cook on low for 4 hours or until cheese is melted, stirring occasionally. Serve with tortilla chips. **Yield:** 3 quarts.

Editor's Note: If you're planning on serving Slow Cooker Cheese Dip at a holiday party or family get-together, make it ahead and freeze it. Then all you need to do is thaw and reheat it.

Rhubarb Strawberry Granita

Prep: 15 min.+ freezing

Fresh rhubarb and strawberries make this sweet and icy dessert such a treat. You'll love how quickly it comes together and that you don't need any special equipment to prepare it. *—Christen Roye, Weatherford, Texas*

3 cups water
1 cup plus 2 tablespoons sugar
1 cup diced fresh *or* frozen rhubarb, thawed
1/2 cup halved fresh strawberries
2 tablespoons orange liqueur *or* orange juice
Fresh mint leaves and orange peel strips, optional

In a large saucepan, bring the water, sugar, rhubarb and strawberries to a boil. Cook and stir until the sugar is dissolved. Strain; discard pulp and seeds.

Transfer syrup to an 8-in. square dish. Stir in orange liqueur; cool to room temperature. Freeze for 1 hour; stir with a fork. Freeze 2-3 hours longer or until completely frozen, stirring every 30 minutes. Stir granita with a fork just before serving; spoon into dessert dishes. Garnish with mint and orange peel if desired. **Yield:** 8 servings.

Editor's Note: If using frozen rhubarb, measure rhubarb while still frozen, then thaw completely. Drain in a colander, but do not press liquid out.

Blueberry Cobbler

(Pictured above)

Prep: 10 min. **Cook:** 3 hours

This comforting, simple-to-make dessert is ready in a jiffy. If you like, you can substitute other flavors, such as apple or cherry, for the blueberry filling.
—Nelda Cronbaugh, Belle Plaine, Iowa

1 can (21 ounces) blueberry pie filling
1 package (9 ounces) yellow cake mix
1/4 cup chopped pecans
1/4 cup butter, melted
Vanilla ice cream, optional

Place pie filling in a greased 1-1/2-qt. slow cooker. Sprinkle with cake mix and pecans. Drizzle with butter. Cover and cook on high for 3 hours or until topping is golden brown. Serve warm with ice cream if desired. **Yield:** 6 servings.

CHAPTER 6

Finished in 15 Minutes

When you're in a rush, there's no time to guess at how long it takes to throw a recipe together. That's where the dishes in this chapter come in handy, because every recipe here takes only 15 minutes or less to make!

Scrumptious appetizers, such as Parmesan-Coated Brie and Cranberry-Chili Cheese Spread, will impress party guests, and take a mere 10 minutes each to prepare. For a quick lunch or light meal, try Smoked Salmon Egg Salad or Orange Turkey Croissants—each ready in 10 minutes! For ready-in-a-flash desserts, try Hot Fudge Sauce or Blueberry Cheesecake Parfait.

No matter what kind of delicious dish you require, these recipes offer you peace of mind and fast, easy recipes that use on-hand ingredients. ■

FAST FIXIN'S. Barbecue Chicken Tacos (p. 100).

Broiled Parmesan Tomatoes

(Pictured above)

Prep/Total Time: 10 min.

Here's the ideal accompaniment to steak. It's a winner every time! —*Mary Price, Youngstown, Ohio*

2 medium tomatoes, halved
2 tablespoons plus 1/4 cup butter, *divided*
4 green onions, chopped
3 tablespoons dry bread crumbs
1 tablespoon grated Parmesan cheese
1/8 teaspoon salt
1/8 teaspoon garlic powder
1/4 cup shredded Swiss cheese

Place tomatoes, cut side up, in ungreased 15-in. x 10-in. x 1-in. baking pan; dot with 2 tablespoons butter. Broil 4 in. from heat for 4-6 minutes or until butter is melted. Meanwhile, in a small microwave-safe bowl, combine remaining butter and onions. Microwave, uncovered, on high for 2-3 minutes or until onions are tender. Stir in bread crumbs, Parmesan, salt and garlic powder; spoon over the tomatoes. Sprinkle with Swiss. Broil 1-2 minutes or until cheese is melted. **Yield:** 4 servings.

Smoked Salmon Egg Salad

Prep/Total Time: 10 min.

Smoked salmon and buttery croissants elevate ordinary egg salad sandwiches to a delicious, definitely grown-up level. I also like to add drained and rinsed capers to it. —*Cathy Tang, Redmond, Washington*

3/4 cup mayonnaise
1 teaspoon dill weed
1/2 teaspoon lemon juice
1/4 teaspoon salt
1/8 teaspoon pepper
6 hard-cooked eggs, chopped
4 ounces smoked salmon, chopped
6 croissants, split
1-1/2 cups fresh baby spinach

In a large bowl, combine the mayonnaise, dill weed, lemon juice, salt and pepper. Stir in the chopped hard-cooked eggs and salmon.

Place 1/3 cup of salmon egg salad on each of the bottom halves of croissants; top with the fresh spinach leaves. Top the egg salad with the croissant tops. **Yield:** 6 servings.

Spinach & Feta Saute

Prep/Total Time: 10 min.

With just the right level of garlic and a pleasant mix of cheese and almonds, this quick side will brighten any plate. You could also try it stuffed in a filet.
—Sharon Delaney-Chronis, South Milwaukee, Wisconsin

2 garlic cloves, minced
2 tablespoons olive oil
1 package (6 ounces) fresh baby spinach
1/4 cup slivered almonds
1/2 cup crumbled feta cheese

In a large skillet, saute garlic in oil for 1 minute. Add spinach and almonds; saute 2 minutes longer or just until spinach is wilted. Sprinkle with cheese. **Yield:** 2 servings.

Raspberry Pomegranate Smoothies

(Pictured below)

Prep/Total Time: 10 min.

Take advantage of the nutritional benefits of pomegranate by sampling this yummy smoothie made in our Test Kitchen. You'll love the unique blend of flavors.

1-1/2 cups pomegranate juice
2 cups frozen unsweetened raspberries
1/4 cup packed brown sugar
2 cups low-fat vanilla frozen yogurt

In a blender, combine the juice, raspberries and brown sugar; cover and process until blended. Add the frozen yogurt; cover and process until blended. Pour into chilled glasses; serve immediately. **Yield:** 4 servings.

Fire-Roasted Salsa

(Pictured above)

Prep/Total Time: 15 min.

Here's the pleasantly fiery treat friends and family won't be able to stray from at your next Cinco de Mayo buffet. Canned tomatoes speed preparation in this restaurant-quality salsa that's table-ready in no time.
—Missy Kampling, Mountain View, California

1 can (14-1/2 ounces) fire-roasted diced tomatoes, drained
1/2 cup sliced onion
1/3 cup fresh cilantro leaves
1 tablespoon lime juice
1 teaspoon sugar
1/4 teaspoon salt

In a food processor, combine the tomatoes, onion, cilantro, lime juice, sugar and salt. Cover and process until desired consistency. **Yield:** 1-1/2 cups.

Lemon-Dill Couscous

Prep/Total Time: 10 min.

I add a touch of lemon and a hint of dill to dress up my couscous with satisfying results. I enjoy serving this as a low-fat side to most any full-flavored meat entree.
—Mary Jo Welch, Brandon, Manitoba

3/4 cup uncooked plain couscous
3-1/4 teaspoons lemon juice
1/4 to 1/2 teaspoon dill weed

Follow couscous package directions for 2 servings, adding salt to the water and omitting the oil or butter from the first step. Stir in the couscous, lemon juice and dill. Cover and remove from the heat; let stand for 5 minutes. Fluff with a fork. **Yield:** 2 servings.

Editor's Note: This recipe was tested with Near East plain couscous.

Orange Turkey Croissants

(Pictured below)

Prep/Total Time: 10 min.

"Orange" you glad it's not the same old crustless ham and cheese? Orange you also glad you don't have to get up early to pack lunch? In less than 10 minutes, you (and five others) will have something to look forward to all morning long. —Jennifer Moore, Centerville, Iowa

6 tablespoons spreadable cream cheese
6 tablespoons orange marmalade
6 croissants, split
1/2 cup chopped pecans
1 pound thinly sliced deli turkey

Spread cream cheese and marmalade onto bottom half of croissants. Sprinkle with pecans. Top with turkey; replace tops. **Yield:** 6 servings.

Italian Snack Mix

(Pictured above right)

Prep/Total Time: 10 min.

A favorite sausage pizza inspired me to create this savory mix. It has great Italian flavors in a fun-to-eat snack version. —Priscilla Yee, Concord, California

7 cups Rice Chex
2 cups miniature pretzels
2 cups Parmesan and garlic-flavored snack crackers
1/4 cup olive oil
1 tablespoon balsamic vinegar
2 teaspoons seasoned salt
2 teaspoons Italian seasoning
1/2 teaspoon fennel seed, crushed
1/2 cup grated Parmesan cheese

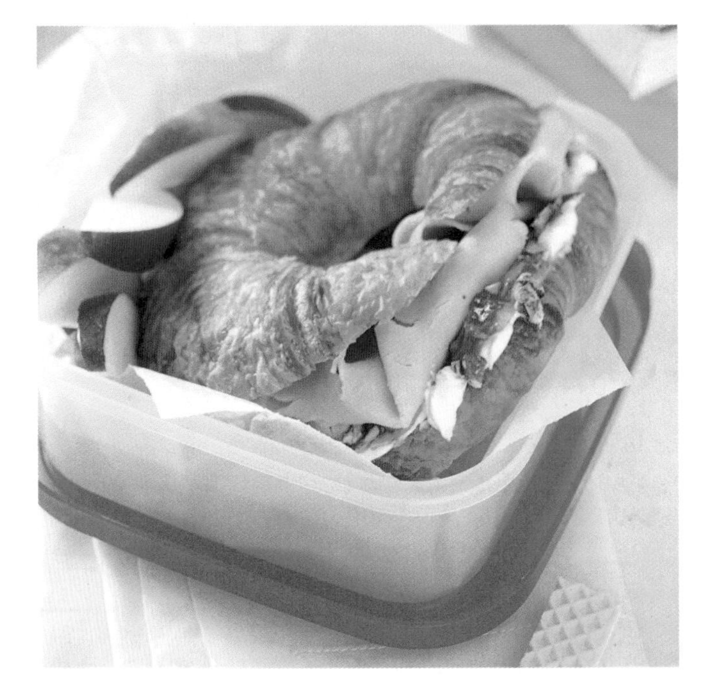

In a 3-qt. microwave-safe bowl, combine the cereal, pretzels and crackers. In a small bowl, combine the oil, vinegar, seasoned salt, Italian seasoning and fennel. Pour over cereal mixture and toss to coat. Stir in the Parmesan cheese.

Microwave the mixture, uncovered, on high for 3 minutes, stirring after each minute. Spread on waxed paper to cool. Store in an airtight container. **Yield:** 14 servings (2-1/2 quarts).

Barbecue Chicken Tacos

(Pictured at right)

Prep/Total Time: 15 min.

Here's a refreshing change from the average taco. Since everything's already prepared, there's practically no prep time involved. It makes dinner on busy nights a breeze. —Amy Krischel, Normal, Illinois

4 cups refrigerated shredded barbecued chicken
8 taco shells, warmed
1 cup (4 ounces) shredded Monterey Jack cheese
1 cup deli coleslaw

Place the chicken in a microwave-safe dish. Microwave, uncovered, on high for 3-5 minutes or until heated through, stirring every minute.

Spoon chicken into taco shells; top with cheese and coleslaw. **Yield:** 4 servings.

Editor's Note: This recipe was tested in a 1,100-watt microwave.

NO-MESS GRATED CHEESE

When shredding a block of cheese, place the base of the box grater inside a rolled-down, gallon-size plastic bag. When finished, pull out the grater, unroll the bag, seal it and store cheese in the refrigerator.

Parmesan-Coated Brie

(Pictured above)

Prep/Total Time: 10 min.

In no time, this wonderful appetizer cooks to a golden exterior with gooey cheese inside. It's delicious with French bread, crackers or fresh fruit.
—Karen Grant, Tulare, California

1 egg
1 tablespoon water
1/2 cup seasoned bread crumbs
1/4 cup grated Parmesan cheese
1 round (8 ounces) Brie cheese *or* Brie cheese with herbs
1/4 cup canola oil
Assorted crackers *and/or* fresh fruit

In a shallow bowl, combine egg and water. In another bowl, combine bread crumbs and Parmesan cheese. Dip Brie in egg mixture, turning to coat all sides; coat with crumb mixture. Repeat.

In a small skillet, cook Brie in oil over medium heat for 2 minutes on each side or until golden brown. Serve with crackers and/or fresh fruit. **Yield:** 8 servings.

Creamy Taco Dressing

Prep/Total Time: 5 min.

Here's a no-fuss alternative to ranch dressing. I use it on salads or as a dip. *—Kim Smith, Alden, New York*

1-1/4 cups mayonnaise
3/4 cup 2% milk
5 teaspoons taco seasoning

In a large bowl, combine all of the ingredients. Cover and refrigerate until serving. **Yield:** 2 cups.

Cranberry-Chili Cheese Spread

(Pictured below)

Prep/Total Time: 10 min.

Appetizers just can't get much easier than this ritzy-looking cheese spread with its refreshing hint of lime. I turn to this recipe whenever unexpected guests drop in.
—Laurie LaClair, North Richland Hills, Texas

2 packages (8 ounces *each*) cream cheese, softened
1 can (14 ounces) whole-berry cranberry sauce
1 can (4 ounces) chopped green chilies, drained
1 green onion, sliced
1 tablespoon lime juice
1/2 teaspoon garlic salt
1/2 teaspoon cayenne pepper
1/2 teaspoon chili powder
Assorted crackers

Place cream cheese on a serving plate. In a small bowl, combine the cranberry sauce, green chilies, onion, lime juice and spices. Spoon over cream cheese. Serve with crackers. **Yield:** 14 servings.

Maple Balsamic Dressing

Prep/Total Time: 5 min.

Sweet maple syrup and zesty balsamic vinegar lend bright flavors to tender grilled pork chops, a crisp summer salad and luscious red strawberries.
—Kim Sumrall, Aptos, California

1/3 cup balsamic vinegar
1/3 cup maple syrup
1/3 cup olive oil
FOR PORK CHOPS:
4 bone-in pork loin chops (8 ounces *each*)
FOR SALAD:
8 cups torn mixed salad greens
FOR STRAWBERRIES:
2 pounds fresh strawberries, hulled

In a blender, combine the vinegar and syrup. While processing, gradually add oil in a steady stream. **Yield:** 1 cup.

For pork chops: Pour 2/3 cup dressing into a large resealable plastic bag; add pork. Seal bag and turn to coat; refrigerate for at least 30 minutes. Cover and refrigerate remaining dressing.

Drain and discard marinade. Grill pork chops, covered, over medium heat for 6-7 minutes on each side or until juices run clear, brushing with 3 tablespoons reserved dressing during the last 5 minutes. Drizzle remaining dressing over chops before serving. **Yield:** 4 servings.

For salad: In a large bowl, toss greens with dressing. Serve immediately. **Yield:** 8 servings.

For strawberries: In a large bowl, toss berries with dressing. Chill until serving. **Yield:** 8 servings.

Hot Fudge Sauce

(Pictured above)

Prep/Total Time: 10 min.

You can whip up this homemade, chocolaty hot fudge sauce in a flash. You might want to make extra because it won't last long! —*Dorothy Floyd, Norton, Ohio*

1 cup miniature marshmallows
1 cup (6 ounces) semisweet chocolate chips
1 can (5 ounces) evaporated milk
Vanilla ice cream
Jimmies, optional

In a small saucepan, combine marshmallows, chocolate chips and milk. Cook and stir over low heat until smooth. Serve over ice cream. Sprinkle with jimmies if desired. **Yield:** about 1 cup.

Blueberry Cheesecake Parfait

(Pictured below)

Prep/Total Time: 10 min.

Whether served as breakfast fare or as a dessert, this cheesecake-flavored parfait will make your mouth water. —*Blair Lonergan, Rochelle, Virginia*

1/2 cup reduced-fat ricotta cheese
1 teaspoon sugar
1/4 teaspoon vanilla extract
3 tablespoons blueberry preserves
1/2 cup fresh *or* frozen blueberries, thawed
1/4 cup graham cracker crumbs
1 tablespoon slivered almonds

In a small bowl, combine the cheese, sugar and vanilla. Spoon 1 tablespoon preserves, 2 tablespoons blueberries, half of the cheese mixture and 2 tablespoons cracker crumbs into a parfait glass. Repeat layers. Top with remaining preserves, blueberries and almonds. **Yield:** 1 serving.

CHOOSING BLUEBERRIES

Look for fresh blueberries that are firm, dry, plump and smooth-skinned and relatively free from leaves and stems. Berries should be deep purple-blue to blue-black in color.

Italian Spinach Salad

(Pictured above)

Prep/Total Time: 15 min.

A simple homemade dressing makes this salad a wonderful option for any meal, but it's ideal alongside lasagna, spaghetti, manicotti and more.
—Cathy Desper, Staunton, Virginia

- **1/3 cup olive oil**
- **1/3 cup balsamic vinegar**
- **2 garlic cloves, minced**
- **2 teaspoons Italian seasoning**
- **2 packages (6 ounces *each*) fresh baby spinach**
- **1 cup grape tomatoes, halved**
- **4 green onions, sliced**
- **1/2 cup shredded part-skim mozzarella cheese**
- **1/2 cup salad croutons**

In a small bowl, whisk the oil, vinegar, garlic and Italian seasoning; set aside.

Divide spinach among 10 salad plates; top with tomatoes and onions. Drizzle with vinaigrette; sprinkle with cheese and croutons. **Yield:** 10 servings (2/3 cup vinaigrette).

Garlic Butter Topping

Prep/Total Time: 5 min.

My mother gave me this microwave recipe several years ago. It's easy and so tasty even my kids eat their veggies with this on them! Also try the garlic-flavored topping over bread as a yummy change of pace, or substitute garlic salt for garlic powder for a bit more zing.
—Marla Pinson, Granbury, Texas

- **3 tablespoons butter, softened**
- **1/2 teaspoon garlic powder**
- **1/4 teaspoon dried thyme**

GARLIC BREAD:

- **4 hoagie buns, split**
- **1/4 cup grated Parmesan cheese**

VEGETABLES:

- **3 cups fresh broccoli florets**
- **3 cups fresh caulifloweretts**
- **1 to 2 tablespoons water**
- **1/4 cup grated Parmesan cheese**

In a small microwave-safe bowl, combine the butter, garlic powder and thyme. Cover and microwave on high until butter is melted. **Yield:** 3 tablespoons.

For garlic bread: Brush butter topping over cut sides of buns. Place cut side down on grill. Grill, uncovered, over medium heat for 1 minute or until toasted. Sprinkle with cheese. **Yield:** 4 servings.

For vegetables: Place broccoli, cauliflower and water in a 2-qt. microwave-safe dish. Cover and microwave on high for 5-7 minutes or until crisp-tender; drain. Drizzle with butter topping; toss to coat. Sprinkle with cheese. Cook, uncovered, on high for 30 seconds or until heated through. **Yield:** 4 servings.

Editor's Note: This recipe was tested in a 1,100-watt microwave.

Sicilian Salad

(Pictured at right)

Prep/Total Time: 15 min.

Loaded with fabulous flavors, this hearty toss comes together in no time. Chop the tomatoes and celery and cube the mozzarella before guests arrive, and you'll have this dish ready in moments.
—Beth Burgmeier, East Dubuque, Illinois

- **1 package (9 ounces) torn iceberg and romaine lettuce blend**
- **1 jar (16 ounces) pickled banana peppers, drained and sliced**
- **1 jar (5-3/4 ounces) sliced green olives with pimientos, drained**
- **3 plum tomatoes, chopped**
- **4 celery ribs, chopped**
- **1 cup chopped pepperoni**
- **1/2 cup cubed part-skim mozzarella cheese**
- **1/2 cup Italian salad dressing**

In a large bowl, combine the first seven ingredients. Drizzle with the salad dressing and toss to coat. **Yield:** 10 servings.

HOMEMADE CROUTONS

To make your own croutons, in a large bowl, combine 1/4 cup melted butter, 1-1/2 teaspoons Italian seasoning and 1/2 teaspoon garlic powder. Cut 5 bread slices into 1/2-inch cubes. Add the bread cubes to the bowl and toss to coat them in the butter mixture. Arrange in a single layer on an ungreased baking sheet and bake at 325° for 15-20 minutes until golden brown, stirring occasionally.

Salsa Roja

(Pictured above)

Prep/Total Time: 15 min.

Preparing homemade salsa lets you alter the flavor to fit your palate. Whip this easy snack together and serve with fresh veggies, or my favorite, lime tortilla chips.
—Amber Massey, Coppell, Texas

- **1 can (28 ounces) whole tomatoes, drained**
- **1 can (14-1/2 ounces) diced tomatoes with garlic and onion, drained**
- **1 can (14-1/2 ounces) Mexican stewed tomatoes, drained**
- **1 can (10 ounces) diced tomatoes and green chilies, drained**
- **1 medium onion, quartered**
- **2 banana peppers, seeded and coarsely chopped**
- **2 jalapeno peppers, seeded and coarsely chopped**
- **3 garlic cloves, minced**
- **2 teaspoons salt**
- **1/4 teaspoon ground cumin**
- **1/2 cup minced fresh cilantro**
- **1/4 cup lime juice**
- **2 medium ripe avocados, peeled and cubed**
- **Tortilla chips**

Place the tomatoes, onion, peppers, garlic, salt and cumin in a food processor; cover and process until chopped. Add the cilantro and lime juice; cover and process until combined.

Transfer to a bowl and stir in the avocados. Serve with tortilla chips. **Yield:** 7 cups.

Editor's Note: Wear disposable gloves when cutting hot peppers; the oils can burn skin. Avoid touching your face.

BANANA PEPPERS

The flavor of banana peppers is sweet and mild. Look for peppers with evenly colored skins that are free of blemishes. They stay fresh in a plastic bag in the refrigerator for about 1 week.

Zesty Lemon Broccoli

Prep/Total Time: 15 min.

I invented this recipe when I began changing my eating habits to incorporate more vegetables into my diet. This broccoli tastes so decadent, you won't know it's healthy.
—Brooke Szczepanski, Gloucester, Virginia

4 cups fresh broccoli florets
1 tablespoon butter, melted
1 tablespoon grated lemon peel
1 tablespoon lemon juice
1 garlic clove, minced
1/2 teaspoon Dijon mustard
1/4 teaspoon salt
1/8 teaspoon pepper
1/4 cup pine nuts, toasted

Place the broccoli in a steamer basket; place in a large saucepan over 1 in. of water. Bring to a boil; cover and steam for 3-4 minutes or until crisp-tender.

Meanwhile, in a large bowl, combine the butter, lemon peel, juice, garlic, mustard, salt and pepper. Add broccoli and pine nuts; toss to coat. **Yield:** 4 servings.

Minted Sugar Snap Peas

(Pictured below)

Prep/Total Time: 15 min.

In 15 minutes, you'll bring spring flavors to the table with this praise-worthy side.
—Karen Adams, Cleveland, Tennessee

3 cups fresh *or* frozen sugar snap peas, thawed
3 green onions, chopped
1 garlic clove, minced
1/4 teaspoon salt

1/4 teaspoon pepper
2 teaspoons olive oil
1 tablespoon minced fresh mint

In a large skillet, bring 1 in. of water to a boil. Add the snap peas; cover and cook for 1-2 minutes. Drain and immediately place the snap peas in ice water. Drain and pat dry.

In the same skillet, saute the peas, onions, garlic, salt and pepper in oil until crisp-tender. Sprinkle with mint. **Yield:** 4 servings.

Chesapeake Snack Mix

(Pictured above)

Prep/Total Time: 10 min.

Plain pretzels pale in comparison to this jazzy concoction that microwaves in moments. Pack a pouch to go for an easy at-work or on-the-road snack.
—JoAnne Geiger, Baltimore, Maryland

2-1/2 cups Corn Chex
2 cups Wheat Chex
2 cups cheddar-flavored snack crackers
1 cup miniature pretzels
1/4 cup butter, cubed
1 teaspoon white vinegar
1 teaspoon Worcestershire sauce
3/4 teaspoon garlic powder
3/4 teaspoon seafood seasoning
1/2 teaspoon celery seed
1/2 teaspoon ground mustard

In a 3-qt. microwave-safe bowl, combine the cereals, crackers and pretzels. In a small microwave-safe bowl, melt butter. Stir in the vinegar, Worcestershire sauce, garlic powder, seafood seasoning, celery seed and mustard. Pour over cereal mixture and toss to coat.

Cook, uncovered, on high for 3-4 minutes, stirring once. Spread onto waxed paper to cool. Store in an airtight container. **Yield:** 2 quarts.

Editor's Note: This recipe was tested in a 1,100-watt microwave.

CHAPTER 7

Shop Once...Eat All Week

Does a weeks' worth of shopping lists and recipes sound too good to be true? Believe it or not, this chapter features six weeks of weeknight dinners that have already been planned for you.

Our Test Kitchen experts organized their own recipe creations for five days of the week. Each day features a new family-friendly entree, such as Shrimp Risotto, Mini Reuben Casseroles or Whole Wheat Pasta Bake.

To streamline prep, some of the recipes make use of leftovers from dishes made for other days of the week. The order of the meals throughout each week is up to you, so personalize them to your own schedule.

To make things even easier, each weekly menu comes with a complete grocery list! How fantastic is that? ■

A TASTY MONDAY MEAL. Creole Shrimp & Sausage (p. 125).

Week 1

SHOPPING LIST

Check for these staples:

- brown sugar
- butter
- chicken broth
- cider vinegar
- cornstarch
- dried parsley flakes
- dried sage leaves
- dried thyme
- eggs
- garlic cloves
- garlic powder
- ground ginger
- lemon juice
- olive oil
- onions
- paprika
- pepper
- prepared mustard
- salt
- soy sauce
- sugar
- white wine

Shop for these items:

1 package (8 ounces) panko (Japanese) bread crumbs
1 package (24 ounces) refrigerated mashed potatoes
1 jar (12 ounces) seedless raspberry preserves
1 package (16 ounces) rigatoni
1 bottle (50.7 ounces) apple cider
1 package (5 ounces) shredded Parmesan cheese
1 package (8 ounces) smoked mozzarella cheese
1 carton (8 ounces) heavy whipping cream
2 medium pears
3/4 pound fresh green beans
3 medium sweet potatoes
1 bunch small carrots
4 beef tenderloin steaks (6 ounces each)
4 tilapia fillets (6 ounces each)
4 bone-in pork loin chops (7 ounces each)
4 boneless skinless chicken breast halves (5 ounces each)
1 package (4 ounces) chopped walnuts
1 package (2.25 ounces) slivered almonds
1 package (16 ounces) frozen puff pastry

MAKE IT EASY

- For extra convenience, simply scan or copy the above grocery list.
- Jazz up the Parmesan-Sage Potatoes even more by stirring in freshly snipped chives.
- Choose ripe Anjou or Bosc pears for the best results when making the Chicken & Pear Bundles.
- Halve brussels sprouts and toss with olive oil, salt and pepper to lightly coat. Roast with the carrots in baking pan for an earthy addition to the pork chops.

MEAL 1

Broiled Steaks with Parmesan-Sage Potatoes

(Pictured above)

Prep: 20 min. **Broil:** 15 min.

This five-star meal would likely cost you about $25 in a restaurant, and that's without the tip! Serve this to guests, and they're sure to personally thank the chef.

1 teaspoon paprika
1 teaspoon pepper
1 teaspoon salt, *divided*
1/2 teaspoon sugar
1/2 teaspoon garlic powder
1/2 teaspoon dried sage leaves, *divided*
4 beef tenderloin steaks (6 ounces *each*)
1 large onion, halved and thinly sliced
2 tablespoons butter
2 teaspoons brown sugar
1 package (24 ounces) refrigerated mashed potatoes
1/2 cup shredded Parmesan cheese

In a large resealable plastic bag, combine the paprika, pepper, 1/2 teaspoon salt, sugar, garlic powder and 1/4 teaspoon sage. Add the steaks, two at a time, and shake to coat.

Broil steaks 4 in. from the heat for 7-9 minutes on each side or until meat reaches desired doneness (for medium-rare, a meat thermometer should read 145°; medium, 160°; well-done, 170°).

Meanwhile, in a large skillet, saute the onion in butter until tender. Add brown sugar and remaining salt; saute 1 minute longer.

In a small microwave-safe bowl, combine the potatoes, cheese and remaining sage. Microwave, uncovered, on high for 2-3 minutes or until heated through. Serve with steaks and onion. **Yield:** 4 servings.

MEAL 2

Chicken & Pear Bundles

(Pictured below)

Prep: 20 min. **Bake:** 20 min.

Filled with smoked mozzarella and sweet pears, these creative bundles are elegance at its easiest. A simple raspberry sauce finishes the dish nicely.

4 boneless skinless chicken breast halves (5 ounces *each*)
1/4 teaspoon salt
1/4 teaspoon pepper
1 sheet frozen puff pastry, thawed
4 slices smoked mozzarella cheese
2 medium ripe pears, thinly sliced
1 egg, beaten
1/2 cup seedless raspberry preserves
1 teaspoon cider vinegar

Flatten chicken breasts evenly; sprinkle with salt and pepper. On a lightly floured surface, roll pastry sheet into a 14-in. square. Cut into four squares. Place a chicken breast in the center of each square; top each with cheese and pear slices.

Lightly brush pastry edges with egg. Bring opposite corners of pastry over each bundle; pinch seams to seal. Place seam side down on a greased baking sheet; brush with remaining egg.

Bake at 400° for 20-25 minutes or until golden brown and a meat thermometer reads 170°.

In a small microwave-safe bowl, combine preserves and vinegar. Microwave, uncovered, on high for 20-25 seconds or until melted. Serve with the bundles. **Yield:** 4 servings.

MEAL 3

Rigatoni with Roasted Sweet Potatoes

(Pictured above)

Prep: 30 min. **Cook:** 15 min.

A rich and buttery cream sauce coats pasta and sweet potatoes in this impressive entree. Walnuts and wine give the dish its special flavor, while sage offers just the right seasoning.

3 medium sweet potatoes, peeled and cubed
1 medium onion, halved and sliced
3 garlic cloves, minced
1 tablespoon olive oil
3/4 teaspoon salt
1/2 teaspoon dried sage leaves
1/8 teaspoon pepper
2 cups uncooked rigatoni
2 tablespoons butter
1 cup heavy whipping cream
1/2 cup white wine *or* chicken broth
1/2 cup chopped walnuts, toasted
Shredded Parmesan cheese

Place sweet potatoes and onion in an ungreased 15-in. x 10-in. x 1-in. baking pan. Combine the garlic, olive oil, salt, sage and pepper; drizzle over the vegetables and toss to coat.

Bake, uncovered, at 400° for 20-25 minutes or until potatoes are tender, stirring occasionally.

Meanwhile, cook the rigatoni according to package directions. In a small saucepan, melt butter; stir in cream and wine. Bring to a gentle boil; cook for 10-12 minutes or until slightly thickened.

Drain the rigatoni; place in a large bowl. Add cream sauce, vegetables and walnuts; toss to coat. Sprinkle with cheese. **Yield:** 4 servings.

MEAL 4

Cider-Glazed Pork Chops With Carrots

(Pictured above)

Prep: 20 min. **Cook:** 15 min.

Treat your family to a dinner that will please them so much, they'll think you took cooking classes. They'll never guess this simple dish cost about $2 a serving!

4 bone-in pork loin chops (7 ounces *each*)
4 teaspoons olive oil, *divided*
3/4 cup apple cider *or* juice
2 tablespoons brown sugar
2 tablespoons cider vinegar
2 tablespoons soy sauce
3 garlic cloves, minced
2 teaspoons prepared mustard
1/2 teaspoon ground ginger
8 small carrots, halved lengthwise
1/2 teaspoon salt
1/4 teaspoon pepper

In a large skillet, brown the pork chops in 3 teaspoons oil on both sides.

In a small bowl, combine the cider, brown sugar, vinegar, soy sauce, garlic, mustard and ginger; pour over chops. Bring to a boil. Reduce heat; cover and simmer for 15-20 minutes or until tender.

Meanwhile, place carrots in a greased 15-in. x 10-in. x 1-in. baking pan. Drizzle with remaining oil. Sprinkle with salt and pepper; toss to coat.

Bake, uncovered, at 425° for 15-20 minutes or until tender, turning once. Serve with the pork chops. **Yield:** 4 servings.

Tilapia with Green Beans Amandine

(Pictured below)

Prep: 20 min. **Cook:** 15 min.

Japanese bread crumbs give tilapia a light, crispy coating that doesn't overpower the delicate fish. Lemony green beans are the ideal complement to this delightful entree.

4 tilapia fillets (6 ounces *each*)
1/2 teaspoon salt
1 egg
1-1/4 cups panko (Japanese) bread crumbs
3/4 teaspoon dried parsley flakes
3/4 teaspoon dried thyme
2 tablespoons butter
1 tablespoon plus 2 teaspoons olive oil, *divided*
1 teaspoon cornstarch
1 can (14-1/2 ounces) chicken broth
4 garlic cloves, minced
4 teaspoons lemon juice
3/4 pound fresh green beans, trimmed
1/4 cup slivered almonds, toasted

Sprinkle the fillets with salt. In a shallow bowl, whisk the egg. In another shallow bowl, combine bread crumbs, parsley and thyme. Dip fillets in egg, then coat with the crumb mixture.

In a large skillet, cook fillets in butter and 1 tablespoon oil over medium heat for 5-6 minutes on each side or until golden brown and fish flakes easily with a fork. Remove and keep warm.

In a small bowl, combine the cornstarch, broth, garlic and lemon juice until blended; set aside.

In the same skillet, saute beans in remaining oil until crisp-tender. Stir the cornstarch mixture and pour over beans. Bring to a boil; cook and stir for 1-2 minutes or until slightly thickened. Sprinkle with almonds. Serve with fish. **Yield:** 4 servings.

Week 2

SHOPPING LIST

Check for these staples:

- baking cocoa
- brown sugar
- butter
- cayenne
- chicken broth
- chili powder
- coriander
- cornmeal
- cumin
- Dijon mustard
- dried basil
- dried rosemary
- dried thyme
- eggs
- garlic cloves
- garlic powder
- instant rice
- Italian seasoning
- lemon juice
- mayonnaise
- milk
- olive oil
- onion salt
- onions
- Parmesan cheese
- pepper
- salt

Shop for these items:

1 loaf (1 pound) French bread
4 cans (5 ounces each) white water-packed tuna
2 jars (14 ounces each) spaghetti sauce
1 can (10-3/4 ounces) condensed cream of onion soup, undiluted
1 can (14-1/2 ounces) diced tomatoes with basil, oregano and garlic
1 can (14 ounces) water-packed artichoke hearts
1 jar (16 ounces) chunky salsa
1 package (8 ounces) no-cook lasagna noodles
1 carton (16 ounces) 1% cottage cheese
1 package (8 ounces) shredded Colby-Monterey Jack cheese
1 package (8 ounces) shredded part-skim mozzarella cheese
1 tube (10.2 ounces) large refrigerated flaky biscuits
1 package (6 ounces) fresh baby spinach
1 medium green pepper
3 plum tomatoes
3/4 pound ground beef
1-3/4 pounds boneless skinless chicken breasts
1 pound peeled and deveined cooked medium shrimp
1 package (16 ounces) frozen broccoli florets
1 package (16 ounces) frozen corn

CHANGE IT UP

- The flavor of Skillet Lasagna will change depending on the type of tomatoes used. Fire-roasted tomatoes, or tomatoes with roasted garlic also work well.

MEAL 1

Artichoke Tuna Melt

(Pictured above)

Prep/Total Time: 25 min.

Artichokes, spinach and a lemony mayonnaise give this melt an advantage over ordinary tuna salad sandwiches.

1 loaf (1 pound) French bread
1 tablespoon olive oil
1 garlic clove, halved
3/4 cup mayonnaise
1 tablespoon lemon juice
1 tablespoon Dijon mustard
1/2 teaspoon garlic powder
1/2 teaspoon pepper
4 cans (5 ounces *each*) white water-packed tuna, drained and flaked
1 can (14 ounces) water-packed artichoke hearts, rinsed, drained and chopped
1 cup fresh baby spinach
2 plum tomatoes, sliced
1 cup (4 ounces) shredded part-skim mozzarella cheese

Cut bread in half lengthwise (save one half for another use). Brush bread with the oil. Place cut side up on an ungreased baking sheet. Broil 4-6 in. from the heat for 2-3 minutes or until golden brown. Rub cut sides of garlic clove over bread; discard garlic.

In a large bowl, combine the mayonnaise, lemon juice, mustard, garlic powder and pepper. Stir in tuna and artichokes.

Arrange spinach over bread; top with tuna mixture, tomatoes and cheese. Broil 1-2 minutes longer or until cheese is melted. Cut into six slices. **Yield:** 6 servings.

MEAL 2

Chicken Cheese Strata

(Pictured below)

Prep/Total Time: 30 min.

The spices in this simple strata with chicken, broccoli and cheese offer an extra-special taste.

3/4 pound boneless skinless chicken breasts, cut into 1/2-inch cubes
4 tablespoons butter, *divided*
3 cups frozen broccoli florets, thawed
1/2 teaspoon onion salt
1/2 teaspoon dried thyme
1/2 teaspoon dried rosemary, crushed
1/4 teaspoon pepper
6 cups cubed French bread
2 eggs
3/4 cup 2% milk
2/3 cup condensed cream of onion soup, undiluted
1 cup (4 ounces) shredded Colby-Monterey Jack cheese

In a 10-in. ovenproof skillet, saute the chicken in 2 tablespoons butter until no longer pink. Add broccoli, onion salt, thyme, rosemary and pepper; heat through. Remove from skillet and keep warm.

In the same skillet, toast bread cubes in remaining butter until lightly browned. In a small bowl, combine the eggs, milk and soup; pour over bread cubes. Stir in chicken mixture. Sprinkle with cheese.

Bake, uncovered, at 400° for 15-20 minutes or until a knife inserted near the center comes out clean. Let stand for 5 minutes before cutting. **Yield:** 8 servings.

MEAL 3

Chicken Mole Casserole

(Pictured above)

Prep: 25 min. **Bake:** 20 min.

The key to a good mole is its rich, brown sauce with a hint of chocolate. The baking cocoa in this recipe lends a richness without sweetness.

1 pound boneless skinless chicken breasts, cut into 1/2-inch cubes
1 medium green pepper, cut into strips
1 small onion, chopped
1 tablespoon butter
2 tablespoons baking cocoa
2 teaspoons brown sugar
1 teaspoon chili powder
1/2 teaspoon ground cumin
1/4 teaspoon salt
1/4 teaspoon ground coriander
1/4 teaspoon cayenne pepper
2-1/2 cups frozen corn, thawed
1 jar (16 ounces) chunky salsa
1 tube (10.2 ounces) large refrigerated flaky biscuits
2 teaspoons butter, melted
3/4 teaspoon cornmeal

In a large skillet, saute the chicken, green pepper and onion in butter until the chicken juices run clear and the vegetables are tender.

Add the cocoa, brown sugar and spices; cook and stir over medium heat for 1 minute. Stir in the corn and salsa; heat through. Transfer to a greased 11-in. x 7-in. baking dish.

Cut each biscuit in half. Arrange biscuit pieces over chicken mixture with cut sides facing outer edge of dish, overlapping slightly. Brush with melted butter; sprinkle with cornmeal.

Bake, uncovered, at 375° for 20-25 minutes or until biscuits are golden brown. **Yield:** 6 servings.

MEAL 4

Shrimp Risotto

(Pictured below)

Prep/Total Time: 30 min.

This colorful main dish will make family meals seem a little more elegant. It comes together so quickly, it's just right for a warming weeknight supper.

1 small onion, chopped
2 tablespoons butter
1-3/4 cups uncooked instant rice
2 garlic cloves, minced
1/2 teaspoon dried basil
1/4 teaspoon pepper
2 cans (14-1/2 ounces *each*) chicken broth
1 pound peeled and deveined cooked medium shrimp
2 cups fresh baby spinach, coarsely chopped
1 cup frozen corn, thawed
1 plum tomato, chopped
1/4 cup grated Parmesan cheese
2 tablespoons 2% milk

In a large skillet, saute onion in butter until tender. Add the rice, garlic, basil and pepper; cook 2 minutes longer. Stir in one can of broth. Cook and stir until most of the liquid is absorbed.

Add the remaining broth, 1/2 cup at a time, stirring constantly. Allow the liquid to absorb between additions. Cook until risotto is creamy and rice is tender.

Stir in the remaining ingredients; cook and stir until spinach is wilted and shrimp are heated through. **Yield:** 4 servings.

MEAL 5

Skillet Lasagna

(Pictured above)

Prep/Total Time: 30 min.

This is hands-down one of the best skillet lasagna recipes our testing panel has ever tasted. With classic flavors and cheesy layers, it's definitely kid-friendly.

3/4 pound ground beef
2 garlic cloves, minced
1 can (14-1/2 ounces) diced tomatoes with basil, oregano and garlic, undrained
2 jars (14 ounces *each*) spaghetti sauce
2/3 cup condensed cream of onion soup, undiluted
2 eggs, lightly beaten
1-1/4 cups 1% cottage cheese
3/4 teaspoon Italian seasoning
9 no-cook lasagna noodles
1/2 cup shredded Colby-Monterey Jack cheese
1/2 cup shredded part-skim mozzarella cheese

In a large skillet, cook the beef and garlic over medium heat until the meat is no longer pink; drain. Stir in tomatoes and spaghetti sauce; heat through. Transfer to a large bowl.

In a small bowl, combine the soup, eggs, cottage cheese and Italian seasoning.

Return 1 cup meat sauce to the skillet; spread evenly. Layer with 1 cup cottage cheese mixture, 1-1/2 cups meat sauce and half of the noodles, breaking to fit. Repeat layers of cottage cheese mixture, meat sauce and noodles. Top with remaining meat sauce. Bring to a boil. Reduce heat; cover and simmer for 15-17 minutes or until noodles are tender.

Remove the heat. Sprinkle with shredded cheeses; cover and let stand for 2 minutes or until melted. **Yield:** 6 servings.

Week 3

SHOPPING LIST

Check for these staples:

- all-purpose flour
- beef broth
- butter
- brown sugar
- canola oil
- cayenne pepper
- chili powder
- cornstarch
- dried marjoram
- dried thyme
- garlic cloves
- garlic powder
- ground cinnamon
- ground ginger
- honey
- ketchup
- mayonnaise
- milk
- olive oil
- onion powder
- onions
- peanut butter
- pepper
- rice vinegar
- salt
- soy sauce
- Worcestershire sauce

Shop for these items:

1 loaf (1 pound) rye bread
1 bottle stout beer
1 can (12 ounces) root beer
1 can (14 ounces) coconut milk
1 can (10-3/4 ounces) condensed cream of chicken soup, undiluted
1 can (14 ounces) sauerkraut
1 bottle (16 ounces) Thousand Island dressing
1 cup fresh salsa
1 package (8 ounces) shredded Mexican cheese blend
1 package (5 ounces) shredded Swiss cheese
1 bunch fresh cilantro
1 package (1 pound) medium carrots
2 medium green peppers
1 medium sweet yellow pepper
2-1/2 pounds small red potatoes
1 boneless beef chuck roast (4 pounds)
4 bone-in pork loin chops (7 ounces each)
1 broiler/fryer chicken (3 to 4 pounds)

MAKE IT EASY

- Try the filling ingredients for the Mexican Grilled Cheese Sandwiches in a quesadilla. Simply layer ingredients on flour tortillas and toast 1-2 minutes on each side or until the cheese is melted.
- Using leftover beef from the Stout & Honey Beef Roast gives you a leg up on preparation for the Mini Reuben Casseroles.
- Use any leftover coconut milk in tropical smoothies and milk shakes, or use it in place of water in rice.

MEAL 1

Mexican Grilled Cheese Sandwiches

(Pictured above)

Prep/Total Time: 25 min.

A little salsa goes a long way in these quick, no-fuss sandwiches. Perked up with sweet peppers, they're flavorful, fun and ideal on busy weeknights.

1 medium sweet yellow pepper, chopped
1 medium green pepper, chopped
2 teaspoons olive oil
8 slices rye bread
2 tablespoons mayonnaise
1 cup fresh salsa, well drained
3/4 cup shredded Mexican cheese blend
2 tablespoons butter, softened

In a small skillet, saute peppers in oil until tender. Spread four bread slices with mayonnaise. Layer with peppers, salsa and cheese. Top with the remaining bread. Butter outsides of sandwiches.

In a small skillet over medium heat, toast sandwiches for 2-4 minutes on each side or until cheese is melted. **Yield:** 4 servings.

MEAL 2

Mini Reuben Casseroles

(Pictured below)

Prep: 20 min. **Bake:** 20 min.

These cute and creamy individual roast beef casseroles have the classic flavors of a Reuben sandwich.

1 medium onion, chopped
1 medium green pepper, chopped
2 teaspoons olive oil
2 cups cubed cooked beef roast
1 can (14 ounces) sauerkraut, rinsed and well drained
1 can (10-3/4 ounces) condensed cream of chicken soup, undiluted
1-1/4 cups (5 ounces) shredded Swiss cheese, *divided*
1/3 cup 2% milk
1/2 cup Thousand Island salad dressing
2 slices rye bread, cubed
1 tablespoon butter, melted
1/2 teaspoon onion powder

In a large skillet, saute the onion and green pepper in oil until tender. Stir in roast, sauerkraut, soup, 1 cup cheese, milk and salad dressing; heat through. Transfer to four greased 10-oz. ramekins or custard cups. Place ramekins on a baking sheet.

In a small bowl, toss the bread cubes with butter and onion powder. Arrange over tops. Bake, uncovered, at 350° for 15 minutes. Sprinkle with remaining cheese. Bake 5-10 minutes longer or until cheese is melted. **Yield:** 4 servings.

MEAL 3

Soda Pop Chops With Smashed Potatoes

(Pictured above)

Prep: 25 min. **Cook:** 20 min.

Root beer gives this family-friendly recipe a tangy taste kids will love. Served alongside the yummy smashed potatoes, this makes a scrumptious stick-to-the-ribs meal any weeknight.

1-1/2 pounds small red potatoes, halved
1 cup root beer
1 cup ketchup
1 tablespoon brown sugar
2 teaspoons chili powder
2 teaspoons Worcestershire sauce
1/4 teaspoon garlic powder
2 tablespoons all-purpose flour
3/4 teaspoon pepper, *divided*
1/2 teaspoon salt, *divided*
4 bone-in pork loin chops (7 ounces *each*)
2 tablespoons olive oil
2 tablespoons butter
1/4 teaspoon garlic powder

Place potatoes in a large saucepan and cover with water. Bring to a boil. Reduce heat; cover and cook for 15-20 minutes or until tender.

Meanwhile, in a small bowl, combine the root beer, ketchup, brown sugar, chili powder, Worcestershire sauce and garlic powder; set aside. In a large resealable plastic bag, combine flour, 1/2 teaspoon pepper and 1/4 teaspoon salt. Add pork chops, one at a time, and shake to coat.

In a large skillet, brown chops in oil. Add root beer mixture. Bring to a boil. Reduce heat; cover and cook for 10-15 minutes or until meat is tender, turning once. Remove pork and keep warm.

Bring sauce to a boil; cook until liquid is reduced by half. Meanwhile, drain the potatoes; mash with butter, garlic powder and remaining salt and pepper. Serve with pork chops and sauce. **Yield:** 4 servings.

MEAL 4

Stout & Honey Beef Roast

(Pictured above)

Prep: 15 min. **Cook:** 8 hours

Here's a heartwarming meal that's ideal for chilly days and hectic nights. Honey, beer and seasonings make the sauce different and oh, so good.

8 small red potatoes
4 medium carrots, cut into 1-inch pieces
2 medium onions, quartered
1 boneless beef chuck roast (4 pounds), trimmed
1 can (14-1/2 ounces) beef broth
1 cup stout beer *or* additional beef broth
1/2 cup honey
3 garlic cloves, minced
1 teaspoon dried marjoram
1 teaspoon dried thyme
1/2 teaspoon salt
1/2 teaspoon pepper
1/4 teaspoon ground cinnamon
2 tablespoons cornstarch
1/4 cup cold water

Place the potatoes, carrots and onions in a 5-qt. slow cooker. Cut roast in half; transfer to slow cooker. In a small bowl, combine the broth, beer, honey, garlic, marjoram, thyme, salt, pepper and cinnamon; pour over top. Cover and cook on low for 8-10 hours or until meat and vegetables are tender.

Remove roast and cut a portion of the meat into cubes, measuring 2 cups; cover and save for another use. Slice the remaining beef and keep warm. Strain cooking juices, reserving vegetables and 1 cup juices; skim fat from reserved juices.

Transfer to a small saucepan. Bring to a boil. Combine cornstarch and water until smooth; gradually stir into the pan. Bring to a boil; cook and stir for 2 minutes or until thickened. Serve with beef and vegetables. **Yield:** 4 servings plus leftovers.

MEAL 5

Thai Fried Chicken

(Pictured below)

Prep: 30 min. **Bake:** 25 min.

Nothing says "comfort food" more than homemade fried chicken. We gave it an Asian flair, creating an amazing combo of tastes your family will love.

1-1/2 cups all-purpose flour, *divided*
1 cup coconut milk
1/2 teaspoon salt
1/2 teaspoon garlic powder
1/2 teaspoon ground ginger
1/4 teaspoon cayenne pepper
1 broiler/fryer chicken (3 to 4 pounds), cut up
1/4 cup canola oil

SAUCE:

1 cup water
1/3 cup packed brown sugar
1/4 cup soy sauce
3-1/2 teaspoons cornstarch
2 teaspoons rice vinegar
2 teaspoons peanut butter
1/4 teaspoon cayenne pepper
1/4 teaspoon ground ginger
3 tablespoons minced fresh cilantro

Place 1/2 cup flour and coconut milk in separate shallow bowls. In another shallow bowl, combine the salt, garlic powder, ginger, cayenne and remaining flour. Dip the chicken in the flour, coconut milk, then flour mixture.

In a large skillet, brown the chicken in oil in batches; drain. Transfer to a greased 13-in. x 9-in. baking dish. Bake, uncovered, at 400° for 25-35 minutes or until a meat thermometer reads 180°.

Meanwhile, in a small saucepan, combine the water, brown sugar, soy sauce, cornstarch, vinegar, peanut butter, cayenne and ginger. Bring to a boil; cook and stir for 2 minutes or until thickened. Stir in cilantro. Serve with chicken. **Yield:** 6 servings.

Week 4

■ SHOPPING LIST ■

Check for these staples:

- butter
- dried thyme
- olive oil
- pepper
- salt

Shop for these items:

1 can (14-1/2 ounces) fire-roasted diced tomatoes
1 jar (12 ounces) garlic-herb mayonnaise
1 box (9.5 ounces) fire-roasted tomato Triscuits
1 jar (1.0 ounces) Caribbean Jerk seasoning
1 package (16 ounces) fusilli pasta
1 package (6-1/4 ounces) curry rice pilaf mix
4 slices part-skim mozzarella cheese
1 fresh small pineapple
4 medium limes
1 package (.75 ounces) fresh basil
1 bunch fresh parsley
1 package (6 ounces) fresh baby spinach
1 pint grape tomatoes
4 beef tenderloin steaks (1-1/4 inches thick and 6 ounces each)
1 package (17 ounces) refrigerated beef tips with gravy
4 bone-in pork loin chops (3/4 inches thick)
4 boneless skinless chicken breast halves (6 ounces each)
1-1/2 pounds sea scallops
1 package (12 ounces) frozen garlic baby peas and mushrooms
1 package (15 ounces) frozen Parmesan and garlic red potatoes
1 package (14 ounces) frozen pepper strips

■ MAKE IT EASY ■

- When cooking steak, check the internal temperature by inserting a meat thermometer from the side into the meat's center.
- You'll have about 3 cups of baby spinach left over this week. Use it to toss together a side salad with your favorite toppings and serve it with Beef Tip Stew over Fusilli.
- If you'd like to fix Grilled Jerk Chops on a Monday, and you're shopping on Sunday, before putting the pineapple in the fridge, quarter it. The supper will be a cinch to fix on Monday.
- If you're not a fan of curry, for the Curry Scallops and Rice, feel free to use a brown rice pilaf mix in the speedy main dish.

MEAL 1

Basil-Butter Steaks With Roasted Potatoes

(Pictured below)

Prep/Total Time: 30 min.

A few ingredients and 30 minutes are all you'll need for this incredibly satisfying meal. A simple basil butter gives these steaks a very special taste.

1 package (15 ounces) frozen Parmesan and roasted garlic red potato wedges
4 beef tenderloin steaks (1-1/4 inches thick and 6 ounces *each*)
1/2 teaspoon salt
1/2 teaspoon pepper
5 tablespoons butter, *divided*
2 cups grape tomatoes
1 tablespoon minced fresh basil

Bake potato wedges according to package directions.

Meanwhile, sprinkle steaks with salt and pepper. In a 10-inch cast-iron skillet, brown steaks in 2 tablespoons butter. Add tomatoes to the skillet. Bake, uncovered, at 425° for 15-20 minutes or until meat reaches desired doneness (for medium-rare, a meat thermometer should read 145°; medium, 160°; well-done, 170°).

In a small bowl, combine basil and remaining butter. Spoon over the steaks and serve with potato wedges. **Yield:** 4 servings.

MEAL 2

Beef Tip Stew over Fusilli

(Pictured below)

Prep/Total Time: 25 min.

Fire-roasted tomatoes add bright color and delightful flair to this hearty entree with a well-seasoned veggie blend.

2-1/2 cups uncooked fusilli pasta
1 package (17 ounces) refrigerated beef tips with gravy
1 package (12 ounces) frozen garlic baby pea and mushroom blend
1 can (14-1/2 ounces) fire-roasted diced tomatoes, undrained
1/2 teaspoon dried thyme
1/4 teaspoon pepper

Cook pasta according to package directions. Meanwhile, in a large skillet, combine the beef tips with gravy, vegetable blend, tomatoes, thyme and pepper; heat through. Drain pasta. Serve with beef mixture. **Yield:** 4 servings.

MEAL 3

Curry Scallops and Rice

(Pictured above)

Prep/Total Time: 30 min.

Buttery scallops, colorful pepper strips and a fast rice mix tinged with curry...what's not to love about this stress-free main dish?

1 package (6-1/4 ounces) curry rice pilaf mix
1/4 cup butter, *divided*
1-1/2 pounds sea scallops
1 package (14 ounces) frozen pepper strips, thawed and chopped
1/4 cup minced fresh parsley
1/4 teaspoon salt

Prepare pilaf mix according to package directions using 1 tablespoon butter.

Meanwhile, in a large skillet, saute the scallops in remaining butter until firm and opaque. Remove and keep warm. In the same skillet, saute the peppers until tender. Stir in the scallops, rice, parsley and salt. **Yield:** 4 servings.

MEAL 4

Grilled Jerk Chops

(Pictured below)

Prep: 15 min. + marinating **Grill:** 10 min.

Moist and tender chops are treated to a quick, tangy marinade that gives this fresh meal weeknight ease.

4 medium limes
1 tablespoon Caribbean jerk seasoning
1 tablespoon olive oil
4 bone-in pork loin chops (3/4 inch thick)
1 small fresh pineapple

Finely grate the peel from one lime; set aside. Squeeze juice from two limes. Cut remaining two limes in half; set aside.

In a small bowl, combine the jerk seasoning, oil, lime peel and half of the juice; rub over pork chops. Refrigerate for at least 30 minutes. Meanwhile, peel and quarter pineapple; drizzle with remaining lime juice.

Moisten a paper towel with cooking oil; using long-handled tongs, lightly coat the grill rack. Grill chops and pineapple, covered, over medium heat for 4-5 minutes on each side or until a meat thermometer reads 160° and pineapple is tender. Grill lime halves for 2-3 minutes or until heated through.

Chop pineapple; serve with pork and lime halves. **Yield:** 4 servings.

MEAL 5

Smothered Italian Chicken

(Pictured above)

Prep: 15 min. **Bake:** 20 min.

A crispy cracker coating and flavored mayo make these savory chicken breasts downright delicious.

22 fire-roasted tomato Triscuits, crushed
3/4 cup plus 3 tablespoons garlic-herb mayonnaise, *divided*
4 boneless skinless chicken breast halves (6 ounces *each*)
4 cups fresh baby spinach
4 slices part-skim mozzarella cheese
Dash pepper

Place the crushed crackers and 3/4 cup mayonnaise in separate shallow bowls. Dip chicken in mayonnaise and then coat with crackers.

Transfer to a greased 13-in. x 9-in. baking dish. Bake, uncovered, at 375° for 20-25 minutes or until no longer pink inside.

Meanwhile, in a large microwave-safe bowl, combine spinach and remaining mayonnaise. Microwave on high for 30-40 seconds or just until spinach is wilted. Spoon spinach mixture over chicken; top each with a cheese slice. Bake 5-7 minutes longer or until cheese is melted. Sprinkle with pepper. **Yield:** 4 servings.

Week 5

SHOPPING LIST

Check for these staples:

- all-purpose flour
- balsamic vinegar
- butter
- canola oil
- chicken bouillon granules
- chili powder
- dijon mustard
- dried basil
- dried marjoram
- dried rosemary
- dried thyme
- eggs
- garlic cloves
- ground allspice
- ground coriander
- ground cumin
- ground ginger
- ground turmeric
- honey
- instant brown rice
- lemon juice
- olive oil
- onions
- pepper
- red wine vinegar
- salt
- sweet-and-sour sauce

Shop for these items:

1 can (13.66 ounces) coconut milk
1 package (4.7 ounces) spring roll wrappers or rice papers (8 inches)
1 can (11 ounces) mandarin oranges
1 package (4 ounces) chopped walnuts
1 package (16 ounces) penne pasta
1 container (1 quart) half-and-half cream
1 container (8 ounces) garlic-herb cheese spread
1 medium avocado
1 pint fresh blueberries
1 bunch broccoli
1 head Chinese or napa cabbage
1 package (5 ounces) spring mix salad greens
4 large portobello mushrooms (4 to 4-1/2 inches)
1 bunch green onions
2 jalapeno peppers
2 medium red peppers
1 bunch small carrots
2 medium zucchini
6 plum tomatoes
1-1/2 pounds ground beef
1 package (17.6 ounces) turkey breast cutlets
1 pound uncooked medium shrimp
1 package (11.2 ounces) frozen garlic Texas toast

MAKE IT EASY

- You'll end the week with 4 slices of leftover garlic bread—perfect for open-faced sandwiches. Layer with mango chutney, thinly sliced havarti and cooked steak. Top each with a fried egg...yum!

MEAL 1

Caribbean Shrimp Spring Rolls

(Pictured above)

Prep/Total Time: 30 min.

Kids will love helping wrap up these delicate rolls filled with bright, beautiful ingredients. And you'll love the burst of flavors in every bite.

1 pound uncooked medium shrimp, peeled, deveined and chopped
3 teaspoons canola oil, *divided*
2 cups fresh broccoli florets
2 garlic cloves, minced
1/4 cup coconut milk
1/2 teaspoon salt
1/2 teaspoon ground ginger
1/2 teaspoon ground coriander
1/4 teaspoon ground turmeric
Dash ground allspice
4 cups shredded Chinese *or* napa cabbage
1/2 cup mandarin oranges
3 green onions, thinly sliced
8 spring roll wrappers *or* rice papers (8 inches)
Hot cooked rice and sweet-and-sour sauce

In a large skillet or wok, stir-fry shrimp in 2 teaspoons oil until shrimp turn pink. Remove and keep warm. In the same skillet, stir-fry broccoli in remaining oil until tender. Add garlic; cook 1 minute longer.

Stir in the coconut milk and seasonings. Bring to a boil. Add cabbage; cook 1-2 minutes longer or until cabbage is tender. Remove from the heat; stir in the shrimp, oranges and onions.

Soak each spring roll wrapper in cool water for 1 minute; place on a flat surface. Place 1/2 cup shrimp mixture down the center of each wrapper to within 1-1/2 in. of ends.

Fold both ends over filling; fold one long side over the filling, then carefully roll up tightly. Place seam side down on serving plates. Serve immediately with rice and sweet-and-sour sauce. **Yield:** 4 servings.

MEAL 2

Summer Turkey Salads

(Pictured below)

Prep/Total Time: 25 min.

Tender turkey is treated to a yummy walnut coating in this dressy salad that just begs to be served outside. Add a cold glass filled with a mix of lemonade and iced tea.

1/4 cup all-purpose flour
1/2 teaspoon salt
1 egg, beaten
3/4 cup finely chopped walnuts
1/2 teaspoon dried rosemary, crushed
8.8 ounces turkey breast cutlets, cut into strips
1 tablespoon olive oil
1 package (5 ounces) spring mix salad greens
2 plum tomatoes, cut into wedges
1 cup fresh blueberries
1/2 cup mandarin oranges
2 green onions, thinly sliced

BLUEBERRY VINAIGRETTE:

1/4 cup red wine vinegar
1/2 cup fresh blueberries
1 tablespoon honey
2 teaspoons Dijon mustard
1/4 cup olive oil

Combine flour and salt in a shallow bowl. Place egg in a separate shallow bowl. Combine walnuts and rosemary in another shallow bowl. Coat turkey in flour mixture, then dip in egg and coat with walnut mixture.

In a large skillet over medium heat, cook turkey in oil in batches for 2-3 minutes on each side or until meat is no longer pink.

Divide the salad greens among four serving plates; top with tomatoes, blueberries, oranges, onions and turkey strips.

In a blender, combine the vinegar, blueberries, honey and mustard. While processing, gradually add oil in a steady stream. Serve with salad. **Yield:** 4 servings.

MEAL 3

Turkey Penne with Lemon Cream Sauce

(Pictured above)

Prep/Total Time: 30 min.

You'll please every picky palate at the table with this colorful pasta dish. Creamy, satisfying and loaded with lively flavors, it's the perfect way to sneak some fresh veggies into little tummies.

2 cups uncooked penne pasta
1/2 pound turkey breast cutlets, cut into 3/4-inch pieces
3 tablespoons butter, *divided*
2 cups fresh broccoli florets
3 small carrots, thinly sliced
2 garlic cloves, minced
2 tablespoons all-purpose flour
1-1/2 teaspoons chicken bouillon granules
1/2 teaspoon dried thyme
1/4 teaspoon pepper
1/8 teaspoon salt
2-1/2 cups half-and-half cream
1/4 cup lemon juice
2 plum tomatoes, seeded and chopped

Cook pasta according to package directions. Meanwhile, in a large skillet, saute turkey in 1 tablespoon butter until no longer pink. Remove and keep warm.

In the same skillet, saute the broccoli and carrots in remaining butter until crisp-tender. Add the garlic; cook 1 minute longer. Stir in the flour, bouillon granules, thyme, pepper and salt until blended. Combine the cream and lemon juice; gradually stir into the broccoli mixture. Bring to a boil; cook and stir for 2-3 minutes or until thickened.

Drain pasta; add to skillet. Stir in turkey and tomatoes and heat through. **Yield:** 4 servings.

MEAL 4

Unstuffed Jalapeno Popper Burgers

(Pictured above)

Prep/Total Time: 30 min.

This sassy, grown-up burger has a little bit of bite and a whole lot of flavor! Our taste panel couldn't stop eating this knife-and-fork sandwich.

2 jalapeno peppers, seeded and finely chopped
4 teaspoons chili powder
2 teaspoons ground cumin
3/4 teaspoon salt
1/4 teaspoon pepper
1-1/2 pounds ground beef
4 slices frozen garlic Texas toast
2 medium onions, halved and thinly sliced
1 medium sweet red pepper, halved and thinly sliced
2 tablespoons butter
1 medium ripe avocado, peeled and sliced
1/2 cup garlic-herb cheese spread

In a large bowl, combine the first five ingredients. Crumble beef over mixture and mix well. Shape into four oval patties.

Grill the burgers, covered, over medium heat or broil 4 in. from the heat for 5-7 minutes on each side or until a meat thermometer reads 160° and juices run clear.

Meanwhile, prepare Texas toast according to package directions. In a large skillet, saute onions and red pepper in butter until tender. Spoon onion mixture onto toast slices; top each with a burger, avocado slices and cheese spread. **Yield:** 4 servings.

Editor's Note: Wear disposable gloves when cutting hot peppers; the oils can burn your skin. Avoid touching your face.

MEAL 5

Vegetable-Stuffed Grilled Portobellos

(Pictured below)

Prep: 20 min. + marinating **Grill:** 10 min.

Mushrooms, tomatoes, zucchini, onions? The garden-fresh gang's all here! A luscious cheese spread, garlic and balsamic vinegar beautifully complement the grilled flavor in this totally delish dish.

1/2 cup olive oil
1/2 cup balsamic vinegar
6 garlic cloves, minced
1/2 teaspoon salt
1/2 teaspoon *each* dried thyme, marjoram and basil
4 large portobello mushrooms (4 to 4-1/2 inches), stems removed
2 medium onions, halved and sliced
2 medium zucchini, halved and sliced
1 medium sweet red pepper, cut into 3/4-inch pieces
2 plum tomatoes, halved and sliced
5 small carrots, halved lengthwise and cut in half
1/2 cup garlic-herb cheese spread

In a small bowl, combine the oil, vinegar, garlic, salt and herbs. Pour half of the marinade into a large resealable plastic bag. Add mushrooms; seal bag and turn to coat. Pour remaining marinade into another large resealable plastic bag. Add remaining vegetables; seal bag and turn to coat. Refrigerate for at least 1 hour.

Drain the vegetables and discard marinade. Grill the mushrooms, covered, over medium heat for 3-4 minutes on each side or until tender. Place remaining vegetables in a grill wok or basket. Grill, covered, over medium heat for 8-12 minutes or until tender, stirring frequently.

Spread cheese over mushrooms; top with vegetables. **Yield:** 4 servings.

Editor's Note: If you do not have a grill wok or basket, use a disposable foil pan. Poke holes in the bottom of the pan with a meat fork to allow liquid to drain.

Week 6

SHOPPING LIST

Check for these staples:

- all-purpose flour
- apricot preserves
- butter
- chicken broth
- chili powder
- crushed red pepper flakes
- Dijon mustard
- dried basil
- dried oregano
- dried sage leaves
- dried thyme
- garlic cloves
- garlic powder
- ground ginger
- Italian seasoning
- olive oil
- onions
- pepper
- reduced-sodium soy sauce
- rice vinegar
- salt
- whole wheat bread crumbs
- Worcestershire sauce

Shop for these items:

1 jar (3.25 ounces) Creole seasoning
1 can (14-1/2 ounces) diced tomatoes
1 package (6 ounces) dried apricots
1 can (16 ounces) kidney beans
1 jar (6 ounces) pitted Greek olives
1 envelope pork gravy mix
1 package (16 ounces) process cheese (Velveeta)
1 box (11 ounces) quick-cooking barley
1 package (28 ounces) quick-cooking bulgur
1 box (12 ounces) quinoa
1 package (8.8 ounces) ready-to-serve whole grain brown and wild rice medley
1 package (16 ounces) whole wheat spiral pasta
1 container (16 ounces) half-and-half cream
1 bunch fresh parsley
1 medium green pepper
3 medium zucchini
2 plum tomatoes
1-1/2 pounds boneless skinless chicken breasts
2 pork tenderloins (1 pound each)
1 package (16 ounces) smoked sausage
1-3/4 pounds uncooked jumbo shrimp
1 package (16 ounces) frozen broccoli, carrots and water chestnuts

SIMPLE SECRETS

- The Whole Grains Council says consuming three servings of whole grains a day offers the most benefits, but health experts agree that as little as one daily serving of whole grains can contribute to your health. Find healthy choices fast by choosing products that have the Whole Grain stamp. For more information, go to *wholegrainscouncil.org*.

MEAL 1

Creole Shrimp & Sausage

(Pictured below)

Prep/Total Time: 30 min.

Add diversity to weeknight meals and get a taste of low-country cuisine with this simple take on a Louisiana Creole classic that uses bulgur instead of rice.

1/2 cup water
1/2 cup chicken broth
1 cup quick-cooking bulgur
1/2 teaspoon chili powder
3/4 teaspoon Creole seasoning, *divided*
1/2 pound smoked sausage, cut into 1/4-inch slices
2 teaspoons olive oil, *divided*
1 medium onion, chopped
1 medium green pepper, chopped
2 garlic cloves, minced
1 can (16 ounces) kidney beans, rinsed and drained
1 can (14-1/2 ounces) diced tomatoes, undrained
1/2 pound uncooked jumbo shrimp, peeled and deveined
1/2 teaspoon Worcestershire sauce

In a small saucepan, bring water and broth to a boil. Stir in the bulgur, chili powder and 1/4 teaspoon Creole seasoning. Reduce heat; cover and simmer for 15 minutes or until tender.

Meanwhile, in a large skillet, brown sausage in 1 teaspoon oil. Remove and keep warm.

In the same skillet, saute onion and green pepper in remaining oil until tender. Add garlic; cook 1 minute longer. Stir in the beans, tomatoes, shrimp, Worcestershire sauce, sausage and remaining Creole seasoning. Cook for 3-5 minutes or until shrimp turn pink. Fluff bulgur with a fork; serve with sausage mixture. **Yield:** 4 servings.

Editor's Note: The following spices may be substituted for the 1 teaspoon Creole seasoning: 1/4 teaspoon ***each*** salt, garlic powder and paprika; and a pinch ***each*** of dried thyme, ground cumin and cayenne pepper.

MEAL 2

Pork Tenderloins with Wild Rice

(Pictured below)

Prep: 25 min. **Bake:** 25 min. + standing

Apricots say sweet things to herbs in this gravy-licious meal. This recipe is worthy of special weekends, too.

2 pork tenderloins (1 pound *each*)
1 package (8.8 ounces) ready-to-serve whole grain brown and wild rice medley
1-3/4 cups frozen broccoli, carrots and water chestnuts, thawed and coarsely chopped
1/2 cup chopped dried apricots
1/2 cup minced fresh parsley
1/2 teaspoon salt
1/2 teaspoon garlic powder
1/2 teaspoon dried thyme
1/2 teaspoon dried sage leaves
1/4 teaspoon pepper

GRAVY:

1 cup water
1 envelope pork gravy mix
1 tablespoon Dijon mustard
1/4 teaspoon dried sage leaves
1 tablespoon minced fresh parsley

Make a lengthwise slit down center of each tenderloin to within 1/2 in. of bottom. Open tenderloins so they lie flat; cover with plastic wrap. Flatten to 3/4-in. thickness.

Prepare the rice according to package directions. In a small bowl, combine the rice, vegetables, apricots, parsley and seasonings.

Remove plastic; spread rice mixture over meat. Close tenderloins; tie with kitchen string. Place in an ungreased 15-in. x 10-in. x 1-in. baking pan. Bake, uncovered, at 425° for 15 minutes.

Meanwhile, in a small saucepan, combine the water, gravy mix, mustard and sage. Bring to a boil; cook and stir for 2 minutes or until thickened. Stir in parsley.

Brush 2 tablespoons gravy over tenderloins. Bake 10-15 minutes longer or until a meat thermometer reads 160°. Let stand for 15 minutes. Discard string; cut each tenderloin into nine slices. Serve with remaining gravy. **Yield:** 6 servings.

MEAL 3

Whole Wheat Pasta Bake

(Pictured above)

Prep/Total Time: 25 min.

With a casserole this rich and saucy, it's tempting to skip the crunchy topping and dip a fork straight into the skillet. But as one taster noted, the bread crumbs on top make this one extra special.

2 cups uncooked whole wheat spiral pasta
1/2 pound boneless skinless chicken breasts, cubed
3 tablespoons butter, *divided*
1 medium zucchini, chopped
1/4 cup chopped onion
2 tablespoons all-purpose flour
1-1/2 cups half-and-half cream
3/4 pound process cheese (Velveeta), cubed
1/2 teaspoon Italian seasoning

TOPPING:

1-1/2 cups dry whole wheat bread crumbs
3 tablespoons butter, melted
1/2 teaspoon Italian seasoning
1/4 teaspoon salt

Cook pasta according to package directions. Meanwhile, in a large skillet, saute the chicken in 1 tablespoon butter until no longer pink. Remove and keep warm.

In the same skillet, saute the zucchini and onion in remaining butter. Stir in flour until blended; gradually add cream. Bring to a boil; cook and stir for 2 minutes or until thickened. Reduce heat. Stir in cheese and Italian seasoning until cheese is melted; add chicken.

Drain pasta; add to the cheese mixture. Transfer to a greased 8-in. square baking dish. In a small bowl, combine the bread crumbs, butter, Italian seasoning and salt; sprinkle over top. Bake, uncovered, at 350° for 10-15 minutes or until heated through and topping is golden brown. **Yield:** 4 servings.

MEAL 4

Mediterranean Chicken Stir-Fry

(Pictured below)

Prep/Total Time: 30 min.

Barley is a chewier and more flavorful alternative to white rice. Try making the switch in this quick and colorful garden-fresh stir-fry.

2 cups water
1 cup quick-cooking barley
1 pound boneless skinless chicken breasts, cubed
3 teaspoons olive oil, *divided*
1 medium onion, chopped
2 medium zucchini, chopped
2 garlic cloves, minced
1 teaspoon dried oregano
1/2 teaspoon dried basil
1/4 teaspoon salt
1/4 teaspoon pepper
Dash crushed red pepper flakes
2 plum tomatoes, chopped
1/2 cup pitted Greek olives, chopped
1 tablespoon minced fresh parsley

In a small saucepan, bring water to a boil. Stir in barley. Reduce heat; cover and simmer for 10-12 minutes or until barley is tender. Remove from the heat; let stand for 5 minutes.

Meanwhile, in a large skillet or wok, stir-fry chicken in 2 teaspoons oil until no longer pink. Remove and keep warm.

Stir-fry onion in remaining oil for 3 minutes. Add the zucchini, garlic, oregano, basil, salt, pepper and pepper flakes; stir-fry 2-4 minutes longer or until vegetables are crisp-tender. Add the chicken, tomatoes, olives and parsley. Serve with barley. **Yield:** 4 servings.

MEAL 5

Shrimp Skewers with Asian Quinoa

(Pictured above)

Prep/Total Time: 30 min.

Quinoa is a more complete protein than most other grains. We think you'll be hearing more requests for this flavorful Asian-inspired dish.

1/4 cup rice vinegar
3 tablespoons apricot preserves
2 tablespoons olive oil
2 garlic cloves, minced
1/2 teaspoon reduced-sodium soy sauce
1/4 teaspoon salt
1/4 teaspoon ground ginger
1/4 teaspoon pepper
1 cup water
2/3 cup quinoa, rinsed
1-3/4 cups frozen broccoli, carrots and water chestnuts, thawed and coarsely chopped
1-1/4 pounds uncooked jumbo shrimp, peeled and deveined

In a small bowl, combine the first eight ingredients. In a small saucepan, combine the water, quinoa and 1/3 cup vinegar mixture. Bring to a boil. Reduce heat; cover and simmer for 12-15 minutes or until liquid is absorbed. Remove from the heat. Stir in the vegetables. Cover and let stand for 10 minutes.

Meanwhile, on four metal or soaked wooden skewers, thread shrimp. If grilling the shrimp, moisten a paper towel with cooking oil; using long-handled tongs, lightly coat the grill rack.

Grill shrimp, covered, over medium heat or broil 4 in. from the heat for 6-8 minutes or until shrimp turn pink, basting frequently with remaining vinegar mixture and turning once. Serve with quinoa. **Yield:** 4 servings.

Editor's Note: Look for quinoa in the cereal, rice or organic food aisle.

CHAPTER 8

Speedy Sides & Salads

Finding quick, colorful and simple accompaniments to an entree can truly balance out a meal. And, of course, you don't want to spend too much time on a side dish, which is why the pairings in this chapter are so appealing for family cooks.

Roasted Winter Vegetables and Maple-Glazed Green Beans are two swift recipes that make perfect sides to a meat-centered main course. And they add flair to a festive tablescape, too!

You'll also find side salads for dinner or gatherings. The Caesar Tortellini Salad and Provencal Bean Salad are great potluck dishes, while the Caramelized Grapefruit Salad is holiday-special. Whatever your needs, this is your go-to chapter for super suppertime sidekicks! ■

EASY ADDITION. Tangerine Tabouleh (p. 136).

Almond Rice Pilaf

(Pictured above)

Prep/Total: 15 min.

With quick-cooking rice, this is a speedy recipe, and the almonds make it special enough to serve to company. It goes well with all kinds of meats.
—Sharon Adamczyk, Wind Lake, Wisconsin

1 medium onion, chopped
1/2 cup slivered almonds
1 tablespoon butter
2 cups chicken broth
2 cups uncooked instant rice

In a large saucepan, saute onion and almonds in butter until onion is tender and almonds are lightly browned. Add broth; bring to a boil. Stir in rice. Cover and remove from the heat. Let stand for 5-8 minutes or until the liquid is absorbed. **Yield:** 6 servings.

Tequila-Lime Fruit Salad

(Pictured at right)

Prep/Total Time: 20 min.

Looking for a fast, colorful side to round out any meal? My refreshing fruit salad is pure perfection!
—Angela Howland, Haynesville, Maine

3/4 cup sugar
1/4 cup water
1/4 cup lime juice
3 tablespoons tequila ***or*** **additional lime juice**
2 cups cubed fresh pineapple
2 cups sliced fresh strawberries
2 cups chopped peeled kiwifruit
2 cups seedless red grapes, halved

In a small saucepan, bring sugar and water to a boil over medium heat. Remove from the heat; cool completely. Stir in lime juice and tequila.

In a large bowl, combine the fruit. Drizzle with syrup and toss gently to coat. **Yield:** 10 servings.

Crunchy Romaine Strawberry Salad

(Pictured at right)

Prep/Total Time: 30 min.

This is such an impressive dish! It's been a hit with people of all ages every time we've brought it to a get-together. In addition to being pretty and colorful, it's a snap to make. And the mouthwatering combination of textures and tastes seems to please every palate.
—Leslie Lancaster, Zachary, Louisiana

1 package (3 ounces) ramen noodles
1 cup chopped walnuts
1/4 cup butter
1/4 cup sugar
1/4 cup canola oil
2 tablespoons red wine vinegar
1/2 teaspoon soy sauce
8 cups torn romaine
1/2 cup chopped green onions
2 cups fresh strawberries, sliced

Discard seasoning packet from ramen noodles or save for another use. Break noodles into small pieces. In a large skillet, cook noodles and walnuts in butter over medium heat for 8-10 minutes or until golden; cool.

For dressing, in a small bowl, whisk the sugar, oil, vinegar and soy sauce. Just before serving, combine the romaine, onions, strawberries and noodle mixture in a large bowl. Drizzle with dressing and toss gently. **Yield:** 12 servings.

Citrus Steak Salad

(Pictured below)

Prep/Total Time: 25 min.

Your family will think you spent hours on this beautiful main dish salad with its from-scratch dressing, but our Test Kitchen thinks it's an absolute cinch!

6 tablespoons olive oil
1/4 cup cider vinegar
1/4 cup orange juice
2 tablespoons minced fresh parsley
2 tablespoons honey
1 garlic clove, minced
1 teaspoon chili sauce
1/2 teaspoon salt
8 cups torn romaine
3/4 pound cooked beef sirloin steak, sliced
2 cups sliced fresh strawberries
1 medium red onion, sliced
1 can (11 ounces) mandarin oranges, drained
1 cup pecan halves, toasted
1/2 cup fresh goat cheese, crumbled

In a small bowl, whisk the first eight ingredients; set aside. Divide romaine among four plates; top with steak, strawberries, onion, oranges, pecans and cheese. Serve with vinaigrette. **Yield:** 4 servings (1 cup vinaigrette).

Garlic Carrots

(Pictured above)

Prep/Total Time: 30 min.

While making the main course, it's easy to prepare these simple veggies. I use bite-sized carrots that don't need to be cut or peeled and keep a jar of prepared minced garlic on hand to save on prep and cleanup time.
—Chris Rentmeister, Ripon, Wisconsin

1 pound baby carrots
2 garlic cloves, minced
2 tablespoons olive oil
1/4 cup hot water
1/2 teaspoon salt
1/4 teaspoon dried thyme
Dash pepper

In a large skillet, saute carrots and garlic in oil for 5 minutes. Add water, salt, thyme and pepper. Bring to a boil. Reduce heat; cover and cook for 8-12 minutes or until carrots are tender. **Yield:** 6 servings.

Slow-Cooked Broccoli

Prep: 10 min. **Cook:** 2-1/2 hours

My crumb-topped dinner addition is quick to assemble and full of flavor. Since it simmers in a slow cooker, it frees up my oven for other things—a great help when I'm preparing several items for a big meal at home.
—Connie Slocum, Antioch, Tennessee

6 cups frozen chopped broccoli, partially thawed
1 can (10-3/4 ounces) condensed cream of celery soup, undiluted
1-1/2 cups (6 ounces) shredded sharp cheddar cheese, *divided*
1/4 cup chopped onion

1/2 teaspoon Worcestershire sauce
1/4 teaspoon pepper
1 cup crushed butter-flavored crackers (about 25)
2 tablespoons butter

In a large bowl, combine broccoli, soup, 1 cup cheese, onion, Worcestershire sauce and pepper. Pour into a greased 3-qt. slow cooker. Sprinkle the crackers on top; dot with butter.

Cover and cook on high for 2-1/2 to 3 hours. Sprinkle with remaining cheese. Cook 10 minutes longer or until the cheese is melted. **Yield:** 8-10 servings.

Lemonade Fruit Salad

(Pictured below)

Prep/Total Time: 25 min.

Here's a no-fuss medley that lets fresh fruit shine. I've taken it to several picnics, where it's always been well received. Any combination of fruit will work well.
—Claire L. Watson, Cape Girardeau, Missouri

1/2 cup water
3 tablespoons sugar
2 teaspoons grated lemon peel
1 teaspoon grated orange peel
1 tablespoon lemon juice
1 fresh pineapple, peeled and cubed
1-1/2 pounds seedless red grapes
1 pound fresh dark sweet cherries, pitted

In a small saucepan, bring water and sugar to a boil; add lemon and orange peels. Remove from the heat; cool completely. Stir in lemon juice.

In a large bowl, combine the fruit. Drizzle with syrup and toss gently to coat. **Yield:** 16 servings (3/4 cup each).

Roasted Winter Vegetables

(Pictured above)

Prep: 25 min. **Bake:** 30 min.

A few seasonings enhance the natural goodness of your fresh fall harvest. —Donna Lamano, Olathe, Kansas

3 small red potatoes, cubed
2 medium carrots, chopped
2 medium parsnips, peeled and chopped
1 medium turnip, peeled and chopped
1 cup cubed peeled butternut squash
3 shallots, peeled and halved
1 whole garlic bulb, cloves separated and peeled
4-1/2 teaspoons olive oil
1/4 teaspoon salt
1/4 teaspoon dried thyme
1/4 teaspoon pepper

Place the first seven ingredients in a greased 15-in. x 10-in. x 1-in. baking pan. Combine the oil, salt, thyme and pepper; drizzle over vegetables and toss to coat.

Bake, uncovered, at 425° for 30-35 minutes or until tender, stirring occasionally. **Yield:** 6 servings.

POTATO POINTERS

When buying potatoes, look for those that are firm, well shaped and free of blemishes. If kept in a cool, dark, well-ventilated place, most potatoes will keep for up to 2 weeks.

Fresh Tomato & Cucumber Salad

(Pictured above)

Prep/Total Time: 20 min.

This bright, fresh recipe is so easy to prepare. It helps us find a use for the various vegetables we accumulate from our garden and from friends who kindly share their own vegetables, too. —Jodie Gharbi, Shreveport, Louisiana

1/4 cup lemon juice
1/4 cup olive oil
1 tablespoon minced fresh basil *or* 1 teaspoon dried basil
1 tablespoon white wine vinegar
1 garlic clove, minced
1 teaspoon minced fresh mint *or* 1/4 teaspoon dried mint
1/8 teaspoon kosher salt
1/8 teaspoon coarsely ground pepper
4 plum tomatoes, seeded and chopped
2 medium cucumbers, chopped
1/2 cup Greek olives, sliced
2 cups torn mixed salad greens
3/4 cup crumbled feta cheese
1/4 cup pine nuts, toasted

In a small bowl, whisk the first eight ingredients; set aside.

In a large bowl, combine the tomatoes, cucumbers and olives. Drizzle with half of the dressing; toss to coat. Arrange salad greens on a large serving plate; spoon the tomato mixture over top. Sprinkle with cheese and pine nuts and drizzle with remaining dressing. **Yield:** 6 servings.

Roasted Rosemary Potatoes

Prep: 15 min. **Bake:** 40 min.

Here is one of my family's all-time favorites, and you won't believe how simple it is. You can alter it to fit whatever meal you dream up.
—Melissa Graham, Savannah, Texas

6 medium potatoes (about 2 pounds), peeled and cut into 1-inch cubes
1/2 cup mayonnaise
1 tablespoon garlic powder
1 tablespoon onion powder
1 tablespoon dried rosemary, crushed
1 tablespoon water
1 teaspoon salt

In a large bowl, combine all ingredients; toss to coat. Transfer to a greased 15-in. x 10-in. x 1-in. baking pan.

Bake, uncovered, at 425° for 40-45 minutes or until tender, stirring occasionally. **Yield:** 6 servings.

Maple-Glazed Green Beans

(Pictured below)

Prep/Total Time: 25 min.

After picking my first green beans years ago, I wanted to try a new dish, so I began to experiment. The results were so yummy, I couldn't stop eating, so I picked more. Guess what happened? —Merry Graham, Newhall, California

3 cups cut fresh green beans
1 large onion, chopped
4 bacon strips, cut into 1-inch pieces
1/2 cup dried cranberries
1/4 cup maple syrup
1 tablespoon bourbon, optional
1/4 teaspoon salt
1/4 teaspoon pepper

Place beans in a steamer basket; place in a large saucepan over 1 in. of water. Bring to a boil; cover and steam for 4-5 minutes or until crisp-tender.

Meanwhile, in a large skillet, cook onion and bacon over medium heat until bacon is crisp; drain. Add the beans, cranberries, syrup, bourbon if desired, salt and pepper; heat through. **Yield:** 4 servings.

Grilled Potato Packets

(Pictured at right)

Prep: 20 min. **Grill:** 45 min.

Potatoes require a little extra time on the grill, so remember to give these pouches first dibs on the flames. There's little prep and easy cleanup. —Anna Bjornn, Rexburg, Idaho

- **7 medium red potatoes**
- **6 slices ready-to-serve fully cooked bacon, chopped**
- **1/4 cup thinly sliced green onions**
- **3/4 teaspoon salt**
- **1/8 teaspoon pepper**
- **2 tablespoons butter**
- **1 cup (4 ounces) shredded cheddar cheese**

Cut the potatoes into wedges. In a large bowl, combine the potatoes, bacon, onions, salt and pepper. Divide between two double thicknesses of greased heavy-duty foil (about 18 in. square). Dot with butter.

Fold foil around mixture and seal tightly. Grill, covered, over medium heat for 40-45 minutes or until potatoes are tender, turning once.

Carefully open the foil; sprinkle with cheese. Grill 3-5 minutes longer or until the cheese is melted. **Yield:** 8 servings.

Poppy Seed Slaw

(Pictured at right)

Prep: 10 min. + chilling

This crisp, colorful side can be put together in minutes for a tasty accompaniment to any backyard barbecue.
—Mary McRae, Coldwater, Michigan

- **1 package (10 ounces) angel hair coleslaw**
- **3/4 cup dried cranberries**
- **3/4 cup honey-roasted sliced almonds**
- **3/4 cup poppy seed salad dressing**
- **1/2 teaspoon salt**
- **1/2 teaspoon pepper**

In a large bowl, combine the coleslaw, cranberries and almonds. Combine the salad dressing, salt and pepper; drizzle over salad and toss to coat. Refrigerate for 1 hour before serving. **Yield:** 5 servings.

DRIED CRANBERRIES

Dried cranberries are often substituted for raisins in recipes. Commercially dried cranberries contain added sugar, making them a sweet-tart snack by the handful or a tasty addition to salads, breads, stuffings and trail mixes.

Tangerine Tabbouleh

(Pictured above)

Prep: 35 min. + chilling

Citrus really comes through in this interesting mix of fruit, nuts and chickpeas. It makes a hearty and flavorful side dish alongside grilled chicken, pork or beef.
—Vivian Levine, Summerfield, Florida

1 cup bulgur
1 cup boiling water
1 can (15 ounces) garbanzo beans *or* chickpeas, rinsed and drained
2 tangerines, peeled, sectioned and chopped
2/3 cup chopped dates
1/2 cup pistachios, coarsely chopped
1/3 cup dried cranberries
1/2 cup tangerine juice
2 tablespoons olive oil
1 teaspoon grated tangerine peel
1/4 teaspoon ground ginger
1/8 teaspoon salt

Place bulgur in a large bowl. Stir in water. Cover and let stand for 30 minutes or until most of the liquid is absorbed. Drain well.

Stir in the garbanzo beans, tangerines, dates, pistachios and cranberries. In a small bowl, combine the tangerine juice, oil, tangerine peel, ginger and salt. Pour over the bulgur mixture and toss to coat. Cover and refrigerate for at least 1 hour. Stir before serving. **Yield:** 8 servings.

Squash & Carrot Saute

Prep/Total Time: 20 min.

This bright and cheerful saute offers a delightful new way to prepare summer squash and carrots.
—Sarah Gamboa, Holland, Michigan

2 medium carrots, sliced
4-1/2 teaspoons olive oil
2 yellow summer squash, sliced
1 medium onion, chopped
1 teaspoon garlic powder
1/4 teaspoon salt
1/4 teaspoon pepper

In a large skillet, saute carrots in oil until crisp-tender. Add the remaining ingredients; saute 3-4 minutes longer or until vegetables are tender. **Yield:** 5 servings.

Peachy Green Beans

Prep/Total Time: 20 min.

Apricot preserves lend a sweetness to tender green beans, while cayenne pepper gives them a slight kick.
—Lisa Ruehlow, Blaine, Minnesota

1/2 pound fresh green beans, trimmed
3 tablespoons peach preserves
Dash cayenne pepper

Place beans in a steamer basket; place in a large saucepan over 1 in. of water. Bring to a boil; cover and steam for 8-10 minutes or until crisp-tender.

In a small microwave-safe bowl, combine preserves and cayenne. Cook, uncovered, on high for 30 seconds or until preserves are melted. Transfer beans to a serving bowl; add peach mixture and toss to coat. **Yield:** 2 servings.

Caesar Tortellini Salad

(Pictured below)

Prep/Total Time: 25 min.

I dress to impress when it comes to topping tortellini. Creamy, melt-in-your-mouth avocado matched with rich ripe olives and fresh chopped tomatoes make this the ultimate summer salad.

—Diane Macey, New Lenox, Illinois

3-1/2 cups frozen cheese tortellini
3 plum tomatoes, chopped
1 can (3.8 ounces) sliced ripe olives, drained
1 medium ripe avocado, peeled and chopped
1/2 cup shredded cheddar cheese
1/2 cup creamy Caesar salad dressing
8 thinly sliced hard salami, cut into 2-inch strips

Cook tortellini according to package directions; drain and rinse in cold water. In a large bowl, combine the tortellini and remaining ingredients. Refrigerate until serving. **Yield:** 5 servings.

Caramelized Grapefruit Salad

(Pictured above)

Prep/Total Time: 25 min.

Grapefruit segments are treated to a slight caramelization in a hot skillet just before topping this colorful mix. It's finished with a light honey mustard dressing, bacon and avocado. *—Maria Davis, Flower Mound, Texas*

1/3 cup pecan halves
2 tablespoons plus 1/4 cup sugar, *divided*
1 medium grapefruit, peeled and cut into segments
4 cups spring mix salad greens
3/4 cup chopped cucumber
2 green onions, sliced
1/2 medium ripe avocado, peeled and cubed
2 bacon strips, cooked and crumbled
3 tablespoons reduced-fat honey mustard salad dressing
1/4 teaspoon coarsely ground pepper

In a small nonstick skillet over medium heat, cook and stir pecans and 2 tablespoons sugar for 2-4 minutes or until sugar is melted. Spread on foil to cool.

Coat grapefruit segments with remaining sugar. Coat the same skillet with cooking spray; cook grapefruit over medium heat for 2-3 minutes on each side or until browned.

In a large bowl, combine the salad greens, cucumber, onions, avocado and bacon. Drizzle with salad dressing and toss to coat.

Divide salad among four serving plates. Top with the grapefruit and pecans; sprinkle with pepper. **Yield:** 4 servings.

Provencal Bean Salad

(Pictured above)

Prep/Total Time: 25 min.

Lightly coated in reduced-fat tarragon mayonnaise, this refreshing three-bean medley perks up summer meals. Every bite bursts with flavor.

—Suzanne Banfield, Basking Ridge, New Jersey

3/4 pound fresh green beans, trimmed
3/4 pound fresh wax beans, trimmed
1 pound grape tomatoes, halved
1 can (15 ounces) white kidney *or* cannellini beans, rinsed and drained
1/2 cup pitted Greek olives
1/2 cup reduced-fat mayonnaise
1 tablespoon minced fresh tarragon *or* 1 teaspoon dried tarragon
1 tablespoon lemon juice
1 garlic clove, minced
1/2 teaspoon salt
Dash pepper

In a large saucepan, bring 4 cups water to a boil. Add green and wax beans; cover and cook for 3 minutes. Drain and immediately place beans in ice water. Drain and pat dry.

Place the beans, tomatoes, kidney beans and olives in a large bowl. In a small bowl, whisk the remaining ingredients; pour over the salad and toss to coat. **Yield:** 12 servings (3/4 cup each).

Italian Mushrooms

(Pictured at right)

Prep: 10 min. **Cook:** 4 hours

Only four ingredients create a rich and flavorful side dish that goes great with beef and mashed potatoes.

—Kim Reichert, St. Paul, Minnesota

1 pound medium fresh mushrooms
1 large onion, sliced
1/2 cup butter, melted
1 envelope Italian salad dressing mix

In a 3-qt. slow cooker, layer mushrooms and onion. Combine the butter and salad dressing mix; pour over vegetables. Cover and cook on low for 4-5 hours or until vegetables are tender. Serve with a slotted spoon. **Yield:** 6 servings.

Brussels Sprouts with Bacon

(Pictured below)

Prep/Total Time: 25 min.

Brussels sprouts are an absolute treat when cooked this way. Short on time? Substitute ready-to-serve cooked bacon for the cooked bacon.

—Lisa Daniell, Loveland, Colorado

1 pound fresh *or* frozen brussels sprouts, thawed and halved
1/4 cup butter, cubed
6 bacon strips, cooked and crumbled
2/3 cup chopped walnuts
3 garlic cloves, minced

In a large skillet, saute the brussels sprouts in butter until tender. Add the bacon, walnuts and garlic; cook 1-2 minutes longer or until heated through. **Yield:** 6 servings.

CHAPTER 9

Effortless Entertaining

Don't let party planning stress you out, because we've got you covered! Holding a cozy, indoor get-together? Check out the Coffeehouse at Home section, chock-full of sweet delights and coffee treats that rival those at your favorite espresso shop. For savory dishes, thumb through the Greats for Game Day section for casual party fare.

We even have recipes for the great outdoors, whether you're grilling out or camping out. Our Cooked by the Campfire section offers lip-smacking recipes that can be toted around while on a backcountry trip or cooked over a fire. Gathering at the Grill features a delicious menu that's ideal for backyard parties. No matter what the occasion, these speedy recipes are sure to make hostess duties a snap! ■

CAMPFIRE TREATS. Pudgy Pies: S'more; Cherry-Chocolate; Ham & Jack (pages 148-149).

COFFEEHOUSE AT HOME

Indulging in cafe treats and espresso drinks doesn't have to be a luxury. We've pulled together these sweet delights and liquid coffee confections so you can create a decadent-laden coffeehouse in the comfort of your own home!

Don't let the sophisticated appearance of these goodies fool you, because most of the delicious recipes use down-to-earth ingredients and have straightforward preparations. What a great excuse to host an afternoon get-together with friends! ■

Butter Pecan Biscotti

Prep: 25 min. **Bake:** 40 min. + cooling

These crunchy, Test Kitchen-created cookies are perfect for dunking and have a subtle coffee flavor and sweetness. For those who are huge fans of butter and pecan flavors, these traditional Italian cookies are the ticket!

- **1 package (18-1/4 ounces) butter pecan cake mix**
- **1 cup all-purpose flour**
- **1/2 cup butter, melted**
- **2 eggs**
- **3 tablespoons maple syrup**
- **2-1/2 teaspoons instant coffee granules**
- **1 teaspoon vanilla extract**
- **1 cup white baking chips**
- **1 cup confectioners' sugar**
- **2 tablespoons brewed coffee**
- **1 cup finely chopped pecans**

In a large bowl, beat cake mix, flour, butter, eggs, syrup, coffee granules and vanilla until well blended (dough will be very thick). Fold in chips. Divide dough in half. On an ungreased baking sheet, shape each portion into a 12-in. x 2-in. rectangle. Bake at 350° for 30-35 minutes or until golden brown.

Place the pans on wire racks. When cool enough to handle, transfer to a cutting board; cut diagonally with a serrated knife into 3/4-in. slices. Place cut side down on ungreased baking sheets.

Bake for 10-15 minutes or until firm. Remove to wire racks to cool completely. Combine confectioners' sugar and coffee. Drizzle over biscotti; sprinkle with pecans. Let stand until set. Store in an airtight container. **Yield:** about 2 dozen.

Coffee Cake Muffins

Prep: 15 min. **Bake:** 20 min.

Everyone who tries these moist muffins will delight in the surprise that's inside. The rich streusel topping adds an extra layer of yumminess.
—Caroline Wamelink, Cleveland Heights, Ohio

1-1/2 cups all-purpose flour
1/2 cup packed brown sugar
2 teaspoons baking powder
3/4 teaspoon ground cinnamon
1/4 teaspoon baking soda
1/4 teaspoon salt
3/4 cup strong brewed coffee
1/3 cup canola oil
1 egg
1/4 cup apricot preserves

TOPPING:

1/4 cup all-purpose flour
1/4 cup packed brown sugar
1/4 teaspoon ground cinnamon
3 tablespoons cold butter
1/4 cup chopped walnuts

In a large bowl, combine the flour, brown sugar, baking powder, cinnamon, baking soda and salt. In another bowl, combine the coffee, oil and egg. Stir into the dry ingredients just until moistened.

Fill paper-lined muffin cups half full. Drop 1 teaspoon preserves into center of each muffin; cover with the remaining batter. In a small bowl, combine the flour, brown sugar and cinnamon; cut in butter until crumbly. Stir in walnuts. Sprinkle over tops.

Bake at 400° for 18-20 minutes or until a toothpick inserted in muffin comes out clean. Cool for 5 minutes before removing from pan to a wire rack. Serve warm. **Yield:** 1 dozen.

Coffee & Cream Doughnuts

(Pictured on page 143)

Prep/Total Time: 30 min.

Craving something sweet? Our Test Kitchen made these delicious doughnuts in no time, and so can you!

Oil for deep-fat frying
2 tubes (10.2 ounces *each*) large refrigerated buttermilk biscuits
1/4 cup heavy whipping cream
1 tablespoon plus 1 teaspoon instant coffee granules
2 packages (3 ounces *each*) cream cheese, softened
2/3 cup Nutella
Confectioners' sugar and baking cocoa

In an electric skillet or deep fryer, heat oil to 375°. Drop biscuits, a few at a time, into hot oil. Fry until golden brown on both sides. Drain on paper towels.

Meanwhile, place cream in a small microwave-safe bowl. Microwave, uncovered, on high for 1 minute; stir in coffee granules until dissolved. Add cream cheese and Nutella; beat until smooth.

Cut a small hole in the corner of a pastry or plastic bag; insert a very small tip. Fill bag with coffee mixture. Push the tip through the side of each doughnut to fill with cream. Dust tops with confectioners' sugar and cocoa. Serve immediately. **Yield:** 10 doughnuts.

Cherry Cordial Cake Balls

(Pictured on page 143)

Prep: 1 hour **Bake:** 35 min. + standing

Coffee and brandy add mild flavor to these scrumptious cherry cake balls. They're the perfect bite-size treat when you want something rich without indulging too much.
—Susan Westerfield, Albuquerque, New Mexico

1 package (18-1/4 ounces) fudge marble cake mix
1-1/4 cups plus 3 tablespoons strong brewed coffee, *divided*
1/4 cup canola oil
3 eggs
1 jar (10 ounces) maraschino cherries without stems, well drained
1/3 cup brandy
1/4 cup cherry preserves
1 cup canned chocolate frosting
4 pounds milk chocolate candy coating, chopped
2 tablespoons shortening

In a large bowl, combine the cake mix, cocoa packet, 1-1/4 cups coffee, oil and eggs; beat on low speed for 30 seconds. Beat on medium for 2 minutes. Pour batter into a greased and floured 13-in. x 9-in. baking pan.

Bake at 350° for 30-35 minutes or until a toothpick inserted near center comes out clean. Cool completely. Place cherries in a food processor; cover and process until coarsely chopped. Transfer to a small bowl; stir in the brandy, preserves and remaining coffee. Crumble cake into a large bowl. Add frosting and cherry mixture; beat well. Shape into 1-in. balls.

In a microwave, melt candy coating and shortening; stir until smooth. Dip balls in chocolate mixture; allow excess to drip off. Place on waxed paper; let stand until set. Store in an airtight container overnight before serving. **Yield:** 6 dozen.

Iced Skinny Hazelnut Latte

Prep/Total Time: 10 min.

After trying a friend's iced hazelnut latte, I was hooked. This homemade version has less than 150 calories.
—Marie Fibelstad, Storm Lake, Iowa

3 cups fat-free milk, *divided*
1/4 cup hazelnut Belgian cafe coffee drink mix
2 tablespoons refrigerated hazelnut coffee creamer
Crushed ice

Place 1 cup milk in a large microwave-safe bowl. Microwave, uncovered, on high for 1-2 minutes or until hot. Stir in drink mix until dissolved. Add coffee creamer and remaining milk. Serve over ice. **Yield:** 4 servings.

Caramel Macchiato Floats

Prep/Total Time: 20 min.

I made these creamy, caramel-flavored floats for a party, and everyone loved them! It's much more affordable than going to the local coffee shop.
—Melissa Heller, Santa Maria, California

6 cups cold brewed coffee
1 cup 2% milk
1/3 cup caramel flavoring syrup
1/4 cup sugar
8 scoops coffee ice cream
8 scoops dulce de leche caramel ice cream
Whipped cream and caramel sundae syrup

In a large pitcher combine the first four ingredients. Divide ice cream among eight chilled glasses; pour coffee mixture over top. Garnish servings with whipped cream and sundae syrup. **Yield:** 8 servings.

Editor's Note: This recipe was tested with Torani brand flavoring syrup. Look for it in the coffee section.

French Vanilla Mocha

Prep/Total Time: 10 min.

My husband and I have spent hours trying to create coffeehouse drinks. This is the closest we've come. You can use any creamer to change the taste.
—Lori Stickling, Bloomington, Illinois

2 tablespoons instant coffee granules
2 teaspoons chocolate syrup
1-1/2 cups 2% milk
1/2 cup refrigerated French vanilla coffee creamer

Pictured left to right: Iced Skinny Hazelnut Latte, Caramel Macchiato Floats, Whipped Banana Latte, French Vanilla Mocha and Spanish Coffee.

Divide coffee granules and chocolate syrup between two mugs; set aside. In a small microwave-safe bowl, combine the milk and coffee creamer. Microwave, uncovered, on high for 1-2 minutes or until hot. Ladle into mugs; stir until coffee granules are dissolved. Serve immediately. **Yield:** 2 servings.

Whipped Banana Latte

Prep/Total Time: 10 min.

Save ripe bananas to use in this refreshing, frothy beverage that'll take moments to fix on a hot day.
—Mary Tallman, Arbor Vitae, Wisconsin

1-1/2 cups cold strong brewed coffee
3/4 cup half-and-half cream
2 medium ripe bananas, frozen
1/2 cup ice cubes
1/4 cup sugar
2 tablespoons chocolate syrup

Place all ingredients in a blender; cover and process for 15 seconds or until smooth. Pour into chilled glasses. Serve immediately. **Yield:** 5 servings.

Spanish Coffee

Prep/Total Time: 5 min.

You'll look forward to dessert even more when this warm and welcoming after-dinner delight is on the menu. It tastes fancier than it is to make.
—Sharon Tipton, Winter Garden, Florida

6 ounces coffee liqueur
6 teaspoons sugar
4 cups hot brewed coffee
Whipped cream and chocolate curls

Divide liqueur and sugar among four mugs. Add coffee. Top with whipped cream and chocolate curls. Serve immediately. **Yield:** 6 servings.

GATHERING AT THE GRILL

These recipes are perfectly suited for warm, sunny weather, when you want to break out the grill. Citrusy grilled chicken and deliciously seasoned kabobs create the centerpiece of a tantalizing outdoor menu, with zippy fresh salsa as a super sidekick. A cool and quick butter pecan refrigerator pie is, last but not least, the ultimate summertime dessert. ■

Tomatillo Salsa

(Pictured below)

Prep/Total Time: 20 min.

Dare to deviate from tomato salsa, and try this tomatillo-based version for a deliciously addictive change of pace. It's fantastic on its own with tortilla chips or served as a condiment alongside a variety of meats.

—Lori Kostecki, Wausau, Wisconsin

8 tomatillos, husks removed
1 medium tomato, quartered
1 small onion, cut into chunks
1 jalapeno pepper, seeded
3 tablespoons fresh cilantro leaves
3 garlic cloves, peeled
1 tablespoon lime juice
1/2 teaspoon salt
1/4 teaspoon ground cumin
1/8 teaspoon pepper
Tortilla chips

In a large saucepan, bring 4 cups water to a boil. Add tomatillos. Reduce heat; simmer, uncovered, for 5 minutes. Drain.

Place the tomatillos, tomato, onion, jalapeno, cilantro, garlic, lime juice and seasonings in a food processor. Cover and process until blended. Serve with the chips. **Yield:** 2-1/4 cups.

Editor's Note: Wear disposable gloves when cutting hot peppers; the oils can burn skin. Avoid touching your face.

Orange-Spiced Chicken

(Pictured above)

Prep: 10 min. + marinating **Grill:** 10 min.

Five ingredients are all you will need for this fast and extremely flavorful marinade. With one bite, it'll become your most-requested chicken recipe!

—Debra Stevens, Lutz, Florida

1/2 cup thawed orange juice concentrate
1/4 cup honey
1/4 cup soy sauce
1 teaspoon Chinese five-spice powder
1/2 teaspoon garlic powder
4 boneless skinless chicken breast halves (5 ounces *each*)

In a small bowl, combine the first five ingredients. Pour 1/2 cup marinade into a large resealable plastic bag; add chicken. Seal bag and turn to coat; refrigerate for 2 hours. Cover and refrigerate remaining marinade.

Drain and discard marinade. Moisten a paper towel with cooking oil; using long-handled tongs, lightly coat the grill rack. Grill chicken, covered, over medium heat or broil 4 in. from the grill for 5-7 minutes on each side or until a thermometer reads 170°, basting frequently with reserved marinade. **Yield:** 4 servings.

Lemon-Sesame Veggie Kabobs

(Pictured below)

Prep: 30 min. + marinating **Grill:** 10 min.

Lemon and sesame star in this fresh veggie combination. The tasty marinade turns plain veggie kabobs into an irresistible side dish.

—Kimberly Hammond, Kingwood, Texas

1/4 cup lemon juice
1/4 cup soy sauce
2 tablespoons sesame oil
3 garlic cloves, minced
1 tablespoon minced chives
1-1/2 teaspoons ground ginger
1 pound medium fresh mushrooms
1 pound cherry tomatoes
1 large sweet yellow pepper, cut into 1-inch pieces
1 small red onion, cut into wedges
Hot cooked brown rice, optional

In a large resealable plastic bag, combine the first six ingredients. Add the mushrooms, tomatoes, pepper and onion; seal bag and turn to coat. Refrigerate for at least 1 hour. Drain and reserve marinade.

Thread the vegetables onto eight metal or soaked wooden skewers. Grill, covered, over medium heat or broil 4 in. from the heat for 6-8 minutes or until tender, basting frequently with reserved marinade and turning once. Serve with rice if desired. **Yield:** 8 servings.

Butter Brickle Ice Cream Pie

(Pictured above)

Prep: 20 min. + freezing

This is my husband's absolute favorite summertime dessert. I often serve it to company in warm-weather months. Everyone loves the rich nutty flavor.

—Brenda Jackson, Garden City, Kansas

1/2 gallon vanilla ice cream, softened, *divided*
1 graham cracker crust (9 inches)
1/2 cup English toffee bits *or* almond brickle chips

SAUCE:
1 cup sugar
1 can (5 ounces) evaporated milk, *divided*
1/4 cup dark corn syrup
1/4 cup butter, cubed
1/8 teaspoon salt
1 tablespoon cornstarch
1/2 cup English toffee bits *or* almond brickle chips

Spread half the ice cream into crust. Sprinkle with toffee bits. Spoon remaining ice cream over top. Cover and freeze until firm.

In a large saucepan, combine the sugar, 3 tablespoons milk, corn syrup, butter and salt. Bring to a boil over medium heat. Combine cornstarch and remaining milk until smooth; gradually add to sugar mixture.

Return to a boil, stirring constantly. Cook and stir for 1-2 minutes or until thickened. Cool until room temperature, stirring several times. Stir in toffee bits. Refrigerate until serving.

Just before serving, transfer the sauce to a small microwave-safe bowl. Microwave, uncovered, on high for 30-60 seconds or until heated through, stirring once. Serve with pie. **Yield:** 8 servings.

COOKED BY THE CAMPFIRE

Little ones and adults alike can't wait until the sun goes down to gather around the campfire for special treats. The cookies and bars below travel well and can be easily packed in anticipation of hungry campers and backpackers. Or, with a sandwich iron, create panini-style sandwiches with savory and sweet fillings—including fruit, hazelnut spread, ham and cheese—that will hit the spot on starry nights. ■

Double Chip Cookies

(Pictured below)

Prep: 15 min. **Bake:** 10 min./batch

I first made these cookies and sent them to my stepson in the Marines. The next time he phoned, guess what he requested? More of these cookies! They pack well and are great for taking on overnight trips, too.

—Marcella Moore, Washburn, Illinois

- **1/2 cup butter, softened**
- **3/4 cup packed brown sugar**
- **1 egg**
- **1 teaspoon vanilla extract**
- **1-1/4 cups all-purpose flour**
- **1/2 teaspoon baking soda**
- **1/2 teaspoon salt**
- **2/3 cup semisweet chocolate chips**
- **1/3 cup butterscotch chips**

In a large bowl, cream butter and brown sugar until light and fluffy. Beat in the egg and vanilla. Combine the flour, baking soda and salt; gradually add to the creamed mixture and mix well. Stir in chocolate and butterscotch chips.

Drop by rounded tablespoonfuls 2 in. apart onto greased baking sheets. Bake at 350° for 10-12 minutes or until golden brown (tops will feel soft). Cool for 3 minutes before removing to wire racks to cool completely. Store in an airtight container. **Yield:** 2-1/2 dozen.

Fruit & Nut Cereal Bars

(Pictured below left)

Prep: 15 min. + cooling

This is a sweet and yummy treat for summer picnics or outdoor adventures. I had to get the recipe from a friend because my husband enjoys them so much.

—Erin Climenhaga, Cadillac, Saskatchewan

- **8 cups cornflakes**
- **1 package (6 ounces) dried apricots, chopped**
- **1 cup dry roasted peanuts**
- **1 cup chopped dates**
- **1/2 cup flaked coconut**
- **1/2 cup sesame seeds**
- **1/3 cup butter**
- **1 package (16 ounces) large marshmallows**

In a large bowl, combine cornflakes, apricots, peanuts, dates, flaked coconut and sesame seeds. In a large saucepan over low heat, melt butter and marshmallows; stir until smooth. Pour over cereal mixture; toss to coat. Press into a greased 13-in. x 9-in. dish. Cool. Cut into bars. Store in an airtight container. **Yield:** 18 servings.

Cherry-Chocolate Pudgy Pie

(Pictured in center on next page)

Prep/Total Time: 10 min.

Here's a popular campfire classic from our Test Kitchen. Now all you need to make this ooey-gooey treat is the sandwich iron and a roaring fire.

- **2 slices white bread**
- **3 tablespoons cherry pie filling**
- **1 tablespoon chopped almonds**
- **1 tablespoon semisweet chocolate chunks**
- **1 teaspoon sugar**

Place one slice of bread in a greased sandwich iron. Spread with pie filling; sprinkle with almonds, chocolate chunks and sugar. Top with the remaining bread slice. Close the iron.

Cook sandwich over a hot campfire for 1 to 1-1/2 minutes or until golden brown, turning occasionally. **Yield:** 1 serving.

S'more Pudgy Pie

(Pictured above left)

Prep/Total Time: 10 min.

Simply sinful is how tasters described this fresh take on s'mores. —Joanne Surfus, Sturgeon Bay, Wisconsin

2 slices cinnamon bread
2 tablespoons Nutella
1/2 graham cracker, crushed
1 tablespoon miniature marshmallows

Place one slice of bread in a greased sandwich iron. Spread with Nutella; sprinkle with cracker crumbs and marshmallows. Top with the remaining bread slice. Close iron.

Cook sandwich over a hot campfire for 1 to 1-1/2 minutes or until golden brown, turning occasionally. **Yield:** 1 serving.

Ham & Jack Pudgy Pie

(Pictured above right)

Prep/Total Time: 10 min.

Pepper Jack cheese adds spicy flavor to these warm, melty sandwiches. —Terri McKitrick, Delafield, Wisconsin

2 slices sourdough bread
2 tablespoons diced fully cooked ham
2 tablespoons canned sliced mushrooms
3 tablespoons shredded pepper Jack cheese
1 tablespoon salsa

Place one slice of bread in a greased sandwich iron. Top with ham, mushrooms, cheese and salsa. Top with remaining bread slice. Close iron.

Cook sandwich over a hot campfire for 1 to 1-1/2 minutes or until golden brown, turning occasionally. **Yield:** 1 serving.

GREATS FOR GAME DAY

Excitement abounds when your favorite sports team is duking it out with their rival. Although being at the game is great, a party at home with friends gathered around the TV can be just as enthusiastic.

All the finger food you need to make sure your sports fans are satisfied can be found on the following pages. And many of the dips and snacks here can be made in only 5 minutes! Now that's a good reason to hoot and holler! ■

Red Pepper & Feta Dip

(Pictured below)

Prep/Total Time: 5 min.

This creamy classic dip with red peppers and feta cheese will deliver on flavor before the football game's coin drops. Even better, it's made with four ingredients!

—Melody Landaiche, Lafayette, Colorado

1 package (8 ounces) cream cheese, softened
1 tablespoon 2% milk
1/2 cup chopped roasted sweet red peppers
1/2 cup crumbled feta cheese
Baked pita chips

In a large bowl, beat the cream cheese and milk until smooth; gently stir in red peppers and feta cheese. Serve with pita chips. **Yield:** 1-1/2 cups.

Rocky Road Cookie Pizza

(Pictured at left)

Prep: 15 min. **Bake:** 20 min. + cooling

Short and sweet, this recipe will win big with guests no matter how the game winds up. It's chock-full of tasty toppings, including chocolate, nuts and caramel.
—Loraine Meyer, Bend, Oregon

1 tube (16-1/2 ounces) refrigerated sugar cookie dough
1 cup miniature marshmallows
1 cup (6 ounces) semisweet chocolate chips
1/2 cup chopped salted peanuts
1/3 cup hot caramel ice cream topping, warmed

Let dough stand at room temperature for 5-10 minutes to soften. Press dough onto a greased 12-in. pizza pan. Bake at 350° for 15-20 minutes or until a deep golden brown color.

Sprinkle with marshmallows, chips and peanuts. Bake 5-10 minutes longer or until marshmallows are puffed. Drizzle with the caramel topping. Cool on a wire rack. **Yield:** 16 slices.

STICKY MARSHMALLOWS

To separate sticky marshmallows, place a spoonful of powdered sugar in the bag, close and shake it well. A few stubborn marshmallows may still need to be separated by hand, but this generally works great.

Candied Pumpkin Spice Pecans

(Pictured at left)

Prep: 5 min. **Cook:** 20 min. + cooling

You'll be tempted to take possession of the bowl and eat up all of these sweet and spicy nuts. Before you know it, they'll be gone! *—Julie Puderbaugh, Berwick, Pennsylvania*

1/4 cup butter, cubed
1/2 cup sugar
1 teaspoon pumpkin pie spice
1 teaspoon vanilla extract
2 cups pecan halves

In a large heavy skillet, melt the butter. Add sugar; cook and stir over medium heat until sugar is dissolved. Reduce heat; cook until dark reddish brown, about 15-20 minutes, stirring occasionally.

Stir in pie spice and vanilla; add pecans. Cook and stir 3-5 minutes longer or until pecans are toasted. Spread onto foil to cool. **Yield:** 2 cups.

Simmered Smoked Links

(Pictured below)

Prep: 5 min. **Cook:** 4 hours

An appetizing sweet-spicy sauce glazes these bite-size sausages. Serve the effortless appetizers with toothpicks at parties or holiday get-togethers.
—Maxine Cenker, Weirton, West Virginia

2 packages (16 ounces *each*) miniature smoked sausage links
1 cup packed brown sugar
1/2 cup ketchup
1/4 cup prepared horseradish

Place the miniature sausages in a 3-qt. slow cooker. Combine the brown sugar, ketchup and horseradish; pour over the sausages. Cover and cook on low for 4 hours. **Yield:** 16-20 servings.

Seafood Cheese Dip

(Pictured above)

Prep: 15 min. **Cook:** 1-1/2 hours

This cheesy recipe has a nice combination of crab and shrimp tastes. Its rich and thick texture clings well to slices of French or Italian bread.
—Michelle Domm, Atlanta, New York

1 package (32 ounces) process cheese (Velveeta), cubed
2 cans (6 ounces *each*) lump crabmeat, drained
1 can (10 ounces) diced tomatoes and green chilies, undrained
1 cup frozen cooked salad shrimp, thawed
French bread baguettes, sliced and toasted

In a greased 3-qt. slow cooker, combine the cheese, crab, tomatoes and shrimp. Cover and cook on low for 1-1/2 to 2 hours or until the cheese is melted, stirring occasionally. Serve with baguettes. **Yield:** 5 cups.

Hot Fruit Punch

(Pictured at far right)

Prep/Total Time: 20 min.

You don't need a special occasion to serve this warming drink. It's great after a football game or fall hayride. Kids will enjoy it as much as adults.
—Maggie Wind, Grand Rapids, Michigan

6 cups water, *divided*
2 individual tea bags
1 cup sugar
1 cup orange juice
1/2 cup lemon juice
1/2 cup white grape juice

Bring 1 cup water to a boil. Add tea bags; steep for 5 minutes. Discard tea bags. Stir in sugar until dissolved.

In a Dutch oven, combine the remaining water, juices and tea; heat through. Serve warm. **Yield:** 2 quarts.

Colorful Spiral Pasta Salad

(Pictured at far right)

Prep/Total Time: 20 min.

Tackle potlucks with a bright pasta salad. This tricolor toss-up with broccoli, tomatoes, olives and a hardworking dressing is an easy-to-make dish to bring.
—Amanda Cable, Boxford, Massachusetts

1 package (12 ounces) tricolor spiral pasta
4 cups fresh broccoli florets
1 pint grape tomatoes
1 can (6 ounces) pitted ripe olives, drained
1/8 teaspoon salt
1/8 teaspoon pepper
1-1/2 cups Italian salad dressing with roasted red pepper and Parmesan

In a Dutch oven, cook pasta according to package directions, adding the broccoli during the last 2 minutes of cooking. Drain and rinse in cold water.

Transfer to a large bowl. Add tomatoes, olives, salt and pepper. Drizzle with salad dressing; toss to coat. Chill until serving. **Yield:** 14 servings (3/4 cup each).

Cheddar & Bacon Burgers

(Pictured at right)

Prep/Total Time: 25 min.

Bacon and onion soup flavor these satisfying handhelds from the inside out. One taste tester called them her "favorite bacon burgers ever!"
—Teresa Euken, Red Oak, Iowa

1/2 cup shredded cheddar cheese
1/2 cup crumbled cooked bacon
1 envelope onion soup mix
2 pounds ground beef
8 hamburger buns, split
Lettuce leaves and tomato slices, optional

In a large bowl, combine the cheese, bacon and soup mix. Crumble beef over mixture and mix well. Shape into eight patties.

Grill burgers, covered, over medium heat or broil 4 in. from the heat for 5-7 minutes on each side or until a thermometer reads 160° and the juices run clear. Serve on buns with the lettuce and tomato if desired. **Yield:** 8 servings.

MAKING HAMBURGERS

To keep hamburgers moist, first combine the filling ingredients, then add the meat and mix just until combined. Overmixing can cause the burgers to be dense and heavy.

Oktoberfest

CHAPTER 10

Slow-Cooked Sensations

Having a home-cooked meal ready for you when you return from a hard day's work or a full afternoon of activities is a wonderful welcome!

You'll find plenty of hearty, flavorful entrees here to help put a wholesome dinner on the table no matter how busy your day. Cranberry-Ginger Pork Ribs and Slow Cooker Chicken Curry take just 20 minutes to prepare. And Sweet-and-Sour Beef Stew takes only 25 minutes to throw together and slow cooks for 8 hours, so it's ready at the end of a long day.

And for those who truly love their slow cooker, we even have a bevy of desserts. Simply check out the Minty Hot Fudge Sundae Cake—it's ooey-gooey, easy and oh, so irresistible! ■

IT'S "SLOW" GOOD. Slow-Cooker Bread Pudding (p. 172).

Hawaiian Kielbasa Sandwiches

(Pictured above)

Prep: 15 min. **Cook:** 3 hours

If you are looking for a different way to use kielbasa, the sweet and mildly spicy flavor of these satisfying sandwiches is a nice change of pace.
—Judy Dames, Bridgeville, Pennsylvania

3 pounds smoked kielbasa *or* Polish sausage, cut into 3-inch pieces
2 bottles (12 ounces *each*) chili sauce
1 can (20 ounces) pineapple tidbits, undrained
1/4 cup packed brown sugar
12 hoagie buns, split

Place the kielbasa in a 3-qt. slow cooker. Combine the chili sauce, pineapple tidbits and brown sugar; pour over the kielbasa. Cover and cook on low for 3-4 hours or until heated through. Serve on hoagie buns. **Yield:** 12 servings.

MEASURING BROWN SUGAR

The moisture in brown sugar tends to trap air between the crystals, so it should be firmly packed when you are measuring it. Taste of Home recipes specify packed brown sugar in the ingredients.

Green Olive Dip

(Pictured below)

Prep: 30 min. **Cook:** 3 hours

Olive fans will love this dip. It's cheesy and full of beef and beans. It could even be used to fill taco shells.
—Beth Dunahay, Lima, Ohio

1 pound ground beef
1 medium sweet red pepper, chopped
1 small onion, chopped
1 can (16 ounces) refried beans
1 jar (16 ounces) mild salsa
2 cups (8 ounces) shredded part-skim mozzarella cheese
2 cups (8 ounces) shredded cheddar cheese
1 jar (5-3/4 ounces) sliced green olives with pimientos, drained
Tortilla chips

In a large skillet, cook the beef, pepper and onion over medium heat until meat is no longer pink; drain.

Transfer to a greased 3-qt. slow cooker. Add the beans, salsa, cheeses and olives. Cover and cook on low for 3-4 hours or until the cheese is melted, stirring occasionally. Serve with chips. **Yield:** 8 cups.

Southern Pulled Pork

(Pictured above right)

Prep: 20 min. **Cook:** 6-1/4 hours

With molasses and brown sugar, this sweet and tangy pork takes just a few minutes of prep and offers plenty of hands-free time. It's even more rewarding served with yummy sweet potatoes.
—Katie Grady, West Boylston, Massachusetts

1 boneless pork shoulder butt roast (3 pounds)
1/3 cup spicy brown mustard
1/3 cup molasses
1/4 cup packed brown sugar
1-1/2 teaspoons soy sauce
1 tablespoon cornstarch
1/4 cup cold water
Baked sweet potatoes, optional

Cut roast in half; place in a 3- or 4-qt. slow cooker. In a small bowl, combine the mustard, molasses, brown sugar and soy sauce; pour over roast.

Cover and cook on low for 6-8 hours or until the meat is tender.

Remove meat; cool slightly. Skim fat from cooking juices; transfer to a large saucepan. Bring to a boil. Combine cornstarch and water until smooth; gradually stir into the juices. Return to a boil; cook and stir for 2 minutes or until thickened.

Shred meat with two forks; return to the slow cooker. Stir in gravy. Cover and cook 15 minutes longer or until heated through. Serve with sweet potatoes if desired. **Yield:** 10 servings.

Vegetarian Stuffed Peppers

(Pictured at right)

Prep: 30 min. **Cook:** 3-1/2 hours

These filling and flavorful peppers are an updated version of my mom's stuffed peppers, which were a favorite when I was growing up in upstate New York. Whenever I make them, I'm reminded of home.
—Melissa McCabe, Long Beach, California

6 large sweet peppers
2 cups cooked brown rice
3 small tomatoes, chopped
1 cup frozen corn, thawed
1 small sweet onion, chopped
1/3 cup canned red beans, rinsed and drained
1/3 cup canned black beans, rinsed and drained
3/4 cup cubed Monterey Jack cheese
1 can (4-1/4 ounces) chopped ripe olives
4 fresh basil leaves, thinly sliced
3 garlic cloves, minced
1 teaspoon salt
1/2 teaspoon pepper
3/4 cup meatless spaghetti sauce
1/2 cup water
4 tablespoons grated Parmesan cheese, *divided*

Cut tops off peppers and remove seeds; set aside. In a large bowl, combine the rice, tomatoes, corn, onion and beans. Stir in the Monterey Jack cheese, olives, basil, garlic, salt and pepper. Spoon into peppers.

Combine spaghetti sauce and water; pour half into an oval 5-qt. slow cooker. Add the stuffed peppers. Top with the remaining sauce. Sprinkle with 2 tablespoons Parmesan cheese.

Cover and cook on low for 3-1/2 to 4 hours or until peppers are tender and filling is heated through. Sprinkle with remaining Parmesan cheese. **Yield:** 6 servings.

Baked Vegetarian Stuffed Peppers: Fill peppers as directed. Spoon half of the sauce mixture into an ungreased 3-qt. baking dish. Add the peppers; top with remaining sauce mixture. Sprinkle with cheese as directed. Cover and bake at 350° for 30-35 minutes or until peppers are tender and filling is heated through.

Italian Sausages with Provolone

(Pictured below)

Prep: 15 min. **Cook:** 4 hours

Here's an easy recipe everyone will rave about. The tangy sausages with their pepper and onion topping will go fast. Better make a double batch!

—Shelly Bevington-Fisher, Hermiston, Oregon

10 Italian sausage links (4 ounces *each*)
1 tablespoon canola oil
1 *each* small sweet red, yellow and orange pepper, cut into strips
2 medium onions, halved and sliced
2 cups Italian salad dressing
10 brat buns
10 slices provolone cheese

In a large skillet, brown sausages in oil in batches on all sides. Drain. Transfer to a 5-qt. slow cooker. Add the peppers, onions and salad dressing. Cover and cook on low for 4-5 hours or until sausages are no longer pink and vegetables are tender.

Place brats and cheese in buns; using a slotted spoon, top with pepper mixture. **Yield:** 10 servings.

Mulled Dr. Pepper

(Pictured above right)

Prep: 10 min. **Cook:** 2 hours

When neighbors or friends visit us on a chilly evening, I'll serve this warm beverage with ham sandwiches and deviled eggs. —Bernice Morris, Marshfield, Missouri

8 cups Dr. Pepper
1/4 cup packed brown sugar
1/4 cup lemon juice
1/2 teaspoon ground allspice
1/2 teaspoon whole cloves
1/4 teaspoon salt
1/4 teaspoon ground nutmeg
3 cinnamon sticks (3 inches)

In a 3-qt. slow cooker, combine all ingredients. Cover and cook on low for 2 hours or until heated through.

Discard the cloves and cinnamon sticks. **Yield:** 8-10 servings.

Mom's Scalloped Potatoes and Ham

Prep: 20 min. **Cook:** 8 hours

When I have leftover ham to use up, this is the most-requested recipe in the house!

—Kelly Graham, St. Thomas, Ontario

10 medium potatoes, peeled and thinly sliced
3 cups cubed fully cooked ham
2 large onions, thinly sliced
2 cups (8 ounces) shredded cheddar cheese
1 can (10-3/4 ounces) condensed cream of mushroom soup, undiluted
1/2 teaspoon paprika
1/4 teaspoon pepper

In a greased 6-qt. slow cooker, layer half of the potatoes, ham, onions and cheese. Repeat layers. Pour soup over top. Sprinkle with paprika and pepper.

Cover and cook on low for 8-10 hours or until the potatoes are tender. **Yield:** 9 servings.

Bacon-Beef Barley Soup

(Pictured below)

Prep: 40 min. **Cook:** 8 hours

Here's a robust dish that's perfect for hungry teenage boys! Served over creamy mashed potatoes, this quick, comforting soup will really hit the spot.
—Cathy Peterson, Menominee, Michigan

4 bacon strips, chopped
1-1/2 pounds beef stew meat, cut into 1/2-inch pieces
1 medium onion, chopped
4 medium red potatoes, cut into 1/2-inch cubes
1-1/2 cups fresh baby carrots, cut in half lengthwise
1 cup frozen corn
1/4 cup medium pearl barley
2 cans (14-1/2 ounces *each*) beef broth
1 can (14-1/2 ounces) diced tomatoes with basil, oregano and garlic, undrained
1 jar (12 ounces) home-style beef gravy
1/2 teaspoon pepper
Mashed potatoes, optional

In a large skillet, cook bacon over medium heat until crisp. Using a slotted spoon, remove to paper towels to drain. In the drippings, cook beef and onion until meat is no longer pink; drain.

In a 5-qt. slow cooker, layer potatoes, carrots, corn and barley. Top with beef mixture and bacon. Combine the broth, tomatoes, gravy and pepper; pour over top (do not stir).

Cover and cook on low for 8 to 10 hours or until meat and vegetables are tender. Stir before serving. Serve over mashed potatoes if desired. **Yield:** 7 servings.

Cranberry-Dijon Pork Roast

(Pictured above)

Prep: 15 min. **Cook:** 4 hours

Five everyday ingredients are all you need for this sweet and tangy pork roast. I like to serve it with a side of mashed sweet potatoes and slices of corn bread.
—Mary-Ellen Steele, Bristol, Connecticut

1 boneless pork loin roast (2 to 3 pounds)
2 tablespoons butter
1 envelope golden onion soup mix
1 can (14 ounces) whole-berry cranberry sauce
2 teaspoons Dijon mustard

In a large skillet, brown the roast in butter on all sides. Transfer to a 5-qt. slow cooker; sprinkle with soup mix. Add cranberry sauce to skillet, stirring to loosen browned bits from pan. Pour over roast.

Cover and cook on low for 4-5 hours or until the meat is tender. Remove the roast to a serving platter and keep warm. Strain the cooking juices and stir in the Dijon mustard. Slice the roast and serve with the sauce. **Yield:** 6 servings.

WHAT ARE BROWN BITS?

When a recipe method states "stirring to loosen browned bits," it's referring to the little flecks of browned food that are left in the bottom of a pan after browning or cooking meat or poultry.

Moroccan Chicken

(Pictured above)

Prep: 25 min. **Cook:** 6 hours

With squash, chickpeas, tomatoes and olives, this dish is packed with flavor. Most of the ingredients are pantry staples, but they combine to make a fun and unique meal your family will enjoy. —Lily Julow, Gainesville, Florida

1-1/2 pounds butternut squash, peeled, seeded and cut into 2-inch cubes
1 can (15 ounces) garbanzo beans *or* chickpeas, rinsed and drained
1 medium onion, chopped
1 cup chicken broth
1/3 cup raisins
2 garlic cloves, minced
2 teaspoons ground coriander
2 teaspoons ground cumin
1/2 teaspoon ground cinnamon
1/2 teaspoon salt
1/4 teaspoon pepper
8 bone-in chicken thighs (about 3 pounds), skin removed
2 medium tomatoes, chopped
1/2 cup pitted green olives
1 tablespoon cornstarch
1 tablespoon cold water
Hot cooked couscous

In a 6-qt. slow cooker, place the squash, beans, onion, broth, raisins and garlic. Combine the coriander, cumin, cinnamon, salt and pepper; rub over chicken. Place in slow cooker.

Cover and cook on low for 6-8 hours or until chicken is tender, adding tomatoes and olives during the last 20 minutes of cooking.

Remove chicken and vegetables to a serving platter; keep warm. Skim fat from cooking juices; transfer to a small saucepan. Bring to a boil. Combine cornstarch and water until smooth; gradually stir into cooking juices. Return to a boil; cook and stir for 2 minutes or until thickened. Serve with chicken, vegetables and couscous. **Yield:** 8 servings.

Tangy Tomato Pork Chops

(Pictured below)

Prep: 20 min. **Cook:** 8 hours

These tender chops are smothered in a delightfully rich sauce. I've used a chuck roast instead of pork loin chops, stewed tomatoes instead of diced and served it over rice. It's always good. —Lea Ann Schalk, Garfield, Arkansas

6 bone-in pork loin chops (8 ounces *each*)
1 tablespoon canola oil
1 large onion, sliced
1 large sweet red pepper, sliced
1 jar (4-1/2 ounces) sliced mushrooms, drained
1 can (28 ounces) diced tomatoes, undrained
1 tablespoon brown sugar
1 tablespoon balsamic vinegar
2 teaspoons Worcestershire sauce
1/4 teaspoon salt
1/4 teaspoon pepper
Hot cooked egg noodles, optional

In a large skillet, brown pork chops in oil. Transfer to a 5-qt. slow cooker. Layer the onion, red pepper and mushrooms over pork chops.

In a large bowl, combine the tomatoes, brown sugar, vinegar, Worcestershire sauce, salt and pepper; pour over pork and vegetables.

Cover and cook on low for 8-9 hours or until pork is tender. Serve with noodles if desired. **Yield:** 6 servings.

Beef & Tortellini Marinara With Green Beans

(Pictured above)

Prep: 30 min. **Cook:** 6-1/2 hours

This hearty stew made with fresh green beans is a meal in itself. It's great served with crusty Italian bread to dip in the sauce and a big green salad.
—Joyce Frey, Macksville, Kansas

1 pound beef stew meat
2 tablespoons olive oil
2 garlic cloves, minced
1 jar (26 ounces) marinara *or* spaghetti sauce
2 cups dry red wine *or* beef broth
1 pound fresh green beans, trimmed
1 can (14-1/2 ounces) Italian diced tomatoes, undrained
1/2 pound small fresh mushrooms
2 envelopes thick and zesty spaghetti sauce mix
2 tablespoons minced fresh parsley
1 tablespoon dried minced onion
2 teaspoons minced fresh rosemary
1 teaspoon coarsely ground pepper
1/4 teaspoon salt
1 package (9 ounces) refrigerated cheese tortellini

In a large skillet, brown beef in oil until no longer pink. Add the garlic; cook 1 minute longer. Transfer to a 5- or 6-qt. slow cooker. Stir in marinara sauce, wine, green beans, tomatoes, mushrooms, sauce mix, parsley, onion, rosemary, pepper and salt. Cover and cook on low for 6-8 hours or until meat is tender.

Stir in tortellini. Cover and cook on high 30 minutes longer or until the tortellini are heated through. **Yield:** 11 servings.

Herb Stuffed Chops

(Pictured below)

Prep: 25 min. **Cook:** 8 hours

Guests will think you stayed home all day when you serve these savory stuffed chops. I often share this recipe with new brides because I know it will become one of their favorites. *—Diana Seeger, New Springfield, Ohio*

3/4 cup chopped onion
1/4 cup chopped celery
2 tablespoons butter
2 cups day-old bread cubes
1/2 cup minced fresh parsley
1/3 cup evaporated milk
1 teaspoon fennel seed, crushed
1-1/2 teaspoons salt, *divided*
1/2 teaspoon pepper, *divided*
6 bone-in pork rib *or* loin chops (8 ounces *each*)
1 tablespoon canola oil
3/4 cup white wine *or* chicken broth

In a small skillet, saute onion and celery in butter until tender. Add the bread cubes, parsley, milk, fennel, 1/4 teaspoon salt and 1/8 teaspoon pepper; toss to coat.

Cut a pocket in each chop by slicing from the fat side almost to the bone. Spoon about 1/4 cup stuffing into each pocket. Combine the remaining salt and pepper; rub over chops.

In a large skillet, brown chops in oil; transfer to a 3-qt. slow cooker. Pour wine over top. Cover and cook on low for 8-9 hours or until a meat thermometer reads 160°. **Yield:** 6 servings.

Fiesta-Twisted Brunswick Stew

(Pictured at right)

Prep: 20 min. **Cook:** 5 hours

Traditionally made with game meat, this updated take on Brunswick stew, using spicy sausage, is a modern mom's best friend.
—Donna Marie Ryan, Topsfield, Massachusetts

1/2 pound uncooked chorizo *or* bulk spicy pork sausage
1 large potato, cubed
1 large onion, chopped
1 large green pepper, chopped
3 jalapeno peppers, seeded and chopped
1 can (28 ounces) crushed tomatoes
1 jar (26 ounces) marinara sauce
1 can (14-3/4 ounces) cream-style corn
1 tablespoon Cajun seasoning
1 garlic clove, minced
1/2 teaspoon sugar
1/2 teaspoon pepper
1/4 teaspoon salt
1/3 cup all-purpose flour
1 can (14-1/2 ounces) chicken broth
4 bone-in chicken breast halves (8 ounces *each*), skin removed
1 cup cut fresh green beans
2 tablespoons minced fresh cilantro
Shredded Asiago cheese

Crumble chorizo into a small skillet; cook over medium heat for 6-8 minutes or until fully cooked. Drain. Transfer to a 6-qt. slow cooker. Add the potato, onion, green pepper, jalapenos, tomatoes, marinara sauce, corn, Cajun seasoning, garlic, sugar, pepper and salt.

In a small bowl, combine the flour and broth until smooth; stir into slow cooker. Add the chicken. Cover and cook on low for 5-6 hours or until the chicken and vegetables are tender; adding green beans and cilantro during the last 2 hours of cooking.

Remove chicken from slow cooker. When cool enough to handle, remove meat from bones; discard bones. Cut meat into bite-size pieces and return to the slow cooker; heat through. Sprinkle servings with cheese. **Yield:** 9 servings (3-1/2 quarts).

Editor's Note: Wear disposable gloves when cutting hot peppers; the oils can burn skin. Avoid touching your face.

Sweet-and-Sour Beef Stew

(Pictured at far right)

Prep: 25 min. **Cook:** 8 hours

This chunky meal in a bowl makes terrific use of nutrient-packed vegetables. Pineapple and brown sugar provide the sweetness. *—Frances Conklin, Grangeville, Idaho*

2 pounds beef top round steak, cut into 1-inch cubes
2 tablespoons olive oil
1 can (15 ounces) tomato sauce
2 large onions, chopped
4 medium carrots, thinly sliced
1 large green pepper, cut into 1-inch pieces
1 cup canned pineapple chunks, drained
1/2 cup cider vinegar
1/4 cup packed brown sugar
1/4 cup light corn syrup
2 teaspoons chili powder
2 teaspoons paprika
1/2 teaspoon salt
Hot cooked rice

In a large skillet, brown beef in oil in batches; drain. Transfer to a 4- or 5-qt. slow cooker.

In a large bowl, combine the tomato sauce, onions, carrots, green pepper, pineapple chunks, vinegar, brown sugar, corn syrup, chili powder, paprika and salt; pour over the beef.

Cover and cook on low for 8-10 hours or until beef is tender. Serve with rice. **Yield:** 8 servings.

Harvest Butternut & Pork Stew

(Pictured at top right)

Prep: 20 min. **Cook:** 7-1/2 hours

Cure your craving for something different with a savory stew that's delicious with warm bread.
—Erin Chilcoat, Smithtown, New York

1/3 cup plus 1 tablespoon all-purpose flour, *divided*
1 tablespoon paprika
1 teaspoon salt
1 teaspoon ground coriander
1-1/2 pounds boneless pork shoulder butt roast, cut into 1-inch cubes
1 tablespoon canola oil
2-3/4 cups cubed peeled butternut squash
1 can (14-1/2 ounces) diced tomatoes, undrained
1 cup frozen corn, thawed
1 medium onion, chopped
2 tablespoons cider vinegar
1 bay leaf
2-1/2 cups reduced-sodium chicken broth
1-2/3 cups frozen shelled edamame, thawed

In a large resealable plastic bag, combine 1/3 cup flour, paprika, salt and coriander. Add pork, a few pieces at a time, and shake to coat.

In a large skillet, brown pork in oil in batches; drain. Transfer to a 5-qt. slow cooker. Add squash, tomatoes, corn, onion, vinegar and bay leaf. In a small bowl, combine broth and remaining flour until smooth; stir into slow cooker.

Cover and cook on low for 7-9 hours or until pork and vegetables are tender. Stir in the edamame; cover and cook 30 minutes longer. Discard bay leaf. **Yield:** 6 servings (2 quarts).

Slow-Cooked Pork Tacos

(Pictured above)

Prep: 20 min. **Cook:** 4 hours

Sometimes I'll substitute Bibb lettuce leaves for the tortillas to make crunchy lettuce wraps, and I find that leftovers are perfect for burritos.
—Kathleen Wolf, Naperville, Illinois

1 boneless pork sirloin roast (2 pounds), cut into 1-inch pieces
1-1/2 cups salsa verde
1 medium sweet red pepper, chopped
1 medium onion, chopped
1/4 cup chopped dried apricots
2 tablespoons lime juice
2 garlic cloves, minced
1 teaspoon ground cumin
1/2 teaspoon salt
1/4 teaspoon white pepper
Dash hot pepper sauce
10 flour tortillas (8 inches), warmed
Reduced-fat sour cream, thinly sliced green onions, cubed avocado, shredded reduced-fat cheddar cheese and chopped tomato, optional

In a 3-qt. slow cooker, combine the first 11 ingredients. Cover and cook on high for 4-5 hours or until meat is very tender.

Shred pork with two forks. Place about 1/2 cup pork mixture down the center of each tortilla. Serve with toppings if desired. **Yield:** 10 tacos.

COOKING PORK

Fresh pork needs only to be cooked to an internal temperature of 160° to 170°. At 160°, the internal color of boneless roasts may be faint pink and bone-in roasts may be slightly pink near the bone. But if the juices run clear, the meat is properly cooked.

Tex-Mex Chili with a Cincinnati Twist

(Pictured below)

Prep: 35 min. **Cook:** 6 hours

My husband grew up in Cincinnati, where chili is served over spaghetti, and I grew up in the South. This family-pleaser is a mingling of both worlds—and a great way to make a meal go further. —Stephanie Rabbitt-Schapp, Cincinnati, Ohio

1 pound ground beef
1 cup chopped sweet onion
1/4 cup chili powder
2 tablespoons ground cumin
2 teaspoons baking cocoa
1-1/2 teaspoons ground cinnamon
3/4 teaspoon cayenne pepper
1/2 teaspoon salt
1 can (16 ounces) chili beans, undrained
1 can (16 ounces) kidney beans, rinsed and drained
1 can (14-1/2 ounces) diced tomatoes, undrained
1 can (8 ounces) tomato sauce
1 medium tomato, chopped
1 jalapeno pepper, seeded and chopped
Hot cooked spaghetti
Optional toppings: oyster crackers, hot pepper sauce, chopped sweet onion and shredded cheddar cheese

In a large skillet, cook beef and onion over medium heat until meat is no longer pink; drain. Stir in chili powder, cumin, cocoa, cinnamon, cayenne and salt.

Transfer to a 4- or 5-qt. slow cooker. Stir in the chili beans, kidney beans, diced tomatoes, tomato sauce, tomato and jalapeno.

Cover and cook on low for 6-8 hours or until heated through. Serve over spaghetti. Garnish with toppings of your choice. **Yield:** 7 servings.

Editor's Note: Wear disposable gloves when cutting hot peppers; the oils can burn skin. Avoid touching your face.

Gingered Short Ribs With Green Rice

(Pictured above)

Prep: 25 min. **Cook:** 8 hours

I love the exotic flavors of Korean cooking, so I converted this special recipe for slow cooker convenience.

—Lily Julow, Gainesville, Florida

4 medium carrots, chopped
2 medium onions, chopped
3 pounds bone-in beef short ribs
1/2 teaspoon salt
1/2 teaspoon pepper
1/2 cup reduced-sodium beef broth
1/3 cup sherry *or* additional reduced-sodium beef broth
1/4 cup reduced-sodium soy sauce
3 tablespoons honey
1 tablespoon rice vinegar
1 tablespoon minced fresh gingerroot
3 garlic cloves, minced
3 cups uncooked instant brown rice
3 green onions, thinly sliced
3 tablespoons minced fresh cilantro
2 tablespoons chopped pickled jalapenos
3/4 teaspoon grated lime peel
4-1/2 teaspoons cornstarch
4-1/2 teaspoons cold water

In a 5-qt. slow cooker, layer the carrots, onions and ribs; sprinkle with salt and pepper. In a small bowl, combine the broth, sherry, soy sauce, honey, vinegar, ginger and garlic. Pour over top. Cover and cook on low for 8-10 hours or until meat is tender.

Meanwhile, cook the brown rice according to package directions. Stir in the green onions, cilantro, jalapenos and lime peel.

Remove ribs to a serving platter; keep warm. Skim fat from cooking juices; transfer to a small saucepan. Bring to a boil. Combine cornstarch and water until smooth; gradually stir into the cooking liquid. Bring to a boil; cook and stir for 2 minutes or until thickened. Serve with ribs and rice. **Yield:** 6 servings.

Slow-Cooked Cabbage Rolls

(Pictured below)

Prep: 20 min. **Cook:** 6 hours

I've worked full time for more than 30 years, and this super slow-cooker recipe has been a lifesaver. It cooks while I'm away and smells heavenly when I walk in the door in the evening.

—Rosemary Jarvis, Sparta, Tennessee

1 large head cabbage
1 can (8 ounces) tomato sauce
3/4 cup quick-cooking rice
1/2 cup chopped green pepper
1/2 cup crushed saltines (about 15 crackers)
1 egg, lightly beaten
1 ounce onion soup mix
1-1/2 pounds lean ground beef (90% lean)
1 can (46 ounces) V8 juice
Salt to taste
Grated Parmesan cheese, optional

Cook cabbage in boiling water just until leaves fall off head. Set aside 12 large leaves for rolls; drain well. (Refrigerate remaining cabbage for another use.) Cut out the thick vein from the bottom of each reserved leaf, making a V-shaped cut; set aside.

In a large bowl, combine tomato sauce, rice, green pepper, cracker crumbs, egg and soup mix. Crumble beef over mixture and mix well.

Place about 1/3 cup meat mixture on each cabbage leaf; overlap cut ends of leaf. Fold in sides, beginning from the cut end. Roll up completely to enclose filling. Secure with toothpicks if desired.

Place cabbage rolls in a 3-qt. slow cooker. Pour V8 juice over rolls. Cover and cook on low for 6-7 hours or until filling reaches 160°. Just before serving, sprinkle with salt and cheese if desired. **Yield:** 6 servings.

Family-Favorite Beef Roast

(Pictured below)

Prep: 10 min. **Cook:** 6 hours

Just a few ingredients are all you'll need for this tangy roast that feeds a bunch. The gravy is tasty on mashed potatoes, too. —Jeanie Beasley, Tupelo, Mississippi

1 boneless beef chuck roast (3-4 pounds)
1 can (14-1/2 ounces) stewed tomatoes, cut up
1 can (10-3/4 ounces) condensed cream of mushroom soup, undiluted
1 envelope Lipton beefy onion soup mix
1/4 cup cornstarch
1/2 cup water

Cut roast in half. Transfer to a 5-qt. slow cooker. In a small bowl, combine the tomatoes, soup and soup mix; pour over meat. Cover and cook on low for 6-8 hours or until meat is tender.

Remove meat to a serving platter; keep warm. Skim fat from cooking juices; transfer to a large saucepan. Bring liquid to a boil. Combine cornstarch and water until smooth; gradually stir into the pan. Bring to a boil; cook and stir for 2 minutes or until thickened. Serve with roast. **Yield:** 8 servings.

French Onion Portobello Brisket

Prep: 20 min. **Cook:** 8 hours

I use this recipe when I go to winter potlucks and want something everyone will love. Though I have seen kids who scrape away the mushrooms and onion, they still rave about how the meat tastes and gobble it right up. —Aysha Schurman, Ammon, Idaho

1 fresh beef brisket (4 pounds)
1-3/4 cups sliced baby portobello mushrooms
1 small red onion, sliced
2 garlic cloves, minced
2 tablespoons butter
1 can (10-1/2 ounces) condensed French onion soup
1/4 cup dry white wine *or* beef broth
1/2 teaspoon coarsely ground pepper
Fresh sage, optional

Cut brisket in half; place in a 5-qt. slow cooker.

In a large saucepan, saute the mushrooms, onion and garlic in butter for 3-5 minutes or until onion is crisp-tender. Add the soup, wine and pepper; mix well.

Pour mushroom mixture over beef. Cover and cook on low for 8-10 hours or until meat is tender. Garnish with sage if desired. **Yield:** 9 servings.

Editor's Note: This is a fresh beef brisket, not corned beef.

Butternut Squash Soup

(Pictured above)

Prep: 30 min. **Cook:** 6-1/4 hours

The golden color, creamy texture and wonderful taste of this soup is a welcome addition on a chilly fall day. It has a slightly tangy flavor from the cream cheese, and the cinnamon really comes through. —Jackie Campbell, Stanhope, New Jersey

1 medium onion, chopped
2 tablespoons butter
1 medium butternut squash (about 4 pounds), peeled and cubed
3 cans (14-1/2 ounces *each*) vegetable broth
1 tablespoon brown sugar
1 tablespoon minced fresh gingerroot
1 garlic clove, minced
1 cinnamon stick (3 inches)
1 package (8 ounces) cream cheese, softened and cubed

In a small skillet, saute onion in butter until tender. Transfer to a 5-or 6-quart slow cooker; add squash. Combine the broth, brown sugar, ginger, garlic and cinnamon; pour over squash. Cover and cook on low for 6-8 hours or until squash is tender.

Cool slightly. Discard cinnamon stick. In a blender, process soup in batches until smooth. Return all to slow cooker. Whisk in cream cheese; cover and cook 15 minutes longer or until cheese is melted. **Yield:** 14 servings (2-1/2 quarts).

Slow-Cooked Ham 'n' Broccoli

(Pictured below)

Prep: 10 min. **Cook:** 2 hours + standing

This sensational dish is so fabulous to come home to, especially on a cold winter day. It's a delicious way to use up leftover holiday ham, too.

—Jill Pennington, Jacksonville, Florida

- **3 cups cubed fully cooked ham**
- **3 cups frozen chopped broccoli, thawed**
- **1 can (10-3/4 ounces) condensed cream of mushroom soup, undiluted**
- **1 jar (8 ounces) process cheese sauce**
- **1 can (8 ounces) sliced water chestnuts, drained**
- **1-1/4 cups uncooked instant rice**
- **1 cup 2% milk**
- **1 celery rib, chopped**
- **1 medium onion, chopped**
- **1/8 to 1/4 teaspoon pepper**
- **1/2 teaspoon paprika**

In a 3-qt. slow cooker, combine the first 10 ingredients. Cover and cook on high for 2-3 hours or until the rice is tender. Let stand for 10 minutes before serving. Sprinkle with paprika. **Yield:** 6-8 servings.

Butter & Herb Turkey

(Pictured above)

Prep: 10 min. **Cook:** 5 hours

My kids love turkey, and this one falls off the bone. It's the ideal recipe for special family times, such as the Saturday supper before Easter.

—Rochelle Popovic, South Bend, Indiana

- **1 bone-in turkey breast (6 to 7 pounds)**
- **2 tablespoons butter, softened**
- **1/2 teaspoon dried rosemary, crushed**
- **1/2 teaspoon dried thyme**
- **1/4 teaspoon garlic powder**
- **1/4 teaspoon pepper**
- **1 can (14-1/2 ounces) chicken broth**
- **3 tablespoons cornstarch**
- **1 tablespoon cold water**

Rub turkey with butter. Combine the rosemary, thyme, garlic powder and pepper; sprinkle over turkey. Place in a 6-qt. slow cooker. Pour the broth over top. Cover and cook on low for 5-6 hours or until tender.

Remove turkey to a serving platter; keep warm. Skim fat from cooking juices; transfer to a small saucepan. Bring to a boil. Combine cornstarch and water until smooth. Gradually stir into the pan. Bring to a boil; cook and stir for 2 minutes or until thickened. Serve with turkey. **Yield:** 12 servings (3 cups gravy).

SPICES OF LIFE

Whole bottles of spices can be costly, so to save money, buy spices in bulk a few tablespoons at a time. It's a great way to add variety to your spice collection so you can easily try out new recipes.

Old-World Corned Beef And Vegetables

(Pictured above)

Prep: 25 min. **Cook:** 8 hours

This traditional corned beef dinner is a winner with my husband, family and friends. It's an easy meal-in-one.
—Ruth Burrus, Zionsville, Indiana

2-1/2 pounds red potatoes, quartered
2 cups fresh baby carrots
1 package (10 ounces) frozen pearl onions
1 corned beef brisket with spice packet (3 to 3-1/2 pounds)
1/2 cup water
1 tablespoon marinade for chicken
1/8 teaspoon pepper
3 tablespoons cornstarch
1/4 cup cold water

In a 5-qt. slow cooker, combine the potatoes, carrots and onions. Add the beef; discard spice packet from corned beef or save for another use. Combine the water, marinade for chicken and pepper; pour over meat. Cover and cook on low for 8-10 hours or until meat and vegetables are tender.

Remove meat and vegetables to a serving platter; keep warm. Skim fat from cooking juices; transfer to a small saucepan. Bring the liquid to a boil. Combine cornstarch and cold water until smooth. Gradually stir into the pan. Bring to a boil; cook and stir for 1-2 minutes or until thickened. Serve with meat and vegetables. **Yield:** 8 servings.

Glazed Cinnamon Apples

(Pictured below)

Prep: 20 min. **Cook:** 3 hours

If you are seeking comfort food on the sweet side, this warm and yummy apple dessert, made with cinnamon and nutmeg, fits the bill.
—Megan Maze, Oak Creek, Wisconsin

6 large tart apples
2 tablespoons lemon juice
1/2 cup packed brown sugar
1/2 cup sugar
2 tablespoons all-purpose flour
1 teaspoon ground cinnamon
1/4 teaspoon ground nutmeg
6 tablespoons butter, melted
Vanilla ice cream

Peel, core and cut each apple into eight wedges; transfer to a 3-qt. slow cooker. Drizzle with lemon juice. Combine the sugars, flour, cinnamon and nutmeg; sprinkle over apples. Drizzle with butter.

Cover and cook on low for 3-4 hours or until apples are tender. Serve in dessert dishes with ice cream. **Yield:** 7 servings.

Cranberry-Ginger Pork Ribs

(Pictured above right)

Prep: 20 min. **Cook:** 5 hours

This festive and spicy main dish is wonderful served for weeknight family meals or for entertaining.
—Judy Armstrong, Prairieville, Louisiana

1 can (14 ounces) whole-berry cranberry sauce
2 habanero peppers, seeded and minced
4-1/2 teaspoons minced grated gingerroot
3 garlic cloves, minced
2-1/2 pounds boneless country-style pork ribs
1/2 teaspoon salt
1/2 teaspoon cayenne pepper
1/2 teaspoon pepper
2 tablespoons olive oil
Hot cooked rice

In a small bowl, combine the cranberry sauce, habanero peppers, ginger and garlic. Sprinkle the ribs with salt, cayenne and pepper. In a large skillet, brown ribs in oil on all sides; drain.

Transfer meat to a 3-qt. slow cooker; pour cranberry mixture over ribs. Cover and cook on low for 5-6 hours or until meat is tender. Skim fat from cooking juices. Serve with pork and rice. **Yield:** 8 servings.

Editor's Note: Wear disposable gloves when cutting hot peppers; the oils can burn skin. Avoid touching your face.

Moist Turkey Breast With White Wine Gravy

Prep: 20 min. **Cook:** 6 hours

I modified a favorite dish for slow-cooker ease; and it's moist and tender every time. The wine gravy is a perfect complement. The flavor is best when you use drinking wine, not cooking wine.
—Tina MacKissock, Manchester, New Hampshire

1 cup white wine
1 medium apple, chopped
1/2 cup sliced fennel bulb
1/3 cup chopped celery
1/3 cup chopped carrot
3 garlic cloves, minced
1 teaspoon ground mustard
1 bay leaf
1/2 teaspoon dried rosemary, crushed
1/2 teaspoon dried thyme
1/2 teaspoon rubbed sage
1/4 teaspoon pepper
1 package (3 pounds) frozen boneless turkey roast with gravy, thawed
2 tablespoons plus 1-1/2 teaspoons cornstarch
1/2 cup half-and-half cream

In a 6-qt. slow cooker, combine the wine, apple, fennel, celery, carrot, garlic, mustard and bay leaf. In a small bowl, combine the rosemary, thyme, sage and pepper; rub over the turkey. (Discard gravy packet or save for another use.) Add turkey to slow cooker. Cover and cook on low for 6-8 hours or until meat is tender.

Remove meat to a serving platter and keep warm. Strain drippings into a measuring cup to measure 1 cup. Skim fat. In a small saucepan, combine cornstarch and cream; stir until smooth. Gradually add drippings. Bring to a boil; cook and stir for 2 minutes or until thickened. Serve with turkey. **Yield:** 8 servings.

Spicy Turkey Bean Soup

(Pictured below)

Prep: 20 min. **Cook:** 5 hours

I originally called this recipe "Turkey Dump Soup" because all you have to do is dump all the ingredients into the slow cooker and let them cook!
—Gary Fenski, Huron, South Dakota

2 cans (15 ounces *each*) white kidney *or* cannellini beans, rinsed and drained
2 cups cubed cooked turkey
1 can (14-1/2 ounces) chicken broth
1 can (10 ounces) diced tomatoes and green chilies, undrained
1 cup salsa
1/2 teaspoon ground cumin
1/4 teaspoon curry powder
1/4 teaspoon ground ginger
1/4 teaspoon paprika

In a 3- or 4-qt. slow cooker, combine all ingredients. Cover and cook on low for 5-6 hours or until heated through. **Yield:** 4 servings.

Chicken & Vegetables with Mustard-Herb Sauce

(Pictured below)

Prep: 20 min. **Cook:** 6 hours

Here's an almost effortless recipe that makes a simply delicious, comforting chicken dinner.
—Marie Rizzio, Interlochen, Michigan

- **4 medium red potatoes, quartered**
- **3 medium parsnips, cut into 1-inch pieces**
- **2 medium leeks (white portion only), thinly sliced**
- **3/4 cup fresh baby carrots**
- **4 chicken leg quarters (about 2 pounds), skin removed**
- **1 can (10-3/4 ounces) condensed cream of chicken soup with herbs, undiluted**
- **2 tablespoons minced fresh parsley**
- **1 tablespoon snipped fresh dill *or* 1 teaspoon dill weed**
- **1 tablespoon Dijon mustard**

In a 5- or 6-qt. slow cooker, place the potatoes, parsnips, leeks, carrots and chicken; pour the soup over the top. Cover and cook on low for 6-8 hours or until the chicken is tender.

Remove the chicken and vegetables; cover and keep warm. Stir the parsley, dill and mustard into cooking juices; serve with the chicken and vegetables. **Yield:** 4 servings.

ABOUT PARSNIPS

Parsnips are a root vegetable similar to carrots. Look for small to medium parsnips that are firm and have smooth skin. Store in a plastic bag for up to 2 weeks. Peel and trim ends just before using.

Pulled Pork Taters

(Pictured above)

Prep: 15 min. **Cook:** 6 hours

This recipe is as manly as it gets—part meat, part potatoes, totally satisfying. If there's ever a time to be jealous of a potato, it's now. *—Shannon Harris, Tyler, Texas*

- **1 boneless pork loin roast (2 to 3 pounds)**
- **1 medium onion, chopped**
- **1 cup ketchup**
- **1 cup root beer**
- **1/4 cup cider vinegar**
- **2 tablespoons Worcestershire sauce**
- **1 tablespoon Louisiana-style hot sauce**
- **2 teaspoons salt**
- **2 teaspoons pepper**
- **1 teaspoon ground mustard**
- **6 large potatoes**
- **1 tablespoon cornstarch**
- **1 tablespoon cold water**
- **6 tablespoons butter**
- **1-1/2 cups (6 ounces) shredded cheddar cheese**
- **6 tablespoons sour cream**

Place roast in a 5-qt. slow cooker. Top with onion. Combine ketchup, root beer, vinegar, Worcestershire, hot sauce, salt, pepper and mustard; pour over the top. Cover and cook on low for 6 to 6-1/2 hours or until meat is tender.

Meanwhile, scrub and pierce potatoes. Bake at 400° for 50-55 minutes or until tender.

Remove pork; shred with two forks. Skim fat from cooking juices; transfer to a large saucepan. Bring liquid to a boil. Combine cornstarch and water until smooth; gradually stir into the pan. Bring to a boil; cook and stir for 2 minutes or until thickened. Return meat to cooking juices; heat through.

With a sharp knife, cut an "X" in each potato; fluff with a fork. Top each with the butter and pork mixture; sprinkle with the cheese. Top with sour cream. **Yield:** 6 servings.

Minty Hot Fudge Sundae Cake

(Pictured below)

Prep: 15 min. **Cook:** 4 hours

The best part about dessert from the slow cooker is that when dinner's done, a yummy hot treat is ready to serve. In this case, a chocolaty, gooey, minty treat you can't get enough of! —*Terri McKitrick, Delafield, Wisconsin*

1-3/4 cups packed brown sugar, *divided*
1 cup all-purpose flour
5 tablespoons baking cocoa, *divided*
2 teaspoons baking powder
1/2 teaspoon salt
1/2 cup evaporated milk
2 tablespoons butter, melted
1/2 teaspoon vanilla extract
1/8 teaspoon almond extract
1 package (4.67 ounces) mint Andes candies
1-3/4 cups boiling water
4 teaspoons instant coffee granules
Vanilla ice cream, whipped cream and maraschino cherries

In a large bowl, combine 1 cup brown sugar, the flour, 3 tablespoons cocoa, baking powder and salt. In another bowl, combine the milk, butter and extracts. Stir into dry ingredients just until moistened. Transfer to a 3-qt. slow cooker coated with cooking spray. Sprinkle with Andes candies.

Combine the water, coffee granules and remaining brown sugar and cocoa; pour over batter (do not stir). Cover and cook on high for 4 to 4-1/2 hours or until a toothpick inserted near the center of the cake comes out clean. Serve with ice cream, whipped cream and cherries. **Yield:** 12 servings.

Tex-Mex Chicken with Black Beans & Rice

(Pictured above)

Prep: 15 min. **Cook:** 7 hours

I came up with this recipe for my sister who just got her first slow cooker and cooks mostly by throwing canned goods into a pot. It's a delicious go-to recipe for those busy days. —*Elizabeth Dumont, Boulder, Colorado*

6 chicken leg quarters, skin removed
1 envelope taco seasoning, *divided*
1 can (14-1/2 ounces) Mexican diced tomatoes, undrained
1 can (10-3/4 ounces) condensed cream of chicken soup, undiluted
1 large onion, chopped
1 can (4 ounces) chopped green chilies
1 cup uncooked instant rice
1 cup black beans, rinsed and drained
1 container (8 ounces) sour cream
1 cup (4 ounces) shredded cheddar cheese
1-1/2 cups crushed tortilla chips
Minced fresh cilantro

Sprinkle the chicken with 1 tablespoon taco seasoning; transfer to a 5- or 6-qt. slow cooker. In a large bowl, combine tomatoes, soup, onion, chilies and remaining taco seasoning; pour over chicken. Cover and cook on low for 7-9 hours or until chicken is tender.

Prepare rice according to package directions. Place beans in a small microwave safe-bowl. Microwave on high for 30 seconds or until warmed; stir in rice.

Remove meat and keep warm. Skim fat from cooking juices; stir in sour cream. Serve chicken with rice mixture. Sprinkle servings with cheese, tortilla chips and cilantro. **Yield:** 6 servings.

Slow-Cooker Bread Pudding

(Pictured above)

Prep: 15 min. **Cook:** 3 hours

I like to use my slow cooker to turn day-old cinnamon rolls into this comforting, old-fashioned dessert. It tastes wonderful topped with lemon or vanilla sauce or whipped cream. —*Edna Hoffman, Hebron, Indiana*

8 cups cubed day-old unfrosted cinnamon rolls
4 eggs
2 cups milk
1/4 cup sugar
1/4 cup butter, melted
1/2 teaspoon vanilla extract
1/4 teaspoon ground nutmeg
1 cup raisins

Place cubed cinnamon rolls in a 3-qt. slow cooker. In a small bowl, whisk the eggs, milk, sugar, butter, vanilla and nutmeg. Stir in raisins. Pour over cinnamon rolls; stir gently. Cover and cook on low for 3 hours or until a knife inserted near the center comes out clean. **Yield:** 6 servings.

Editor's Note: 8 slices of cinnamon or white bread, cut into 1-inch cubes, may be substituted for the cinnamon rolls.

Slow Cooker Chicken Curry

(Pictured below)

Prep: 20 min. **Cook:** 4-1/2 hours

This festive twist on traditional chicken curry can be tailored to your tastes. Try replacing green beans with fresh sugar snap peas, or use a spicier salsa to turn up the heat. —*Erin Chilcoat, Smithtown, New York*

4 bone-in chicken breast halves, skin removed (8 ounces *each*)
1 can (15 ounces) white kidney *or* cannellini beans, rinsed and drained
3/4 cup thinly sliced sweet onion
1/2 cup chopped sweet red pepper
1 cup peach salsa
1 tablespoon curry powder
1/2 teaspoon salt
1/4 teaspoon pepper
1 cup fresh green beans, trimmed and cut in half
2 tablespoons cornstarch
1/2 cup cold water
1-1/2 cups chicken broth
1-1/2 cups uncooked instant rice

Place the chicken, kidney beans, onion and red pepper in 4-qt. slow cooker. In a small bowl, combine the salsa, curry powder, salt and pepper; pour over top.

Cover and cook on low for 4-5 hours or until chicken is tender. Stir in the green beans. Combine cornstarch and water until smooth; gradually stir into slow cooker. Cover and cook on high for 30 minutes or until sauce is thickened.

In a large saucepan, bring broth to a boil; stir in rice. Cover and remove from the heat. Let stand for 5 minutes or until liquid is absorbed and rice is tender. Fluff with a fork. Serve with chicken and sauce. **Yield:** 4 servings.

Savory Mushroom & Herb Pork Roast

(Pictured above)

Prep: 25 min. **Cook:** 5 hours

Your family will love this tender pork. I like to crisp up the French-fried onion pieces in a dry skillet, then sprinkle over the top just before serving. Round it out with mashed potatoes or fluffy noodles.

—Judy Clark, Addison, Michigan

2 medium onions, chopped
12 fresh baby carrots
1 boneless pork shoulder butt roast (3 to 4 pounds)
1 can (10-3/4 ounces) condensed cream of mushroom soup, undiluted
3/4 cup chicken broth
1 can (4 ounces) mushroom stems and pieces, drained
1/2 teaspoon dried thyme
1/2 teaspoon Worcestershire sauce
1/4 teaspoon dried rosemary, crushed
1/4 teaspoon dried marjoram
1/4 teaspoon pepper
1 tablespoon cornstarch
2 tablespoons cold water
French-fried onions, optional

Place onions and carrots in a 5-qt slow cooker. Cut roast in half; add to slow cooker. In a small bowl, combine the soup, broth, mushrooms, thyme, Worcestershire sauce, rosemary, marjoram and pepper; pour over pork. Cover and cook on low for 5-6 hours or until meat is tender.

Remove pork to a serving platter; keep warm. Skim fat from cooking juices; transfer to a large saucepan. Bring liquid to a boil. Combine cornstarch and water until smooth; gradually stir into the pan. Bring to a boil; cook and stir for 2 minutes or until thickened.

Serve pork with gravy. Sprinkle servings with French-friend onions if desired. **Yield:** 8 servings.

Mom's Celery Seed Brisket

(Pictured below)

Prep: 20 min. **Cook:** 8 hours

Warning: Keep a close eye on this tangy pot of goodness; it's been fine-tuned to perfection and tends to vanish at gatherings. *—Aysha Schurman, Ammon, Idaho*

1 fresh beef brisket (3 to 4 pounds)
1 can (28 ounces) Italian crushed tomatoes
1 large red onion, chopped
2 tablespoons red wine vinegar
2 tablespoons Worcestershire sauce
4 garlic cloves, minced
1 tablespoon brown sugar
1 teaspoon celery seed
1 teaspoon pepper
1/2 teaspoon salt
1/2 teaspoon ground cumin
1/2 teaspoon Liquid Smoke
4 teaspoons cornstarch
3 tablespoons cold water

Cut the brisket in half; place in a 5-qt. slow cooker. In a large bowl, combine tomatoes, onion, red wine vinegar, Worcestershire sauce, garlic, brown sugar, celery seed, pepper, salt, cumin and Liquid Smoke. Pour over beef. Cover and cook on low for 8-10 hours or until the meat is tender.

Remove the meat to a serving platter; keep warm. In a large saucepan, combine cornstarch and water until smooth. Gradually stir in 4 cups cooking liquid. Bring to a boil; cook and stir for 2 minutes or until thickened. Slice brisket across the grain; serve with gravy. **Yield:** 8 servings.

Editor's Note: This is a fresh beef brisket, not corned beef.

CHAPTER 11

Breakfast & Brunch Favorites

Coffee cakes, scones, muffins, breakfast casseroles and crepes are just a few of the reasons why breakfast is so popular—and we've got recipes for all of them right here!

Check out old standbys with a twist, such as scrumptious Cranberry Orange Pancakes and Banana Macadamia Muffins. Or, if you need something for a potluck, take a peek at the Hash Brown Pancetta Casserole or Tomato Olive Quiche. Not only are they tasty, but they add easy pizzazz to any buffet table.

Whether you're hosting a brunch or want to whip up a special a.m. meal for your family, you'll find a variety of yummy morning treats that everyone will love! ■

BRIGHT & EARLY CHOW TIME. Breakfast Biscuit Cups (p. 182).

Brie and Sausage Brunch Bake

(Pictured above)

Prep: 30 min. + chilling **Bake:** 50 min. + standing

I've made this for holidays as well as for weekends at a friend's cabin, and I always get requests for the recipe. It's make-ahead convenient, reheats well and even tastes great the next day. —*Becky Hicks, Forest Lake, Minnesota*

1 pound bulk Italian sausage
1 small onion, chopped
8 cups cubed day-old sourdough bread
1/2 cup chopped roasted sweet red peppers
1/2 pound Brie cheese, rind removed, cubed
2/3 cup grated Parmesan cheese
2 tablespoons minced fresh basil *or* 2 teaspoons dried basil
8 eggs
2 cups heavy whipping cream
1 tablespoon Dijon mustard
1 teaspoon pepper
1/2 teaspoon salt
3/4 cup shredded part-skim mozzarella cheese
3 green onions, sliced

In a large skillet, cook sausage and onion over medium heat until meat is no longer pink; drain.

Place bread cubes in a greased 13-in. x 9-in. baking dish. Layer with sausage mixture, red peppers, Brie and Parmesan cheeses and basil. In a large bowl, whisk the eggs, cream, mustard, pepper and salt; pour over top. Cover and refrigerate overnight.

Remove from the refrigerator 30 minutes before baking. Bake, uncovered, at 350° for 45-50 minutes or until a knife inserted near the center comes out clean.

Sprinkle with mozzarella cheese. Bake 4-6 minutes longer or until cheese is melted. Let stand for 10 minutes before cutting. Sprinkle with the green onions. **Yield:** 12 servings.

Crab Quiche

(Pictured below)

Prep: 30 min. **Bake:** 40 min. + standing

Rich and elegant, this party-pretty quiche is flecked with minced parsley, chives and cilantro. It's ideal for a weekend brunch but would also be wonderful as a late-night supper. —*Lori Wardoclip, Gibsonia, Pennsylvania*

1 sheet refrigerated pie pastry
4 eggs
2 cups heavy whipping cream
2 tablespoons minced chives
2 tablespoons minced fresh cilantro
2 tablespoons minced fresh parsley *or* 2 teaspoons dried parsley flakes
1/2 teaspoon salt
1/2 teaspoon seafood seasoning
1/4 teaspoon pepper
1/8 teaspoon ground nutmeg
1 can (6-1/2 ounces) lump crabmeat, drained
1/2 cup shredded Swiss cheese
1/2 cup shredded Monterey Jack cheese
Fresh chives, optional

Unroll pastry into a 9-in. pie plate; flute edges. Line unpricked pastry with a double thickness of heavy-duty foil. Bake at 450° for 8 minutes. Remove the foil; bake 5-7 minutes longer or until lightly browned. Cool on a wire rack.

In a large bowl, whisk the eggs, cream, chives, cilantro, parsley, salt, seafood seasoning, pepper and nutmeg; stir in the crabmeat and cheeses. Pour into the crust.

Bake at 375° for 40-45 minutes or until a knife inserted near the center comes out clean. Let stand for 15 minutes before cutting. Garnish with fresh chives if desired. **Yield:** 6 servings.

Crescent Zucchini Pie

(Pictured above)

Prep: 20 min. **Bake:** 20 min.

A tender, flaky crust makes this egg- and zucchini-based pie a special treat. The cheese, herbs and seasonings add delectable flavor. —*Zelda DeHoedt, Cedar Rapids, Iowa*

1 tube (8 ounces) refrigerated crescent rolls
2 teaspoons Dijon mustard
4 cups sliced zucchini
1 cup chopped onion
6 tablespoons butter, cubed
2 eggs, lightly beaten
1 cup (4 ounces) shredded part-skim mozzarella cheese
1 cup (4 ounces) shredded Colby-Monterey Jack cheese
2 tablespoons dried parsley flakes
1/2 teaspoon salt
1/2 teaspoon pepper
1/4 teaspoon dried basil
1/4 teaspoon dried oregano

Separate crescent dough into eight triangles and place in a greased 9-in. deep-dish pie plate with points toward the center. Press the dough onto the bottom and up the sides of the plate to form a crust; seal seams. Spread with mustard.

In a large skillet, saute zucchini and onion in butter until tender. In a large bowl, combine the eggs, cheeses, seasonings and zucchini mixture. Pour into crust.

Bake at 375° for 20-25 minutes or until a knife inserted near the center comes out clean. Cover edges loosely with foil if crust browns too quickly. **Yield:** 6 servings.

Cranberry Orange Pancakes

(Pictured below)

Prep: 20 min. **Cook:** 5 min./batch

As special as can be, these fluffy, flavorful pancakes are drop-dead gorgeous, ready in just minutes and brimming with sweet, tart and tangy flavor. They're perfect for the holidays. Seconds, anyone? —*Nancy Zimmerman, Cape May Court House, New Jersey*

SYRUP:
1 cup fresh *or* frozen cranberries
2/3 cup orange juice
1/2 cup sugar
3 tablespoons maple syrup

PANCAKES:
2 cups biscuit/baking mix
2 tablespoons sugar
2 teaspoons baking powder
2 eggs
1 egg yolk
1 cup evaporated milk
2 tablespoons orange juice
1 teaspoon grated orange peel
1/2 cup chopped fresh *or* frozen cranberries
Orange peel strips, optional

In a small saucepan, bring cranberries, orange juice and sugar to a boil. Reduce heat; simmer, uncovered, for 5 minutes. Cool slightly. With a slotted spoon, remove 1/4 cup cranberries; set aside.

In a blender, process cranberry mixture until smooth. Transfer to a small bowl; stir in maple syrup and reserved cranberries. Keep warm.

In a large bowl, combine the biscuit mix, sugar and baking powder. In another bowl, whisk the eggs, egg yolk, milk, orange juice and peel. Stir into dry ingredients just until blended. Fold in chopped cranberries.

Drop batter by 1/4 cupfuls onto a greased hot griddle; turn when bubbles form on top. Cook until second side is golden brown. Serve with syrup. Garnish with orange peel strips if desired. **Yield:** 12 pancakes (1-1/4 cups syrup).

Tiramisu Crepes

(Pictured below)

Prep: 30 min. + chilling **Cook:** 5 min./batch

Delicate crepes, filled with creamy Mascarpone cheese and laced with vanilla and a hint of coffee liqueur, make for an extra-special, mouthwatering morning treat.
—Karen Shelton, Collierville, Tennessee

4 eggs
3/4 cup 2% milk
1/4 cup club soda
3 tablespoons butter, melted
2 tablespoons strong brewed coffee
1 teaspoon vanilla extract
1 cup all-purpose flour
3 tablespoons sugar
2 tablespoons baking cocoa
1/4 teaspoon salt

FILLING:

1 carton (8 ounces) Mascarpone cheese
1 package (8 ounces) cream cheese, softened
1 cup sugar
1/4 cup coffee liqueur *or* strong brewed coffee
2 tablespoons vanilla extract

Optional toppings: chocolate syrup, whipped cream and baking cocoa

In a large bowl, beat the eggs, milk, soda, butter, coffee and vanilla. Combine the flour, sugar, cocoa and salt; add to milk mixture and mix well. Cover and refrigerate for 1 hour.

Heat a lightly greased 8-in. nonstick skillet over medium heat; pour 2 tablespoons batter into the center of skillet. Lift and tilt pan to coat bottom evenly. Cook until top appears dry; turn and cook 15-20 seconds longer. Remove to a wire rack. Repeat with remaining batter, greasing the skillet as needed. When cool, stack crepes with waxed paper or paper towels in between.

For filling, in a large bowl, beat the cheeses and sugar until fluffy. Add liqueur and vanilla; beat until smooth. Spoon about 2 tablespoons filling down the center of each crepe; roll up. Top with chocolate syrup, whipped cream and cocoa if desired. **Yield:** 22 crepes.

Cranberry-Pecan Coffee Cake

(Pictured above)

Prep: 30 min. **Bake:** 40 min. + cooling

With its nutty, tart topping, this cake will bring smiles as soon as you turn it out of the pan.
—Anne Thompson, Grand Rapids, Michigan

2/3 cup packed brown sugar
1/3 cup butter, cubed
1 cup chopped fresh *or* frozen cranberries, thawed
1/2 cup chopped pecans

CAKE:

1/2 cup butter, softened
3/4 cup sugar
2 eggs
2 tablespoons orange juice
1 teaspoon vanilla extract
1-1/2 cups all-purpose flour
1 teaspoon baking powder
1/2 teaspoon ground cinnamon
1/4 teaspoon baking soda
1/4 teaspoon salt
1 cup (8 ounces) sour cream

In a small saucepan, combine brown sugar and butter. Cook and stir over medium heat until butter is melted. Transfer to a greased 9-in. round baking pan. Sprinkle with cranberries and pecans.

In a large bowl, cream butter and sugar until light and fluffy. Add eggs, one at a time, beating well after each addition. Beat in orange juice and vanilla. Combine flour, baking powder, cinnamon, baking soda and salt; add to creamed mixture alternately with sour cream, beating well after each addition. Pour over cranberries.

Bake at 350° for 40-45 minutes or until a toothpick inserted near the center comes out clean. Cool for 10 minutes before inverting onto a serving plate. Serve warm. **Yield:** 8 servings.

Pull-Apart Caramel Coffee Cake

Prep: 10 min. **Bake:** 25 min.

The first time I made this delightful breakfast treat for a brunch party, it was a huge hit. Now I get requests every time family or friends do anything around the breakfast hour! I always keep the four simple ingredients on hand.
—Jaime Keeling, Keizer, Oregon

- **2 tubes (12 ounces *each*) refrigerated flaky buttermilk biscuits**
- **1 cup packed brown sugar**
- **1/2 cup heavy whipping cream**
- **1 teaspoon ground cinnamon**

Cut each biscuit into four pieces; arrange evenly in a 10-in. fluted tube pan coated with cooking spray. Combine the brown sugar, cream and cinnamon; pour over biscuits.

Bake at 350° for 25-30 minutes or until golden brown. Cool for 5 minutes before inverting onto a serving platter. **Yield:** 12 servings.

Chicken and Egg Hash

Prep/Total Time: 30 min.

This recipe is one of my daughter's favorites. To reduce cooking time and clean out the fridge, dice up leftover potatoes and use cooked chicken or ham instead.
—Joyce Price, Whitefish, Ontario

- **4 bacon strips, diced**
- **1 medium onion, chopped**
- **2 garlic cloves, minced**
- **1 pound boneless skinless chicken breasts, cubed**
- **2 large potatoes, peeled and diced**
- **1 tablespoon canola oil**
- **1/2 cup frozen peas, thawed**
- **1/2 cup frozen corn, thawed**
- **2 tablespoons minced fresh parsley**
- **3/4 teaspoon salt**
- **1/8 teaspoon pepper**
- **4 eggs**

In a large skillet, cook bacon until crisp. Remove with a slotted spoon to paper towels to drain. In the drippings, saute the onion until tender. Add garlic; cook 1 minute longer. Stir in the chicken, potatoes and oil.

Cover and cook for 10 minutes or until the chicken is no longer pink, stirring once. Stir in the peas, corn, parsley, salt and pepper.

Make four wells in the hash; break an egg into each well. Cover and cook over low heat for 8-10 minutes or until eggs are completely set. Sprinkle with bacon. **Yield:** 4 servings.

Crustless Quiche Bake

(Pictured below)

Prep: 30 min. **Bake:** 40 min. + standing

Chock-full of veggies, cheese, bacon, eggs and a touch of sherry, this yummy recipe would be great served with fresh muffins or toasted bread and fruit!
—June Marie Racus, Sun City West, Arizona

- **14 bacon strips, chopped**
- **1 pound sliced fresh mushrooms**
- **1/2 cup chopped green pepper**
- **8 green onions, thinly sliced**
- **1 jar (2 ounces) diced pimientos, drained**
- **2 tablespoons sherry, optional**
- **12 eggs**
- **1-1/2 cups 2% milk**
- **3/4 teaspoon dried thyme**
- **3/4 teaspoon seasoned salt**
- **1/2 teaspoon ground mustard**
- **Dash dill weed**
- **4 cups (16 ounces) shredded Gruyere *or* Swiss cheese, *divided***

In a large skillet, cook the bacon over medium heat until crisp. Remove to paper towels with a slotted spoon; drain, reserving 2 tablespoons drippings.

In the drippings, saute the mushrooms, green pepper and onions until tender. Add pimientos and sherry if desired; cook until liquid is evaporated.

In a large bowl, whisk the eggs, milk, thyme, seasoned salt, mustard and dill. Add bacon, mushroom mixture and 3 cups cheese. Transfer to a greased 13-in. x 9-in. baking dish.

Bake, uncovered, at 350° for 35 minutes. Sprinkle with remaining cheese. Bake 5-10 minutes longer or until a knife inserted near the center comes out clean and cheese is melted. Let stand for 10 minutes before cutting. **Yield:** 12 servings.

Hash Brown Egg Breakfast

(Pictured above)

Prep: 15 min. **Cook:** 3-1/2 hours

I love this hearty, slow-cooked breakfast dish. It's great for potlucks because it's easy to carry and is always very popular. —Nancy Marion, Frostproof, Florida

1 package (32 ounces) frozen cubed hash brown potatoes, thawed
2 cups cubed fully cooked ham
1-1/2 cups (6 ounces) shredded cheddar cheese
1 large green pepper, chopped
1 medium onion, chopped
12 eggs, beaten
1 cup 2% milk
1 teaspoon salt
1 teaspoon pepper

Layer a third of the potatoes, ham, cheese, green pepper and onion in a greased 6-qt. slow cooker. Repeat the layers twice. In a large bowl, whisk the eggs, milk, salt and pepper; pour over the top. Cover and cook on low for 3-1/2 to 4 hours or until a thermometer reads 160°. **Yield:** 12 servings (1-1/3 cups each).

Banana Macadamia Muffins

Prep: 15 min. **Bake:** 20 min.

These muffins taste even better the next day, so to save time, I often make them the night before. They will stay moist for days. —Stasha Wampler, Clinchport, Virginia

3 cups all-purpose flour
2 cups sugar
2 teaspoons ground cinnamon
1 teaspoon baking soda
1 teaspoon salt
3 eggs
1 cup canola oil
1 teaspoon vanilla extract
3 medium ripe bananas, mashed
1 cup flaked coconut
1 can (8 ounces) crushed pineapple, drained
1 cup macadamia nuts, coarsely chopped

In a large bowl, combine the flour, sugar, cinnamon, baking soda and salt. In another bowl, combine the eggs, oil and vanilla extract. Stir into dry ingredients just until moistened. Fold in the the bananas, coconut and pineapple.

Fill greased or paper-lined muffin cups two-thirds full. Sprinkle with nuts. Bake at 375° for 18-20 minutes or until a toothpick inserted near the center comes out clean. Cool for 5 minutes before removing from pans to wire racks. **Yield:** 2 dozen.

Southwest Breakfast Tart

(Pictured below)

Prep: 30 min. **Bake:** 25 min. + standing

Give your breakfast crowd a stick-to-the-ribs jump start in the morning with this cheesy, colorful tart. It's packed with sausage, plenty of heat and hearty Tex-Mex flavor. —Pamela Shank, Parkersburg, West Virginia

1/2 pound bulk spicy pork sausage
4 teaspoons chopped seeded jalapeno pepper
1 tablespoon finely chopped red onion
1 can (4 ounces) chopped green chilies
1 sheet refrigerated pie pastry
1-1/4 cups shredded Monterey Jack cheese, *divided*
6 eggs
1/3 cup half-and-half cream
1/2 teaspoon salt
1/4 teaspoon pepper
1 tablespoon finely chopped sweet red pepper
1 tablespoon finely chopped green pepper
Optional toppings: sour cream, salsa, chopped tomatoes and sliced green onions

In a large skillet, cook the sausage, jalapeno and onion over medium heat until meat is no longer pink; drain. Stir in chilies.

Press pastry onto the bottom and up the sides of an ungreased 9-in. tart pan with removable bottom; trim edges. Sprinkle 1/2 cup cheese over crust; top with the sausage mixture.

In a large bowl, whisk eggs, cream, salt and pepper. Pour over sausage mixture. Sprinkle with red and green peppers and 1/2 cup cheese.

Bake at 350° for 25-30 minutes or until eggs are set and a knife inserted near the center comes out clean. Sprinkle with remaining cheese. Let stand for 10 minutes before cutting. Serve with the toppings of your choice. **Yield:** 6 servings.

Editor's Note: Wear disposable gloves when cutting hot peppers; the oils can burn skin. Avoid touching your face.

Gingerbread Scones With Lemon Butter

(Pictured above)

Prep/Total Time: 30 min.

Busy morning? Fill your kitchen with the warm aroma of these tender gingerbread scones. Then slather on some lip-smacking lemon butter and relax with a steaming cup of coffee. Yum! *—Sharon Delaney-Chronis South Milwaukee, Wisconsin*

2-1/4 cups all-purpose flour
1 teaspoon baking powder
1 teaspoon ground cinnamon
1/2 teaspoon ground ginger
1/4 teaspoon salt
1/4 teaspoon baking soda
1/4 teaspoon ground allspice
1/4 teaspoon ground nutmeg
1/2 cup cold butter
3/4 cup heavy whipping cream
1/3 cup molasses
1/2 cup dried currants
LEMON BUTTER:
1/4 cup butter, softened
1/4 cup confectioners' sugar
1 tablespoon lemon juice
1 teaspoon grated lemon peel

In a large bowl, combine the first eight ingredients. Cut in butter until mixture resembles coarse crumbs. Whisk cream and molasses; stir into crumb mixture just until moistened. Stir in currants.

Turn onto a floured surface; knead 10 times. Pat or roll out to 1/2-in. thickness; cut with a floured 2-in. biscuit cutter.

Place 2 in. apart on a lightly greased baking sheet. Bake at 425° for 8-10 minutes or until golden brown.

Meanwhile, for lemon butter, in a small bowl, beat butter, confectioners' sugar, lemon juice and peel until combined. Serve with warm scones. **Yield:** 16 scones.

Sausage-Apple Puff Pancake

(Pictured below)

Prep: 25 min. **Bake:** 20 min.

Savory sausage and sweet apples combine in this beautiful breakfast dish. The cheesy topping will definitely make you want seconds. *—Carolyn Kumpe, El Dorado, California*

1 pound bulk pork sausage
2 medium apples, peeled and thinly sliced
2 tablespoons brown sugar
2 tablespoons butter
6 eggs
1-1/2 cups 2% milk
1 cup all-purpose flour
2 tablespoons sugar
1/2 teaspoon salt
1 cup (4 ounces) extra sharp shredded cheddar cheese
Sour cream and maple syrup, optional

In a 10-in. ovenproof skillet, cook sausage over medium heat until no longer pink; drain and set aside. In same skillet, cook the apples and brown sugar in butter over medium heat until apples are tender.

In a blender, combine the eggs, milk, flour, sugar and salt; cover and process for 10 seconds or until smooth. Pour over the apple mixture. Sprinkle with the sausage and cheese.

Bake, uncovered, at 425° for 18-23 minutes or until pancake is puffy and golden brown. Cut into wedges. Serve with the sour cream and syrup if desired. **Yield:** 6 servings.

Breakfast Tortas

(Pictured below)

Prep: 25 min. **Bake:** 15 min.

My hubby likes these ciabatta rolls served with pickled jalapenos. Try substituting leftover taco meat, ham, grilled steak or chicken for the bacon. This recipe is a guaranteed crowd-pleaser.

—Carolyn Kumpe, El Dorado, California

4 ciabatta rolls
3/4 cup refried black beans
1/3 cup sour cream
1/4 cup minced fresh cilantro
2 teaspoons lime juice
3 to 5 drops chipotle hot pepper sauce
1/8 teaspoon salt
4 eggs
1/2 cup shredded Monterey Jack cheese
1 teaspoon olive oil
4 cooked bacon strips, halved
1/2 medium ripe avocado, peeled and sliced
1/2 cup salsa
2 green onions, chopped

Cut the top third off each roll; hollow out bottom, leaving a 1/2-in. shell (discard the removed bread or save for another use). Place roll bottoms on an ungreased baking sheet.

In a small bowl, combine the beans, sour cream, cilantro, lime juice, pepper sauce and salt. Spread 1/4 cup inside each roll. Break an egg into each roll. Bake at 400° for 10 minutes.

Sprinkle cheese over eggs. Brush roll tops with olive oil; place on the baking sheet. Bake 5-8 minutes longer or until egg whites are completely set and the yolks begin to thicken but are not firm. Top each with bacon, avocado, salsa and onions. Replace the roll tops. **Yield:** 4 servings.

Baked Fruit Compote

(Pictured above)

Prep/Total Time: 30 min.

Put canned fruit in a fancy, festive mood with a splash of Madeira wine. This dish brightens any winter brunch. Mix and match the canned fruits to suit your family's tastes.

—Myrt Pfannkuche, Pell City, Alabama

1 can (29 ounces) sliced peaches, drained
1 can (20 ounces) pineapple chunks, drained
2 cans (8 ounces *each*) grapefruit sections, drained
1 can (15-1/4 ounces) sliced pears, drained
1 can (11 ounces) mandarin oranges, drained
1 cup pitted dried plums
1/2 cup butter, cubed
1/2 cup packed brown sugar
1/4 cup Madeira wine, optional
Fresh mint leaves, optional

In a 13-in. x 9-in. baking dish, combine the first six ingredients.

In a small saucepan, combine the butter and brown sugar. Bring to a boil over medium heat; cook and stir for 2-3 minutes or until sugar is dissolved. Remove from the heat; stir in wine if desired. Pour over fruit and toss to coat.

Bake, uncovered, at 350° for 20-25 minutes or until heated through. Garnish with mint if desired. **Yield:** 11 servings.

Breakfast Biscuit Cups

(Pictured at right)

Prep: 30 min. **Bake:** 20 min.

The first time I made these biscuit cups, my husband and his assistant basketball coach came in as I was pulling them out of the oven. They loved them!

—Debra Carlson, Columbus Junction, Iowa

1/3 pound bulk pork sausage
1 tablespoon all-purpose flour
1/8 teaspoon salt
1/2 teaspoon pepper, *divided*
3/4 cup plus 1 tablespoon 2% milk, *divided*
1/2 cup frozen cubed hash brown potatoes, thawed
1 tablespoon butter
2 eggs
1/8 teaspoon garlic salt
1 can (16.3 ounces) large refrigerated flaky biscuits
1/2 cup shredded Colby-Monterey Jack cheese

In a large skillet, cook sausage over medium heat until no longer pink; drain. Stir in flour, salt and 1/4 teaspoon pepper until blended; gradually add 3/4 cup milk. Bring to a boil; cook and stir for 2 minutes or until thickened. Remove from the heat and set aside.

In another large skillet over medium heat, cook the potatoes in butter until tender. Whisk the eggs, garlic salt and remaining milk and pepper; add to skillet. Cook and stir until almost set.

Press each biscuit onto the bottom and up the sides of eight ungreased muffin cups. Spoon the egg mixture, half of the cheese and sausage into cups; sprinkle with remaining cheese.

Bake at 375° for 18-22 minutes or until golden brown. Cool for 5 minutes before removing from pan. Serve immediately or allow to cool completely. Tightly wrap the individual biscuit cups in foil; freeze for up to 3 months.

To use one frozen biscuit cup: Unwrap; microwave on high for 50-60 seconds or until heated through. **Yield:** 8 servings.

Berry-Topped Puff Pancake

(Pictured above)

Prep: 20 min. **Bake:** 15 min.

Impressive to look at and even better to taste, this gorgeous pancake is surprisingly simple to make.
—Marie Cosenza, Cortlandt Manor, New York

2 tablespoons butter
2 eggs
1/2 cup 2% milk
1/2 cup all-purpose flour
2 tablespoons sugar
1/4 teaspoon salt

TOPPING:

1/3 cup sugar
1 tablespoon cornstarch
1/2 cup orange juice
2 teaspoons orange liqueur
1 cup sliced fresh strawberries
1 cup fresh blueberries
1 cup fresh raspberries
Confectioners' sugar, optional

Place butter in a 9-in. pie plate. Place in a 425° oven for 4-5 minutes or until melted. Meanwhile, in a large bowl, whisk the eggs and milk. In another bowl, combine the flour, sugar and salt. Whisk into the egg mixture until blended. Pour into prepared pie plate. Bake for 14-16 minutes or until sides are crisp and golden brown.

Meanwhile, in a small saucepan, combine sugar and cornstarch. Gradually stir in orange juice and liqueur. Bring to a boil over medium heat, stirring constantly. Cook and stir 1-2 minutes longer or until thickened. Remove from the heat.

Spoon the berries over pancake and drizzle with sauce. Dust with confectioners' sugar if desired. **Yield:** 4 servings.

Hash Brown Pancetta Casserole

(Pictured above)

Prep: 25 min. **Bake:** 30 min. + standing

Eggs, hash browns, cheese, spinach, pancetta and fabulous flavor—this casserole has everything! You could also substitute provolone or Swiss cheese for the fontina.
—Gilda Lester, Millsboro, Delaware

1 large onion, finely chopped
1 tablespoon olive oil
2 garlic cloves, minced
1 package (10 ounces) frozen chopped spinach, thawed and squeezed dry
1/4 teaspoon salt
1/4 teaspoon pepper
2 ounces sliced pancetta *or* bacon, finely chopped
3 cups frozen shredded hash brown potatoes, thawed
8 eggs
2 cups 2% milk
1 cup (4 ounces) shredded fontina cheese, *divided*
1 cup (4 ounces) shredded cheddar cheese, *divided*
1/4 cup minced fresh parsley
1 tablespoon Worcestershire sauce
1 teaspoon ground mustard
1/4 teaspoon ground nutmeg
Freshly ground pepper and additional fresh parsley, optional

In a large skillet, saute onion in oil until tender. Add garlic; cook 1 minute longer. Stir in the spinach, salt and pepper. Remove from the heat.

In another skillet, cook the pancetta over medium heat until crisp. Remove to paper towels with a slotted spoon; drain.

In a greased 13-in. x 9-in. baking dish, layer the hash browns, spinach mixture and pancetta. In a large bowl, whisk the eggs, milk, 1/2 cup fontina cheese, 1/2 cup cheddar cheese, parsley, Worcestershire sauce, mustard and nutmeg; pour over the casserole. Sprinkle with the remaining cheeses.

Bake, uncovered, at 350° for 30-35 minutes or until a knife inserted near the center comes out clean. Let stand for 10 minutes before cutting. If desired, sprinkle with freshly ground pepper and garnish with additional parsley. **Yield:** 8 servings.

Chai Tea

(Pictured below)

Prep: 20 min. **Cook:** 8 hours

The sweet-spicy aroma that wafts from the slow cooker as this pleasantly flavored chai tea cooks is wonderful.
—Crystal Bruns, Iliff, Colorado

3-1/2 ounces fresh gingerroot, peeled and thinly sliced
25 whole cloves
15 cardamom pods, crushed
3 cinnamon sticks (3 inches)
3 whole peppercorns
3-1/2 quarts water
8 individual black tea bags
1 can (14 ounces) sweetened condensed milk

Place the ginger, cloves, cardamom, cinnamon sticks and peppercorns on a double thickness of cheesecloth; bring up corners of cloth and tie with string to form a bag. Add the spice bag and water to a 5- or 6-qt. slow cooker. Cover and cook on low for 8 hours.

Add the tea bags; cover and steep for 3-5 minutes. Discard tea bags and spice bag. Stir in the milk; heat through. Serve warm. **Yield:** 12 servings (3 quarts).

Cinnamon Roll Coffee Cake

(Pictured above)

Prep: 20 min. **Bake:** 25 min. + standing

Ready in a twinkling, this fresh-from-the-oven treat will be a sensational, no-fuss addition to any weekend or holiday brunch. Your guests will never guess how easy it is to whip up. —Teresa Maag, Leipsic, Ohio

1 tube (17-1/2 ounces) large refrigerated cinnamon rolls with cream cheese icing
2 packages (8 ounces *each*) cream cheese, softened
3 eggs
1/2 cup sugar
1 teaspoon vanilla extract
1/2 cup chopped pecans
1/4 cup all-purpose flour
1/4 cup quick-cooking oats
1/4 cup packed brown sugar
1 teaspoon ground cinnamon
3 tablespoons butter, melted
Whipped cream and additional ground cinnamon, optional

Unroll the tube of cinnamon rolls into one long rectangle. Press onto the bottom of a greased 13-in. x 9-in. baking dish; seal perforations. Set aside icing packet from the cinnamon rolls.

In a large bowl, beat the cream cheese, eggs, sugar and vanilla until smooth. Pour over the crust. In a small bowl, combine the pecans, flour, oats, brown sugar and cinnamon; stir in butter. Sprinkle over the cream cheese layer.

Bake at 350° for 25-30 minutes or until a toothpick inserted near the center comes out clean. Drizzle with the contents of icing packet; let stand for 15 minutes before serving. If desired, serve with a dollop of whipped cream sprinkled with additional ground cinnamon. **Yield:** 12 servings.

Tomato Olive Quiche

(Pictured below)

Prep: 30 min. **Bake:** 40 min. + standing

Salty, savory olives, two kinds of onions, juicy tomatoes and layers of cheese make this quiche memorable. —Stephanie Proebsting, Barrington, Illinois

1 sheet refrigerated pie pastry
1/4 cup all-purpose flour
1/2 teaspoon salt
1/2 teaspoon pepper
2 medium tomatoes, sliced
2 tablespoons olive oil
2 eggs
1 cup heavy whipping cream
1 cup (4 ounces) shredded sharp cheddar cheese
1 can (6 ounces) pitted ripe olives, drained and finely chopped
1/2 cup chopped sweet onion
3 green onions, chopped
4 slices provolone cheese

Unroll pastry into a 9-in. pie plate; flute edges. Line unpricked pastry shell with a double thickness of heavy-duty foil. Bake at 450° for 8 minutes. Remove foil; bake 5 minutes longer.

In a large resealable plastic bag, combine the flour, salt and pepper. Add tomato slices, a few at a time, and shake to coat. In a large skillet, cook tomatoes in oil for 1-2 minutes on each side or until golden brown.

In a small bowl, whisk eggs and cream; stir in cheddar cheese. Sprinkle olives and onions into crust; top with two slices of provolone cheese. Layer with tomatoes and remaining provolone. Pour egg mixture over the top.

Bake at 375° for 40-45 minutes or until a knife inserted near center comes out clean. Let stand for 10 minutes before cutting. **Yield:** 8 servings.

CHAPTER 12

Quick Soups & Sandwiches

Need an express lunch or an easy weeknight meal? The hearty soups and flavorful sandwiches in this chapter create the perfect combination!

These casual comfort foods fix up fast and will easily satisfy the most robust eaters in your family. The Very Best Barbecue Sandwiches and Meat-atarian Sub are just two examples of more-than-a-meal sandwiches.

For food to warm your bones, the Chipotle-Black Bean Chili preps up in only 15 minutes, then simmers all day in a slow cooker for a convenient, stick-to-your-ribs meal. And for a wholesome, homemade lunch or dinner, the Hearty Vegetable Beef Soup cooks up in only half an hour. Served with a chunk of crusty bread slathered in butter, what's not to like? ■

MIDDAY MEAL. Hearty Italian Sandwiches (p. 192).

Cheddar Seafood Chowder

(Pictured above left)

Prep: 15 min. **Cook:** 20 min.

Created by our Test Kitchen, fresh-from-the-sea shrimp and scallops make this cheesy, chunky chowder extra-special. It's packed with fresh veggies, and the crispy bacon makes a yummy garnish.

6 bacon strips, chopped
2 celery ribs, finely chopped
1/2 cup chopped sweet orange pepper
1 small onion, finely chopped
2 garlic cloves, minced
1/4 cup all-purpose flour
1 can (14-1/2 ounces) chicken broth
2 cups 2% milk
2 medium red potatoes, cubed
1 teaspoon seafood seasoning
1/4 teaspoon salt
1/2 pound uncooked medium shrimp, peeled and deveined
1/2 pound bay scallops
1-1/2 cups (6 ounces) shredded cheddar cheese

In a large saucepan, cook the bacon over medium heat until crisp. Remove to paper towels with a slotted spoon; drain, reserving 1 tablespoon drippings.

In the drippings, saute the celery, sweet pepper and onion until crisp-tender. Add the garlic; cook 1 minute longer. Stir in flour until blended; gradually add broth and milk. Bring to a boil; cook and stir for 1 minute or until thickened.

Add the potatoes, seafood seasoning and salt; return to a boil. Reduce the heat; cover and simmer for 10-15 minutes or until potatoes are tender.

Add shrimp and scallops; cook and stir for 3-4 minutes or until shrimp turn pink and scallops are opaque. Stir in cheese until melted. Garnish each serving with bacon. **Yield:** 6 servings.

Italian Sausage Soup

(Pictured above right)

Prep/Total Time: 30 min.

This is definitely a meal on its own. It smells so good while cooking, the men in my family are always glad to walk in the door after work and see this on the stove.
—Joan Oakland, Troy, Montana

5 Italian sausage links (4 ounces *each*), sliced
1 large onion, halved and sliced
6 cups water
1 can (28 ounces) crushed tomatoes, undrained
2 small zucchini, quartered and sliced
1/2 cup chopped green pepper
1 tablespoon beef bouillon granules
1/2 teaspoon dried basil
1/2 teaspoon dried oregano
1/4 teaspoon pepper
3 ounces uncooked linguine, broken into 2-inch pieces
3 tablespoons grated Parmesan cheese

In a Dutch oven, cook sausage and onion over medium heat until sausage is no longer pink; drain.

Stir in the water, tomatoes, zucchini, green pepper, bouillon, basil, oregano and pepper. Bring to a boil. Stir in the linguine. Cover and simmer for 10-15 minutes or until linguine is tender. Sprinkle with the cheese. **Yield:** 10 servings (3 quarts).

Meat-atarian Sub

(Pictured below)

Prep: 20 min. **Bake:** 25 min.

Our Test Kitchen tasters called this meaty sandwich the "ultimate football food," but it's great any time!
—Shanon Mayer, Mountain View, Wyoming

1 cup (4 ounces) shredded part-skim mozzarella cheese
1/2 cup grated Parmesan cheese
1/2 cup butter, softened
1/2 cup mayonnaise
2 garlic cloves, minced
1 teaspoon Italian seasoning
1/4 teaspoon crushed red pepper flakes
1/4 teaspoon pepper
1 loaf (1 pound) French bread, halved lengthwise
1 pound sliced deli ham
2 packages (2.1 ounces *each*) ready-to-serve fully cooked bacon, warmed
4 ounces sliced pepperoni
1/2 cup pizza sauce

In a small bowl, combine the first eight ingredients. Spread over cut sides of bread. Layer with ham, bacon, pepperoni and pizza sauce; replace top.

Wrap in foil; place on a large baking sheet. Bake at 350° for 25-30 minutes or until heated through. Cut into slices. **Yield:** 6 servings.

Three-Cheese Florentine Burgers

(Pictured above)

Prep/Total Time: 30 min.

We love cheese—it's an ingredient we always have in abundance. I came up with this recipe to showcase one of our favorite combinations: spinach and cheese!
—Deborah Biggs, Omaha, Nebraska

1-1/3 cups fresh baby spinach
1 tablespoon plus 1-1/2 teaspoons balsamic vinaigrette

BURGERS:

1 egg
1/3 cup fresh baby spinach, finely chopped
3 tablespoons crumbled feta cheese
3 tablespoons shredded Asiago cheese
3 tablespoons chopped red onion
1 tablespoon plus 1-1/2 teaspoons ketchup
2 teaspoons Worcestershire sauce
1/2 teaspoon salt
1/2 teaspoon pepper
1 pound ground beef
4 ounces fresh mozzarella cheese, sliced
4 whole wheat hamburger buns, split

Place spinach in a small bowl. Drizzle with vinaigrette and toss to coat; set aside.

In a large bowl, combine the egg, spinach, cheeses, onion, ketchup, Worcestershire sauce, salt and pepper. Crumble beef over mixture and mix well. Shape into four patties.

Grill the burgers, covered, over medium heat or broil 4 in. from the heat for 5-7 minutes on each side or until a meat thermometer reads 160° and juices run clear. Top with mozzarella cheese. Grill 1-2 minutes longer or until cheese is melted. Serve on buns with the spinach mixture. **Yield:** 4 servings.

Chipotle-Black Bean Chili

(Pictured above)

Prep: 15 min. **Cook:** 7 hours

This thick, slow-cooked chili is special to me because it "cooks itself" while I'm at work. My family and friends love it, too. It's wonderful served with corn bread.
—Patricia Nieh, Portola Vally, California

2 cans (15 ounces *each*) black beans, rinsed and drained
2 cans (14-1/2 ounces *each*) fire-roasted diced tomatoes, undrained
1 large onion, finely chopped
1 medium green pepper, finely chopped
2 chipotle peppers in adobo sauce, finely chopped
2 tablespoons adobo sauce
2 garlic cloves, minced
1 boneless beef chuck roast (2 pounds), cut into 1-inch cubes
1 tablespoon ground cumin
1 tablespoon dried oregano
1/2 teaspoon salt
1/2 teaspoon pepper
Optional toppings: shredded Monterey Jack cheese, reduced-fat sour cream, minced fresh cilantro and lime wedges

In a large bowl, combine the beans, tomatoes, onion, green pepper, chipotle peppers, adobo sauce and garlic. In another bowl, combine the beef, cumin, oregano, salt and pepper.

Pour half of the tomato mixture in a 4- or 5-qt. slow cooker; add beef. Top with remaining tomato mixture. Cover and cook on low for 7-9 hours or until meat is tender. Serve with toppings of your choice. **Yield:** 8 servings (2-1/2 quarts).

Au Gratin Chicken Chowder

(Pictured below)

Prep/Total Time: 30 min.

Everyone will want more of this quick and rich chowder. The flavor is unbeatable! Canned corn and packaged potatoes make it a snap to prepare.
—Ella Eberly, Englewood, Ohio

6 bacon strips, diced
1 small onion, chopped
1 package (4.9 ounces) au gratin potatoes
2 cups hot water
1-1/2 cups 2% milk
1-1/4 cups chicken broth
1 can (15-1/4 ounces) whole kernel corn, drained
1 bay leaf
3 cups cubed cooked chicken
2/3 cup evaporated milk

In a large saucepan, cook bacon over medium heat until crisp. Remove to paper towels with a slotted spoon; drain, reserving 2 tablespoons drippings.

Saute onion in drippings until tender. Add the potatoes with contents of sauce mix, water, milk, broth, corn and bay leaf. Cook, uncovered, over medium heat for 15-20 minutes or until potatoes are tender, stirring occasionally.

Reduce heat. Stir in the chicken, evaporated milk and bacon; heat through. Discard bay leaf. **Yield:** 6 servings (about 2 quarts).

Very Best Barbecue Beef Sandwiches

(Pictured above)

Prep: 20 min. **Cook:** 8 hours

These sweet and tangy barbecue beef sandwiches, made in our Test Kitchen, definitely live up to their name.

1 boneless beef chuck roast (3 to 4 pounds)
1-1/2 cups ketchup
1 small onion, finely chopped
1/4 cup packed brown sugar
1/4 cup red wine vinegar
1 tablespoon Dijon mustard
1 tablespoon Worcestershire sauce
2 garlic cloves, minced
1/2 teaspoon salt
1/4 teaspoon celery seed
1/4 teaspoon paprika
1/4 teaspoon pepper
2 tablespoons cornstarch
2 tablespoons cold water
12 kaiser rolls, split
Dill pickle slices, optional

Cut roast in half. Place in a 5-qt. slow cooker. In a small bowl, combine the ketchup, onion, brown sugar, vinegar, mustard, Worcestershire sauce, garlic, salt, celery seed, paprika and pepper; pour over roast. Cover and cook on low for 8-10 hours or until meat is tender.

Remove meat. Skim fat from cooking juices; transfer to a large saucepan. Bring to a boil. Combine cornstarch and water until smooth; gradually stir into juices. Return to a boil; cook and stir for 2 minutes or until thickened.

When meat is cool enough to handle, shred with two forks. Return to slow cooker and stir in sauce mixture; heat through. Serve on rolls with pickle slices if desired. **Yield:** 12 servings.

Hoisin Pork Wraps

(Pictured below)

Prep: 25 min. **Cook:** 7 hours

This flavorful pork with its tasty slaw is fun to serve at a buffet because it lets guests make their own wraps. Even my grandchildren like it. —Linda Woo, Derby, Kansas

1 boneless whole pork loin roast (3 pounds)
1 cup hoisin sauce, *divided*
1 tablespoon minced fresh gingerroot
6 cups shredded red cabbage
1-1/2 cups shredded carrots
1/4 cup thinly sliced green onions
3 tablespoons rice vinegar
4-1/2 teaspoons sugar
15 flour tortillas (8 inches), warmed

Cut roast in half. Combine 1/3 cup hoisin sauce and ginger; rub over pork. Transfer to a 3-qt. slow cooker. Cover and cook on low for 7-8 hours or until pork is tender.

Meanwhile, in a large bowl, combine the cabbage, carrots, onions, vinegar and sugar. Chill until serving.

Shred the meat with two forks and return to the slow cooker; heat through. Place 2 teaspoons of remaining hoisin sauce down the center of each tortilla; top with 1/3 cup shredded pork and 1/3 cup coleslaw. Roll up. **Yield:** 15 servings.

GINGERROOT

Fresh gingerroot is available in your grocer's produce section. It should have a smooth skin. If wrinkled and cracked, the root is dry and past its prime. When it's stored in a heavy-duty resealable plastic bag, unpeeled gingerroot can be frozen for up to 1 year.

Creamy Chicken Rice Soup

(Pictured above)

Prep/Total Time: 30 min.

I came up with this thick, flavorful soup while making some adjustments to a favorite stovetop chicken casserole. My family enjoys this dish for lunch with a crisp roll and some fresh fruit. —Janice Mitchell, Aurora, Colorado

- **1/2 cup chopped onion**
- **1 medium carrot, chopped**
- **1 celery rib, chopped**
- **1 tablespoon canola oil**
- **1/2 teaspoon minced garlic**
- **2 cans (14-1/2 ounces *each*) chicken broth**
- **1/3 cup uncooked long grain rice**
- **3/4 teaspoon dried basil**
- **1/4 teaspoon pepper**
- **3 tablespoons all-purpose flour**
- **1 can (5 ounces) evaporated milk**
- **1 package (9 ounces) frozen diced cooked chicken, thawed**

In a large saucepan, saute the onion, carrot, celery in oil until tender. Add the garlic; cook 1 minute longer. Stir in broth, rice, basil and pepper. Bring to a boil. Reduce heat; cover and simmer for 15 minutes or until the rice is tender.

In a small bowl, combine flour and milk until smooth; stir into soup. Bring to a boil; cook and stir for 2 minutes or until thickened. Stir in chicken; heat through. **Yield:** 5 servings.

Lemon-Chicken Velvet Soup

(Pictured below)

Prep/Total Time: 25 min.

Here's the perfect antidote to a chilly spring day. The lively flavor of lemon perks up this rich, brothy soup that's accented with fresh sugar snap peas. —Celeste Buckley, Redding, California

- **2 tablespoons butter**
- **2 tablespoons all-purpose flour**
- **1 can (14-1/2 ounces) chicken broth**
- **3 tablespoons lemon juice**
- **1-1/2 cups cubed cooked chicken breast**
- **10 fresh *or* frozen sugar snap peas**
- **2 tablespoons minced fresh parsley**
- **1 teaspoon grated lemon peel**
- **3 tablespoons heavy whipping cream**

In a small saucepan, melt butter. Stir in the flour until smooth; gradually add broth and lemon juice. Bring to a boil; cook and stir for 1-2 minutes or until thickened.

Stir in chicken, peas, parsley and lemon peel; cook 2-3 minutes longer or until chicken is heated through and peas are crisp-tender. Stir in cream; heat through (do not boil). **Yield:** 2 servings.

Hearty Italian Sandwiches

(Pictured on next page)

Prep: 20 min. **Cook:** 6 hours

I've been making this sweet and spicy sandwich filling for many years. The Italian-flavored meat mixture smells just as good as it tastes. —Elaine Krupsky, Las Vegas, Nevada

- **1-1/2 pounds lean ground beef (90% lean)**
- **1-1/2 pounds bulk Italian sausage**
- **2 large onions, sliced**
- **2 large green peppers, sliced**
- **2 large sweet red peppers, sliced**

In a large bowl, combine the beef, steak sauce and onion soup mix. Shape into four patties.

Moisten a paper towel with cooking oil; using long-handled tongs, lightly coat the grill rack. Grill burgers, covered, over medium heat or broil 4 in. from the heat for 4-5 minutes on each side or until a meat thermometer reads 160° and juices run clear.

Top with Swiss cheese; cover and grill 1-2 minutes longer or until cheese is melted. Place buns, cut side down, on grill for 1-2 minutes or until toasted.

Meanwhile, in a large skillet, saute the mushrooms and green onions in remaining butter until tender. Serve the burgers on buns; top with French-fried onions, mushroom mixture and tomato and lettuce if desired. **Yield:** 4 servings.

Touchdown Brat Sliders

(Pictured above)

Prep/Total Time: 30 min.

You can be sure it's game time when these minis make an appearance. Two things my husband loves to eat —beer and brats—get stepped up a notch with crunchy, flavored potato chips. —Kirsten Shabaz, Lakeville, Minnesota

5 thick-sliced bacon strips, chopped
1 pound uncooked bratwurst links, casings removed
1 large onion, finely chopped
2 garlic cloves, minced
1 package (8 ounces) cream cheese, cubed
1 cup dark beer *or* nonalcoholic beer
1 tablespoon Dijon mustard
1/4 teaspoon pepper
16 dinner rolls, split and toasted
2 cups cheddar and sour cream potato chips, crushed

In a large skillet, cook bacon over medium heat until crisp. Remove to paper towels with a slotted spoon; drain, reserving drippings. Cook bratwurst and onion in drippings over medium heat until meat is no longer pink. Add garlic; cook 1 minute longer. Drain.

Stir in the cream cheese, beer, mustard and pepper. Bring to a boil. Reduce heat; simmer, uncovered, for 8-10 minutes or until thickened, stirring occasionally. Stir in the bacon. Spoon 1/4 cup onto each roll; sprinkle with chips. Replace tops. **Yield:** 16 sliders.

Pepperoni Pizza Chili

(Pictured below)

Prep: 20 min. **Cook:** 30 min.

Pizza and chili go together like dudes and football in this must-try man food that delivers before halftime. —Jennifer Gelormino, Pittsburgh, Pennsylvania

2 pounds ground beef
1 pound bulk hot Italian sausage
1 large onion, chopped
1 large green pepper, chopped
4 garlic cloves, minced
1 jar (16 ounces) salsa
1 can (16 ounces) hot chili beans, undrained
1 can (16 ounces) kidney beans, rinsed and drained
1 can (12 ounces) pizza sauce
1 package (8 ounces) sliced pepperoni, halved
1 cup water
2 teaspoons chili powder
1/2 teaspoon salt
1/2 teaspoon pepper
3 cups (12 ounces) shredded part-skim mozzarella cheese

In a Dutch oven, cook the beef, sausage, onion, green pepper and garlic over medium heat until meat is no longer pink; drain.

Stir in the salsa, beans, pizza sauce, pepperoni, water, chili powder, salt and pepper. Bring to a boil. Reduce heat; cover and simmer for 20 minutes. Sprinkle servings with cheese. **Yield:** 12 servings (3 quarts).

White Chili with a Kick

(Pictured below)

Prep: 20 min. **Cook:** 15 min.

Store-bought rotisserie chicken makes this spicy chili easy, but you could also cook your own. We like it with sour cream, green onions, cheese or salsa on top.
—Emmajean Anderson, Mendota Heights, Minnesota

1 large onion, chopped
6 tablespoons butter, cubed
2 tablespoons all-purpose flour
2 cups chicken broth
3/4 cup half-and-half cream
1 rotisserie chicken, cut up
2 cans (15 ounces *each*) white kidney *or* cannellini beans, rinsed and drained
1 can (11 ounces) white corn, drained
2 cans (4 ounces *each*) chopped green chilies
2 teaspoons ground cumin
1 teaspoon chili powder
1/2 teaspoon salt
1/2 teaspoon white pepper
1/2 teaspoon hot pepper sauce
1-1/2 cups (6 ounces) shredded pepper Jack cheese
Salsa and chopped green onions, optional

In a Dutch oven, saute onion in butter. Stir in flour until blended; cook and stir for 3 minutes or until golden brown. Gradually add broth and cream. Bring to a boil; cook and stir for 2 minutes or until thickened.

Add the chicken, beans, corn, chilies, cumin, chili powder, salt, pepper and pepper sauce; heat through. Stir in cheese until melted.

Garnish each serving with salsa and green onions if desired. **Yield:** 9 servings (2-1/4 quarts).

Satisfying Beef Stew

(Pictured above)

Prep: 30 min. **Cook:** 6 hours

This stew is so hearty and tastes even better the next day, if there are leftovers! It goes great with corn bread or any crusty loaf of bread. *—Abbey Mueller, Enid, Oklahoma*

2 pounds beef stew meat, cut into 1-inch cubes
1 medium onion, chopped
2 tablespoons canola oil
2 cups water
1/4 cup all-purpose flour
3 medium carrots, sliced
3 medium potatoes, peeled and cubed
2 cups frozen corn
1-1/2 cups frozen cut green beans
1 can (15 ounces) Italian tomato sauce
2 teaspoons Worcestershire sauce
1 teaspoon salt
1 teaspoon paprika
1 teaspoon pepper
Dash ground cloves
2 bay leaves

In a large skillet, brown beef and onion in oil; drain. Transfer to a 5-qt. slow cooker. Combine water and flour; pour over beef. Stir in the remaining ingredients.

Cover and cook on low for 6-8 hours or until meat and vegetables are tender. Discard bay leaves. **Yield:** 8 servings.

Zesty Calzone

Prep: 10 min. **Bake:** 20 min. + standing

This family-friendly calzone is great when you need a quick weekend lunch, but it's also perfect when you're watching the big game on TV.
—Mary Ann Saam, Cridersville, Ohio

1 tube (13.8 ounces) refrigerated pizza crust
2 tablespoons grated Parmesan cheese
8 thin slices deli ham
8 thin slices hard salami
1/4 cup chopped onion
1/4 cup chopped green pepper
1/4 cup chopped tomato
1 cup (4 ounces) shredded part-skim mozzarella cheese

In a greased 15-in. x 10-in. x 1-in. baking pan, pat dough into a 13-in. x 8-in. rectangle. Sprinkle Parmesan cheese to within 1/2 in. of edges.

On half of the dough, layer the ham, salami, onion, green pepper and tomato to within 1 in. of the edges. Sprinkle with mozzarella cheese. Fold dough over filling; pinch edges to seal. Cut slits in top.

Bake at 425° for 20-22 minutes or golden brown. Let stand for about 10 minutes. Cut into four pieces. **Yield:** 4 servings.

Hearty Vegetable Beef Soup

(Pictured below)

Prep/Total Time: 30 min.

This soup is packed with flavor. Thanks to convenience products, it's ideal for a weeknight supper or for a tasty, warming lunch some snowy Saturday.
—Joanne Meehan, Shippensburg, Pennsylvania

1 package (17 ounces) refrigerated beef roast au jus
2 cans (14-1/2 ounces *each*) Italian diced tomatoes, undrained
1 package (16 ounces) frozen mixed vegetables
5-1/2 cups water
1/4 teaspoon salt
1-1/2 cups uncooked mini penne pasta

Shred beef with two forks; transfer to a Dutch oven. Add the tomatoes, vegetables, water and salt. Bring to a boil.

Stir in pasta. Reduce heat; simmer, uncovered, for 15 minutes or until flavors are blended and pasta is tender. **Yield:** 8 servings.

Orange Chicken Wraps

(Pictured above)

Prep/Total Time: 20 min.

Oranges give these cool and crunchy wraps a pleasant change of pace. The tasty handhelds come together in a snap. Enjoy them as a simple everyday meal or a filling, on-the-go lunch. *—Jamie Jones, Madison, Georgia*

4 cups coleslaw mix
2 cans (11 ounces *each*) mandarin oranges, drained
1-1/2 cups fresh broccoli florets
1 medium sweet yellow pepper, thinly sliced
1/4 cup chopped celery
1 tablespoon sunflower kernels
1 teaspoon grated orange peel
1/3 cup coleslaw salad dressing
2 packages (6 ounces *each*) ready-to-serve roasted chicken breast strips, chopped
3/4 cup honey barbecue sauce
8 flour tortillas (10 inches)

In a large bowl, combine the first seven ingredients. Add salad dressing; toss to coat. In another bowl, combine chicken and barbecue sauce.

Spoon 3/4 cup coleslaw mixture down the center of each tortilla; top with 1/4 cup chicken mixture. Roll up. **Yield:** 8 servings.

BROCCOLI TIP

When purchasing broccoli, look for bunches that have a deep green color, tightly closed buds and crisp leaves. Store in a resealable plastic bag in the refrigerator for up to 4 days. Wash just before using. One pound of broccoli yields about 2 cups florets.

CHAPTER 13

Express Entrees

In today's busy, hectic world, it helps to have everyday go-to recipes so your week runs smoothly. We've compiled this chapter with main courses that can be prepped and cooked in 30 minutes or less. A hearty, family-pleasing supper can go from the kitchen to the table in only half an hour!

There are plenty of delicious entrees that'll send your family back for seconds, such as Italian Chicken Cordon Bleu and the restaurant-quality Roasted Pepper Chicken Penne.

For kid-friendly meals, check out Zesty Grilled Sandwiches and Family-Favorite Italian Chicken. Not only are they quick and hearty, but they're sure to become your latest, most reliable recipes! ■

DINNER IN A FLASH. Sloppy Joe Pizza (p. 205).

Quicker Chicken and Dumplings

(Pictured above)

Prep/Total Time: 30 min.

Pressed for time? This easy version of the chicken classic takes advantage of convenience items and uses time-saving, drop-style dumplings.
—Willie DeWaard, Coralville, Iowa

1-1/2 cups 2% milk
1-1/2 cups frozen mixed vegetables, thawed
2-1/2 cups cubed cooked chicken
1 can (10-3/4 ounces) condensed cream of chicken soup, undiluted
1/2 teaspoon garlic powder
1/4 teaspoon poultry seasoning
DUMPLINGS:
1 cup biscuit/baking mix
1/3 cup French-fried onions, coarsely chopped
7 tablespoons 2% milk
1/2 teaspoon dried parsley flakes

In a Dutch oven, combine the first six ingredients; bring to a boil, stirring occasionally.

Meanwhile, in a small bowl, combine the biscuit mix, onions, milk and parsley just until moistened. Drop by heaping teaspoonfuls onto the simmering stew. Cook, uncovered, for 10 minutes.

Cover and simmer 10-12 minutes longer or until a toothpick inserted in a dumpling comes out clean (do not lift the cover while simmering). **Yield:** 6 servings.

Zesty Grilled Sandwiches

Prep/Total Time: 25 min.

Store-bought coleslaw adds sweetness and a fun change of pace to these extra-easy grilled sandwiches. Serve chips or veggies alongside, and dinner will be ready on the double! *—Missy Herr, Quarryville, Pennsylvania*

8 slices sourdough bread
16 slices deli ham
4 slices provolone cheese
1 cup deli coleslaw
1 cup (4 ounces) shredded cheddar cheese
2 tablespoons olive oil

On four slices of bread, layer the ham, provolone cheese, coleslaw and cheddar cheese. Top with remaining bread slices. Spread oil on outsides of sandwiches.

On a griddle, toast sandwiches until bread is lightly browned on both sides. **Yield:** 4 servings.

Southern Shrimp & Grits

(Pictured below)

Prep/Total Time: 30 min.

This is just an old Southern stick-to-your-ribs dinner combining fresh shrimp, a medley of peppers and onion, and creamy cheese grits. It's great served with corn bread and sliced tomatoes.
—Melissa Birdsong, Gilbert, South Carolina

2-1/2 cups chicken broth
1 cup quick-cooking grits
1 medium onion, sliced
1 package (14 ounces) frozen pepper strips, thawed
4 teaspoons olive oil
12 uncooked jumbo shrimp, peeled and deveined

1/4 cup minced fresh parsley
1 teaspoon lemon juice
1 cup (4 ounces) shredded sharp cheddar cheese
1/2 cup sour cream

In a large saucepan, bring broth to a boil. Slowly stir in grits. Reduce heat; cook and stir for 5-7 minutes or until thickened.

Meanwhile, in a large skillet, saute onion and pepper strips in oil until crisp-tender. Add the shrimp, parsley and lemon juice; saute 3-4 minutes longer or until shrimp turn pink.

Stir the cheese and sour cream into grits; serve with shrimp mixture. **Yield:** 4 servings.

Honey-Pecan Baked Cod

(Pictured above)

Prep/Total Time: 30 min.

One night at dinner, while vacationing in the Blue Ridge Mountains, we tried a pecan-encrusted trout that we've tried to re-create. We enjoy this tasty version with fresh or frozen cod often.
—Lana German, Lenoir, North Carolina

3 tablespoons honey
2 tablespoons butter, melted
1 tablespoon reduced-sodium soy sauce
1-1/2 teaspoons lemon-pepper seasoning
1/2 teaspoon garlic powder
1/2 teaspoon paprika
1/4 teaspoon seasoned salt
1-1/2 cups finely chopped pecans
6 cod fillets (6 ounces *each*)

In a shallow bowl, combine the first seven ingredients. Place the pecans in another shallow bowl. Dip fillets in honey mixture, then coat with pecans.

Place in a greased 13-in. x 9-in. baking dish. Bake, uncovered, at 400° for 15-20 minutes or until fish flakes easily with a fork. **Yield:** 6 servings.

Coquille St. Jacques

(Pictured below)

Prep/Total Time: 30 min.

Buttery scallops in rich, creamy sauce would be tough to share. Good thing you don't have to.
—Betsy Esley, Lake Alfred, Florida

6 ounces bay scallops
3 tablespoons white wine *or* chicken broth
2 teaspoons butter
1/4 teaspoon dried minced onion
1-1/2 teaspoons all-purpose flour
1/4 cup heavy whipping cream
3 tablespoons shredded cheddar cheese
TOPPING:
4 teaspoons dry bread crumbs
1 teaspoon butter, melted
Paprika

In a small skillet, combine the scallops, wine, butter and onion. Bring to a boil. Reduce heat; cover and simmer for 1-2 minutes or until scallops are firm and opaque. Using a slotted spoon, remove scallops and keep warm.

Bring poaching liquid to a boil; cook until liquid is reduced to about 2 tablespoons, about 3 minutes. Stir in flour until smooth; gradually add the cream. Bring to a boil; cook and stir for 1 minute or until thickened. Remove from the heat. Stir in the cheese until melted. Return scallops to skillet. Pour into a greased 6-oz. ramekin or custard cup.

In a small bowl, combine bread crumbs and butter; sprinkle over top. Sprinkle with paprika. Bake, uncovered, at 400° for 4-5 minutes or until golden brown. **Yield:** 1 serving.

Home-Style Sausage Gravy and Biscuits

(Pictured above)

Prep/Total Time: 30 min.

My mother-in-law introduced me to her hamburger gravy, and I modified it slightly. We have this every weekend.
—Michele Bapst, Jacksonville, North Carolina

1 tube (16.3 ounces) large refrigerated flaky biscuits
1 pound bulk pork sausage
1 cup chopped sweet onion
2 tablespoons butter
1 envelope country gravy mix
1 tablespoon all-purpose flour
Dash *each* garlic powder, Italian seasoning, onion powder and pepper
1-1/2 cups 2% milk
1 cup reduced-sodium chicken broth

Bake biscuits according to package directions.

Meanwhile, in a large skillet, cook sausage and onion over medium heat until sausage is no longer pink; drain. Add the butter, cook until melted. Stir in the gravy mix, flour and seasonings until blended. Gradually add milk and broth. Bring to a boil; cook and stir for 1 minute or until thickened. Serve with biscuits. **Yield:** 8 servings.

SWEET ONIONS

Sweet onions, such as Vidalia, are mild-flavored, high in sugar and water, and low in tear-inducing sulfur compounds. Because of these properties, they are not suited for long-term storage, so you should use them within several weeks of purchase.

Scallops with Thai Sauce

(Pictured below)

Prep/Total Time: 30 min.

Tender scallops and crunchy cashews star at dinnertime tonight! This recipe calls for sea scallops, which are about 1-1/2 inches in diameter. You could also use their sweeter, smaller relative, the bay scallop.
—Joe Hable, Madison, Wisconsin

1 tablespoon cornstarch
1 can (14-1/2 ounces) vegetable broth
2 tablespoons creamy peanut butter
1 to 2 tablespoons Thai chili sauce
1 pound sea scallops
2 tablespoons canola oil, *divided*
1 small onion, sliced
1 large sweet red pepper, julienned
1/2 cup salted cashews
2 garlic cloves, minced
1 can (8-3/4 ounces) whole baby corn, drained
Hot cooked angel hair pasta, optional

In a small bowl, combine the cornstarch, broth, peanut butter and chili sauce until smooth; set aside.

In a large skillet, saute scallops in 1 tablespoon oil for 2-3 minutes on each side or until opaque. Remove with a slotted spoon and keep warm.

In the same pan, saute the onion, red pepper and cashews in the remaining oil for 3-5 minutes or until the vegetables are crisp-tender. Add the garlic; cook for 1 minute longer.

Stir cornstarch mixture and add to the pan. Bring to a boil; cook and stir for 1-2 minutes or until thickened. Add scallops and corn; heat through. Serve over pasta if desired. **Yield:** 5 servings.

Catfish Po'boys

(Pictured above)

Prep/Total Time: 30 min.

This tribute to a great Southern staple does fried catfish serious justice. A creative Cajun coleslaw with a touch of heat tops the fried fish perfectly for a sandwich you won't be able to resist. —*Ann Baker, Texarkana, Texas*

CAJUN COLESLAW:
3-3/4 cups coleslaw mix
1/2 cup mayonnaise
3 tablespoons seafood cocktail sauce
1/2 teaspoon Cajun seasoning
1/4 teaspoon seafood seasoning
SANDWICHES:
1/2 cup cornmeal
1/3 cup all-purpose flour
1 teaspoon salt
1 teaspoon Cajun seasoning
1/4 teaspoon seafood seasoning
2/3 cup buttermilk
4 catfish fillets (6 ounces *each*)
Oil for deep-fat frying
4 hoagie buns, split

In a large bowl, toss together the coleslaw ingredients; set aside.

In a shallow bowl, combine the cornmeal, flour, salt, Cajun seasoning and seafood seasoning. Place buttermilk in another shallow bowl. Dip fish in buttermilk, then coat with cornmeal mixture.

In an electric skillet, heat 1/4 in. of oil to 375°. Cook fillets for 2-3 minutes on each side or until fish flakes easily with a fork. Drain on paper towels.

Place fish and coleslaw on bun bottoms; replace bun tops. **Yield:** 4 servings.

Pumpkin-Curry Chicken Over Cashew Rice

(Pictured above)

Prep/Total Time: 30 min.

Combine international flavors with homespun comfort for this fast, delicious meal. The sweet curry aroma alone will warm hearts on gray-sky days.
—Aysha Schurman, Ammon, Idaho

2 cups uncooked jasmine rice
1-1/2 pounds boneless skinless chicken breasts, cut into 1/2-inch cubes
4 teaspoons curry powder, *divided*
1/4 teaspoon pepper
2 tablespoons olive oil
1 garlic clove, minced
1 cup canned pumpkin
1/2 cup chicken broth
1/2 cup raisins
1/4 cup apple butter
1/2 teaspoon Chinese five-spice powder
1/3 cup chopped cashews, toasted
Minced fresh parsley

Cook rice according to package directions.

Meanwhile, sprinkle chicken with 1 teaspoon curry powder and pepper. In a large skillet, saute chicken in oil for 5-6 minutes or until no longer pink. Add garlic; cook 1 minute longer.

Stir in pumpkin, broth, raisins, apple butter, five-spice powder and remaining curry powder. Bring to a boil. Reduce heat; simmer, uncovered, for 5-7 minutes or until heated through.

Stir cashews into cooked rice and serve with chicken mixture. Sprinkle with parsley. **Yield:** 5 servings.

Editor's Note: Recipe was tested with commercially prepared apple butter.

Pork Chops with Mustard Sauce

Prep/Total Time: 30 min.

Dress up pork chops with a golden, full-flavored reduction sauce comprised of bold ingredients, including Dijon mustard, white wine, Worcestershire sauce and lots of garlic. You won't be disappointed.
—Sharla Reel, St. Charles, Missouri

4 boneless pork loin chops (6 ounces *each*)
1/4 teaspoon salt
1/4 teaspoon pepper
2 tablespoons olive oil
1/4 cup white wine *or* chicken broth
3 garlic cloves, minced
1/2 cup chicken broth
1 tablespoon butter
1 tablespoon lemon juice
1 tablespoon Dijon mustard
1/4 teaspoon Worcestershire sauce

Sprinkle pork chops with salt and pepper. In a large skillet, brown chops in oil. Add wine and garlic, stirring to loosen browned bits from pan. Bring to a boil; cook for 2 minutes.

Add broth; cover and cook for 8-10 minutes or until a meat thermometer reads 160°. Remove the pork and keep warm.

Bring pan juices to a boil; cook until liquid is reduced to 1/3 cup. Stir in the butter, lemon juice, mustard and Worcestershire sauce; heat through. Serve with pork. **Yield:** 4 servings.

Sloppy Joe Pizza

(Pictured below)

Prep/Total Time: 25 min.

If your children like sloppy joes, they're sure to love this change-of-pace pizza. The six-ingredient recipe has kid-pleasing flavor and goes together in a flash.

—Brenda Rohlman, Kingman, Kansas

2 tubes (13.8 ounces *each*) refrigerated pizza crust
1 pound ground beef
1 can (15-1/2 ounces) sloppy joe sauce
2 cups (8 ounces) shredded part-skim mozzarella cheese
1 cup (4 ounces) shredded cheddar cheese
1/2 cup grated Parmesan cheese

Unroll the pizza dough and place on two greased 12-in. pizza pans. Bake at 425° for 6-7 minutes or until the crust is golden brown.

In a large skillet, cook the beef over medium heat until no longer pink; drain. Add the sloppy joe sauce. Spread over the crusts. Sprinkle with cheeses. Bake at 425° for 6-8 minutes or until the cheese is melted. **Yield:** 2 pizzas (8 slices each).

Crumb-Coated Cod Fillets

(Pictured above)

Prep/Total Time: 30 min.

Pantry ingredients and fresh or frozen fish make this tasty entree a snap.

—Candy Summerhill, Alexander, Arkansas

1/4 cup all-purpose flour
1/4 teaspoon pepper
1/8 teaspoon salt
2 eggs
1 teaspoon water
1 cup panko (Japanese) bread crumbs
1/4 cup shredded Parmesan cheese
4-1/2 teaspoons ranch salad dressing mix
1 tablespoon salt-free Italian herb seasoning
4 cod fillets (4 ounces *each*)

In a shallow bowl, combine the flour, pepper and salt. In another shallow bowl, whisk eggs and water. In a third shallow bowl, combine the bread crumbs, cheese, dressing mix and seasoning. Coat the fillets with flour mixture, then dip in the egg mixture and coat with the crumb mixture.

Place fillets on a greased baking sheet. Bake at 425° for 15-20 minutes or until fish flakes easily with a fork, turning once. **Yield:** 4 servings.

STORING FISH

Fresh fish is highly perishable and should be prepared within a day or two after it is caught or purchased. To store, pan-dress, wash in cold water, blot dry with paper towels and place in an airtight container or heavy-duty plastic bag and refrigerate.

Tuna Zucchini Cakes

(Pictured above)

Prep/Total Time: 25 min.

Here's a great combination of seafood and a bountiful garden vegetable! People seem to like its nice color and texture...not to mention the wonderful taste!
—Billie Blanton, Kingsport, Tennessee

1/2 cup finely chopped onion
1 tablespoon butter
1 can (6-1/2 ounces) light water-packed tuna, drained and flaked
1 cup shredded zucchini
2 eggs, lightly beaten
1/3 cup minced fresh parsley
1 teaspoon lemon juice
1/2 teaspoon salt
1/8 teaspoon pepper
1 cup seasoned bread crumbs, *divided*
2 tablespoons canola oil

In a large saucepan, saute onion in butter until tender. Remove from the heat. Add the tuna, zucchini, eggs, parsley, lemon juice, seasonings and 1/2 cup bread crumbs. Stir until well combined. Shape into six 1/2-in.-thick patties; coat with remaining bread crumbs.

In a large skillet, heat the oil. Cook the patties for 3 minutes on each side or until golden brown. **Yield:** 3 servings.

Champagne Salmon & Fettuccine

(Pictured below)

Prep/Total Time: 30 min.

Poached with a Champagne sauce, this quick salmon dish is delish! —Taryn Kuebelbeck, Plymouth, Minnesota

8 ounces uncooked fettuccine
2 cups cut fresh asparagus (1-inch pieces)
1 cup water
1 cup chicken broth
2 cups brut Champagne, *divided*
1 medium onion, sliced
1/2 teaspoon dried tarragon
1/2 teaspoon pepper, *divided*
4 salmon fillets (4 ounces *each*)
2 garlic cloves, minced
1/2 teaspoon dried basil
1/2 teaspoon brown sugar
1/4 teaspoon salt
3/4 cup cold butter, cubed

In a Dutch oven, cook fettuccine according to package directions, adding asparagus during the last 2 minutes of cooking; drain.

In a large skillet, combine the water, broth, 1 cup Champagne, onion, tarragon and 1/4 teaspoon pepper. Bring to a boil. Reduce heat; add the fillets and poach, uncovered, for 8-10 minutes or until fish flakes easily with a fork.

In a small saucepan, bring the remaining champagne, garlic, basil, brown sugar, salt and remaining pepper to a boil; cook until reduced to 1/2 cup. Whisk in butter until melted. Pour over fettuccine mixture; toss to coat. Serve with salmon. **Yield:** 4 servings.

Orange Roughy Italiano

(Pictured above)

Prep/Total Time: 30 min.

I'm usually not a big fan of fish unless it's fried. But this recipe is so simple and good that it has become a favorite! It's also low in fat and packed with vitamin-rich veggies and Italian flavor. —*Sherry Fletcher, Highland, Illinois*

2 cups sliced zucchini
1/2 cup thinly sliced onion
1 teaspoon dried oregano
1 tablespoon olive oil
4 orange roughy fillets (4 ounces *each*)
1/4 teaspoon salt
1/8 teaspoon pepper
1 medium tomato, chopped
1/2 cup shredded part-skim mozzarella cheese

In a large nonstick skillet coated with cooking spray, saute zucchini, onion and oregano in oil for 5 minutes or until onion is tender.

Sprinkle the fillets with salt and pepper; place over zucchini mixture. Sprinkle with the tomato. Reduce heat; cover and simmer for 10 minutes or until fish flakes easily with a fork. Sprinkle with the cheese; cover and let stand for 2 minutes or until cheese is melted. **Yield:** 4 servings.

BUYING ZUCCHINI

Handle zucchini carefully; they're thin-skinned and easily damaged. To pick the freshest zucchini, look for a firm heavy squash with a moist stem end and a shiny skin. Smaller squash are generally sweeter and more tender than larger ones.

Santa Fe Chicken

(Pictured below)

Prep/Total Time: 30 min.

Chicken and rice are dressed up with a zippy sauce for a complete meal that's ready in a dash. Garnished with fresh cilantro, it's a festive weeknight supper or special occasion menu. —*Jon Carole Gilbreath, Tyler, Texas*

1 large onion, chopped
1 to 2 tablespoons chopped seeded jalapeno pepper
1 tablespoon olive oil
1 garlic clove, minced
1-1/4 cups reduced-sodium chicken broth
1 can (10 ounces) diced tomatoes and green chilies, undrained
1 cup uncooked long grain rice
4 boneless skinless chicken breast halves (4 ounces *each*)
1/2 teaspoon salt
1/4 teaspoon pepper
1/4 teaspoon ground cumin
3/4 cup shredded reduced-fat cheddar cheese
Minced fresh cilantro, optional

In a large skillet, saute the onion and jalapeno in oil until tender. Add garlic; cook 1 minute longer. Stir in broth and tomatoes; bring to a boil. Stir in rice.

Sprinkle chicken with salt, pepper and cumin; place over rice mixture. Cover and simmer for 10-15 minutes on each side or until a meat thermometer reads 170°.

Remove from the heat. Sprinkle with cheese; cover and let stand for 5 minutes. Garnish with cilantro if desired. **Yield:** 4 servings.

Editor's Note: Wear disposable gloves when cutting hot peppers; the oils can burn your skin. Avoid touching your face.

Greek Chicken Penne

(Pictured below)

Prep/Total Time: 25 min.

It's hard to believe a recipe this speedy could create such fresh, mouthwatering Mediterranean flavors.
—Dawn Frihauf, Fort Morgan, Colorado

2-1/2 cups uncooked penne pasta
1 pound boneless skinless chicken breasts, cubed
1/2 cup chopped red onion
2 garlic cloves, minced
1 tablespoon olive oil
2 jars (7-1/2 ounces *each*) marinated quartered artichoke hearts, drained and chopped
1 large tomato, chopped
1/2 cup crumbled feta cheese
3 tablespoons minced fresh parsley
2 tablespoons lemon juice
2 teaspoons dried oregano
1/4 teaspoon salt
1/4 teaspoon pepper
Fresh oregano, optional

Cook pasta according to package directions.

Meanwhile, in a large skillet, cook the chicken, onion and garlic in oil over medium heat for 4-5 minutes or until chicken is no longer pink. Stir in the artichokes, tomato, cheese, parsley, lemon juice, oregano, salt and pepper; heat through.

Drain pasta; toss with chicken mixture. Garnish with oregano if desired. **Yield:** 5 servings.

Italian Chicken Cordon Bleu

(Pictured above)

Prep/Total Time: 30 min.

Streamline any weeknight dinner preparation with this pretty main dish full of pleasing flavors. Chop the pepper ahead and pick up sliced mushrooms, and you'll have this microwaved in moments.
—Laura Mahaffey, Annapolis, Maryland

2 tablespoons butter, cubed
1/2 teaspoon rubbed sage
6 boneless skinless chicken breast halves (4 ounces *each*)
1 medium green pepper, julienned
1/3 cup sliced fresh mushrooms
1 can (15 ounces) tomato sauce
1 teaspoon sugar
1 teaspoon dried oregano
1/2 teaspoon salt
1/2 teaspoon garlic powder
1/2 teaspoon lemon-pepper seasoning
6 slices deli ham
6 slices Swiss cheese
Hot cooked rice, optional

Place butter and sage in a microwave-safe 11-in. x 7-in. dish. Microwave, uncovered, on high for 30 seconds or until the butter is melted. Place the chicken in dish; turn to coat. Top with the green pepper and mushrooms. Cook, uncovered, on high for 8-10 minutes or until the chicken juices run clear, turning and rearranging the chicken twice.

Remove chicken and vegetables; keep warm. Add the tomato sauce, sugar and seasonings to cooking juices; mix well. Microwave, uncovered, on high for 2 minutes or until heated through. Return chicken to the dish; top with ham, cheese and green pepper mixture. Cook on high for 2 minutes or until cheese is melted. Serve with rice if desired. **Yield:** 6 servings.

Editor's Note: This recipe was tested in a 1,100-watt microwave.

Creamy Sausage & Bow Ties

(Pictured below)

Prep/Total Time: 25 min.

Just a few ingredients deliciously jazz up a package of noodles for this fast supper. I stumbled across the recipe when I was running late for dinner. My kids love it!
—Linda Nilson, Melrose Park, Illinois

1 package (4.1 ounces) four cheese bow tie pasta mix
1/2 pound fully cooked smoked sausage, cut into 1/4-inch pieces
1 cup frozen peas
1 cup (4 ounces) shredded part-skim mozzarella cheese

Prepare pasta mix according to package directions. Meanwhile, in a large skillet, brown sausage; drain. Add the peas and pasta. Simmer, uncovered, for 1-2 minutes or until heated through. Sprinkle with cheese. Cover and cook for 1-2 minutes or until the cheese is melted. **Yield:** 4 servings.

Asian Chicken Skillet

(Pictured above)

Prep/Total Time: 30 min.

This scrumptious recipe is a meal in itself. It uses a convenient Rice-A-Roni mix and only one pan...so cleanup is as short as the prep time.
—Terri Christensen, Montague, Michigan

1 package (5.9 ounces) chicken and garlic-flavored rice and vermicelli mix
2 tablespoons butter
1 pound boneless skinless chicken breasts, cut into strips
2-1/4 cups water
1/4 cup reduced-sodium teriyaki sauce
1/2 teaspoon ground ginger
1 package (16 ounces) frozen stir-fry vegetable blend, thawed

In a large skillet, saute rice mix in butter until golden brown. Stir in the chicken, water, teriyaki sauce, ginger and contents of rice seasoning packet. Bring to a boil. Reduce heat; cover and simmer for 10 minutes.

Stir in vegetable blend. Cover and cook 5-8 minutes longer or until the rice is tender and chicken is no longer pink. **Yield:** 4 servings.

SPICE SAVVY

Store your dry spices in tightly closed glass or heavy-duty plastic containers in a cool, dry place. Avoid storing them in direct sunlight, over the stove or near other heat sources. For best flavor, keep ground spices for up to 6 months

Chimichurri Shrimp Skillet

(Pictured above)

Prep/Total Time: 30 min.

Fresh fruit adds sweetness to this bright southwestern shrimp entree. The contrast of colors, flavors and textures in this dish is sensational! —Susan Riley, Allen, Texas

2 cups uncooked instant rice
3 cups packed fresh parsley sprigs
1/2 cup olive oil
2 tablespoons lime juice
4 garlic cloves, halved
2 teaspoons red wine vinegar
1-1/2 teaspoons ground cumin
1 teaspoon salt
1 teaspoon dried oregano
1/2 teaspoon pepper
1 pound uncooked large shrimp, peeled and deveined
1 cup chopped sweet red pepper
1 medium onion, chopped
1-1/2 cups seedless red grapes, halved

Cook rice according to package directions. Meanwhile, in a food processor, combine the parsley, oil, lime juice, garlic, vinegar, cumin, salt, oregano and pepper; cover and process until blended.

In a large skillet, saute the shrimp in 1/4 cup parsley mixture for 3-4 minutes or until shrimp turn pink; remove and keep warm.

In the same skillet, saute red pepper and onion in 1/4 cup parsley mixture until tender. Stir in the shrimp, rice, grapes and remaining parsley mixture; heat through. **Yield:** 6 servings.

Pork Chops Normandy

(Pictured below)

Prep/Total Time: 30 min.

Pears and brandy team up to turn ordinary pork chops into a restaurant-quality dish that's good enough for guests. Serve with an upscale side, such as brussels sprouts or asparagus, and a glass of wine for a fantastic meal. —Gina Quartermaine, Alexandria, Virginia

4 boneless pork loin chops (6 ounces *each*)
3 tablespoons butter
3 medium pears, peeled and chopped
3 tablespoons chopped shallots
3 garlic cloves, minced
3 tablespoons brandy *or* chicken broth
1/2 cup heavy whipping cream
1/2 teaspoon salt
1/2 teaspoon rubbed sage
1/2 teaspoon dried thyme
1/2 teaspoon pepper

In a large skillet, brown pork chops in butter. Remove and keep warm. In the same skillet, saute pears and shallots until crisp-tender. Add garlic; saute 1 minute longer. Remove from the heat. Stir in brandy; cook over medium heat until liquid is evaporated.

Stir in the cream and seasonings; cook for 2-3 minutes or until the sauce is slightly thickened. Return the pork chops to skillet; cover and cook for 8-10 minutes or until a meat thermometer reads 160°, turning once. **Yield:** 4 servings.

Tomato and Onion Salmon

(Pictured above)

Prep/Total Time: 30 min.

Tomatoes, onions and lemon juice make this moist, flaky salmon something special. My husband, Frank, and I really enjoy salmon cooked this way.
—Lillian Denchick, Olmstedville, New York

4 salmon fillets (5 ounces *each*)
2 teaspoons olive oil
1/4 teaspoon dill weed
1/4 teaspoon pepper
2 medium tomatoes, thinly sliced
1 medium onion, thinly sliced
4 garlic cloves, minced
1/2 cup reduced-sodium chicken broth
1 tablespoon lemon juice
2 tablespoons minced fresh parsley

Place salmon in a 13-in. x 9-in. baking dish coated with cooking spray. Drizzle with oil; sprinkle with dill and pepper. Top with tomatoes; set aside.

In a small skillet coated with cooking spray, saute onion and garlic. Add the broth, lemon juice and parsley. Bring to a boil; cook for 2-3 minutes or until most of the liquid has evaporated. Spoon over salmon. Cover and bake at 350° for 13-18 minutes or until fish flakes easily with a fork. **Yield:** 4 servings.

Chicken in Lime Butter

Prep/Total Time: 20 min.

It takes just a few ordinary, on-hand ingredients to make everyday chicken breasts taste this extraordinary! The flavor added by the rich, buttery sauce with a splash of lime juice is unmatched. The recipe has been a hands-down winner at our house for many years.
—Denise Segura, Draper, Utah

4 boneless skinless chicken breast halves (4 ounces *each*)
1/8 teaspoon salt
1/8 teaspoon pepper
2 tablespoons canola oil
1/4 cup butter, cubed
1 tablespoon lime juice
1/2 teaspoon dill weed
1/4 teaspoon minced chives

Sprinkle the chicken with salt and pepper. In a large skillet, cook the chicken in oil over medium heat for 5-7 minutes on each side or until a meat thermometer reaches 170°; drain. Remove chicken from the skillet and keep warm.

Add the butter and lime juice to the skillet; cook and stir until the butter is melted. Stir in the dill weed and minced chives. Drizzle butter mixture over the chicken. **Yield:** 4 servings.

Family-Favorite Italian Chicken

(Pictured above)

Prep/Total Time: 30 min.

Crispy chicken is treated to a jazzed-up sauce in this simple main dish that's so comforting and good.
—Carol Heeren, Parker, South Dakota

- **2 cans (8 ounces *each*) tomato sauce**
- **2 teaspoons dried basil**
- **1/2 teaspoon garlic powder**
- **4 boneless skinless chicken breast halves (4 ounces *each*)**
- **3/4 cup dry bread crumbs**
- **2 teaspoons dried oregano**
- **1/4 teaspoon salt**
- **2 eggs**
- **2 tablespoons water**
- **1/2 cup all-purpose flour**
- **1/4 cup olive oil**
- **1 cup (4 ounces) shredded part-skim mozzarella cheese**
- **1/4 cup shredded Parmesan cheese**
- **Hot cooked angel hair pasta**

In a small saucepan, combine the tomato sauce, basil and garlic powder; heat through.

Meanwhile, flatten the chicken breasts to 1/4-in. thickness. In a shallow bowl, combine the bread crumbs, oregano and salt. In a separate shallow bowl, whisk eggs and water. Place flour in another shallow bowl. Coat chicken with flour, then dip in the egg mixture and coat with bread crumb mixture.

In a large skillet, cook chicken in oil in batches for 4-6 minutes on each side or until juices run clear. Spoon sauce over chicken; sprinkle with cheeses. Serve with pasta. **Yield:** 4 servings.

Roasted Pepper Chicken Penne

(Pictured below)

Prep/Total Time: 30 min.

My husband calls me an aerobic cook because I can make this Italian dish in just a half hour. No one will accuse you of cutting corners. It tastes like it has been simmering deliciously for hours.
—Regina Cowles, Boulder, Colorado

- **1 pound boneless skinless chicken breasts, cut into 1-inch strips**
- **1/4 cup balsamic vinegar**
- **1 package (16 ounces) penne pasta**
- **1 medium onion, sliced**
- **3 garlic cloves, sliced**
- **1/4 cup olive oil**
- **1 can (28 ounces) crushed tomatoes**
- **1 cup julienned roasted sweet red peppers**
- **1 cup chicken broth**
- **3 teaspoons Italian seasoning**
- **1/4 teaspoon salt**
- **1 cup shredded Parmesan cheese**

Place the chicken in a large resealable plastic bag; add the vinegar. Seal the bag and turn to coat; refrigerate for 15 minutes.

Cook the pasta according to the package directions. Meanwhile, in a large skillet, saute the onion and garlic in oil for 1 minute. Drain and discard vinegar. Add the chicken to skillet; cook for 4-5 minutes or until meat is no longer pink.

Stir in tomatoes, red peppers, broth, Italian seasoning and salt. Bring to a boil over medium heat; cook and stir for 4-5 minutes or until heated through. Drain pasta; toss with chicken mixture. Sprinkle with cheese. **Yield:** 8 servings.

Smoky Chicken Enchilada Skillet

(Pictured above)

Prep/Total Time: 25 min.

Here in Texas, we love our Mexican food, and this is a family favorite. It's quick and easy, and requires no rolling up of enchiladas or baking in the oven.
—Carolyn Collins, Freeport, Texas

1 pound boneless skinless chicken breasts, cubed
1 small onion, chopped
1 tablespoon canola oil
1 can (10-3/4 ounces) condensed cream of chicken soup, undiluted
1 can (10 ounces) enchilada sauce
1 can (4 ounces) chopped green chilies
1 tablespoon minced chipotle pepper in adobo sauce
12 corn tortillas (6 inches), cut into 1-inch strips
1-1/4 cups shredded Mexican cheese blend, *divided*
1/4 cup minced fresh cilantro
Sour cream

In a large skillet, cook chicken and onion in oil over medium heat for 6-8 minutes or until the chicken is no longer pink. Stir in the soup, enchilada sauce, chilies and chipotle pepper. Add tortillas and 1 cup cheese.

Bring to a boil. Reduce heat; cover and simmer for 5-7 minutes or until heated through, stirring occasionally. Sprinkle with cilantro and remaining cheese. Serve with sour cream. **Yield:** 5 servings.

CHICKEN BREAST BASICS

Buying skinned and boned chicken breasts can cut up to 15 minutes off your cooking time. Save money by buying larger size packages, and rewrapping the breasts individually or in family-size portions and then freezing.

Shrimp & Avocado Salads

(Pictured below)

Prep/Total Time: 25 min.

This pretty salad has such authentic flavor, you'll think you're sitting at a beachside cantina in Acapulco.
—Heidi Hall, North St. Paul, Minnesota

1 pound uncooked large shrimp, peeled and deveined
1 small garlic clove, minced
1/2 teaspoon chili powder
1/4 teaspoon salt
1/4 teaspoon ground cumin
2 teaspoons olive oil
5 cups hearts of romaine salad mix
1 cup fresh *or* frozen corn, thawed
1 cup frozen peas, thawed
1/2 cup chopped sweet red pepper
1 medium ripe avocado, peeled and thinly sliced

CILANTRO VINAIGRETTE:
7 tablespoons olive oil
1/4 cup minced fresh cilantro
1/4 cup lime juice
1-1/2 teaspoons sugar
1 small garlic clove, minced
1/2 teaspoon salt
1/4 teaspoon pepper

In a large skillet, cook the shrimp, garlic, chili powder, salt and cumin in oil over medium heat for 3-4 minutes or until shrimp turn pink; set aside.

In a large bowl, combine the romaine, corn, peas and red pepper; divide among four serving plates. Top each with shrimp and avocado. In a small bowl, whisk the vinaigrette ingredients; drizzle over the salads. **Yield:** 4 servings.

Beef Chow Mein

(Pictured below)

Prep/Total Time: 30 min.

My grandma used to make a fabulous chop suey with pork, but I found this recipe that uses ground beef and has a similar flavor. It's quick and tasty—and the leftovers are wonderful, too. —*Ann Nolte, Tampa, Florida*

2 cups uncooked instant rice
1 pound ground beef
1 can (14-1/2 ounces) beef broth
1-1/2 cups chopped celery
1 can (14 ounces) bean sprouts, drained
1 can (8 ounces) sliced water chestnuts, drained
1 jar (4-1/2 ounces) sliced mushrooms, drained
1 jar (2 ounces) pimientos, drained and diced
2 tablespoons soy sauce
1/2 teaspoon ground ginger
2 tablespoons cornstarch
3 tablespoons water

Cook rice according to package directions.

Meanwhile, in a large skillet, cook beef over medium heat until no longer pink; drain. Add the broth, celery, bean sprouts, water chestnuts, mushrooms, pimientos, soy sauce and ginger. Bring to a boil. Reduce heat; cover and simmer for 10 minutes, stirring occasionally.

In a small bowl, combine cornstarch and water until smooth. Gradually stir into skillet. Bring to a boil; cook and stir for 2 minutes or until thickened. Serve with rice. **Yield:** 5 servings.

Ravioli with Creamy Squash Sauce

(Pictured above)

Prep/Total Time: 20 min.

Store-bought ravioli speeds up assembly of this cozy, restaurant-quality dish created by our Test Kitchen. It tastes so good, your family won't notice it's meatless.

1 package (9 ounces) refrigerated cheese ravioli
3 garlic cloves, minced
2 tablespoons butter
1 package (12 ounces) frozen cooked winter squash, thawed
1 package (6 ounces) fresh baby spinach
1 cup heavy whipping cream
1/3 cup vegetable broth
1/4 teaspoon salt
1 cup chopped walnuts, toasted

Cook ravioli according to package directions. Meanwhile, in a Dutch oven, saute garlic in butter for 1 minute. Add squash and spinach; cook 2-3 minutes longer or until spinach is wilted. Stir in cream, broth and salt. Bring to a gentle boil; cook for 6-8 minutes or until slightly thickened.

Drain ravioli; add to squash mixture. Toss to coat. Sprinkle with walnuts. **Yield:** 4 servings.

Barbecue Pork and Penne Skillet

Prep/Total Time: 25 min.

I'm the proud mother of wonderful and active children. Simple, delicious and quick meals like this are perfect for us to enjoy together following our after-school activities, errands and sports.

—*Judy Armstrong, Prairieville, Louisiana*

1 package (16 ounces) penne pasta
1 cup chopped sweet red pepper
3/4 cup chopped onion

1 tablespoon butter
1 tablespoon olive oil
3 garlic cloves, minced
1 carton (18 ounces) refrigerated fully cooked barbecued shredded pork
1 can (14-1/2 ounces) diced tomatoes with mild green chilies, undrained
1/2 cup beef broth
1 teaspoon ground cumin
1 teaspoon pepper
1/4 teaspoon salt
1-1/4 cups shredded cheddar cheese
1/4 cup chopped green onions

Cook pasta according to package directions. Meanwhile, in a large skillet, saute the red pepper and onion in butter and oil until tender. Add garlic; saute 1 minute longer. Stir in the pork, tomatoes, broth, cumin, pepper and salt; heat through.

Drain pasta. Add pasta and cheese to pork mixture. Sprinkle with green onions. **Yield:** 8 servings.

Serve desired amount of pasta. Cool remaining pasta; transfer to freezer containers. Cover and freeze for up to 3 months.

To use frozen pasta: Thaw in the refrigerator. Place in an ungreased shallow microwave-safe dish. Cover and microwave on high until heated through.

Southwestern Vegetables & Rice

(Pictured below)

Prep/Total Time: 20 min.

Short on time? Straight from our Test Kitchen, here's a spicy, satisfying supper that comes together in moments.

1 can (14-1/2 ounces) fire-roasted diced tomatoes, undrained
1 package (12 ounces) frozen vegetarian meat crumbles, thawed
1 package (12 ounces) frozen Southwestern corn, thawed

1 can (10-3/4 ounces) condensed tomato soup, undiluted
1 cup water
1 teaspoon ground cumin
1/4 teaspoon salt
1 cup uncooked instant rice
1 cup (4 ounces) shredded Monterey Jack cheese

In a Dutch oven, combine the first seven ingredients. Bring to a boil. Stir in rice. Remove from the heat; cover and let stand for 5-7 minutes or until rice is tender. Sprinkle with cheese. **Yield:** 4 servings.

Squash Fajitas with Goat Cheese

(Pictured above)

Prep/Total Time: 30 min.

When we visit New Mexico, we always try new and exciting cuisine. The last time we were there, I tried a few traditional foods with new twists, like pumpkin tamales and goat cheese enchiladas. With an abundance of squash and onions from the garden, I wanted to create a new and healthy fajita. This is a great meatless dish.
—Debra Keil, Owasso, Oklahoma

2 pounds yellow summer squash, sliced
1 large sweet onion, chopped
2 tablespoons olive oil
4 garlic cloves, minced
1 teaspoon pepper
1/2 teaspoon salt
8 flour tortillas (8 inches)
1 log (4 ounces) fresh goat cheese, crumbled
2 tablespoons minced fresh parsley

In a large skillet, saute the squash and onion in olive oil until tender. Add the garlic, pepper and salt; cook 1 minute longer.

Spoon onto tortillas. Top with cheese and sprinkle with parsley. Fold in sides. **Yield:** 4 servings.

CHAPTER 14

Delectable Desserts

The cakes, cookies, bars and other treats in this chapter are so tempting and scrumptious that you won't need any other dessert recipes in your recipe file. Whether you need tempting bites for bake sales, potlucks or after dinner, sweets such as rich and chewy German Chocolate Bars and Caramel-Pecan Dream Bars will make you the most popular baker on the block!

We also have desserts on the elegant side, including Double Chocolate Truffles and Almond Chocolate Torte. And, don't forget the cookies...and boy are there some amazing cookie ideas here! From tangy Lemon Shortbreads to comforting Raisin Sweet Potato Cookies, your delightful bites will be the talk of the town. ■

SINFULLY SWEET. Rocky Road Grilled Banana Splits (p. 232).

Fluffy Lemon Squares

(Pictured above)

Prep: 25 min. + chilling

A few handy convenience items hurry along preparation of these bright, lemony bars. They're not only fun to create with children but also so delectable.
—Joyce Speerbrecher, Grafton, Wisconsin

1-1/2 cups crushed vanilla wafers (about 45 wafers)
1/3 cup chopped pecans
6 tablespoons butter, melted
1/2 cup heavy whipping cream
2 packages (3 ounces *each*) lemon gelatin
1-1/4 cups boiling water
1 package (3.4 ounces) instant lemon pudding mix
1 pint lemon sherbet, softened

In a small bowl, combine the wafer crumbs, pecans and butter; set aside 1/4 cup for topping. Press remaining crumb mixture into an ungreased 11-in. x 7-in. dish. Cover and refrigerate for 30 minutes.

Meanwhile, in a small bowl, beat the cream until stiff peaks form; set aside. In a large bowl, dissolve gelatin in boiling water. Add pudding mix; beat on low speed for 2 minutes. Add sherbet; beat on low for 1 minute or until soft-set. Fold in whipped cream.

Spread over the crust; sprinkle with the reserved crumb mixture. Refrigerate for 1 hour or until set. **Yield:** 12 servings.

READING A RECIPE

When measuring nuts for a recipe, if the word "chopped" comes before the ingredient when listed, then chop the ingredient before measuring. If the word "chopped" comes after the ingredient, then chop after measuring.

Over-the-Top Blueberry Bread Pudding

(Pictured below)

Prep: 15 min. + standing **Bake:** 50 min.

Delicious warm or at room temp, this dessert is out of this world. It's a favorite for family celebrations. For a change, top it with fresh mint and sweetened whipped cream.
—Marilyn Haynes, Sylacauga, Alabama

3 eggs
4 cups heavy whipping cream
2 cups sugar
3 teaspoons vanilla extract
2 cups fresh *or* frozen blueberries
1 package (10 to 12 ounces) white baking chips
1 loaf (1 pound) French bread, cut into 1-inch cubes

SAUCE:

1 package (10 to 12 ounces) white baking chips
1 cup heavy whipping cream

In a large bowl, combine the eggs, cream, sugar and vanilla. Stir in the blueberries and baking chips. Stir in the bread cubes; let stand for 15 minutes or until bread is softened.

Transfer to a greased 13-in. x 9-in. baking dish. Bake, uncovered, at 350° for 50-60 minutes or until a knife inserted near the center comes out clean. Let stand for 5 minutes before serving.

For sauce, place baking chips in a small bowl. In a small saucepan, bring cream just to a boil. Pour over baking chips; whisk until smooth. Serve with bread pudding. **Yield:** 12 servings.

Fluted Tiramisu Cake

(Pictured above)

Prep: 20 min. **Bake:** 35 min. + cooling

Melted coffee ice cream adds a decadent depth of flavor to white cake mix. A simple yet impressive dessert, this bundt cake will rise above your highest expectations.
—Carol Gillespie, Chambersburg, Pennsylvania

1 package (18-1/4 ounces) white cake mix
2 cups coffee ice cream, melted
3 eggs
1 tablespoon water
1 teaspoon instant coffee granules
1 can (12 ounces) whipped vanilla frosting
1/2 teaspoon ground cinnamon
1 tablespoon cinnamon-sugar

In a large bowl, beat the cake mix, ice cream and eggs at low speed for 30 seconds. Beat on medium for 2 minutes. Pour into a greased and floured 10-in. fluted tube pan.

Bake at 350° for 35-40 minutes or until a toothpick inserted near the center comes out clean. Cool for 10 minutes before removing from pan to a wire rack to cool completely.

Place water and coffee granules in a large bowl; stir until dissolved. Add frosting and cinnamon; beat until smooth. Frost cake. Sprinkle with cinnamon-sugar. **Yield:** 12 servings.

Cinnamon & Sugar Cake

(Pictured below)

Prep: 25 min. **Bake:** 20 min. + cooling

This winning combination makes everything nice with sugar and spice. You'd never guess it came from a box.
—Maiah Albi, Carlsbad, California

1 package (18-1/4 ounces) white cake mix
1 cup 2% milk
1/2 cup sour cream
6 tablespoons butter, melted
3 eggs
2-1/2 teaspoons ground cinnamon
1-1/2 teaspoons vanilla extract
FROSTING:
1 cup butter, softened
5 cups confectioners' sugar
2 tablespoons 2% milk
1 teaspoon ground cinnamon
1 teaspoon vanilla extract
1 tablespoon cinnamon-sugar

In a large bowl, combine the first seven ingredients; beat on low speed for 30 seconds. Beat on medium for 2 minutes. Transfer to two greased and floured 9-in. round baking pans.

Bake at 350° for 20-25 minutes or until a toothpick inserted near the center comes out clean. Cool for 10 minutes before removing from pans to wire racks to cool completely.

In a large bowl, beat the butter until fluffy. Add the confectioners' sugar, milk, cinnamon and extract; beat until smooth. Spread frosting between layers and over top and sides of cake. Sprinkle with cinnamon-sugar. Store in the refrigerator. **Yield:** 12 servings.

Waffle Cookies

(Pictured above)

Prep: 15 min. **Bake:** 5 min./batch + cooling

Making cookies was never so much fun! Kids will love the flavor and novelty, while you appreciate their smiles. (And, of course, a cookie or two!)
—Susan Westerfield, Albuquerque, New Mexico

1/2 cup packed brown sugar
1/4 cup sugar
1/2 cup butter, melted
1 egg
1 teaspoon vanilla extract
1 cup plus 2 tablespoons all-purpose flour
1/2 teaspoon salt
1/4 teaspoon baking soda
1/2 cup flaked coconut
1/2 cup chopped cashews
1/2 cup miniature semisweet chocolate chips
Confectioners' sugar, optional

In a large bowl, combine the sugars, butter, egg and vanilla. Combine the flour, salt and baking soda; gradually add to sugar mixture. Stir in the coconut, cashews and chocolate chips.

Drop batter by tablespoonfuls 1 in. apart onto a preheated waffle iron coated with cooking spray. Bake for 1-2 minutes or until golden brown. Carefully remove to wire racks; cool completely. Dust with confectioners' sugar if desired. **Yield:** 3 dozen.

Chocolate Chip Cheesecake

(Pictured above)

Prep: 20 min. + chilling

A neighbor gave me this microwave cheesecake recipe several years ago and jokingly said it serves one.
—Susan Visser, Champaign, Illinois

3/4 cup all-purpose flour
3/4 cup graham cracker crumbs
6 tablespoons sugar
3 tablespoons baking cocoa
1/2 cup butter, melted
FILLING:
1 package (8 ounces) cream cheese, softened
2 tablespoons sugar
2 tablespoons 2% milk
1 egg, beaten
1/2 cup plus 2 tablespoons miniature semisweet chocolate chips, *divided*

In a large bowl, combine the flour, cracker crumbs, sugar and cocoa; stir in butter. Set aside 3/4 cup for topping. Press remaining mixture into a greased 9-in. microwave-safe pie plate. Microwave, uncovered, on high for 1-2 minutes or until set.

In a small bowl, beat the cream cheese, sugar and milk until smooth. Add egg; beat on low speed just until combined. Stir in 1/2 cup chocolate chips. Spread over crust. Sprinkle with the reserved crumb mixture and remaining chocolate chips.

Microwave, uncovered, on high for 3-4 minutes or until a thermometer inserted near the center reads 160°. Cool on a wire rack for 1 hour. Refrigerate until chilled. Let stand at room temperature for 10 minutes before cutting. **Yield:** 8 servings.

Editor's Note: This recipe was tested in a 1,100-watt microwave.

Cranberry-Pear Crisp

(Pictured below)

Prep: 20 min. **Bake:** 30 min. + standing

Delicately spiced fruits are topped with scrumptious crunch —a clever use of oatmeal cookie mix.
—Toni Pendley, Somerset, Kentucky

3 cans (15-1/4 ounces *each*) sliced pears, drained
1 cup fresh *or* frozen cranberries, thawed
1/4 cup sugar
3 tablespoons all-purpose flour
1/2 teaspoon ground cinnamon
1/4 teaspoon ground ginger
1 package (17-1/2 ounces) oatmeal cookie mix
Vanilla ice cream

In a large bowl, combine pears and cranberries. Combine the sugar, flour, cinnamon and ginger; sprinkle over pear mixture and toss to coat. Transfer to a greased 11-in. x 7-in. baking dish.

Prepare cookie mix batter according to package directions. Sprinkle over fruit mixture. Bake at 375° for 30-35 minutes or until fruit is bubbly and topping is golden brown. Serve warm with ice cream. **Yield:** 9 servings.

Autumn Harvest Cobbler

(Pictured above)

Prep: 35 min. **Bake:** 15 min.

Saying goodbye to summer peach crisp doesn't have to be sorrowful when there's a delicious fall cobbler waiting to comfort you. *—Nancy Foust, Stoneboro, Pennsylvania*

1/2 cup sugar
1 teaspoon ground cinnamon
1/2 teaspoon salt
1/2 teaspoon ground nutmeg
2 cups cold water, *divided*
6 large tart apples, peeled and thinly sliced
1 cup golden raisins
1 cup dried apricots, halved
1 tablespoon lemon juice
2 tablespoons cornstarch

TOPPING:

2 cups biscuit/baking mix
3/4 cup 2% milk
1 tablespoon coarse sugar
2 teaspoons grated lemon peel
Whipped cream

In a large saucepan, combine the sugar, cinnamon, salt, nutmeg and 1-3/4 cups water. Bring to a boil. Stir in the apples, raisins, apricots and lemon juice. Return to a boil. Reduce heat; simmer, uncovered, for 10 minutes, stirring occasionally.

Combine the cornstarch and remaining water until smooth. Stir into pan. Bring to a boil; cook and stir for 2 minutes or until thickened. Transfer to a greased 13-in. x 9-in. baking dish.

In a small bowl, combine biscuit mix and milk just until blended. Drop by tablespoonfuls onto hot apple mixture. Sprinkle with coarse sugar and lemon peel.

Bake at 400° for 15-20 minutes or until topping is golden brown. Serve warm with whipped cream. **Yield:** 12 servings.

Double Chocolate Truffles

(Pictured above)

Prep: 30 min. + chilling

Milk chocolate chips enhance the bittersweet flavor of these decadent, melt-in-your-mouth treats made in our Test Kitchen. Tie up a few in pretty cellophane and ribbons for an easy, elegant last-minute holiday gift.

1 cup 60% cacao bittersweet chocolate baking chips
3/4 cup whipped topping
1/4 teaspoon ground cinnamon
1 cup milk chocolate chips
1 teaspoon shortening
Optional toppings: crushed peppermint candies, sprinkles and chopped nuts

In a small saucepan, melt bittersweet chips over low heat. Transfer to a bowl; cool to lukewarm, about 7 minutes.

Beat in whipped topping and cinnamon. Place in the freezer for 15 minutes or until firm enough to form into balls. Shape mixture into 1-in. balls.

In a microwave, melt the milk chocolate chips and shortening; stir until smooth. Dip truffles in chocolate and place on waxed paper-lined baking sheets. Immediately sprinkle with toppings of your choice. Refrigerate until firm. Store in an airtight container in the refrigerator. **Yield:** 1-1/2 dozen.

S'more-Dipped Cherries

(Pictured at left)

Prep: 25 min. + chilling

Dress up any Christmas cookie tray with these cute bites. Dark chocolate chips plus four other ingredients are all you'll need! —*Aysha Schurman, Ammon, Idaho*

2 jars (10 ounces *each*) maraschino cherries with stems
1-1/2 cups marshmallow creme
2/3 cup graham cracker crumbs
1-1/2 cups dark chocolate chips
2-1/4 teaspoons shortening

Drain the cherries, reserving 1/3 cup juice. Pat cherries dry with paper towels. Pour reserved juice into a small saucepan; stir in marshmallow creme. Cook and stir over low heat until smooth. Remove from the heat.

Place cracker crumbs in a shallow bowl. Coat each cherry with marshmallow creme mixture; allow excess to drip off. Dip in the cracker crumbs. Place on waxed paper-lined baking sheets; cover and refrigerate for at least 15 minutes.

In a microwave, melt chocolate chips and shortening; stir until smooth. Partially dip cherries into chocolate; allow excess to drip off. Return to baking sheets; refrigerate until set. **Yield:** 5 dozen.

Best Lime Tart

Prep: 35 min. **Bake:** 15 min. + chilling

This treat is the perfect balance between tart and sweet, and the almonds in the crust are just wonderful. Enjoy! —*Charis O'Connell, Mohnton, Pennsylvania*

1-1/4 cups graham cracker crumbs
5 tablespoons butter, melted
1/4 cup ground almonds
3 tablespoons sugar
FILLING:
4 egg yolks
1 can (14 ounces) sweetened condensed milk
1/2 cup lime juice
2 teaspoons grated lime peel
TOPPING:
1/2 cup heavy whipping cream
1 tablespoon sugar
1/2 cup sour cream
1 teaspoon grated lime peel
Fresh raspberries and lime wedges

Combine crumbs, butter, almonds and sugar. Press onto bottom and up sides of a greased 9-in. tart pan. Bake at 325° for 15-18 minutes or until edges are lightly browned.

In a large bowl, whisk the egg yolks, milk, lime juice and peel. Pour over crust. Bake for 12-14 minutes or until center is almost set. Cool on a wire rack. Refrigerate for at least 2 hours.

In a large bowl, beat cream until it begins to thicken. Add sugar; beat until stiff peaks form. Fold in sour cream and grated lime peel. Spread over tart. Garnish with raspberries and lime wedges. **Yield:** 12 servings.

Raisin Sweet Potato Cookies

(Pictured above)

Prep: 25 min. **Bake:** 10 min./batch

Cozy up to the fire with a plate of these satisfyingly sweet cookies that taste like the comforts of home. Serve them with a hot chai tea or cold milk, and no one will be able to resist them. —Jacque Sue Meyer, Lohman, Missouri

1 cup butter, softened
1 cup sugar
1 egg
1 cup mashed sweet potato
1 teaspoon vanilla extract
2 cups all-purpose flour
1 teaspoon baking powder
1 teaspoon ground cinnamon
1/2 teaspoon baking soda
1/2 teaspoon salt
1/2 teaspoon ground allspice
1 cup chopped pecans
1 cup raisins

In a large bowl, cream butter and sugar until light and fluffy. Beat in the egg, sweet potato and vanilla. Combine the flour, baking powder, cinnamon, baking soda, salt and allspice; gradually add to creamed mixture and mix well. Fold in pecans and raisins.

Drop by tablespoonfuls 1 in. apart onto ungreased baking sheets. Bake at 375° for 10-12 minutes or until the edges begin to brown. Cool for 1 minute before removing to wire racks. Store in an airtight container. **Yield:** 5 dozen.

Lemon & Rosemary Shortbread Cookies

(Pictured below)

Prep: 25 min. + freezing **Bake:** 10 min./batch

Lemon and rosemary make these luscious treats a sweet surprise to share with friends and family.
—Malorie Harris, Wildomar, California

1 cup butter, softened
1/2 cup sugar
3 tablespoons lemon juice
1 teaspoon grated lemon peel
1/2 teaspoon vanilla extract
2 cups all-purpose flour
4-1/2 teaspoons minced fresh rosemary
1/4 teaspoon salt

In a large bowl, cream butter and sugar until light and fluffy. Beat in the lemon juice, peel and vanilla. Combine the flour, rosemary and salt; gradually add to creamed mixture and mix well.

Shape into two 12-in. rolls; wrap each in plastic wrap. Freeze for 30 minutes or until firm. Cut into 1/4-in. slices. Place 2 in. apart on ungreased baking sheets. Bake at 350° for 8-10 minutes or until edges begin to brown. Cool for 2 minutes before removing from pans to wire racks. Store in an airtight container. **Yield:** 8 dozen.

Chocolate Cannoli Cake Roll

(Pictured below)

Prep: 20 min. + chilling **Bake:** 15 min. + cooling

Creamy ricotta cheese filling with a hint of cinnamon rolls up beautifully in this fluffy chocolate cake.
—Tammy Rex, New Tripoli, Pennsylvania

1-3/4 cups chocolate cake mix
1/3 cup water
2 tablespoons canola oil
3 eggs

FILLING:

2 cups ricotta cheese
1 package (8 ounces) cream cheese, softened
1 cup confectioners' sugar
1 teaspoon vanilla extract
1/2 teaspoon ground cinnamon
1/2 cup miniature semisweet chocolate chips

Line a greased 15-in. x 10-in. x 1-in. baking pan with waxed paper and grease the paper; set aside.

In a large bowl, combine the cake mix, water, oil and eggs; beat on low speed for 30 seconds. Beat on medium for 2 minutes. Pour into prepared pan.

Bake at 350° for 12-14 minutes or until cake springs back when lightly touched. Cool for 5 minutes. Invert onto a kitchen towel dusted with confectioners' sugar. Gently peel off waxed paper. Roll up cake in the towel jelly-roll style, starting with a short side. Cool completely on a wire rack.

In a small bowl, beat the cheeses, confectioners' sugar, vanilla and cinnamon until smooth; stir in chips. Unroll cake; spread filling over cake to within 1/2 in. of edges. Roll up again. Place seam side down on a serving platter. Refrigerate for 2 hours before serving. **Yield:** 12 servings.

German Chocolate Bars

(Pictured above)

Prep: 20 min. **Bake:** 25 min. + cooling

Sweet, salty, chewy and sensational, these moist bars are pretty, very rich and finger-lickin' good.
—Margaret Wilson, Sun City, California

1 package (18-1/4 ounces) German chocolate cake mix
1/2 cup coarsely crushed pretzels
1 egg, lightly beaten
1/2 cup butter, melted

FILLING:

1/4 cup sugar
2 eggs
1 cup dark corn syrup
2-1/4 cups flaked coconut
1 cup butterscotch chips
1 cup semisweet chocolate chips
1 cup chopped pecans

In a large bowl, combine the cake mix, pretzels, egg and butter. Press into a greased 13-in. x 9-in. baking pan. Bake at 350° for 12-15 minutes or until edges are lightly browned. Cool on a wire rack.

In a large bowl, beat the sugar, eggs and corn syrup until blended. Fold in coconut, chips and pecans; pour over crust. Bake for 25-35 minutes or until edges are brown and center is almost set. Cool on a wire rack. Cut into bars. **Yield:** 4 dozen.

Kahlua Fudge

Prep: 20 min. + chilling

Here's a tasty variation on the popular sweet. The five-ingredient recipe makes serving up treats easy and scrumptious. —Laura Hanks, Harleysville, Pennsylvania

1 teaspoon plus 2 tablespoons butter, *divided*
24 ounces Baker's white baking chocolate, coarsely chopped
1 cup sweetened condensed milk
1/2 cup chopped pecans, toasted
1/3 cup Kahlua (coffee liqueur)

Line a 9-in. square pan with foil and grease the foil with 1 teaspoon butter; set aside. In a large saucepan over low heat, cook and stir white chocolate until melted. Add milk and remaining butter; stir until blended. Remove from the heat; stir in pecans and Kahlua.

Pour into prepared pan. Cover and refrigerate for 2 hours or until firm.

Using foil, lift fudge out of pan. Gently peel off foil; cut the fudge into 1-in. squares. **Yield:** about 2-1/2 pounds.

Deep-Fried Candy Bars on a Stick

(Pictured below)

Prep: 20 min. **Cook:** 5 min./batch

Why wait in line for this state fair novelty when you can satisfy your curious taste buds in your very own home? Our Test Kitchen knows you'll love these!

1-1/2 cups all-purpose flour
4-1/2 teaspoons baking powder
1 tablespoon sugar
1 tablespoon brown sugar
1/8 teaspoon salt
1/8 teaspoon ground cinnamon
1 egg
1/2 cup water
1/2 cup 2% milk
1/4 teaspoon vanilla extract
24 fun-size Snickers *and/or* Milky Way candy bars, frozen
Oil for deep-fat frying
Wooden skewers
Confectioners' sugar, optional

In a small bowl, combine the first six ingredients. In another bowl, whisk the egg, water, milk and vanilla; add to dry ingredients just until moistened. Dip candy bars into batter.

In an electric skillet or deep fryer, heat oil to 375°. Drop candy bars, a few at a time, into hot oil. Fry until golden brown, about 30 seconds on each side. Drain on paper towels. Insert skewers into the bars; dust with confectioners' sugar if desired. **Yield:** 2 dozen.

Caramel-Pecan Dream Bars

(Pictured above)

Prep: 15 min. **Bake:** 20 min. + cooling

These ooey-gooey cake bars that pull ever so gently from the pan and hold a firm cut are a baker's and sweet lover's dream come true. —*Cay Keppers, Nisswa, Minnesota*

1 package (18-1/4 ounces) yellow cake mix
1/2 cup butter, softened
1 egg

FILLING:
1 can (14 ounces) sweetened condensed milk
1 egg
1 teaspoon vanilla extract
1 cup chopped pecans
1/2 cup brickle toffee bits

In a large bowl, beat the cake mix, butter and egg until crumbly. Press onto the bottom of a greased 13-in. x 9-in. baking pan.

In a small bowl, beat the milk, egg and vanilla until combined. Stir in the pecans and toffee bits. Pour over the crust.

Bake at 350° for 20-25 minutes or until golden brown. Cool on a wire rack. Cut into bars. **Yield:** 2 dozen.

Very Berry Bruschetta

(Pictured above)

Prep/Total Time: 25 min.

Watch out, Mr. Bagel, there's more than one way to spread strawberry cream cheese. You could also try the tasty topping on toast and waffles, too.
—Debbie Limas, North Andover, Massachusetts

1 carton (8 ounces) spreadable strawberry cream cheese
6 tablespoons orange juice
1 teaspoon grated orange peel
2 cups sliced fresh strawberries
1 cup *each* fresh blueberries, blackberries and raspberries
6 slices pound cake
Whipped cream in a can

In a small bowl, beat the cream cheese, orange juice and peel until blended. In a large bowl, combine the berries. Place a cake slice on each of six dessert plates; top with cream cheese mixture and berries. Garnish with whipped cream. **Yield:** 6 servings.

EASY-ACCESS JUICE

When a recipe calls for a small amount of juice, it's simple to make from frozen concentrate, since the ratio to reconstitute the juice is 3 parts water to 1 part concentrate. Plus, the concentrate doesn't freeze hard, so it's easy to scoop out.

Chocolate Cookie Cheesecake

(Pictured below)

Prep: 15 min. **Bake:** 1 hour + chilling

I used to think cheesecake sounded intimidating, but since I started making them I can't stop! This simple but special cookie-topped version will make your family feel fussed over. Seconds, anyone?
—Rose Yoder, Middlebury, Indiana

1-1/2 cups crushed cream-filled chocolate sandwich cookies (about 20 cookies)
2 tablespoons butter, melted
3 packages (8 ounces *each*) cream cheese, softened
1 cup sugar
1 cup (8 ounces) sour cream
1/4 cup all-purpose flour
2 teaspoons vanilla extract
1/4 teaspoon salt
3 eggs, lightly beaten
15 coarsely chopped cream-filled chocolate sandwich cookies (about 2-1/4 cups), *divided*

In a large bowl, combine crushed cookies and butter. Press onto the bottom and 1 in. up the sides of a greased 9-in. springform pan; set aside.

In a large bowl, beat cream cheese and sugar until smooth. Beat in the sour cream, flour, vanilla and salt. Add eggs; beat on low speed just until combined. Fold in 3/4 cup chopped cookies. Pour into crust. Top with remaining chopped cookies.

Place on a baking sheet. Bake at 325° for 60-65 minutes or until center is almost set. Cool on a wire rack for 10 minutes. Carefully run a knife around the edge of pan to loosen; cool 1 hour longer. Refrigerate overnight. Remove sides of pan. **Yield:** 12 servings.

Almond Chocolate Torte

(Pictured above)

Prep: 30 min. **Bake:** 35 min. + chilling

I've been making this torte since the 1970s, and it's often requested by family and friends. It's popular not only for the wonderful eye appeal and taste, but for the short time it takes to create. —Elaine Gairy, Chester, Maryland

1 package (18-1/4 ounces) chocolate cake mix
12 ounces German sweet chocolate, chopped
3/4 cup butter, cubed
1/2 cup chopped almonds, toasted
1 carton (8 ounces) frozen whipped topping, thawed
Chocolate curls

Prepare and bake cake according to package directions, using two greased and floured 9-in. round baking pans. Cool for 10 minutes before removing from pans to wire racks to cool completely.

Meanwhile, in a small saucepan, melt chocolate and butter; stir until smooth. Stir in almonds (mixture will be thin); set aside.

Split each cake into two horizontal layers. Place the bottom layer on a serving plate; spread with half of the chocolate mixture. Top with second cake layer; spread with half of the whipped topping. Repeat layers. Sprinkle with chocolate curls. Chill at least 1 hour before serving. Refrigerate leftovers. **Yield:** 12 servings.

Asti & Strawberries Dessert

(Pictured below)

Prep: 10 min. + chilling

Remember this luscious dessert next time you're hosting a special supper. The combination of sweetened strawberries and dark chocolate mousse is simply outstanding. —Sherry Thompson, Seneca, South Carolina

1 envelope unflavored gelatin
3/4 cup cold Asti Spumante, *divided*
1/2 cup dark chocolate chips
1 package (3 ounces) cream cheese, softened
1-1/2 cups whipped topping, *divided*
2-1/2 cups sliced fresh strawberries
1 tablespoon sugar
1/4 teaspoon vanilla extract
4 pizzelle cookies
Additional whipped topping

In a small microwave-safe bowl, sprinkle gelatin over 1/2 cup Asti Spumante. Let stand for 1 minute. Microwave on high for 30 seconds; stir until gelatin is dissolved. In a microwave, melt chocolate chips; set aside to cool.

In a large bowl, beat cream cheese until smooth. Add the gelatin mixture, melted chocolate and 2/3 cup whipped topping. Beat until combined; fold in the remaining whipped topping. Cover and refrigerate for 30 minutes.

Meanwhile, in another bowl, combine strawberries, sugar, vanilla and remaining Asti Spumante. Beat the mousse until light and fluffy. Serve with strawberries, cookies and the additional whipped topping. **Yield:** 4 servings.

Triple-Chocolate Cake with Raspberry Sauce

(Pictured below)

Prep: 20 min. **Bake:** 1 hour + cooling

Chocolate lovers, brace yourselves. This cocoa creation and its saucy accompaniment make a heavenly combo.
—Jenny Staniec, Oak Grove, Minnesota

- **1 package (18-1/4 ounces) chocolate cake mix**
- **1 package (3.4 ounces) instant vanilla pudding mix**
- **1 package (3.4 ounces) instant chocolate pudding mix**
- **4 eggs**
- **1-1/2 cups water**
- **1/2 cup canola oil**
- **1 cup (6 ounces) semisweet chocolate chips**

RASPBERRY SAUCE:

- **1 cup water**
- **2 packages (10 ounces *each*) frozen sweetened raspberries, thawed**
- **1 tablespoon sugar**
- **3 tablespoons cornstarch**
- **2 tablespoons lemon juice**

Confectioners' sugar

In a large bowl, combine the cake mix, pudding mixes, eggs, water and oil; beat on low speed for 30 seconds. Beat on medium for 2 minutes. Fold in chocolate chips.

Pour into a well-greased 10-in. fluted tube pan. Bake at 325° for 60-65 minutes or until a toothpick inserted near center comes out clean. Cool for 10 minutes before removing from pan to a wire rack to cool completely.

Meanwhile, place the water, raspberries and sugar in a blender; cover and process until well blended. In a small saucepan, combine cornstarch and lemon juice; stir in raspberry puree. Bring to a boil. Cook and stir for 2 minutes or until thickened. Refrigerate until serving.

Dust cake with confectioners' sugar. Serve with sauce. **Yield:** 12 servings (2-2/3 cups sauce).

Strawberry Ginger Tart

(Pictured above)

Prep: 25 min. **Bake:** 20 min. + chilling

This tart heralds lazy summer days when strawberries are at their sweetest and juiciest. It's entirely customizable, too. You can substitute any refrigerated cookie dough for the crust. *—Chantal Bourbon, Montreal, Quebec*

- **1/4 cup butter, softened**
- **2/3 cup sugar**
- **1 egg white**
- **1 tablespoon minced fresh gingerroot**
- **1-1/4 cups all-purpose flour**
- **1/4 teaspoon baking soda**
- **1/4 teaspoon salt**
- **1 cup milk chocolate chips**

FILLING:

- **1 package (8 ounces) reduced-fat cream cheese**
- **3 tablespoons confectioners' sugar**
- **2 tablespoons 2% milk**
- **4 cups halved fresh strawberries**

GLAZE:

- **1/4 cup seedless strawberry jam**
- **1 tablespoon crystallized ginger, finely chopped**

In a large bowl, cream butter and sugar until light and fluffy. Beat in egg white and ginger. Combine the flour, baking soda and salt; gradually add to creamed mixture and mix well. Press onto the bottom and up the sides of a greased 9-in. tart pan.

Bake at 350° for 12-15 minutes or until edges are lightly browned. Sprinkle with chips. Bake 4-5 minutes longer or until chocolate is melted; spread over crust. Cool on a wire rack.

In a small bowl, beat the cream cheese, confectioners' sugar and milk until smooth; spread over chocolate. Top with the strawberries. In a small microwave-safe bowl, microwave the jam in 10-second intervals until melted; brush over strawberries. Sprinkle with ginger. Refrigerate for at least 2 hours before serving. **Yield:** 12 servings.

Lemon Shortbreads

(Pictured below)

Prep: 25 min. + chilling
Bake: 10 min./batch + cooling

Every year my mom and I collect cookie recipes we want to try and then get together in early December for an afternoon of baking. These no-fail lemon cookies have become an annual tradition. They make a wonderful holiday gift from our kitchen.
—Kristen Johnson, Waukesha, Wisconsin

1 cup butter, softened
1/2 cup confectioners' sugar
1/4 cup sugar
1 teaspoon grated lemon peel
2 cups all-purpose flour
1 teaspoon salt
GLAZE:
2 cups confectioners' sugar
3 tablespoons lemon juice
2 teaspoons grated lemon peel
Yellow, green *or* red colored sugar

In a large bowl, cream butter and sugars until light and fluffy. Beat in lemon peel. Combine the flour and salt; gradually add to creamed mixture and mix well.

Divide dough in half. Shape each into a ball, then flatten into a disk. Wrap in plastic wrap and refrigerate for 30 minutes.

Let the dough stand at room temperature for 5-10 minutes to soften. Roll out each portion between two sheets of waxed paper to 1/4-in. thickness. Cut with a floured 1-1/2-in. diamond-shaped cookie cutter. Place 1 in. apart on lightly greased baking sheets.

Bake at 325° for 6-8 minutes or until bottoms of cookies are lightly browned. Remove to wire racks so they can cool completely.

Combine the confectioners' sugar, lemon juice and peel; spread over cookies. Sprinkle with colored sugar. **Yield:** 4 dozen.

Hugs 'n' Kisses Brownie

(Pictured above)

Prep: 20 min. **Bake:** 35 min. + cooling

When I needed a dessert in a hurry, I dressed up a brownie mix and came up with this impressive treat.
—Kristi Van Batavia, Kansas City, Missouri

1 package fudge brownie mix (8-inch square pan size)
1 egg
1/4 cup canola oil
1/4 cup water
1-1/2 cups vanilla *or* white chips, *divided*
14 to 16 milk chocolate kisses
14 to 16 striped chocolate kisses
1-1/2 teaspoons shortening

In a large bowl, stir brownie mix, egg, oil and water until well blended. Fold in 1 cup vanilla chips.

Pour into a greased 9-in. heart-shaped or round springform pan. Bake at 350° for 35-40 minutes or until a toothpick inserted 2 in. from the edge of pan comes out clean.

Let stand for 10 minutes; alternate milk chocolate and striped kisses around edge of the pan with points toward center. Melt shortening and remaining chips; stir until smooth. Drizzle over brownie. Cool completely. Remove sides of springform pan before cutting. **Yield:** 12 servings.

CUTTING BROWNIES

If you have trouble cutting baked items like sheet cakes or brownies, because too much of the goodies sticks to the knife, try a pizza cutter! It rolls through brownies and other baked goods smoothly and simply, cutting clean wedges or squares.

Lemon Cream Cake

(Pictured above)

Prep: 20 min. **Bake:** 25 min. + cooling

Drizzling limoncello liqueur over the layers before frosting adds a puckery punch to this refreshing confection.
—Amy Frederick, Island City, Oregon

1 package (18-1/4 ounces) yellow cake mix
1-1/4 cups water
3 eggs
1/3 cup canola oil
1 teaspoon lemon extract
1 carton (8 ounces) Mascarpone cheese
1 cup heavy whipping cream
1/2 cup lemon curd
1/4 cup limoncello, optional
Fresh raspberries and lemon peel strips

In a large bowl, combine the cake mix, water, eggs, oil and extract; beat on low speed for 30 seconds. Beat on medium for 2 minutes. Pour into two greased and floured 9-in. round baking pans.

Bake at 350° for 22-26 minutes or until a toothpick inserted near the center comes out clean. Cool for 10 minutes before removing from pans to wire racks to cool completely.

In a small bowl, beat the cheese, cream and lemon curd until smooth. Place one cake layer on a serving plate. Drizzle with half the limoncello if desired; spread with half the cheese mixture. Repeat layers. Garnish with raspberries and lemon peel. Store in the refrigerator. **Yield:** 12 servings.

German Chocolate Thumbprint Cookies

(Pictured below)

Prep: 45 min. + chilling **Bake:** 10 min./batch

I love anything with the German chocolate combination of chocolate, pecans and coconut. The taste is most often associated with cake —until now!
—Kathleen Morrow, Hubbard, Ohio

1 cup sugar
1 cup evaporated milk
1/2 cup butter, cubed
3 egg yolks
1-1/2 cups flaked coconut
1-1/2 cups chopped pecans
1 teaspoon vanilla extract
1 package (18-1/4 ounces) German chocolate cake mix
1/2 cup all-purpose flour
1/3 cup butter, melted

In a large heavy saucepan, combine the sugar, milk, butter and egg yolks. Cook and stir over medium-low heat until mixture is thickened and coats the back of a spoon. Remove from the heat. Stir in coconut, pecans and vanilla. Set aside 1-1/4 cups for topping.

In a large bowl, combine the cake mix, flour, melted butter and remaining coconut mixture. Cover and refrigerate for at least 1 hour.

Shape dough into 1-in. balls. Place 2 in. apart on greased baking sheets. Using the end of a wooden spoon handle, make an indentation in the center of each cookie. Fill each cookie with a teaspoonful of reserved topping.

Bake at 350° for 10-12 minutes or until set. Let stand for 2 minutes before removing to wire racks to cool. Store in an airtight container. **Yield:** 5 dozen.

Chocolate-Peanut Cheesecake Bars

(Pictured above)

Prep: 25 min. **Bake:** 15 min. + chilling

You won't hear any complaints about these rich bars layered with a can't-go-wrong combination of flavors.
—Diane Nemitz, Ludington, Michigan

1 package (17-1/2 ounces) peanut butter cookie mix
1/4 cup butter, melted
1 cup chopped salted peanuts
2 packages (8 ounces *each*) cream cheese, softened
1 cup sugar
2 eggs, beaten
1 teaspoon vanilla extract
GANACHE:
4 ounces semisweet chocolate, chopped
1/2 cup heavy whipping cream

In a large bowl combine the cookie mix and butter; stir in peanuts. Press onto the bottom of a greased 13-in. x 9-in. baking pan. Bake at 350° for 10-12 minutes or until edges are lightly browned.

Meanwhile, in a large bowl, beat cream cheese and sugar until smooth. Add eggs and vanilla; beat on low speed just until combined. Pour over crust.

Bake for 15-20 minutes or until the center is almost set. Cool on a wire rack for 1 hour. Refrigerate for at least 2 hours.

Place chocolate in a small bowl. In a small saucepan, bring cream just to a boil. Pour over chocolate; whisk until smooth. Cool, stirring occasionally, to room temperature or until ganache reaches a spreading consistency, about 40 minutes. Spread over top. Refrigerate until firm. Cut into bars. Refrigerate leftovers. **Yield:** 2 dozen.

Citrus Pound Cake

(Pictured below)

Prep: 20 min. **Bake:** 55 min. + cooling

Moist and tender, this gorgeous classic has a refreshing taste of sunshine.
—Lisa Varner, Charleston, South Carolina

1 cup butter, softened
2 cups sugar
6 eggs
2 teaspoons vanilla extract
1 teaspoon grated lemon peel
1 teaspoon grated orange peel
3 cups all-purpose flour
1 teaspoon baking powder
1/2 teaspoon salt
1/2 teaspoon baking soda
1 cup (8 ounces) lemon yogurt
GLAZE:
1-1/2 cups confectioners' sugar
2 to 3 tablespoons lemon juice
2 tablespoons finely chopped candied lemon peel
2 tablespoons finely chopped candied orange peel

In a large bowl, cream butter and sugar until light and fluffy, about 5 minutes. Add eggs, one at a time, beating well after each addition. Beat in the vanilla, lemon peel and orange peel. Combine the flour, baking powder, salt and baking soda; add to creamed mixture alternately with yogurt. Beat just until combined.

Transfer to a greased and floured 10-in. fluted tube pan. Bake at 325° for 55-65 minutes or until a toothpick inserted near the center comes out clean. Cool for 10 minutes before removing from pan to a wire rack to cool completely.

In a small bowl, combine the confectioners' sugar and enough lemon juice to achieve desired consistency. Drizzle over cake. Sprinkle with candied lemon and orange peel. **Yield:** 12 servings.

Pumpkin Streusel Cupcakes

(Pictured below)

Prep: 25 min. **Bake:** 20 min. + cooling

A delicious crumb filling is the center of attention inside these yummy confections that taste like pumpkin bread.
—Donna Gish, Blue Springs, Missouri

1 package (18-1/4 ounces) spice cake mix
1-1/4 cups water
3 eggs
1/2 cup canned pumpkin
STREUSEL:
1/2 cup packed brown sugar
1/2 teaspoon ground cinnamon
1 tablespoon butter
FROSTING:
1 package (8 ounces) cream cheese, softened
2 tablespoons butter
2 cups confectioners' sugar
1/2 teaspoon vanilla extract

In a large bowl, combine the cake mix, water, eggs and pumpkin. Beat on low speed just until moistened. Beat on medium for 2 minutes.

In a small bowl, combine brown sugar and cinnamon; cut in butter until crumbly. Fill paper-lined muffin cups one-fourth full with batter. Drop streusel by heaping teaspoonfuls into center of each cupcake. Cover with remaining batter.

Bake at 350° for 18-20 minutes or until a toothpick inserted in the cake portion comes out clean. Cool for 10 minutes before removing from pans to wire racks to cool completely.

In a small bowl, beat cream cheese and butter until fluffy. Add the confectioners' sugar and vanilla; beat until smooth. Frost cupcakes. Store in the refrigerator. **Yield:** 2 dozen.

Rocky Road Grilled Banana Splits

(Pictured above)

Prep/Total Time: 20 min.

There's no wrong turn when you travel down this rocky road. Toasty-warm bananas filled with gooey goodness and topped with heaping scoops of (pause for drool) creamy perfection are a new cookout must-have.
—Loretta Ouellette, Pompano Beach, Florida

4 medium firm bananas, unpeeled
1 dark chocolate candy bar with almonds (3-1/2 ounces)
3/4 cup miniature marshmallows, *divided*
1 quart rocky road ice cream
Whipped cream in a can

Place each banana on a 12-in. square of foil; crimp and shape foil around bananas so they sit flat.

Cut each banana lengthwise about 1/2 in. deep, leaving 1/2 in. uncut at both ends. Gently pull each banana peel open, forming a pocket. Finely chop half of the candy bar. Fill pockets with chopped chocolate and 1/2 cup marshmallows.

Grill bananas, covered, over medium heat for 8-10 minutes or until marshmallows are melted and golden brown. Transfer each banana to a serving plate; top with scoops of ice cream. Break remaining chocolate into pieces. Sprinkle chocolate pieces and remaining marshmallows over tops. Garnish with whipped cream. **Yield:** 4 servings.

Coconut Citrus Bars

(Pictured below)

Prep: 30 min. **Bake:** 20 min. + cooling

Sweet oranges are the key to these amazing bars with loads of orange flavor in every bite. The unique crust and vibrant zing makes them unlike regular lemon bars.
—Heather Rotunda, St. Cloud, Minnesota

3/4 cup butter, softened
1/3 cup confectioners' sugar
1-1/2 cups all-purpose flour
1/2 cup crisp rice cereal
FILLING:
4 eggs
1-1/2 cups sugar
1 cup flaked coconut
1/3 cup orange juice
1/4 cup lemon juice
2 tablespoons lime juice
2 tablespoons all-purpose flour
3 teaspoons grated orange peel
2 teaspoons grated lemon peel
1-1/2 teaspoons grated lime peel
Confectioners' sugar

In a small bowl, cream butter and confectioners' sugar until light and fluffy; gradually beat in flour until crumbly. Stir in cereal. Press into a greased 13-in. x 9-in. baking pan. Bake at 350° for 18-22 minutes or until lightly browned.

Meanwhile, in a large bowl, beat the eggs, sugar, coconut, juices, flour and peels until frothy. Pour over the hot crust. Bake for 18-22 minutes or until lightly browned. Cool on a wire rack. Dust with confectioners' sugar; cut into bars. Store in the refrigerator. **Yield:** 2 dozen.

Pumpkin Walnut Squares

(Pictured above)

Prep: 15 min. **Bake:** 45 min. + cooling

My mother-in-law gave me this as a way to keep my husband happy during the holidays. It's his favorite childhood dessert. *—Melissa Conchieri, Northport, New York*

1 package (18-1/4 ounces) yellow cake mix, *divided*
1/4 cup canola oil
4 eggs
1 cup chopped walnuts, *divided*
1 can (15 ounces) solid-pack pumpkin
1 can (14 ounces) sweetened condensed milk
1 teaspoon vanilla extract
1/2 teaspoon salt
1/2 teaspoon ground cinnamon

Set aside 1/2 cup cake mix for filling. In a small bowl, combine the oil, 1 egg and remaining cake mix. Press into a greased 13-in. x 9-in. baking pan. Sprinkle with 1/2 cup walnuts.

In a large bowl, combine the pumpkin, milk, vanilla, salt, cinnamon, reserved cake mix and remaining eggs. Pour over crust; sprinkle with remaining walnuts.

Bake at 350° for 45-50 minutes or until a knife inserted near the center comes out clean. Cool on a wire rack. Cut into squares. Store the leftovers in the refrigerator. **Yield:** 12 servings.

OH, NUTS!

Buy large bags of walnuts, pecans and other nuts from wholesale stores, pour them into freezer bags, label them and store them in the freezer. When fixing a recipe, just pour out the amount of nuts called for and put the rest back in the freezer.

Cranberry Orange Cake

(Pictured above)

Prep: 30 min. + chilling **Bake:** 25 min. + cooling

Here's a bright and lovely addition for your dessert table, from our Test Kitchen! Mayonnaise is the secret ingredient that gives this cake its marvelous, moist texture.

1 package (18-1/4 ounces) yellow cake mix
1-1/4 cups mayonnaise
4 eggs
1/4 cup orange juice

FILLING:

1/3 cup whole-berry cranberry sauce
1/4 cup cranberry juice
4 teaspoons cranberry gelatin powder
1/2 cup whipped topping
1/2 teaspoon grated orange peel

FROSTING:

1 package (8 ounces) cream cheese, softened
1 jar (7 ounces) marshmallow creme
1/8 teaspoon almond extract
1-1/2 cups whipped topping

In a large bowl, beat cake mix, mayonnaise, eggs and orange juice until well blended. Transfer to two greased and floured 9-in. round baking pans.

Bake at 350° for 25-30 minutes or until a toothpick inserted near the center comes out clean. Cool for 10 minutes; remove from the pans to wire racks to cool completely.

For filling, in a large saucepan, bring cranberry sauce and juice to a boil; cook and stir until blended. Stir in gelatin powder until dissolved. Cool slightly; transfer to a small bowl. Refrigerate for 30 minutes or until mixture begins to thicken. Fold in the whipped topping and orange peel.

For frosting, in a large bowl, beat cream cheese until fluffy. Add marshmallow creme and extract; beat until smooth. Beat in whipped topping.

Place one cake layer on a serving plate; spread with half of the filling. Top with remaining cake layer. Spread 2 cups frosting over top and sides of the cake. Spread remaining filling over top of cake to within 1 in. of edges. Pipe remaining frosting around edge of cake. Store in the refrigerator. **Yield:** 14 servings.

Double-Chocolate Holiday Pie

(Pictured below)

Prep: 25 min. + chilling

Smooth and creamy, this Test Kitchen-created velvety pie will be a festive change of pace on the dessert table. A hint of orange in the cranberry topping adds extra pizzazz that's too delish to resist.

1/2 cup dark chocolate chips
1/4 cup sweetened condensed milk
1 extra-servings graham cracker crust (9 ounces)
2 tablespoons plus 1/3 cup slivered almonds, *divided*
1 cup cold 2% milk
1 package (3.3 ounces) instant white chocolate pudding mix
1 envelope unflavored gelatin
2 cups heavy whipping cream, *divided*
2 tablespoons sugar
1/4 teaspoon almond extract
1 can (14 ounces) whole-berry cranberry sauce
1/4 teaspoon grated orange peel

Place chocolate chips and milk in a small microwave-safe bowl. Microwave, uncovered, on high for 30-60 seconds or until chocolate is melted; stir until smooth. Spread into crust; sprinkle with 2 tablespoons almonds.

In a large bowl, whisk milk and pudding mix for 2 minutes; set aside. In a small saucepan, sprinkle gelatin over 1/2 cup cream; let stand for 1 minute. Heat over low heat, stirring until gelatin is completely dissolved. Remove from the heat.

In a large bowl, beat the remaining cream until it begins to thicken. Add sugar and almond extract; beat until soft peaks form. Gradually beat in gelatin mixture. Fold into the pudding. Pour into crust. Refrigerate for 4 hours or until firm.

Place cranberry sauce in a food processor; cover and process until blended. Stir in orange peel. Spoon over top; sprinkle with the remaining almonds. Refrigerate leftovers. **Yield:** 8 servings.

Elegant Pumpkin Pie

(Pictured top right)

Prep: 20 min. **Bake:** 50 min. + cooling

Here's the easiest pumpkin pie you'll ever bake. In fact, why not prepare two? Refrigerated pie pastry, pumpkin pie filling and convenient cheesecake filling make this slice of heaven from our Test Kitchen a breeze to whip up.

- **1 package (14.1 ounces) refrigerated pie pastry**
- **1 can (30 ounces) pumpkin pie filling**
- **3/4 cup evaporated milk**
- **2 eggs, lightly beaten**
- **1 carton (24.3 ounces) Philadelphia ready-to-serve cheesecake filling**
- **2 cups whipped topping**
- **1/8 teaspoon salt**
- **1/2 cup glazed pecans**

Unroll each sheet of pastry into a 9-in. pie plate; flute the edges. In a large bowl, beat the pie filling, milk and eggs until smooth; pour into the crusts. Cover edges loosely with foil.

Bake at 425° for 15 minutes. Reduce heat to 350°; bake 35-40 minutes longer or until a knife inserted near the center comes out clean. Remove the foil. Cool on wire racks.

In a large bowl, combine the cheesecake filling, whipped topping and salt. Spread over pies; sprinkle with the pecans. Refrigerate leftovers. **Yield:** 2 pies (8 servings each).

Tipsy Apple Pie

(Pictured above right)

Prep: 15 min. **Bake:** 50 min. + cooling

I turned a cobbler recipe into a pie, adding brandy and crystallized ginger to the filling and a simple crumb topping. It looks complicated and tastes homemade, but it's super easy! —*Debra Keil, Owasso, Oklahoma*

- **1 sheet refrigerated pie pastry**
- **1 can (21 ounces) apple pie filling**
- **1/4 cup brandy**
- **1 teaspoon crystallized ginger, finely chopped**
- **1/2 cup packed brown sugar**
- **1/3 cup all-purpose flour**
- **1/3 cup old-fashioned oats**
- **1/4 cup cold butter, cubed**
- **1/4 teaspoon ground cinnamon**
- **1/8 teaspoon salt**

Unroll pastry into a 9-in. pie plate; flute edges. In a large bowl, combine the pie filling, brandy and ginger. Pour into crust.

Place the brown sugar, flour, oats, butter, cinnamon and salt in a food processor. Cover and pulse until coarse crumbs form; sprinkle over pie. Cover edges of pastry loosely with foil.

Bake at 450° for 10 minutes. Reduce heat to 350°; remove foil and bake for 40-45 minutes or until crust is golden brown and filling is bubbly. Cool on a wire rack. **Yield:** 8 servings.

Pistachio Cake

(Pictured below)

Prep: 20 min. **Bake:** 40 min. + cooling

This precious recipe has been under lock and key for years in our family. Everyone who's ever tried this moist, one-of-a-kind cake can't believe that it starts with a mix. It's perfect for St. Patrick's Day, but you won't need the luck of the Irish to whip it up!
—Suzanne Winkhart, Bolivar, Ohio

1 package (18-1/4 ounces) yellow cake mix
1 package (3.4 ounces) instant pistachio pudding mix
4 eggs
1 cup club soda
1/2 cup canola oil
1/2 cup chopped walnuts
ICING:
1 cup cold heavy whipping cream
3/4 cup cold 2% milk
1 package (3.4 ounces) instant pistachio pudding mix
2 teaspoons confectioners' sugar
1/2 cup chopped walnuts

In a large bowl, combine the cake mix, pudding mix, eggs, soda and oil; beat on low speed for 30 seconds. Beat on medium for 2 minutes. Stir in walnuts.

Pour into a greased and floured 10-in. fluted tube pan. Bake at 350° for 40-45 minutes or until a toothpick inserted near the center comes out clean. Cool for 10 minutes before removing from pan to a wire rack to cool completely.

In a large bowl, beat the cream, milk, pudding mix and confectioners' sugar on high until stiff peaks form. Frost cake. Sprinkle with the walnuts. Refrigerate until serving. **Yield:** 12 servings.

Eggnog Pie

(Pictured above)

Prep: 15 min. + freezing

With pumpkin pie spice and eggnog, this creamy, dreamy pie has fantastic flavor. I created this one day when trying to use up a few things I had on hand. Everyone loved it!
—Shirley Darger, Colorado City, Arizona

4 ounces cream cheese, softened
1 tablespoon butter, softened
1/2 cup confectioners' sugar
1/4 cup eggnog
2 tablespoons sour cream
1 teaspoon pumpkin pie spice
1-1/2 cups whipped topping
1 graham cracker crust (9 inches)
1/8 teaspoon ground nutmeg

In a small bowl, beat the cream cheese, butter and confectioners' sugar until smooth. Beat in the eggnog, sour cream and pie spice. Fold in whipped topping; spread into crust. Sprinkle with nutmeg.

Cover the pie and freeze for 4 hours or until firm. Remove from the freezer 15 minutes before slicing. **Yield:** 8 servings.

Editor's Note: Recipe was tested with commercially prepared eggnog.

Key Lime Bites

Prep: 20 min. **Bake:** 10 min./batch + standing

Key limes don't provide much peel, so sometimes I cheat and use regular limes. —Joni Larsen, Wellington, Utah

1 cup butter, softened
1/4 cup confectioners' sugar
2 teaspoons key lime juice

2 teaspoons grated key lime peel
2 cups all-purpose flour
1/4 teaspoon salt
1/2 cup chopped macadamia nuts

ICING:

2 cups confectioners' sugar
1/4 cup key lime juice
1 teaspoon grated key lime peel

In a large bowl, cream butter and confectioners' sugar until light and fluffy. Beat in lime juice and peel. Combine flour and salt; gradually add to creamed mixture and mix well. Stir in nuts.

Shape into 1-in. balls. Place 2 in. apart on ungreased baking sheets; flatten slightly.

Bake at 400° for 8-10 minutes or until the bottoms are lightly browned. Remove to wire racks to cool completely.

In a small bowl, combine the icing ingredients. Dip cookies in icing; allow excess to drip off. Place on a wire rack; let stand until set. Store in an airtight container. **Yield:** 2-1/2 dozen.

Sunshine Cobbler

Prep: 25 min. **Bake:** 15 min.

This scrumptious cobbler is a refreshing change of pace from everyday desserts. With a crispy homemade topping and a juicy filling, this recipe is a golden success!
—Angela Leinenbach, Mechanicsvlle, Virginia

2 cans (8 ounces *each*) citrus salad, undrained
1/2 cup packed brown sugar
3 tablespoons all-purpose flour
1 can (11 ounces) mandarin oranges, undrained
3 tablespoons butter

TOPPING:

1 cup all-purpose flour
3 tablespoons sugar, *divided*
1-1/2 teaspoons baking powder
1/4 teaspoon salt
1/4 cup cold butter
1 egg, lightly beaten
1/4 cup 2% milk
1/8 teaspoon ground cinnamon
6 pecan halves
Half-and-half cream, optional

Drain citrus salad, reserving 1/4 cup juice. In a large bowl, combine the brown sugar, flour and reserved juice. Stir in citrus salad and oranges. Divide among six 6-oz. ramekins or custard cups; dot with butter.

In a small bowl, combine the flour, 2 tablespoons sugar, baking powder and salt; cut in butter until mixture resembles coarse crumbs. Stir in egg and milk. Drop by spoonfuls over fruit mixture. Combine cinnamon and remaining sugar; sprinkle over tops.

Bake at 425° for 15-18 minutes or until the filling is bubbly and a toothpick inserted in topping comes out clean. Top each with a pecan half. Serve with cream if desired. **Yield:** 6 servings.

Cherry Nut Cookies

(Pictured below)

Prep: 25 min. **Bake:** 20 min./batch

So pretty with a dusting of confectioners' sugar, these cute cookies are fabulous!
—Susan Westerfield, Albuquerque, New Mexico

1 package (6 ounces) golden raisins and cherries
1/4 cup sugar
3 tablespoons cherry juice blend
Dash ground cinnamon
1/2 cup butter, softened
1 package (3 ounces) cream cheese, softened
1-1/4 cups all-purpose flour
1 white chocolate Toblerone candy bar (3.52 ounces), finely chopped
1/4 cup finely chopped walnuts, toasted
2 teaspoons water
1/4 cup confectioners' sugar

In a small saucepan, combine the first four ingredients. Bring to a boil. Reduce heat; simmer, uncovered, for 6-8 minutes or until most of the liquid is absorbed, stirring occasionally. Cool.

Meanwhile, in a large bowl, beat butter and cream cheese until smooth. Gradually add flour.

Turn dough onto a lightly floured surface; knead until smooth, about 3 minutes. Roll into a 12-1/2-in. square; cut into 2-1/2-in. squares.

Stir candy and walnuts into fruit mixture. Drop filling by tablespoonfuls onto the center of each square. Bring two opposite corners to center; moisten the edges with water and pinch together.

Place 1 in. apart on lightly greased baking sheets. Bake at 350° for 16-18 minutes or until lightly browned. Remove to wire racks to cool.

Sprinkle with confectioners' sugar. Store in an airtight container. **Yield:** 25 cookies.

CHAPTER 15

Make-Ahead Marvels

For cooks who are also planners, these hearty and convenient recipes are for you. Each entree can either be assembled the night before or doubled the day you prepare it, so you can cook one dish now and freeze the other for later.

There's no doubt your family will flip for the flavorful main courses featured here, such as Creamy Chicken Enchiladas and Sausage Fettuccine Bake, which are both make-once-eat-twice casseroles.

And when you don't want to get up too early to prepare a hearty breakfast, simply whip up Spring Morning Casserole the night before. The following morning all you have to do is pop the eye-opening dish in the oven until it's hot and bubbly. How handy is that? ■

ONE STEP AHEAD. Blue Cheese Walnut Tart (p. 247).

Tiramisu

(Pictured above)

Prep: 25 min. + chilling

A fix-ahead dessert is just what a fantastic meal needs for maximum ease. This Italian delight is the perfect way to cap it off. —*Linda Finn, Louisville, Mississippi*

1/2 cup strong brewed coffee
2 tablespoons coffee liqueur
2 packages (8 ounces *each*) cream cheese, softened
2/3 cup sugar
2 cups (16 ounces) sour cream
1/4 cup 2% milk
1/2 teaspoon vanilla extract
2 packages (3 ounces *each*) ladyfingers, split
1 tablespoon baking cocoa

In a small bowl, combine the coffee and liqueur; set aside. In a large bowl, beat cream cheese and sugar until smooth. Beat in the sour cream, milk and vanilla extract until blended.

Layer one package of ladyfingers in an ungreased 11-in. x 7-in. dish; brush with half of coffee mixture. Top with half of cream cheese mixture. Repeat layers (dish will be full).

Cover and refrigerate for 8 hours or overnight. Just before serving, place cookie stencil on top of dessert, if desired, and sprinkle with cocoa. **Yield:** 12 servings.

VANILLA EXTRACT

Double-strength imitation vanilla is double the strength of pure or imitation vanilla. If you are using double-strength, add only half of the amount of vanilla. Regular-strength imitation vanilla can be used interchangeably with pure vanilla extract.

Creamy Chicken Enchiladas

(Pictured below)

Prep: 30 min. **Bake:** 30 min.

This is one of the first recipes I created and cooked for my husband right after we got married. He was so impressed! We fix these creamy enchiladas for friends regularly. —*Melissa Rogers, Tuscaloosa, Alabama*

1 rotisserie chicken
2 cans (14-1/2 ounces *each*) diced tomatoes with mild green chilies, undrained
2 cans (10-3/4 ounces *each*) condensed cream of chicken soup, undiluted
1 can (10-3/4 ounces) condensed cheddar cheese soup, undiluted
1/4 cup 2% milk
1 tablespoon ground cumin
1 tablespoon chili powder
2 teaspoons garlic powder
2 teaspoons dried oregano
1 package (8 ounces) cream cheese, cubed
20 flour tortillas (8 inches), warmed
4 cups shredded Mexican cheese blend

Shred the cooked chicken and set aside. In a large bowl, combine tomatoes, soups, milk and seasonings. Transfer 3-1/2 cups to another bowl; add the chicken and cream cheese.

Spread 1/4 cup soup mixture into each of two greased 13-in. x 9-in. baking dishes. Place 1/3 cup chicken mixture down center of each tortilla. Roll up and place seam side down in baking dishes. Pour remaining soup mixture over tops; sprinkle with cheese.

Bake one casserole, uncovered, at 350° for 30-35 minutes or until heated through and the cheese is melted. Cover and freeze remaining casserole for up to 3 months.

To use frozen casserole: Thaw in the refrigerator overnight. Cover and bake at 350° for 45 minutes. Uncover; bake 5-10 minutes longer or until heated through and cheese is melted. **Yield:** 2 casseroles (5 servings each).

Elegant Smoked Salmon Strata

(Pictured above)

Prep: 30 min. + chilling **Bake:** 55 min. + standing

This fancy overnight egg bake is ideal for guests. In the morning, you can simply let it come to room temperature and whip up side dishes as it bakes. Then get ready for compliments! —Lisa Speer, Palm Beach, Florida

4 cups cubed ciabatta bread
2 tablespoons butter, melted
2 tablespoons olive oil
2 cups (8 ounces) shredded Gruyere *or* Swiss cheese
2 cups (8 ounces) shredded white cheddar cheese
10 green onions, sliced
1/2 pound smoked salmon *or* lox, coarsely chopped
8 eggs
4 cups 2% milk
4 teaspoons Dijon mustard
1/4 teaspoon salt
1/4 teaspoon pepper
Creme fraiche *or* sour cream and minced chives

In a large bowl, toss the bread cubes with butter and olive oil; transfer to a greased 13-in.x 9-in. baking dish. Sprinkle with the shredded cheeses, onions and smoked salmon. In another bowl, whisk the eggs, milk, Dijon mustard, salt and pepper; pour over the top. Cover and refrigerate overnight.

Remove from the refrigerator 30 minutes before baking. Cover and bake at 350° for 30 minutes. Uncover; bake 25-30 minutes longer or until a knife inserted near the center comes out clean. Let stand for 10 minutes before serving. Serve with creme fraiche and chives. **Yield:** 12 servings.

Spring Morning Casserole

(Pictured below)

Prep: 25 min. + chilling **Bake:** 40 min. + standing

My mom gave me this recipe, and it has quickly become my favorite breakfast casserole. I love that it can be made the night before and popped in the oven for a special breakfast. —Melody Holland, Lebanon, Pennsylvania

2 cups cut fresh asparagus (1-inch pieces)
1 small sweet red pepper, chopped
1 small onion, chopped
3 tablespoons butter
8 cups cubed day old French bread
1 cup cubed fully cooked ham
2 cups (8 ounces) shredded cheddar cheese
8 eggs, beaten
2 cups 2% milk
1/3 cup honey
1/2 teaspoon salt
1/2 teaspoon pepper

In a large skillet, saute the asparagus, red pepper and onion in butter until tender; set aside.

Place bread in a greased 13-in. x 9-in. baking dish. Layer with ham, 1 cup cheese and vegetable mixture. Sprinkle with remaining cheese. In a large bowl, combine the eggs, milk, honey, salt and pepper. Pour over the top. Cover and refrigerate overnight.

Remove from the refrigerator 30 minutes before baking. Bake, uncovered, at 350° for 40-45 minutes or until a knife inserted near center comes out clean. Let the casserole stand for 10 minutes before cutting. **Yield:** 12 servings.

Company Lasagna

(Pictured below)

Prep: 40 min. + chilling **Bake:** 50 min. + standing

I love having this in the fridge when guests come over. It's so easy, I can focus on socializing instead of stressing about dinner. —Renee Vaughan, Galena, Ohio

- **1 pound bulk pork sausage**
- **2 cans (one 28 ounces, one 14-1/2 ounces) stewed tomatoes, undrained**
- **1 can (6 ounces) tomato paste**
- **2 tablespoons dried oregano**
- **4 garlic cloves, minced**
- **1/4 teaspoon salt**
- **1/4 teaspoon pepper**
- **4 cups (16 ounces) shredded part-skim mozzarella cheese, *divided***
- **3 cups (24 ounces) 2% cottage cheese**
- **1 cup grated Parmesan cheese**
- **2 eggs, lightly beaten**
- **3 tablespoons dried parsley flakes**
- **12 no-cook lasagna noodles**

In a Dutch oven, cook the sausage over medium heat until no longer pink; drain. Stir in tomatoes, tomato paste, oregano, garlic, salt and pepper. Bring to a boil. Reduce heat; simmer, uncovered, for 15-20 minutes or until thickened.

Meanwhile, in a large bowl, combine 2 cups mozzarella cheese, cottage cheese, Parmesan cheese, eggs and parsley.

Spread 1 cup meat mixture into a greased 13-in. x 9-in. baking dish. Layer with three noodles, 1-1/4 cups meat mixture and 1 cup cheese mixture. Repeat three times. Top with remaining mozzarella cheese. Cover and refrigerate for 8 hours or overnight.

Remove from the refrigerator 30 minutes before baking. Cover and bake at 350° for 30 minutes. Uncover and bake 20-25 minutes longer or until bubbly and cheese is melted. Let stand for 10 minutes before cutting. **Yield:** 12 servings.

Chicken & Cheese Noodle Bake

Prep: 20 min. **Bake:** 25 min.

This is the recipe my daughters and I often make for new parents when they come home from the hospital. With its creamy spaghetti filling and melted cheese topping, this casserole holds a nice cut and comforts hungry tummies. —Fancheon Resler, Bluffton, Indiana

- **1 package (16 ounces) spaghetti, broken**
- **2 medium onions, chopped**
- **1 medium green pepper, chopped**
- **1 medium sweet red pepper, chopped**
- **1/2 cup butter, cubed**
- **6 tablespoons all-purpose flour**
- **2 cups 2% milk**
- **4 cups cubed cooked chicken**
- **1 can (10-3/4 ounces) condensed cream of chicken and mushroom soup, undiluted**
- **1 can (10-3/4 ounces) condensed cream of mushroom soup, undiluted**
- **1 cup (8 ounces) sour cream**
- **1/2 teaspoon celery salt**
- **1/2 teaspoon pepper**
- **2 cups (8 ounces) shredded part-skim mozzarella cheese**
- **1 cup (4 ounces) shredded cheddar cheese**

Cook the spaghetti according to package directions. Meanwhile, in a Dutch oven, saute the onions and green and red peppers in butter until tender. Stir in flour until blended; gradually add milk. Bring to a boil; cook and stir for 2 minutes or until thickened. Stir in the chicken, soups, sour cream, celery salt and pepper.

Drain spaghetti; add to sauce mixture and toss to coat. Transfer to two greased 11-in. x 7-in. baking dishes. Sprinkle with cheeses. Cover and freeze one casserole for up to 3 months. Cover and bake the remaining casserole at 350° for 20 minutes. Uncover and bake 5-10 minutes longer or until bubbly.

To use frozen casserole: Thaw in the refrigerator overnight. Remove from the refrigerator 30 minutes before baking. Cover and bake at 350° for 40 minutes. Uncover and bake 5-10 minutes longer or until bubbly. **Yield:** 2 casseroles (6 servings each).

Tater Tot Casseroles

Prep: 25 min. **Bake:** 55 min.

Ground beef, sausage, cheese and, of course, Tater Tots make this homey casserole a crowd-pleaser. Cayenne pepper and hot Italian sausage give it a pleasant kick. —Ryan Jones, Chillicothe, Illinois

- **3/4 pound bulk hot Italian sausage**
- **3/4 pound lean ground beef (90% lean)**
- **1 small onion, chopped**
- **2 cans (10-3/4 ounces *each*) condensed cream of celery soup, undiluted**
- **2 cups frozen cut green beans, thawed**
- **1 can (15-1/4 ounces) whole kernel corn, drained**

2 cups (8 ounces) shredded Colby-Monterey Jack cheese, *divided*
1/2 cup 2% milk
1 teaspoon garlic powder
1/4 teaspoon seasoned salt
1/4 to 1/2 teaspoon cayenne pepper
1 package (32 ounces) frozen Tater Tots

In a Dutch oven, cook the sausage, beef and onion over medium heat until meat is no longer pink; drain. Add the soup, beans, corn, 1 cup cheese, milk, garlic powder, seasoned salt and cayenne. Transfer to two greased 11-in. x 7-in. baking dishes. Top with Tater Tots; sprinkle with remaining cheese.

Cover and freeze one casserole for up to 3 months. Cover and bake the remaining casserole at 350° for 40 minutes. Uncover and bake 5-10 minutes longer or until bubbly.

To use frozen casserole: Thaw in the refrigerator overnight. Remove from the refrigerator 30 minutes before baking. Cover and bake at 350° for 50 minutes. Uncover and bake 5-10 minutes longer or until bubbly. **Yield:** 2 casseroles (6 servings each).

Watermelon Spritzer

Prep: 5 min. + chilling

It couldn't get much easier than this bright spritzer! Watermelon blended with limeade is cool and refreshing. It's a wonderful thirst-quencher on a hot summer day.
—Geraldine Saucier, Albuquerque, New Mexico

4 cups cubed seedless watermelon
3/4 cup frozen limeade concentrate, thawed
2-1/2 cups carbonated water
Lime slices

Place watermelon in a blender. Cover and process until blended. Strain and discard pulp; transfer juice to a pitcher. Stir in limeade concentrate. Refrigerate for 6 hours or overnight.

Just before serving, stir in carbonated water. Garnish servings with lime slices. **Yield:** 5 servings.

Greek Grilled Chicken Pitas

(Pictured above right)

Prep: 20 min. + marinating **Grill:** 10 min.

I switched up my mom's recipe to create this tasty variation. It's delicious and perfect for warm days. It takes advantage of fresh summer veggies and keeps my kitchen cool. *—Blair Lonergan, Rochelle, Virginia*

1/2 cup balsamic vinaigrette
1 pound boneless skinless chicken breast halves
CUCUMBER SAUCE:
1 cup plain Greek yogurt
1/2 cup finely chopped cucumber
1/4 cup finely chopped red onion
1 tablespoon minced fresh parsley
1 tablespoon lime juice
1 garlic clove, minced
1/4 teaspoon salt
1/8 teaspoon pepper
PITAS:
8 pita pocket halves
1/2 cup sliced cucumber
1/2 cup grape tomatoes, chopped
1/2 cup sliced red onion
1/2 cup crumbled feta cheese

Pour vinaigrette into a large resealable plastic bag. Add the chicken; seal bag and turn to coat. Refrigerate for at least 4 hours or overnight. In a small bowl, combine the sauce ingredients; chill until serving.

Drain and discard marinade. If grilling the chicken, moisten a paper towel with cooking oil; using long-handled tongs, lightly coat the grill rack. Grill chicken, covered, over medium heat or broil 4 in. from the heat for 4-7 minutes on each side or until a meat thermometer reads 170°.

Cut chicken into strips. Fill each pita half with chicken, cucumber, tomatoes, onion and cheese; drizzle with sauce. **Yield:** 4 servings.

Editor's Note: If Greek yogurt is not available in your area, line a strainer with a coffee filter and place over a bowl. Place 2 cups fat-free yogurt in prepared strainer; refrigerate overnight. Discard liquid from bowl; proceed as directed.

FRESH CUCUMBERS

Use a plastic "lettuce keeper" to keep cucumbers fresh. Place the cucumbers inside just as you would any other vegetable. Storing cucumbers this way prevents them from getting soft spots and keeps them fresh and crisp for almost two weeks.

Country Chicken Casserole

(Pictured above)

Prep: 45 min. + chilling **Bake:** 45 min. + standing

This hearty entree offers a great way to use up leftover turkey or chicken. Whenever I make it, someone asks for the recipe. Best of all, you can fix it ahead to simplify mealtime. —*Sue Kennedy, Galloway, Ohio*

1 package (6 ounces) Stove Top chicken stuffing mix
1/2 pound sliced fresh mushrooms
1 small onion, chopped
1 tablespoon butter
3 garlic cloves, minced
3 cups cubed cooked chicken
1 package (16 ounces) frozen corn, thawed
1 package (16 ounces) frozen chopped broccoli, thawed
1 can (10-3/4 ounces) reduced-fat reduced-sodium condensed cream of mushroom soup, undiluted
1 cup 2% milk
1 cup reduced-fat sour cream
1 cup reduced-fat mayonnaise
3/4 teaspoon pepper

Prepare the stuffing according to package directions. Meanwhile, in a large skillet, saute mushrooms and onion in the butter until tender. Add the garlic; cook 1 minute longer.

In a large bowl, combine the chicken, corn, broccoli, soup, milk, sour cream, mayonnaise, pepper and mushroom mixture; transfer to a greased 13-in x 9-in. baking dish. Top with stuffing. Cover and refrigerate overnight.

Remove from the refrigerator 30 minutes before baking. Cover and bake at 350° for 35 minutes. Uncover and bake 10-15 minutes longer or until stuffing is lightly browned. Let stand for 10 minutes before serving. **Yield:** 8 servings.

Veggie Calzones

(Pictured below)

Prep: 25 min. + rising **Bake:** 35 min.

Bread dough makes it a breeze to assemble these savory turnovers. They freeze well, and once frozen, they can be heated in half an hour. If you have a favorite pizza dough, you can use it instead. —*Lee Ann Arey, Gray, Maine*

1/2 pound fresh mushrooms, chopped
1 medium onion, chopped
1 medium green pepper, chopped
2 tablespoons canola oil
3 plum tomatoes, seeded and chopped
1 can (6 ounces) tomato paste
1 cup (4 ounces) shredded Monterey Jack cheese
1 cup (4 ounces) shredded part-skim mozzarella cheese
1/2 cup grated Parmesan cheese
2 loaves (1 pound *each*) frozen bread dough, thawed
1 egg
1 tablespoon water

In a large skillet, saute the mushrooms, onion and green pepper in oil until tender. Add tomatoes; cook and stir for 3 minutes. Stir in tomato paste; set aside. Combine cheeses and set aside.

On a lightly floured surface, divide dough into eight pieces. Roll each piece into a 7-in. circle. Spoon a scant 1/2 cup of vegetable mixture and 1/4 cup of cheese mixture over one side of each circle. Brush edges of dough with water; fold dough over filling and press

edges with a fork to seal. Place calzones 3 in. apart on greased baking sheets. Cover and let rise in a warm place for 20 minutes.

Whisk egg and water; brush over calzones. Bake at 375° for 15 minutes. Cool desired number of calzones; place in freezer bags. Seal and freeze for up to 3 months. Bake the remaining calzones 18-22 minutes longer or until golden brown. Serve immediately.

To use frozen calzones: Place 2 in. apart on a greased baking sheet. Bake at 350° for 30-35 minutes or until golden brown. **Yield:** 8 servings.

Burrito Pie

Prep: 40 min. **Bake:** 30 min.

Layers of cheese, meat sauce and tortillas make up this satisfying Mexican lasagna that kids of all ages will love. The recipe yields two casseroles, so you'll have an easy meal later, too. —Renee Starret, Benton, Louisiana

- **2 pounds ground beef**
- **1 medium onion, chopped**
- **2 garlic cloves, minced**
- **2 cans (15 ounces *each*) Ranch Style beans (pinto beans in seasoned tomato sauce)**
- **1 bottle (16 ounces) taco sauce**
- **1 can (10 ounces) diced tomatoes and green chilies, undrained**
- **1 can (4 ounces) chopped green chilies**
- **1 can (3.8 ounces) sliced ripe olives, drained**
- **12 flour tortillas (8 inches), halved**
- **4 cups (16 ounces) shredded Colby-Monterey Jack cheese**

In a large skillet, cook the beef, onion and garlic over medium heat until meat is no longer pink; drain. Stir in the beans, taco sauce, tomatoes, chilies and olives. Bring to a boil. Reduce heat; simmer, uncovered, for 20-25 minutes or until slightly thickened.

Spread 1 cup meat mixture in each of two greased 11-in. x 7-in. baking dishes. Layer with 4 tortilla halves, 1 cup meat mixture and 2/3 cup cheese. Repeat twice.

Cover and freeze one casserole for up to 3 months. Cover and bake the remaining casserole at 350° for 20 minutes. Uncover; bake 10-15 minutes longer or until bubbly and cheese is melted. Let stand for 5 minutes before serving.

To use frozen casserole: Thaw in the refrigerator overnight. Remove from the refrigerator 30 minutes before baking. Cover and bake at 350° for 25 minutes. Uncover; bake 10-15 minutes longer or until bubbly and cheese is melted. Let stand for 5 minutes before serving. **Yield:** 2 casseroles (6 servings each).

GARLIC GALORE

Finely chopped fresh garlic and store-bought minced garlic (often sold in a jar) can be used interchangeably with garlic cloves that have been put through a press. Choose whichever form is the easiest and most convenient for you.

Make-Ahead Lasagna

(Pictured above)

Prep: 35 min. + chilling **Bake:** 55 min. + standing

This is an old standby when time's limited and guests are expected for dinner. It's a combination of several easy lasagna recipes I have tried over the years. —Mary Grimm, Williamsburg, Iowa

- **1 pound ground beef**
- **1 pound bulk hot Italian sausage**
- **1 can (15 ounces) pizza sauce**
- **1 jar (14 ounces) marinara sauce**
- **2 eggs, lightly beaten**
- **1 carton (15 ounces) ricotta cheese**
- **1/2 cup grated Parmesan cheese**
- **1 tablespoon dried parsley flakes**
- **1/2 teaspoon pepper**
- **12 no-cook lasagna noodles**
- **4 cups (16 ounces) shredded part-skim mozzarella cheese**

In a large skillet, cook beef and sausage over medium heat until no longer pink; drain. Stir in pizza and marinara sauces. In a large bowl, combine the eggs, ricotta, Parmesan, parsley and pepper.

Spread 1 cup meat sauce into a greased 13-in. x 9-in. baking dish. Layer with four noodles, half of the cheese mixture, 1 cup meat sauce and 1 cup mozzarella. Repeat layers. Top with the remaining noodles, meat sauce and mozzarella. Cover and refrigerate for 8 hours or overnight.

Remove from the refrigerator 30 minutes before baking. Bake, covered, at 375° for 45 minutes. Uncover; bake 10-15 minutes longer or until cheese is melted. Let casserole stand for 10 minutes before cutting. **Yield:** 12 servings.

Italian Brunch Bake

(Pictured above)

Prep: 30 min. + chilling **Bake:** 55 min. + standing

This is a great overnight recipe to make when you have company coming over for brunch. I often make it during the holidays. All I have to do is pop it into the oven, and in no time, the troops are fed.
—Vivian Taylor, Middleburg, Florida

1 pound bulk Italian sausage
1 pound baby portobello mushrooms, quartered
1 large onion, chopped
1 medium sweet red pepper, chopped
1 medium green pepper, chopped
2 garlic cloves, minced
2 packages (6 ounces *each*) fresh baby spinach
8 slices Italian bread (1 inch thick)
12 eggs
1 cup 2% milk
1 teaspoon Italian seasoning
1/2 teaspoon salt
1/2 teaspoon pepper
1/4 teaspoon ground nutmeg
4 cups (16 ounces) shredded Italian cheese blend

In a large skillet, cook sausage, mushrooms, onion, peppers and garlic over medium heat until meat is no longer pink; drain and set aside.

In a large skillet coated with cooking spray, saute spinach until wilted. Place bread on a baking sheet. Broil 2-3 in. from the heat for 1-2 minutes or until lightly browned. Transfer to a greased 13-in. x 9-in. baking dish.

In a large bowl, combine eggs, milk, Italian seasoning, salt, pepper and nutmeg. Layer the sausage mixture and spinach over bread; pour egg mixture over top. Sprinkle with cheese; cover and refrigerate overnight.

Remove from refrigerator 30 minutes before baking. Cover and bake at 350° for 50 minutes. Uncover; bake 5-10 minutes longer or until a knife inserted near the center comes out clean. Let stand for 10 minutes before cutting. **Yield:** 12 servings.

Chicken Club Casseroles

Prep: 20 min. **Bake:** 35 min.

Here's a warm and welcoming casserole that tastes just as fresh and delicious after it's frozen as it does right out of the oven! —Janine Smith, Columbia, South Carolina

4 cups uncooked spiral pasta
4 cups cubed cooked chicken
2 cans (10-3/4 ounces *each*) condensed cheddar cheese soup, undiluted
1 cup crumbled cooked bacon
1 cup 2% milk
1 cup mayonnaise
4 medium tomatoes, seeded and chopped
3 cups fresh baby spinach, chopped
2 cups (8 ounces) shredded Colby-Monterey Jack cheese

Cook the pasta according to package directions. Meanwhile, in a large bowl, combine the chicken, soup, bacon, milk and mayonnaise. Stir in the tomatoes and baby spinach.

Drain pasta; stir into chicken mixture. Transfer to two greased 8-in. square baking dishes. Sprinkle with cheese.

Cover and freeze one casserole for up to 3 months. Cover and bake remaining casserole at 375° for 35-40 minutes or until bubbly and cheese is melted.

To use frozen casserole: Thaw in the refrigerator overnight. Remove from the refrigerator 30 minutes before baking. Cover and bake at 375° for 60-70 minutes or until bubbly. **Yield:** 2 casseroles (5 servings each).

Southwest Enchilada Bake

Prep: 30 min. **Bake:** 20 min. + standing

The whole family will love this comforting, cheese-topped casserole. It has just the right touch of heat.
—Dixie Terry, Goreville, Illinois

30 corn tortillas (6 inches)
3 pounds lean ground beef (90% lean)
2 large onions, chopped
1 jalapeno pepper, seeded and chopped
4 garlic cloves, minced
2 cans (15 ounces *each*) black-eyed peas, rinsed and drained
2 cans (10-3/4 ounces *each*) condensed cream of chicken soup, undiluted
2 cans (10-3/4 ounces *each*) condensed cream of mushroom soup, undiluted
2 cans (10 ounces *each*) diced tomatoes and green chilies, undrained

2 cans (10 ounces *each*) enchilada sauce
1/2 teaspoon hot pepper sauce
4 cups (16 ounces) shredded sharp cheddar cheese

Cut the tortillas into eighths; set aside. In a Dutch oven, cook the beef, onions, jalapeno and garlic over medium heat until meat is no longer pink; drain. Stir in the black-eyed peas, soups, tomatoes, enchilada sauce and pepper sauce; heat through.

Spread 2-2/3 cups meat mixture into each of two greased 13-in. x 9-in. baking dishes. Top each with 2 cups cut tortillas. Repeat layers. Top with the remaining meat mixture; sprinkle with cheese.

Cover and freeze one casserole for up to 3 months. Cover and bake the remaining casserole at 350° for 20-25 minutes or until bubbly and cheese is melted. Let stand for 10 minutes before cutting.

To use frozen casserole: Thaw in the refrigerator overnight. Remove from the refrigerator 30 minutes before baking. Cover and bake at 350° for 55 minutes. Uncover; bake 10-15 minutes longer or until cheese is melted. Let stand for 10 minutes before cutting. **Yield:** 2 casseroles (8 servings each).

Editor's Note: Wear disposable gloves when cutting hot peppers; the oils can burn your skin. Avoid touching your face.

Easy Beef-Stuffed Shells

Prep: 45 min. + chilling **Bake:** 45 min.

Here's a rich and comforting dish that's terrific right away or made ahead and baked the next day. Pesto makes a surprising filling for these cheesy, satisfying shells.
—Blair Lonergan, Rochelle, Virginia

20 uncooked jumbo pasta shells
1 pound ground beef
1 large onion, chopped
1 carton (15 ounces) ricotta cheese
2 cups (8 ounces) shredded Italian cheese blend, *divided*
1/2 cup grated Parmesan cheese
1/4 cup prepared pesto
1 egg
1 jar (26 ounces) spaghetti sauce, *divided*

Cook pasta shells according to package directions to al dente; drain and rinse in cold water. In a large skillet, cook beef and onion over medium heat until meat is no longer pink; drain. In a large bowl, combine the ricotta cheese, 1-1/2 cups Italian cheese blend, Parmesan cheese, pesto, egg and half of the beef mixture.

Spread 3/4 cup spaghetti sauce into a greased 13-in x 9-in. baking dish. Spoon cheese mixture into pasta shells; place in baking dish. Combine remaining beef mixture and spaghetti sauce; pour over the shells. Sprinkle with remaining cheese. Cover and refrigerate overnight.

Remove from refrigerator 30 minutes before baking. Cover and bake at 350° for 40 minutes. Uncover; bake 5-10 minutes longer or until the cheese is melted. **Yield:** 10 servings.

Blue Cheese Walnut Tart

(Pictured below)

Prep: 30 min. **Bake:** 15 min.

This simple yet elegant tart gives any casual get-together a touch of class. It's wonderful as a lunch entree and also perfect as part of a springtime brunch buffet.
—Erin Chilcoat, Smithtown, New York

1 sheet refrigerated pie pastry
1 package (8 ounces) cream cheese, softened
1/3 cup crumbled blue cheese
1 garlic clove, minced
1/4 cup heavy whipping cream
1 egg
1/4 teaspoon cayenne pepper
1/4 teaspoon coarsely ground pepper
1/3 cup chopped roasted sweet red peppers
3 tablespoons chopped walnuts, toasted
2 tablespoons minced fresh parsley

Press pastry onto the bottom and up the sides of an ungreased 9-in. fluted tart pan with removable bottom; trim edges. Bake at 425° for 8-10 minutes or until lightly browned. Cool completely on a wire rack.

In a large bowl, beat the cream cheese, blue cheese and garlic until blended. Add the cream, egg, cayenne and pepper; beat well. Spread the mixture into crust. Sprinkle with red peppers, walnuts and parsley. Cover and freeze for up to 3 months, or bake, uncovered, at 375° for 15-20 minutes or until center is set.

To use frozen tart: Remove from the freezer 30 minutes before baking (do not thaw). Uncover; place on a baking sheet. Bake at 375° for 30-35 minutes or until center is set. **Yield:** 12 servings.

Sausage Fettuccine Bake

(Pictured below)

Prep: 25 min. **Bake:** 25 min. + standing

Rich and loaded with sausage, veggies and cheese, this family-pleasing casserole will soon become a favorite.
—Lisa Varner, Charleston, South Carolina

- **1-1/2 pounds uncooked fettuccine**
- **2 pounds bulk Italian sausage**
- **2 large onions, chopped**
- **1 medium green pepper, chopped**
- **2 cans (28 ounces *each*) diced tomatoes, undrained**
- **2 jars (4-1/2 ounces *each*) sliced mushrooms, drained**
- **4 teaspoons Italian seasoning**
- **4 cups (1 pound) shredded part-skim mozzarella cheese, *divided***
- **2 cans (10-3/4 ounces *each*) condensed cream of mushroom soup, undiluted**
- **1/2 cup beef broth**
- **1 cup grated Parmesan cheese**

Cook the fettuccine according to package directions. Meanwhile, in a Dutch oven, cook the sausage, onions and green pepper over medium heat until meat is no longer pink; drain. Add the tomatoes, mushrooms and Italian seasoning. Bring to a boil. Reduce heat; simmer, uncovered, for 5 minutes.

Drain fettuccine; stir into meat mixture. Transfer half of sausage mixture to two greased 13-in. x 9-in. baking dishes. Sprinkle each with 1 cup mozzarella cheese; top with remaining sausage mixture.

In a small bowl, whisk the soup and broth; spread over casseroles. Sprinkle with Parmesan and remaining mozzarella.

Cover and freeze one casserole for up to 3 months. Cover and bake the remaining casserole at 350° for 20 minutes. Uncover; bake 5-10 minutes longer or until bubbly and cheese is melted. Let stand for 10 minutes before serving.

To use frozen casserole: Remove from the freezer 30 minutes before baking (do not thaw). Cover and bake at 350° for 70 minutes. Uncover; bake 5-10 minutes longer or until heated through. Let stand for 10 minutes before serving. **Yield:** 2 casseroles (6 servings each).

Sausage Lasagna Rolls

(Pictured above)

Prep: 45 min. **Bake:** 45 min.

Who said lasagna noodles have to lie flat? This artful interpretation of layered comfort food is what we like to call "casser-roll."—Kali Wraspir, Olympia, Washington

- **12 lasagna noodles**
- **1 pound bulk Italian sausage**
- **2 jars (26 ounces *each*) spaghetti sauce**
- **1 carton (15 ounces) ricotta cheese**
- **2 cups (8 ounces) shredded part-skim mozzarella cheese, *divided***
- **3/4 cup shredded Parmesan cheese, *divided***
- **1 egg**
- **2 tablespoons minced fresh parsley *or* 2 teaspoons dried parsley flakes**
- **2-1/2 teaspoons minced fresh rosemary *or* 3/4 teaspoon dried rosemary, crushed**
- **2 teaspoons lemon juice**
- **1-1/2 teaspoons minced fresh thyme *or* 1/2 teaspoon dried thyme**
- **1 teaspoon grated lemon peel**
- **1 teaspoon coarsely ground pepper**
- **1/2 teaspoon salt**

Cook the noodles according to package directions. Meanwhile, in a large skillet, cook sausage over medium heat until no longer pink; drain. Stir in spaghetti sauce.

In a large bowl, combine the ricotta, 1 cup mozzarella, 1/4 cup Parmesan, egg, parsley, rosemary, lemon juice, thyme, lemon peel, pepper and salt. Drain the noodles. Spread 2 tablespoons cheese mixture on each noodle; carefully roll up.

Spread 2/3 cup meat sauce into each of two greased 11-in. x 7-in. baking dishes. Place roll-ups seam side down over sauce. Top with remaining meat sauce. Sprinkle with remaining mozzarella and Parmesan cheeses.

Cover and freeze one casserole for up to 3 months. Cover and bake remaining casserole at 350° for 45-50 minutes or until bubbly.

To use frozen casserole: Thaw in the refrigerator overnight. Remove from the refrigerator 30 minutes before baking. Cover and bake at 350° for 50-60 minutes or until bubbly. **Yield:** 2 casseroles (6 servings each).

Three-Cheese & Pepper Penne

Prep: 40 min. **Bake:** 30 min.

This creamy pasta dish comes together in a snap. It makes two casseroles, so you can freeze one or share it with friends. —Jasey McBurnett, Rock Springs, Wyoming

- **1 package (16 ounces) penne pasta**
- **1-1/2 pounds boneless skinless chicken breasts, cut into 1/2-inch pieces**
- **1-1/4 teaspoons salt**
- **1/2 teaspoon pepper**
- **3 teaspoons olive oil, *divided***
- **1 pound sliced fresh mushrooms**
- **4 garlic cloves, minced**
- **1/4 cup butter, cubed**
- **1/2 cup all-purpose flour**
- **4 cups 2% milk**
- **2 jars (7 ounces *each*) roasted sweet red peppers, drained and chopped**
- **2 cups (8 ounces) shredded mozzarella and provolone cheese**
- **2 cups grated Parmesan cheese, *divided***

Cook pasta according to package directions. Meanwhile, sprinkle chicken with salt and pepper. In a large skillet, saute chicken in 1 teaspoon oil until no longer pink. Remove from the skillet. In the same skillet, saute mushrooms in remaining oil until tender.

In a Dutch oven, saute garlic in butter for 1 minute. Stir in flour until blended; gradually add milk. Bring to a boil; cook and stir for 1-2 minutes or until thickened. Stir in the red peppers, mozzarella and provolone cheese, 1/2 cup Parmesan cheese, mushrooms and chicken.

Drain pasta; stir into sauce. Divide between two greased 8-in. square baking dishes. Sprinkle each with remaining Parmesan cheese. Cover and freeze one casserole for up to 3 months. Cover and bake the remaining casserole at 350° for 30-35 minutes or until bubbly.

To use frozen casserole: Thaw in the refrigerator overnight. Remove from the refrigerator 30 minutes before baking. Cover and bake at 350° for 60-70 minutes or until bubbly, stirring once. **Yield:** 2 casseroles (5 servings each).

Mexican Chicken Alfredo

(Pictured above)

Prep: 25 min. **Bake:** 30 min.

One family member likes Italian; another likes Mexican. They will never have to compromise when this entree is on the menu. —Tia Woodley, Stockbridge, Georgia

- **1 package (16 ounces) gemelli *or* spiral pasta**
- **2 pounds boneless skinless chicken breasts, cubed**
- **1 medium onion, chopped**
- **1/4 teaspoon salt**
- **1/4 teaspoon pepper**
- **1 tablespoon canola oil**
- **2 jars (15 ounces *each*) Alfredo sauce**
- **1 cup grated Parmesan cheese**
- **1 cup medium salsa**
- **1/4 cup 2% milk**
- **2 teaspoons taco seasoning**

Cook pasta according to package directions. Meanwhile, in a large skillet over medium heat, cook the chicken, onion, salt and pepper in oil until chicken is no longer pink. Stir in Alfredo sauce; bring to a boil. Stir in the cheese, salsa, milk and taco seasoning.

Drain pasta; toss with the chicken mixture. Divide between two greased 8-in. square baking dishes.

Cover and freeze one casserole for up to 3 months. Cover and bake remaining casserole at 350° for 30-35 minutes or until bubbly.

To use frozen casserole: Thaw in the refrigerator overnight. Remove from the refrigerator 30 minutes before baking. Cover and bake at 350° for 50-60 minutes or until bubbly. **Yield:** 2 casseroles (4 servings each).

CHAPTER 16

Casseroles & Oven Suppers

There's no better way to please a group of hungry people than with a comforting, piping-hot dinner straight from the oven. This chapter is full of wholesome main dishes that are more fuss-free than you think!

For family-friendly fare, try the Mexican Lasagna or Stuffed Burger Bundles. Or, there's the Baja Chicken Taco Pizza, which both kids and adults will enjoy.

Or if you're looking for an elegant meal with a special touch, try the Bacon & Tomato-Topped Haddock or the Roast Pork with Cherry-Almond Glaze...both restaurant-quality meals. Best of all, these dishes offer simple sophistication that can be made in your oven without too much effort or hard-to-find ingredients! ■

HOT DISH HEAVEN. Reunion Casserole (p. 256).

Harvest Vegetable Bake

(Pictured above)

Prep: 10 min. **Bake:** 1-1/2 hours

This delicious bake is packed with a large assortment of vegetables. Served with a green salad, it makes an excellent entree. —Janet Weisser, Seattle, Washington

2-1/2 to 3 pounds boneless skinless chicken thighs
2 bay leaves
4 small red potatoes, cut into 1-inch pieces
4 small onions, quartered
4 small carrots, cut into 2-inch pieces
2 celery ribs, cut into 2-inch pieces
2 small turnips, peeled and cut into 1-inch pieces
1 medium green pepper, cut into 1-inch pieces
12 small fresh mushrooms
2 teaspoons salt
1 teaspoon dried rosemary, crushed
1/2 teaspoon pepper
1 can (14-1/2 ounces) diced tomatoes, undrained

Place chicken in a greased 13-in. x 9-in. baking dish; add bay leaves. Top with potatoes, onions, carrots, celery, turnips, green pepper and mushrooms. Sprinkle with salt, rosemary and pepper. Pour tomatoes over all.

Cover and bake at 375° for 1-1/2 hours or until chicken juices run clear and vegetables are tender. Discard bay leaves before serving. **Yield:** 6-8 servings.

Mimosa Roasted Chicken

Prep: 15 min. **Bake:** 2-1/4 hours + standing

This aromatic seasoned chicken made in our Test Kitchen with a buttery Champagne gravy will impress everyone.

2 medium navel oranges
1 roasting chicken (6 to 7 pounds)
3/4 teaspoon pepper, *divided*
1/4 cup butter, softened
4 garlic cloves, minced
1 tablespoon dried basil
1 teaspoon salt
1/2 teaspoon onion powder
1/2 teaspoon dried marjoram
2 cups brut Champagne
2 medium onions, cut into wedges
1/2 cup chicken broth
1/2 cup orange juice
GRAVY:
Chicken broth *or* water
1 tablespoon butter
2 tablespoons all-purpose flour

Cut one orange into slices; cut remaining orange into wedges. With fingers, carefully loosen the skin from both sides of chicken breast. Place orange slices under the skin. Place orange wedges inside cavity and sprinkle with 1/4 teaspoon pepper.

Tuck wings under chicken. Place breast side up on a rack in a shallow roasting pan. Combine butter, garlic, basil, salt, onion powder, marjoram and the remaining pepper; rub over chicken.

Bake, uncovered, at 350° for 30 minutes. Meanwhile, in a large bowl, combine the champagne, onions, broth and orange juice; pour into pan. Bake 1-1/2 to 2 hours longer or until a meat thermometer reads 180°, basting occasionally with pan juices. Cover loosely with foil if chicken browns too quickly. Cover and let stand for 15 minutes before slicing.

For gravy, pour drippings and loosened browned bits into a measuring cup. Skim fat, reserving 1 tablespoon. Add enough broth to the drippings to measure 1 cup. In a small saucepan, melt butter and reserved fat. Stir in flour until smooth, gradually add broth mixture. Bring to a boil; cook and stir for 2 minutes or until thickened. Serve with chicken. **Yield:** 6 servings.

Spinach-Stuffed Beef Tenderloin

Prep:30 min. **Bake:** 40 min. + standing

Serve this elegant but easy main course from our Test Kitchen. It'll be the centerpiece of Christmas dinner.

1/2 pound fresh mushrooms, chopped
4 green onions, sliced
2 tablespoons olive oil, *divided*
2 garlic cloves, minced, *divided*
2 packages (10 ounces *each*) fresh spinach leaves
1 teaspoon salt, *divided*
1/8 to 1/4 teaspoon cayenne pepper

1 beef tenderloin roast (3-1/2 pounds)
1/4 teaspoon onion powder
1/4 teaspoon coarsely ground pepper

In a large nonstick skillet, saute mushrooms and onions in 1 tablespoon oil until mushrooms are tender. Add half of the garlic; cook 1 minute longer. Add spinach, 1/2 teaspoon salt and cayenne. Cook until the spinach is wilted. Remove from the heat; set aside.

Cut a lengthwise slit down the center of tenderloin to within 3/4 in. of bottom. Open so meat lies flat. Spread with spinach stuffing. Fold one side of meat over stuffing; tie several times with kitchen string. Rub remaining oil over beef. Combine the onion powder, pepper and remaining garlic and salt; rub over beef. Place on a rack in a shallow roasting pan.

Bake, uncovered, at 425° for 40-55 minutes or until a meat thermometer reaches desired doneness (for medium-rare, meat thermometer should read 145°; medium, 160°; well-done, 170°). Let stand for 10 minutes. Remove string before slicing. **Yield:** 12 servings.

Crab-Stuffed Tilapia

Prep: 20 min. **Bake:** 25 min.

Make a reservation for four at your dining room table. With this lovely, restaurant-quality dish, you can turn an ordinary Tuesday night into a supper celebration.
—Linda Stemen, Monroeville, Indiana

1 small onion, finely chopped
1 celery rib, finely chopped
1/4 cup plus 6 tablespoons butter, *divided*
2 packages (3.53 ounces *each*) premium crabmeat, drained
1/3 cup dry bread crumbs
1/3 cup mayonnaise
1 egg, beaten
2 tablespoons diced pimientos, drained
1/4 teaspoon seafood seasoning
4 tilapia fillets (6 ounces *each*)
1/4 teaspoon salt
1/4 teaspoon paprika

In a large skillet, saute the onion and celery in 1/4 cup butter until tender. Remove from the heat; stir in the crab, bread crumbs, mayonnaise, egg, pimientos and seafood seasoning. Spread 1/3 cup crab mixture over fillets. Roll up each from the pointed end; secure with toothpicks.

Place seam side down in a greased 9-in. square baking pan. Melt remaining butter; drizzle over fish. Sprinkle with salt and paprika.

Bake, uncovered, at 400° for 25-30 minutes or until fish flakes easily with a fork. Discard toothpicks. Spoon pan juices over fish. **Yield:** 4 servings.

TENDER TILAPIA

If you're looking for a type of fish that doesn't taste "fishy," we recommend tilapia. Overall, it has a very mild and appealing flavor. Most of the larger grocery stores carry fresh or frozen tilapia.

Hearty Alfredo Potatoes

(Pictured below)

Prep: 20 min. **Bake:** 1-1/4 hours + standing

With turkey and broccoli, this special scalloped potato recipe is a meal in itself. Using a jar of Alfredo sauce makes the preparation time minimal.
—Lissa Hutson, Phelan, California

1 jar (16 ounces) Alfredo sauce
1 cup whole milk
1 teaspoon garlic powder
3 pounds potatoes, peeled and thinly sliced
5 tablespoons grated Parmesan cheese, *divided*
Salt and pepper to taste
2 to 3 cups cubed cooked turkey
3 cups frozen chopped broccoli, thawed
2 cups (8 ounces) shredded Swiss cheese, *divided*

In a large bowl, combine the Alfredo sauce, milk and garlic powder. Pour a fourth of the mixture into a greased 13-in. x 9-in. baking dish. Layer with a fourth of the potatoes; sprinkle with 1 tablespoon Parmesan cheese, salt and pepper.

In a large bowl, combine the turkey, broccoli and 1-1/2 cups Swiss cheese; spoon a third over potatoes. Repeat layers twice. Top with the remaining potatoes. Sprinkle with remaining Swiss and Parmesan cheeses. Spread with remaining Alfredo sauce mixture.

Cover and bake at 400° for 45 minutes. Reduce heat to 350°. Bake, uncovered, 30 minutes longer or until potatoes are tender. Let stand for 15 minutes before serving. **Yield:** 6-8 servings.

Mexican Smothered Chicken Thighs

(Pictured below)

Prep: 20 min. **Bake:** 30 min.

Chicken thighs are a juicier, less expensive alternative to boneless, skinless chicken breasts. This Mexican-inspired entree uses them to perfection.
—Jeanne Trudell, Del Norte, Colorado

1 cup all-purpose flour
1 tablespoon seasoned salt
1 teaspoon salt
1 teaspoon pepper
3/4 cup 2% milk
8 bone-in chicken thighs (about 3 pounds), skin removed
3 tablespoons olive oil
1 medium onion, chopped
2 jalapeno peppers, seeded and chopped
2 cans (8 ounces *each*) tomato sauce
1 cup water
1 tablespoon chili powder
2 teaspoons garlic powder
2 teaspoons ground cumin

In a shallow bowl, combine the flour, seasoned salt, salt and pepper. Place milk in a separate shallow bowl. Coat chicken with flour mixture, then dip in milk and coat again with flour mixture.

In a large skillet, brown chicken in oil in batches. Transfer to a greased 13-in. x 9-in. baking dish.

In the same skillet, saute onion and jalapenos until tender. Add the tomato sauce, water and spices. Bring to a boil. Reduce the heat; simmer, uncovered, for 5 minutes or until thickened, stirring occasionally. Pour over the chicken.

Cover and bake at 350° for 30-35 minutes or until chicken juices run clear. **Yield:** 8 servings.

Editor's Note: Wear disposable gloves when cutting hot peppers; the oils can burn your skin. Avoid touching your face.

Stuffed Burger Bundles

(Pictured above)

Prep: 30 min. **Bake:** 35 min.

I changed up my mom's recipe a bit to make it my own. Add a side of mashed potatoes and pour the sauce over both the potatoes and the bundles. This is comfort food at its best! *—Debbie Carter, Kingsburg, California*

1 cup stuffing mix
1/3 cup evaporated milk
1/2 teaspoon salt
1/2 teaspoon dried thyme
1 pound ground beef

MUSHROOM SAUCE:

1 cup sliced fresh mushrooms
1 tablespoon butter
1 can (10-3/4 ounces) condensed cream of mushroom soup, undiluted
1 tablespoon ketchup
2 teaspoons Worcestershire sauce
1/4 teaspoon dried thyme

Prepare stuffing according to the package directions. Meanwhile, in a large bowl, combine the milk, salt and thyme. Crumble beef over milk mixture and mix well. Shape mixture into eight thin patties. Divide stuffing between four patties; top with remaining patties and press edges firmly to seal.

Place in an ungreased 13-in. x 9-in. baking dish. Bake, uncovered, at 350° for 35-40 minutes or until a meat thermometer reads 160° and juices run clear.

For sauce, in a large skillet, saute mushrooms in butter until tender. Stir in the remaining ingredients; heat through. Serve with burgers. **Yield:** 4 servings.

Cajun Shrimp Lasagna Roll-Ups

(Pictured below)

Prep: 30 min. **Bake:** 25 min. + standing

If you enjoy Creole and Cajun dishes, you'll love this one. The seasoning and andouille sausage give it a nice kick, and seafood fans will appreciate the shrimp.
—Mary Beth Harris-Murphree, Tyler, Texas

1-1/4 pounds uncooked medium shrimp, peeled and deveined
1 medium onion, chopped
2 tablespoons olive oil
4 medium tomatoes, seeded and chopped
2 tablespoons Cajun seasoning
3 garlic cloves, minced
1/4 cup butter, cubed
1/4 cup all-purpose flour
2 cups milk
1-1/2 cups (6 ounces) shredded cheddar cheese
1 cup diced fully cooked andouille sausage
12 lasagna noodles, cooked and drained
4 ounces pepper Jack cheese, shredded
1 teaspoon paprika

In a large skillet, saute the shrimp and onion in oil until shrimp turn pink. Stir in tomatoes and Cajun seasoning; set aside.

In a large saucepan, saute garlic in butter for 1 minute. Stir in flour until blended. Gradually add milk. Bring to a boil over medium heat; cook and stir for 2 minutes or until thickened. Remove from the heat; stir in cheddar cheese until smooth. Add sausage; set aside.

Spread 1/3 cup shrimp mixture over each noodle. Carefully roll up; place seam side down in a greased 13-in. x 9-in. baking dish. Top with the cheese sauce. Sprinkle with pepper Jack cheese and paprika.

Cover and bake at 350° for 15 minutes. Uncover; bake 10-15 minutes longer or until bubbly. Let stand 15 minutes before serving. **Yield:** 6 servings.

Bacon & Tomato-Topped Haddock

(Pictured above)

Prep: 25 min. **Cook:** 10 min.

Bacon presents a compelling argument for anyone who doesn't like fish. And for those who do, it just got better.
—Sherri Melotik, Oak Creek, Wisconsin

6 bacon strips, chopped
1 medium onion, thinly sliced
1 garlic clove, minced
1 cup panko (Japanese) bread crumbs
2 plum tomatoes, chopped
1/4 cup minced fresh parsley
2 tablespoons olive oil
1 tablespoon butter, melted
5 haddock fillets (6 ounces *each*)
2 tablespoons lemon juice
1/4 teaspoon salt

In a large skillet, cook bacon over medium heat until partially cooked but not crisp. Add onion and garlic; cook for 10-15 minutes or until golden brown, stirring occasionally. Remove from the heat; stir in the bread crumbs, tomatoes and parsley. Set aside.

Spread oil and butter in an ungreased 15-in. x 10-in. x 1-in. baking pan. Place fillets in pan. Drizzle with lemon juice and sprinkle with salt. Top with bread crumb mixture. Bake, uncovered, at 400° for 10-15 minutes or until fish flakes easily with a fork. **Yield:** 5 servings.

Reunion Casserole

(Pictured above)

Prep: 15 min. **Bake:** 45 min.

This is a noodle casserole just like Mom used to make! Its down-home taste has great appeal at a family gathering or as a dish to pass. It's also easy to prepare and can be assembled ahead of time. No leftovers!

—Bernice Morris, Marshfield, Missouri

1 pound ground beef
1/2 pound bulk spicy pork sausage
1 cup chopped onion
2 cups (8 ounces) shredded cheddar cheese, *divided*
1 medium green pepper, chopped
1 can (11 ounces) whole kernel corn, drained
1 can (10-3/4 ounces) condensed tomato soup, undiluted
1 can (8 ounces) tomato sauce
1/3 cup sliced pimiento-stuffed olives
1 garlic clove, minced
1/2 teaspoon salt
8 ounces wide noodles, cooked and drained

In a large Dutch oven, cook the beef, sausage and onion over medium heat until meat is no longer pink; drain. Stir in 1 cup cheese, green pepper, corn, soup, tomato sauce, olives, garlic, salt and noodles.

Transfer to a greased 13-in. x 9-in. baking dish. Sprinkle with remaining cheese. Cover and bake at 350° for 35 minutes or until bubbly. Uncover; bake 10 minutes longer or until cheese is melted. **Yield:** 8-10 servings.

Sausage & Mushroom Stuffed Squash

(Pictured below)

Prep: 45 min. **Bake:** 20 min.

Familiar ingredients make this entree comforting for me. The cheddar cheese is the same kind my family has used for years to make grilled cheese sandwiches. And the croutons remind me of Thanksgiving dinners.

—Eliane Oneyear, River Forest, Illinois

3 medium acorn squash
1-1/2 cups water
1 pound bulk pork sausage
1/2 pound sliced baby portobello mushrooms
1 large onion, chopped
1 celery rib, chopped
1 garlic clove, minced
1/2 cup white wine *or* beef broth
1 can (10-3/4 ounces) condensed cream of mushroom soup, undiluted
1 cup salad croutons
1/2 cup 2% milk
1/3 cup shredded Parmesan cheese
1 cup (4 ounces) sharp shredded cheddar cheese, *divided*

Cut squash in half; discard seeds. Place cut side down in an ungreased 15-in. x 10-in. x 1-in. baking pan. Add the water. Cover and bake at 350° for 40-50 minutes or until tender.

Meanwhile, in a large skillet, cook the sausage, mushrooms, onion, celery and garlic over medium heat until the meat is no longer pink; drain. Add the wine. Bring to a boil; cook until the liquid is reduced by half. Stir in the soup, croutons, milk, Parmesan and 3/4 cup cheddar cheese.

Drain water from squash. Turn squash over; stuff with sausage mixture. Sprinkle with remaining cheddar cheese. Bake, uncovered, for 20-25 minutes or until heated through. **Yield:** 6 servings.

Lattice Chicken Potpie

(Pictured above)

Prep: 10 min. **Bake:** 35 min.

My sister shared this great recipe with me. Because it features all four food groups, it's the only dish you have to prepare for dinner. —*Angie Cottrell, Sun Prairie, Wisconsin*

1 package (16 ounces) frozen California-blend vegetables
2 cups cubed cooked chicken
1 can (10-3/4 ounces) condensed cream of potato soup, undiluted
1 cup 2% milk
1 cup (4 ounces) shredded cheddar cheese
1 can (2.8 ounces) french-fried onions
1/2 teaspoon seasoned salt
1 tube (8 ounces) refrigerated crescent rolls

In a large saucepan, combine the vegetables, chicken, soup and milk; bring to a boil. Remove from the heat. Stir in the cheese, onions and seasoned salt. Transfer to a greased shallow 2-qt. baking dish.

Unroll the crescent roll dough and separate into two rectangles. Seal the perforations; cut each rectangle lengthwise into 1/2-in. strips. Form a lattice crust over the chicken mixture. Bake, uncovered, at 375° for 35-40 minutes or until golden brown. **Yield:** 4-6 servings.

PREHEATED OVENS

Baked items depend on the correct oven temperature to help them rise and cook properly. All Taste of Home recipes are tested in preheated ovens. This takes about 15 to 20 minutes and can be done while preparing the recipe.

Mexican Lasagna

(Pictured below)

Prep: 25 min. **Bake:** 40 min. + standing

No-cook lasagna noodles ease preparation in this hearty classic. I make it with rotisserie chicken when time is short. The robust lasagna is a meal in itself, and the encilada sauce adds great southwestern flavor.
—*Valonda Seward, Hanford, California*

1 cup chopped onion
1 tablespoon canola oil
1 garlic clove, minced
4 cups cubed cooked chicken
3 cans (10 ounces *each*) enchilada sauce
2 eggs
1 carton (15 ounces) ricotta cheese
1/2 cup minced fresh cilantro
12 no-cook lasagna noodles
4 cups (16 ounces) shredded Mexican cheese blend

In a large skillet, cook the chopped onion in oil over medium heat until tender. Add the garlic; cook 1 minute longer. Stir in the cooked chicken and enchilada sauce. Bring to a boil.

Reduce heat; simmer, uncovered, for 5 minutes or until slightly thickened. Meanwhile, in a small bowl, combine the eggs, ricotta cheese and cilantro.

Spread 3/4 cup chicken mixture into a greased 13-in. x 9-in. baking dish. Layer with three noodles, 2/3 cup ricotta mixture, 3/4 cup chicken mixture and 1 cup shredded cheese. Repeat the layers twice. Top with remaining noodles, sauce and shredded cheese.

Cover and bake at 375° for 30 minutes. Uncover; bake 10-15 minutes longer or until bubbly. Let stand for 10 minutes before cutting. **Yield:** 10-12 servings

In a small saucepan, cook and stir the cream cheese and 2 tablespoons butter over low heat until melted and smooth; set aside.

In a large skillet, saute the onion, celery and green pepper in remaining butter until tender. Stir in shrimp, crab, soup, rice, mushrooms, garlic salt, pepper sauce, cayenne and reserved cream cheese mixture.

Transfer to a greased 2-qt. baking dish. Combine cheddar cheese and cracker crumbs; sprinkle over the top. Bake, uncovered, at 350° for 25-30 minutes or until bubbly. **Yield:** 6-8 servings.

Blend of the Bayou

(Pictured above)

Prep: 20 min. **Bake:** 25 min.

My sister-in-law shared this recipe when I first moved to Louisiana. It has been handed down in my husband's family for generations. It's quick to prepare, nutritious and beautiful. I've passed it on to my children, too.
—Ruby Williams, Bogalusa, Louisiana

1 package (8 ounces) cream cheese, cubed
4 tablespoons butter, *divided*
1 large onion, chopped
2 celery ribs, chopped
1 large green pepper, chopped
1 pound cooked medium shrimp, peeled and deveined
2 cans (6 ounces *each*) crabmeat, drained, flaked and cartilage removed
1 can (10-3/4 ounces) condensed cream of mushroom soup, undiluted
3/4 cup cooked rice
1 jar (4-1/2 ounces) sliced mushrooms, drained
1 teaspoon garlic salt
3/4 teaspoon hot pepper sauce
1/2 teaspoon cayenne pepper
3/4 cup shredded cheddar cheese
1/2 cup crushed butter-flavored crackers (about 12 crackers)

Roast Pork with Cherry-Almond Glaze

(Pictured below)

Prep: 10 min. **Bake:** 65 min. + standing

Your pork roast will never dry out during cooking with this sweet cherry glaze. You can also spoon the sauce over slices of baked ham. —Joan Laurenzo, Johnstown, Ohio

1 boneless whole pork loin roast (3-1/2 pounds)
1 teaspoon salt
1 jar (12 ounces) cherry preserves
1/4 cup cider vinegar
2 tablespoons light corn syrup
1/4 teaspoon *each* ground cinnamon, nutmeg and cloves
1/4 cup slivered almonds

Sprinkle roast with salt; place on a rack in a shallow roasting pan. Bake, uncovered, at 350° for 30 minutes.

In a small saucepan, bring the preserves, vinegar, corn syrup and spices to a boil. Reduce heat; simmer, uncovered, for 2 minutes. Set aside 3/4 cup for serving. Stir almonds into remaining mixture.

Brush roast with some of the glaze. Bake 35-50 minutes longer or until a meat thermometer reads 160°, brushing frequently with remaining glaze. Let stand for 10 minutes before slicing. Serve with reserved cherry mixture. **Yield:** 10 servings.

Baja Chicken Taco Pizza

(Pictured top right)

Prep: 20 min. **Bake:** 20 min. + standing

With cilantro, taco seasoning, chicken, avocado and lots of cheese, this flavorful pizza is filling and so refreshing. It's a wonderful warm-weather pizza.
—Jenny Flake, Newport Beach, California

- **1 cup ranch salad dressing**
- **1/4 cup salsa**
- **1 tablespoon lime juice**
- **3 tablespoons minced fresh cilantro**
- **2 cups cubed cooked chicken breast**
- **1 envelope taco seasoning**
- **1 prebaked 12-inch thin pizza crust**
- **1/2 cup chopped tomato**
- **1/2 cup finely chopped red onion**
- **2 cups (8 ounces) shredded part-skim mozzarella cheese**
- **2 cups shredded lettuce**
- **2 medium ripe avocados, peeled and thinly sliced**

In a blender or food processor, combine the salad dressing, salsa, lime juice and cilantro. Cover and process on high for 1-2 minutes or until smooth; set aside. In a small bowl, combine the cooked chicken and taco seasoning; set aside.

Place crust on an ungreased 12-in. pizza pan. Spread salsa mixture over crust. Sprinkle with the chicken mixture, tomato, onion and cheese. Bake at 425° for 17-20 minutes or until crust is golden brown and cheese is melted. Let stand for 10 minutes before cutting. Sprinkle with lettuce; top with avocado slices. Serve immediately. **Yield:** 6 servings.

Smoked Turkey Sausage Pizza

(Pictured bottom right)

Prep: 25 min. **Bake:** 10 min.

Turkey sausage gives this easy, cheesy classic a smoky flavor. It's so simple, you can fix it any weeknight.
—Ruth Ann Bott, Lake Wales, Florida

- **1 package (6-1/2 ounces) pizza crust mix**
- **1/2 cup chopped green pepper**
- **1/2 cup chopped sweet red pepper**
- **2/3 cup pizza sauce**
- **1 package (14 ounces) smoked turkey sausage, sliced**
- **1 jar (6 ounces) sliced mushrooms, drained**
- **1/4 cup chopped green onions**
- **1/2 cup shredded part-skim mozzarella cheese**
- **1/2 cup shredded cheddar cheese**
- **1/4 cup grated Parmesan cheese**
- **1/2 teaspoon dried oregano**

Prepare pizza dough according to package directions. Place dough on a greased baking sheet. With floured hands, press into a 12-in. x 10-in. rectangle. Bake at 425° for 3 minutes.

Meanwhile, in a small nonstick skillet coated with cooking spray, saute peppers until crisp-tender.

Spread the pizza sauce over crust to within 1 in. of the edges. Top with the sauteed vegetables, sausage, mushrooms and onions. Combine cheeses and oregano; sprinkle over pizza.

Bake for 10-15 minutes or until cheese is melted and crust is golden brown. **Yield:** 6 servings.

PIZZA WITH PIZZAZZ

To make a delicious herbed pizza crust, just add 1 teaspoon basil and 1 teaspoon oregano to a boxed pizza crust mix. It's an excellent way to give a little zip to "homemade" pizza crust. Brushing the crust edges with olive oil also adds richness.

Apple-Stuffed Pork Tenderloins

(Pictured above)

Prep: 25 min. **Bake:** 25 min. + standing

This impressive entree is oven-ready in just 25 minutes. Garnish with extra sliced apple and fresh parsley for a special dish when unexpected guests drop in.

—Suzanne Earl, Spring, Texas

1 medium apple, peeled and chopped
1 small onion, chopped
1 tablespoon olive oil
1 garlic clove, minced
1/2 teaspoon salt
1/4 teaspoon pepper
2 pork tenderloins (1 pound *each*)

SAUCE:

1 cup unsweetened apple juice
1 cup pomegranate juice
1 tablespoon Dijon mustard
2 tablespoons cornstarch
2 tablespoons cold water
1 tablespoon minced fresh parsley

In a small skillet, the saute apple and onion in oil until tender. Add the garlic, salt and pepper; cook 1 minute longer. Remove from the heat.

Make a lengthwise slit down center of each tenderloin to within 1/2 in. of bottom. Open so they lie flat; cover with plastic wrap. Flatten to 3/4-in. thickness.

Remove plastic; spread apple mixture over meat. Close tenderloins. Tie with kitchen string. Secure ends with toothpicks. Place in an ungreased 13-in. x 9-in. baking dish. Bake, uncovered, at 425° for 15 minutes.

Meanwhile, in a small saucepan, combine the juices and mustard. Bring to a boil; cook for 5 minutes, stirring occasionally. Combine the cornstarch and water until smooth; gradually stir into the juice mixture. Bring to a boil; cook and stir for 2 minutes or until thickened. Stir in the parsley.

Pour 3/4 cup sauce over the tenderloins. Bake 10-15 minutes longer or until a meat thermometer reads 160°. Let stand for 10 minutes before slicing. Serve with remaining sauce. **Yield:** 8 servings.

Big Daddy's BBQ Ribs

(Pictured below)

Prep: 30 min. + chilling **Bake:** 1-1/2 hours

There's nothing left on the platter when the "Big E" makes these for the guys at work. A hint of cinnamon lends a little sweetness to this manly favorite. And trust me, make plenty, because there won't be any leftovers.

—Eric Brzostek, East Islip, New York

3/4 cup packed brown sugar
2 tablespoons mesquite seasoning
4-1/2 teaspoons garlic powder
4-1/2 teaspoons paprika
1 tablespoon dried minced onion
1 tablespoon seasoned salt
1 tablespoon ground cinnamon
1 tablespoon ground cumin
1 tablespoon pepper
1 teaspoon salt
8 pounds pork spareribs, cut into serving size pieces
3-1/2 cups barbecue sauce

In a small bowl, combine the first 10 ingredients. Rub over ribs; cover and refrigerate overnight.

Place the ribs bone side down on a rack in a shallow roasting pan. Cover and bake at 350° for 1 hour; drain. Brush some of the barbecue sauce over ribs. Bake, uncovered, for 30-45 minutes or until tender, basting occasionally with barbecue sauce. **Yield:** 8 servings.

Apricot Baked Ham

(Pictured above)

Prep: 10 min. **Bake:** 1 hour 40 min.

Ham is a super choice for a holiday meal because once you put it in the oven, it practically takes care of itself until dinnertime. I have it because everyone in my family loves it! The sugary crust on this ham makes it beautiful to serve. —Marge Clark, West Lebanon, Indiana

1/2 fully cooked bone-in ham (5 to 7 pounds)
20 whole cloves
1/2 cup apricot preserves
3 tablespoons ground mustard
1/2 cup packed light brown sugar

Place ham on a rack in a shallow roasting pan. Score the surface of the ham, making diamond shapes 1/2 in. deep; insert a clove in each diamond. Combine preserves and mustard; spread over ham. Pat brown sugar into apricot mixture.

Bake at 325° for 20 minutes per pound or until a meat thermometer reads 140°. **Yield:** 10-14 servings.

Chicken Loaf with Mushroom Gravy

(Pictured at right)

Prep: 25 min. **Bake:** 55 min. + standing

Try a twist on traditional meat loaf with this chicken version that begins in the food processor. Here, ketchup is replaced with an easy mushroom sauce for a more upscale topping. —Keri Schofield Lawson, Brea, California

1-1/4 pounds boneless skinless chicken breast halves
1-1/4 pounds boneless skinless chicken thighs
2 eggs, lightly beaten
1/2 cup panko (Japanese) bread crumbs
1/2 cup mayonnaise
1 envelope onion soup mix
2 tablespoons minced fresh parsley
1 tablespoon prepared horseradish
1/2 teaspoon salt
1/2 teaspoon garlic powder
1/2 teaspoon dried sage leaves
1/2 teaspoon dried thyme
1/2 teaspoon pepper

GRAVY:

2 cups sliced fresh mushrooms
1 tablespoon butter
3 cups reduced-sodium chicken broth
1 teaspoon dried rosemary, crushed
1/2 teaspoon salt
1/4 teaspoon white pepper
3 tablespoons cornstarch
1/4 cup white wine *or* additional reduced-sodium chicken broth

Place chicken in the freezer for 15-20 minutes or until it begins to freeze. Cut it into 1-in. pieces. In a food processor, cover and process chicken in batches until ground.

In a large bowl, combine the eggs, bread crumbs, mayonnaise, soup mix, parsley, horseradish, salt, garlic powder, sage, thyme and pepper. Crumble chicken over mixture and mix well.

Shape into a loaf; place in a greased 13-in. x 9-in. baking dish. Bake, uncovered, at 350° for 55-60 minutes or until no pink remains and a meat thermometer reads 165°. Let stand for 10 minutes.

Meanwhile, in a large saucepan, saute mushrooms in butter until tender. Add the broth, rosemary, salt and white pepper. Bring to a boil. Combine cornstarch and wine until smooth; gradually stir into the mushroom mixture. Bring to a boil; cook and stir for 2 minutes or until thickened.

Slice the chicken loaf and serve with the gravy. **Yield:** 10 servings.

Roasted Chicken with Veggies

(Pictured below)

Prep: 20 min. **Bake:** 1-1/2 hours

Thyme—one of my favorite herbs—flavors this moist chicken surrounded by vegetables.
—Mary Beth Hansen, Columbia, Tennessee

- **1 broiler/fryer chicken (3 to 3-1/2 pounds)**
- **1 tablespoon canola oil**
- **1/8 teaspoon salt**
- **1/8 teaspoon pepper**
- **6 medium carrots, cut into 1-inch pieces**
- **4 celery ribs, cut into 1-inch pieces**
- **3 medium baking potatoes, cut into 1-1/2-inch pieces**
- **2 medium onions, cut into wedges**
- **2 tablespoons butter, melted**
- **4 teaspoons minced fresh thyme *or* 1 teaspoon dried thyme**

Place chicken, breast side up, in a shallow roasting pan. Rub with oil; sprinkle with salt and pepper. Bake, uncovered, at 375° for 45 minutes.

Arrange the carrots, celery, potatoes and onions around chicken. Combine butter and thyme; drizzle over chicken and vegetables.

Cover and bake 45-60 minutes longer or until a meat thermometer reads 180° and vegetables are tender. **Yield:** 6 servings.

Porcini-Crusted Pork with Polenta

(Pictured above)

Prep: 20 min. **Bake:** 20 min.

Hints of rosemary and Parmesan meet earthy mushroom undertones in this restaurant-quality dish you can proudly call your own.
—Casandra Rittenhouse, North Hollywood, California

- **1 package (1 ounce) dried porcini mushrooms**
- **1/4 teaspoon salt**
- **1/4 teaspoon pepper**
- **4 bone-in pork loin chops (7 ounces *each*)**
- **2 teaspoons olive oil**
- **1 tube (1 pound) polenta**
- **1/2 cup grated Parmesan cheese**
- **1/4 teaspoon dried rosemary, crushed**

Process the porcini mushrooms in a food processor until coarsely chopped. Transfer to a shallow bowl; stir in the salt and pepper. Press one side of each pork chop into mushroom mixture.

In a large ovenproof skillet coated with cooking spray, heat oil over medium-high heat. Place chops, mushroom side down, in skillet; cook for 2 minutes. Turn over; cook 2 minutes longer. Bake, uncovered, at 375° for 20-25 minutes or until a meat thermometer reads 160°.

Prepare polenta according to package directions for soft polenta. Stir in cheese and rosemary. Serve with pork chops. **Yield:** 4 servings.

Jim's Honey-Glazed Ham

Prep: 10 min. **Bake:** 1 hour

The aroma of this ham baking in the oven is absolutely wonderful. It always comes out moist, juicy and lightly browned. *—Jim Whelan, Sebastian, Florida*

- **1 boneless fully cooked ham (3 to 4 pounds)**
- **1/2 cup water**
- **1 cup honey**

1/2 cup packed brown sugar
1 teaspoon ground cloves
1/2 teaspoon ground mustard

Score the ham, making diamond shapes 1/2 in. deep. Place on a rack in a well-greased foil-lined roasting pan. Add water to pan. In a small bowl, combine the honey, brown sugar, cloves and mustard; pour over ham.

Bake, uncovered, at 325° for 1 to 1-1/2 hours or until a meat thermometer reads 140°, basting with pan juices often. Add additional water to the pan if necessary. **Yield:** 10 servings.

Halibut with Orange Salsa

(Pictured below)

Prep: 25 min. + marinating **Bake:** 15 min.

Crispy orange halibut is topped with a homemade salsa featuring tomatoes, oranges, kalamata olives and basil for a company-worthy dish that'll bring raves.
—Gloria Bradley, Naperville, Illinois

1 cup orange juice
1-1/4 teaspoons Caribbean jerk seasoning, *divided*
4 halibut fillets (6 ounces *each*)
1/2 cup panko (Japanese) bread crumbs
2 teaspoons grated orange peel
1/2 teaspoon salt

SALSA:
2 plum tomatoes, seeded and chopped
1 large navel orange, peeled, sectioned and chopped
1/4 cup pitted Greek olives, chopped
2 tablespoons minced fresh basil
1 tablespoon olive oil
1 garlic clove, minced
1/8 teaspoon salt
1/8 teaspoon pepper

In a large resealable plastic bag, combine orange juice and 1 teaspoon jerk seasoning. Add the halibut; seal bag and turn to coat. Set aside for 15 minutes.

Meanwhile, in a shallow bowl, combine the bread crumbs, orange peel, salt and remaining jerk seasoning. Drain and discard marinade. Coat halibut with bread crumb mixture. Place on a greased baking sheet.

Bake at 400° for 15-20 minutes or until fish flakes easily with a fork. Broil 4-6 in. from the heat for 3-4 minutes or until lightly browned.

In a small bowl, combine the salsa ingredients. Serve with halibut. **Yield:** 4 servings.

Beef 'n' Turkey Meat Loaf

(Pictured above)

Prep: 15 min. **Bake:** 50 min. + standing

Shredded potatoes bulk up this hefty meat loaf, seasoned with garlic and thyme.
—Fern Nead, Florence, Kentucky

2 egg whites
2/3 cup ketchup, *divided*
1 medium potato, peeled and finely shredded
1 medium green pepper, finely chopped
1 small onion, grated
3 garlic cloves, minced
1 teaspoon salt
1 teaspoon dried thyme
1/2 teaspoon pepper
3/4 pound lean ground beef (90% lean)
3/4 pound lean ground turkey

In a large bowl, combine the egg whites and 1/3 cup ketchup. Stir in the potato, green pepper, onion, garlic, salt, thyme and pepper. Crumble the beef and turkey over mixture and mix well. Shape into a 10-in. x 4-in. loaf.

Line a 15-in. x 10-in. x 1-in. baking pan with heavy-duty foil and coat the foil with cooking spray. Place loaf in pan. Bake, uncovered, at 375° for 45 minutes; drain. Brush with the remaining ketchup. Bake 5-10 minutes longer or until no pink remains and a meat thermometer reads 165°. Let stand for 10 minutes before slicing. **Yield:** 6 servings.

Hearty Barley Bake

(Pictured above)

Prep: 20 min. **Bake:** 45 min.

Barley is a nice change of pace from the usual pasta or rice in this colorful casserole. It's chock-full of spicy sausage and a variety of vegetables including spinach, carrots and corn. —Jenny Browning, Cypress, Texas

2 cups sliced fresh mushrooms
1 cup thinly sliced carrots
1/2 cup chopped onion
2 teaspoons canola oil
1 garlic clove, minced
12 ounces bulk pork sausage
1-1/2 cups cooked barley
1 can (14-3/4 ounces) cream-style corn
1 package (10 ounces) frozen chopped spinach, thawed and squeezed dry
3 green onions, sliced
1 teaspoon dried savory
1 teaspoon dried thyme
1/2 teaspoon dried marjoram
1/8 teaspoon pepper
1/2 cup shredded Parmesan cheese

In a large skillet, saute the mushrooms, carrots and onion in oil until tender. Add garlic; cook 1 minute longer. Transfer to a large bowl.

In the same skillet, cook sausage over medium heat until no longer pink; drain. Add to mushroom mixture. Stir in the barley, corn, spinach, onions, savory, thyme, marjoram and pepper.

Transfer to a greased shallow 2-qt. baking dish. Cover and bake at 350° for 40 minutes. Sprinkle with cheese. Bake, uncovered, 5 minutes longer or until the cheese is melted. **Yield:** 6 servings.

Peachy Pork Chops

Prep: 30 min. **Bake:** 1 hour

Pork and peaches team for a palate-pleasing combination in this hearty entree. The sweet peaches dot the stuffing and make an appealing golden glaze. Even the pickiest eaters will love these tempting stuffed chops.
—Brenda DuFresne, Midland, Michigan

1-1/2 cups finely chopped onion
1-1/2 cups finely chopped celery
1/3 cup butter, cubed
6 cups day-old cubed bread
1/2 teaspoon poultry seasoning
1/2 teaspoon rubbed sage
1/8 teaspoon pepper
1 can (8-1/2 ounces) sliced peaches, drained and diced
2 eggs
1 cup water
2 tablespoons minced fresh parsley
6 boneless pork chops (1-1/4 inches thick and 4 ounces *each*)
3 tablespoons olive oil
Garlic salt and pepper to taste
1/4 cup peach preserves

In a large skillet, saute the onion and celery in butter until tender; transfer to a large bowl. Add the bread, poultry seasoning, sage and pepper. Fold in the peaches. Combine the eggs, water and parsley; add to bread mixture; toss to coat.

Cut a large pocket in the side of each pork chop; spoon stuffing loosely into pockets. Tie with string to secure stuffing if necessary. Brush chops with oil. Sprinkle with garlic salt and pepper.

In a large skillet, brown the chops on both sides. Place the remaining stuffing in a greased 13-in. x 9-in. baking dish. Top with pork chops. Spoon preserves over the chops. Cover and bake at 350° for 45 minutes. Uncover; bake 15 minutes longer or until meat juices run clear. If string was used, remove before serving. **Yield:** 6 servings.

KEEPING PARSLEY FRESH

To keep fresh parsley in the refrigerator for several weeks, wash the entire bunch in warm water, shake off all excess moisture, wrap in paper towel and seal in a plastic bag. If you need longer storage time, remove the paper towel and place the sealed bag in the freezer. Then simply break off and crumble the amount of parsley you need for soups, stews and other cooked dishes.

Roasted Chicken with Lemon Sauce

(Pictured above)

Prep: 20 min. **Bake:** 2 hours + standing

Our family loves chicken cooked many ways, but this roasted version is one of our favorites. If your family likes lemon, try this. It's so simple to make.
—Geneva Garrison, Jacksonville, Florida

1 roasting chicken (6 to 7 pounds)
1 medium lemon
1 garlic clove, minced
1/2 teaspoon salt
1/2 teaspoon pepper
6 medium carrots, cut into chunks
1 large onion, quartered

LEMON SAUCE:
1/2 cup sugar
4-1/2 teaspoons cornstarch
1 cup cold water
2 tablespoons lemon juice
2 tablespoons grated lemon peel
1 to 2 drops yellow food coloring, optional
1 green onion, thinly sliced

Pat chicken dry. Cut lemon in half; squeeze juice over chicken. Place lemon in cavity. Rub garlic over chicken; sprinkle with salt and pepper.

Place chicken on a rack in a shallow roasting pan. Bake, uncovered, at 350° for 2 to 2-1/2 hours or until a meat thermometer reads 180°, basting occasionally with pan juices and adding carrots and onion during the last hour. Cover loosely with foil if chicken browns too quickly. Cover and let stand for 15 minutes before carving.

Meanwhile, in a small saucepan, combine sugar and cornstarch. Stir in water until smooth. Bring to a boil; cook and stir for 2 minutes or until thickened. Remove from the heat. Stir in the lemon juice, lemon peel and food coloring if desired.

Serve the sauce with chicken and vegetables. Sprinkle with green onion. **Yield:** 6 servings.

Sweet Potato Chili Bake

(Pictured below)

Prep: 30 min. **Bake:** 20 min.

I'm a vegetarian and wanted to develop some dishes that are a little heartier than traditional vegetarian fare. I created this recipe, and even my 1-year-old loves it!
—Jillian Tournoux, Massillon, Ohio

2 cups cubed peeled sweet potato
1 medium sweet red pepper, chopped
1 tablespoon olive oil
1 garlic clove, minced
1 can (28 ounces) diced tomatoes, undrained
2 cups vegetable broth
1 can (15 ounces) black beans, rinsed and drained
4-1/2 teaspoons brown sugar
3 teaspoons chili powder
1 teaspoon salt
1/2 teaspoon pepper
1 package (6-1/2 ounces) corn bread/ muffin mix
1/2 cup shredded cheddar cheese
Optional toppings: sour cream, shredded cheddar cheese and chopped seeded jalapeno pepper

In an ovenproof Dutch oven, saute sweet potato and red pepper in oil until crisp-tender. Add garlic; cook 1 minute longer. Add the tomatoes, broth, beans, brown sugar, chili powder, salt and pepper. Bring to a boil. Reduce heat; simmer, uncovered, for 15-20 minutes or until potatoes are tender.

Meanwhile, prepare corn bread batter according to package directions; stir in cheese. Drop by tablespoonfuls over chili.

Cover and bake at 400° for 18-20 minutes or until a toothpick inserted near the center comes out clean. Serve with toppings of your choice. **Yield:** 7 servings.

Editor's Note: Wear disposable gloves when cutting hot peppers; the oils can burn your skin. Avoid touching your face.

CHAPTER 17

Lightened-Up Delights

No one at the table has to know how healthy these recipes are, because after one bite of these rich, delicious dishes, they will never guess they're light!

Guests may feel as if they're indulging in extra calories when they sample Chili-Apricot Pork Chops or yummy Lemon Pasta with Spinach. Full of irresistible flavor, they'll satisfy even the pickiest palate .

Each dish in this chapter includes Nutrition Facts at the end of the recipe, so you'll have all of the information you need to make the best menu choices for you and your family. You'll even find heart-smart options impressive enough for guests. Cooking up healthy, delicious fare has never been easier!

A GOOD-FOR-YOU MEAL. Crumb-Coated Red Snapper (p. 269).

Saucy Peach-Balsamic Chicken

(Pictured above)

Prep/Total Time: 30 min.

I throw this sweet-savory chicken dish together in no time on a weeknight. I serve it with rice and steamed broccoli, and the whole family loves it.

—Trisha Kruse, Eagle, Idaho

4 boneless skinless chicken breast halves (4 ounces *each*)
1/2 teaspoon salt
1/4 teaspoon pepper
2 tablespoons butter
1/4 cup reduced-sodium chicken broth
1/4 cup sherry *or* additional reduced-sodium chicken broth
1/3 cup peach preserves
2 garlic cloves, thinly sliced
2 teaspoons minced fresh tarragon
1 tablespoon balsamic vinegar

Sprinkle chicken with salt and pepper. In a large skillet, brown chicken on both sides in butter. Remove from the skillet and keep warm.

Add broth and sherry to the skillet, stirring to loosen browned bits from pan. Stir in the preserves, garlic and tarragon. Bring to a boil. Reduce the heat and simmer, uncovered, for 5 minutes, stirring occasionally. Stir in vinegar. Return chicken to the skillet; cover and cook over medium heat for 8-10 minutes or until a meat thermometer reads 170°. **Yield:** 4 servings.

Nutrition Facts: 1 chicken breast half with 1 tablespoon sauce equals 249 calories, 8 g fat (4 g saturated fat), 78 mg cholesterol, 427 mg sodium, 19 g carbohydrate, trace fiber, 23 g protein. **Diabetic Exchanges:** 3 lean meat, 1 starch, 1 fat.

Salsa Black Bean Burgers

(Pictured below)

Prep/Total Time: 30 min.

Meatless meals will be so tasty when these hearty bean burgers are on the menu. Guacamole and sour cream make it seem decadent.

—Jill Reichardt, St. Louis, Missouri

1 can (15 ounces) black beans, rinsed and drained
2/3 cup dry bread crumbs
1 small tomato, seeded and finely chopped
1 jalapeno pepper, seeded and finely chopped
1 egg
1 teaspoon minced fresh cilantro
1 garlic clove, minced
1 tablespoon olive oil
4 whole wheat hamburger buns, split
Reduced-fat sour cream and guacamole, optional

Place beans in a food processor; cover and process until blended. Transfer to a large bowl. Add the bread crumbs, tomato, jalapeno, egg, cilantro and garlic. Mix until combined. Shape into four patties.

In a large nonstick skillet, cook patties in oil in batches over medium heat for 4-6 minutes on each side or until lightly browned. Serve on buns. Top with sour cream and guacamole if desired. **Yield:** 4 servings.

Editor's Note: Wear disposable gloves when cutting hot peppers; the oils can burn your skin. Avoid touching your face.

Nutrition Facts: 1 burger (calculated without optional ingredients) equals 323 calories, 8 g fat (1 g saturated fat), 53 mg cholesterol, 557 mg sodium, 51 g carbohydrate, 9 g fiber, 13 g protein.

Crumb-Coated Red Snapper

(Pictured above)

Prep/Total Time: 30 min.

I always reel in compliments with these moist, crispy-coated fillets whenever I serve them. Heart-healthy omega-3 oils are an added bonus with this simple but delicious entree that's done in mere minutes!
—Charlotte Elliott, Neenah, Wisconsin

1/2 cup dry bread crumbs
2 tablespoons grated Parmesan cheese
1 teaspoon lemon-pepper seasoning
1/4 teaspoon salt
4 red snapper fillets (6 ounces *each*)
2 tablespoons olive oil

In a shallow bowl, combine the bread crumbs, cheese, lemon-pepper and salt; add fillets, one at a time, and turn to coat.

In a heavy skillet over medium heat, cook fillets in oil in batches for 4-5 minutes on each side or until fish flakes easily with a fork. **Yield:** 4 servings.

Nutrition Facts: 1 fillet equals 288 calories, 10 g fat (2 g saturated fat), 62 mg cholesterol, 498 mg sodium, 10 g carbohydrate, trace fiber, 36 g protein. **Diabetic Exchanges:** 5 lean meat, 1 fat, 1/2 starch.

COOKING FISH

For fish fillets, check for doneness by inserting a fork at an angle into the thickest portion of the fish and gently parting the meat. When it is opaque and flakes into sections, the fish is cooked completely. Overcooked fish loses its flavor and becomes tough. As a general guideline, fish should be cooked for 10 minutes for every inch of thickness.

Warm Szechuan Shrimp And Spinach Salad

(Pictured below)

Prep/Total Time: 25 min.

A warm ginger-flavored dressing prepared with just a few ingredients tops this fresh and fun salad that's special enough for guests. The slight hint of heat beautifully complements the shrimp and veggies.
—Roxanne Chan, Albany, California

1 pound uncooked medium shrimp, peeled and deveined
1 tablespoon sesame oil
1 package (6 ounces) fresh baby spinach
1 can (15 ounces) whole baby corn, drained
1 cup bean sprouts
1/4 cup salted roasted almonds, chopped
1/4 cup sliced water chestnuts
1/4 cup chopped sweet red pepper
1/4 cup minced fresh cilantro
1 green onion, finely chopped
1/4 cup rice vinegar
1-1/2 teaspoons minced fresh gingerroot
1-1/2 teaspoons chili garlic sauce
1-1/2 teaspoons soy sauce

In a large skillet, saute shrimp in oil until no longer pink. In a large bowl, combine the spinach, corn, sprouts, almonds, water chestnuts, red pepper, cilantro, onion and shrimp.

In the same skillet, combine vinegar, ginger, garlic sauce and soy sauce. Cook and stir over medium heat until heated through; pour over salad and toss to coat. Serve immediately. **Yield:** 5 servings.

Nutrition Facts: 2 cups equals 187 calories, 8 g fat (1 g saturated fat), 110 mg cholesterol, 468 mg sodium, 10 g carbohydrate, 4 g fiber, 20 g protein. **Diabetic Exchanges:** 2 lean meat, 1 fat, 1/2 starch.

Whole Wheat Blueberry Muffins

(Pictured below)

Prep: 15 min. **Bake:** 20 min.

Whole wheat flour gives nutritious flair to these yummy muffins packed with juicy blueberries. Fresh from the oven, they'll warm you up on cold, winter days.
—Sheila Siem, Calumet, Michigan

1-1/2 cups all-purpose flour
1 cup whole wheat flour
1/2 cup sugar
2 teaspoons baking powder
1/2 teaspoon baking soda
1/2 teaspoon salt
1/8 teaspoon ground nutmeg
2 eggs
1 cup buttermilk
1/2 cup canola oil
2 cups fresh *or* frozen blueberries

In a large bowl, combine the flours, sugar, baking powder, baking soda, salt and nutmeg. In another bowl, beat the eggs, buttermilk and oil. Stir into dry ingredients just until moistened. Fold in blueberries.

Fill greased or paper-lined muffin cups three-fourths full. Bake at 375° for 18-20 minutes or until a toothpick comes out clean. Cool for 5 minutes before removing from pans to wire racks. Serve warm. **Yield:** 1-1/2 dozen.

Editor's Note: If using frozen blueberries, use without thawing to avoid discoloring the batter.

Nutrition Facts: 1 each equals 158 calories, 7 g fat (1 g saturated fat), 24 mg cholesterol, 167 mg sodium, 21 g carbohydrate, 1 g fiber, 3 g protein. **Diabetic Exchanges:** 1-1/2 starch, 1 fat.

Just Peachy Pork Tenderloin

(Pictured above)

Prep/Total Time: 20 min.

I had a pork tenderloin and ripe peaches that begged to be put together. We have a no-plate-licking rule, but I licked my plate clean! *—Julia Gosliga, Addison, Vermont*

1 pork tenderloin (1 pound), cut into 12 slices
1/2 teaspoon salt
1/4 teaspoon pepper
2 teaspoons olive oil
4 medium peaches, peeled and sliced
1 tablespoon lemon juice
1/4 cup peach preserves

Flatten each tenderloin slice to 1/4-in. thickness. Sprinkle with salt and pepper. In a large nonstick skillet over medium heat, cook pork in oil until juices run clear. Remove and keep warm.

Add peaches and lemon juice, stirring to loosen browned bits. Cook and stir over medium heat for 3-4 minutes or until peaches are tender. Stir in the pork and preserves; heat through. **Yield:** 4 servings.

Nutrition Facts: 1 serving equals 241 calories, 6 g fat (2 g saturated fat), 63 mg cholesterol, 340 mg sodium, 23 g carbohydrate, 2 g fiber, 23 g protein. **Diabetic Exchanges:** 3 lean meat, 1 starch, 1/2 fruit, 1/2 fat.

Fiesta Taco Salads

(Pictured at right)

Prep/Total Time: 30 min.

This taco salad has all the flavors, but it's easy to prepare and eat because it's not served in a shell. If you like spicy food, use medium or hot salsa and add a jalapeno.
—Tari Ambler, Shorewood, Illinois

- 1/2 pound lean ground beef (90% lean)
- 1 jalapeno pepper, seeded and finely chopped
- 1/3 cup water
- 2 tablespoons reduced-sodium taco seasoning
- 1 can (15 ounces) black beans, rinsed and drained
- 4 cups hearts of romaine salad mix
- 3/4 cup cherry tomatoes, halved
- 1/2 cup chopped green pepper
- 3 green onions, chopped
- 1/4 cup sliced ripe olives
- 1/3 cup shredded reduced-fat sharp cheddar cheese
- 1/2 cup reduced-fat sour cream
- 1/2 cup salsa
- 1/4 cup 2% milk
- 32 blue tortilla chips

In a large skillet, cook beef and jalapeno over medium heat until the meat is no longer pink; drain. Stir in water and taco seasoning. Bring to a boil. Reduce the heat; simmer, uncovered, for 5 minutes. Remove from the heat. Stir in beans.

Divide the romaine among four serving plates. Top with beef mixture, tomatoes, green pepper, onions, olives and cheese.

In a small bowl, combine the sour cream, salsa and milk. Drizzle over salads. Arrange tortilla chips around edges. **Yield:** 4 servings.

Editor's Note: Wear disposable gloves when cutting hot peppers; the oils can burn your skin. Avoid touching your face.

Nutrition Facts: 1 serving equals 483 calories, 18 g fat (6 g saturated fat), 52 mg cholesterol, 922 mg sodium, 54 g carbohydrate, 8 g fiber, 25 g protein.

Greek Chicken Dinner

(Pictured above)

Prep: 15 min. **Bake:** 50 min.

Feta cheese takes this chicken and potatoes dinner over the top with a bit of tangy saltiness. Our Test Kitchen suggests serving with a side salad tossed with pepperoncinis, black olives and reduced-fat balsamic vinaigrette.

- 7 medium red potatoes, cut into 1-inch cubes
- 6 boneless skinless chicken thighs (about 1-1/2 pounds)
- 1/2 cup reduced-fat sun-dried tomato salad dressing
- 2 teaspoons Greek seasoning
- 1 teaspoon dried basil
- 1/2 cup crumbled reduced-fat feta cheese

In a large bowl, combine the first five ingredients. Transfer to a 13-in. x 9-in. baking dish coated with cooking spray.

Cover and bake at 400° for 40 minutes. Sprinkle with cheese. Bake, uncovered, 10-15 minutes longer or until chicken juices run clear and potatoes are tender. **Yield:** 6 servings.

Nutrition Facts: 1 serving equals 316 calories, 12 g fat (3 g saturated fat), 79 mg cholesterol, 767 mg sodium, 25 g carbohydrate, 2 g fiber, 26 g protein. **Diabetic Exchanges:** 3 lean meat, 1-1/2 starch, 1 fat.

FETA CHEESE

Feta is a white, salty, semi-firm cheese. Traditionally it was made from sheep or goat's milk but is now also made with cow's milk. After feta is formed in a special mold, it's sliced into large pieces, salted and soaked in brine.

Shrimp & Tomato Linguine Toss

(Pictured above)

Prep/Total Time: 15 min.

Looking for lighter fare? Pair this fast and flavorful pasta toss with salad and garlic bread for a stress-free supper.
—Louise Gilbert, Quesnel, British Columbia

6 ounces uncooked linguine
1/3 pound uncooked medium shrimp, peeled and deveined
3 garlic cloves, minced
1 tablespoon olive oil
1 can (14-1/2 ounces) fire-roasted diced tomatoes, undrained
2 teaspoons minced fresh basil *or* 1/2 teaspoon dried basil
Dash pepper
1/2 cup crumbled feta cheese
Additional minced fresh basil, optional

Cook linguine according to package directions.

Meanwhile, in a large skillet, cook shrimp and garlic in oil over medium heat until shrimp turn pink. Add the tomatoes, basil and pepper. Bring to a boil; cook and stir for 1-2 minutes or until heated through.

Drain linguine; toss with tomato mixture. Sprinkle with the feta and additional basil if desired. **Yield:** 3 servings.

Nutrition Facts: 1-1/3 cups equals 376 calories, 10 g fat (3 g saturated fat), 71 mg cholesterol, 611 mg sodium, 51 g carbohydrate, 4 g fiber, 20 g protein.

Skillet Ziti with Chicken and Broccoli

(Pictured below)

Prep/Total Time: 30 min.

Here's an elegant entree you'll be proud to serve. It looks like you spent hours, but it's so simple. I like to add a splash of lemon for a refreshing finishing touch.
—Tammy Diekemper, Marine, Illinois

1 pound boneless skinless chicken breasts, cut into 1/2-inch strips
1/2 teaspoon pepper
1/4 teaspoon salt, *divided*
2 tablespoons butter, *divided*
1 small onion, chopped
3 garlic cloves, minced
1/4 teaspoon crushed red pepper flakes
1/4 teaspoon dried oregano
2 cups reduced-sodium chicken broth
1 cup fat-free milk
2-1/2 cups uncooked ziti
1 bunch broccoli, cut into florets
1 cup julienned roasted sweet red peppers
1/2 cup grated Parmesan cheese

Sprinkle chicken with pepper and 1/8 teaspoon salt. In a large skillet, saute chicken in 1 tablespoon butter until no longer pink. Remove and keep warm.

In the same skillet, saute onion in remaining butter until tender. Add the garlic, pepper flakes, oregano and remaining salt; cook 1 minute longer. Stir in broth and milk; bring to a boil. Add ziti; cook for 7-8 minutes or until ziti is tender, adding the broccoli and red peppers during the last 5 minutes of cooking.

Return chicken to skillet; heat through. Sprinkle with cheese. **Yield:** 4 servings.

Nutrition Facts: 2 cups equals 528 calories, 13 g fat (6 g saturated fat), 88 mg cholesterol, 975 mg sodium, 60 g carbohydrate, 7 g fiber, 43 g protein.

Chili-Apricot Pork Chops

(Pictured above)

Prep/Total Time: 20 min.

With a slightly spicy-sweet glaze created with just four ingredients, these chops are not only tasty, they're super-easy, too. Served with an easy pasta side dish, it's a great meal for everyday or when company visits.
—Lily Julow, Gainesville, Florida

1/4 cup apricot preserves
1/4 cup chili sauce
1 tablespoon spicy brown mustard
1 tablespoon water
4 bone-in pork loin chops (7 ounces *each*)
1/4 teaspoon salt
1/4 teaspoon pepper

In a small bowl, combine the preserves, chili sauce, mustard and water. Sprinkle pork chops with salt and pepper. Brush glaze over both sides of pork.

Broil 3-4 in. from the heat for 4-6 minutes on each side or until a meat thermometer reads 160°. **Yield:** 4 servings.

Nutrition Facts: 1 pork chop equals 271 calories, 8 g fat (3 g saturated fat), 86 mg cholesterol, 497 mg sodium, 17 g carbohydrate, trace fiber, 30 g protein. **Diabetic Exchanges:** 4 lean meat, 1 starch.

Lemon Pasta with Spinach

(Pictured above)

Prep/Total Time: 25 min.

Healthy spinach, garlic and lemon combine to coat angel hair pasta for a lovely side that will freshen any meal.
—Charlene Anderson, Bonney Lake, Washington

8 ounces uncooked angel hair pasta
2 garlic cloves, minced
2 tablespoons butter
1 package (6 ounces) fresh baby spinach
3 tablespoons lemon juice
2 teaspoons grated lemon peel
1/2 teaspoon salt
1/4 teaspoon pepper

Cook pasta according to package directions.

Meanwhile, in a large skillet, saute the garlic in butter until tender. Add the spinach, lemon juice and peel, salt and pepper; cook 2-3 minutes longer or until the spinach is wilted.

Drain the pasta. Add to the skillet; toss to coat. **Yield:** 6 servings.

Nutrition Facts: 3/4 cup equals 184 calories, 4 g fat (3 g saturated fat), 10 mg cholesterol, 249 mg sodium, 30 g carbohydrate, 2 g fiber, 6 g protein. **Diabetic Exchanges:** 2 starch, 1 fat.

Turkey Stir-Fry with Cabbage

(Pictured above)

Prep/Total Time: 30 min.

Crunchy cabbage is a nice change of pace from rice in this sweet and savory stir-fry. You'll especially love the mango chutney and nutty flavor from sesame oil.
—Didi Desjardins, Dartmouth, Massachusetts

- **1 tablespoon cornstarch**
- **1-1/4 cups reduced-sodium chicken broth**
- **1/3 cup plus 2 tablespoons mango chutney**
- **4-1/4 teaspoons reduced-sodium soy sauce**
- **1 teaspoon Chinese five-spice powder**
- **1 garlic clove, minced**
- **1 package (20 ounces) turkey breast tenderloins, cut into thin strips**
- **7 teaspoons sesame oil, *divided***
- **1 large sweet red pepper, julienned**
- **1-1/2 cups fresh snow peas**
- **6 cups shredded cabbage**

In a small bowl, combine cornstarch and broth until smooth; stir in the chutney, soy sauce, five-spice powder and garlic.

In a large skillet, saute turkey in 3 teaspoons oil for 6-8 minutes or until no longer pink; set aside. In the same skillet, saute the red pepper and snow peas in 2 teaspoons oil for 2-3 minutes or until crisp-tender. Stir soy sauce mixture and add to skillet. Bring to a boil; cook and stir for 2 minutes or until thickened. Add turkey; heat through.

Meanwhile, in a large nonstick skillet coated with cooking spray, saute the cabbage in remaining oil for 5 minutes or until crisp-tender. Serve with turkey mixture. **Yield:** 4 servings.

Nutrition Facts: 1-1/4 cups stir-fry with 1 cup cabbage equals 410 calories, 10 g fat (2 g saturated fat), 69 mg cholesterol, 803 mg sodium, 42 g carbohydrate, 5 g fiber, 38 g protein.

Tilapia Tostadas

(Pictured below)

Prep/Total Time: 30 min.

Even my non-fish-loving family enjoys this recipe, so it's a winner in my book.
—Jennifer Kolb, Overland Park, Kansas

- **1/4 cup all-purpose flour**
- **1 teaspoon chili powder**
- **1/2 teaspoon salt**
- **1/2 teaspoon pepper**
- **1/4 teaspoon garlic powder**
- **4 tilapia fillets (6 ounces *each*)**
- **1 tablespoon butter**
- **8 corn tortillas (6 inches)**
- **2 cups angel hair coleslaw mix**
- **2 tablespoons reduced-fat mayonnaise**
- **2 tablespoons reduced-fat sour cream**
- **1 tablespoon lime juice**
- **1 teaspoon grated lime peel**
- **1 cup canned black beans, rinsed and drained**
- **1/2 cup sliced avocado**

In a large resealable plastic bag, combine the flour, chili powder, salt, pepper and garlic powder. Add tilapia fillets, one at a time, and shake to coat.

In a large nonstick skillet over medium heat, cook fillets in butter for 5-6 minutes on each side or until fish flakes easily with a fork. Meanwhile, place tortillas on a baking sheet and spritz with cooking spray. Broil 3-4 in. from the heat for 2-3 minutes on each side or until crisp.

In a small bowl, toss the coleslaw mix, mayonnaise, sour cream, lime juice and peel. Cut the fish into large pieces. On each tortilla, layer coleslaw, black beans, fish and avocado. **Yield:** 4 servings.

Nutrition Facts: 2 tostadas equals 437 calories, 12 g fat (4 g saturated fat), 95 mg cholesterol, 659 mg sodium, 44 g carbohydrate, 7 g fiber, 40 g protein. **Diabetic Exchanges:** 5 lean meat, 3 starch, 1-1/2 fat.

Spiced Pork Medallions With Bourbon Sauce

(Pictured at right)

Prep/Total Time: 30 min.

Our tasting panel simply raved over this tender pork with its spicy-sweet sauce.
—Kathy Kantrud, Fenton, Michigan

- **1/2 cup bourbon *or* reduced-sodium chicken broth**
- **1/4 cup packed dark brown sugar**
- **3 tablespoons white vinegar**
- **3 tablespoons reduced-sodium soy sauce**
- **2 garlic cloves, minced**
- **1/2 teaspoon pepper**
- **1/2 teaspoon chili powder**
- **1/4 teaspoon ground cinnamon**
- **1/8 teaspoon salt**
- **1/8 teaspoon ground allspice**
- **1 pork tenderloin (1 pound), cut into 12 slices**

In a small saucepan, combine bourbon, brown sugar, vinegar, soy sauce, garlic and pepper. Bring to a boil; cook until liquid is reduced to about 1/2 cup, stirring occasionally. Meanwhile, combine the chili powder, cinnamon, salt and allspice; rub over pork slices.

In a large skillet coated with cooking spray, cook pork over medium heat for 4-5 minutes on each side or until a meat thermometer reads 160°. Serve with the sauce. **Yield:** 4 servings.

Nutrition Facts: 3 ounces pork with 2 tablespoons sauce equals 221 calories, 4 g fat (1 g saturated fat), 63 mg cholesterol, 581 mg sodium, 15 g carbohydrate, trace fiber, 23 g protein. **Diabetic Exchanges:** 3 lean meat, 1 starch.

TENDERLOIN TIP

Keep pork tenderloin in the freezer for last-minute meals since it thaws and cooks quickly. It's easy to thaw tenderloin using the "defrost" cycle of your microwave. Follow the guidelines outlined on the manufacturer's directions.

Garlic Green Bean Medley

(Pictured above)

Prep/Total Time: 25 min.

This is one of my favorite ways to cook green beans. Everyone loves it! *—Nancy Daugherty, Cortland, Ohio*

- **2 pounds fresh green beans, trimmed**
- **1 large sweet red pepper, cut into strips**
- **1/2 cup thinly sliced sweet onion**
- **1/4 cup thinly sliced celery**
- **2 tablespoons olive oil**
- **2 garlic cloves, minced**
- **1/2 teaspoon salt**
- **1/2 teaspoon pepper**

Place beans in a steamer basket; place in a Dutch oven over 1 in. of water. Bring to a boil; cover and steam for 6-8 minutes or until crisp-tender.

Meanwhile, in a large skillet, saute the red pepper, onion and celery in oil until tender. Add garlic; cook 1 minute longer. Add the beans, salt and pepper; toss to coat. **Yield:** 10 servings.

Nutrition Facts: 3/4 cup equals 57 calories, 3 g fat (trace saturated fat), 0 cholesterol, 126 mg sodium, 8 g carbohydrate, 3 g fiber, 2 g protein. **Diabetic Exchanges:** 1 vegetable, 1/2 fat.

Banana-Pineapple Ice

(Pictured above)

Prep: 15 min. + freezing

My family loves dessert and fruit, but we're trying to make healthier food choices. This refreshing, five-ingredient summer treat is always a hit.
—Myra Hughes, Donaldson, Arkansas

2 cups unsweetened apple juice
2 cups mashed ripe bananas
1 can (8 ounces) unsweetened crushed pineapple, undrained
2 tablespoons lemon juice
1 teaspoon vanilla extract

In a large bowl, combine all ingredients. Pour into an 8-in. square dish. Cover and freeze for 1-1/2 to 2 hours or until almost firm.

Transfer to a large bowl. Beat for 1-2 minutes or until smooth and creamy. Return mixture to dish; freeze until firm. Remove from the freezer 30 minutes before serving. **Yield:** 10 servings.

Nutrition Facts: 1/2 cup equals 79 calories, trace fat (trace saturated fat), 0 cholesterol, 2 mg sodium, 20 g carbohydrate, 1 g fiber, 1 g protein. **Diabetic Exchange:** 1 fruit.

Garden Tuna Pita Sandwiches

Prep/Total Time: 20 min.

A well-balanced meal packed into a pita is a breeze to whip up. Not a fan of tuna? Try canned chicken.
—Rebecca Clark, Warrior, Alabama

2 pouches (one 5 ounces, one 2-1/2 ounces) light water-packed tuna
3/4 cup 2% cottage cheese
1/2 cup chopped cucumber
1/4 cup reduced-fat mayonnaise
1/4 cup shredded carrot
2 tablespoons minced fresh chives
2 tablespoons minced fresh parsley
1/2 teaspoon dill weed
1/4 teaspoon salt
Dash pepper
6 whole wheat pita pocket halves
1 cup fresh baby spinach
6 slices tomato

In a small bowl, combine the first 10 ingredients. Line pita halves with spinach and tomato; fill each with 1/3 cup tuna mixture. **Yield:** 3 servings.

Nutrition Facts: 2 filled pita halves equals 362 calories, 10 g fat (2 g saturated fat), 36 mg cholesterol, 1,114 mg sodium, 39 g carbohydrate, 5 g fiber, 31 g protein. **Diabetic Exchanges:** 3 lean meat, 2 starch, 1 vegetable, 1 fat.

Orange-Coconut Angel Food Cake

(Pictured below)

Prep: 25 min. **Bake:** 30 min. + cooling

Everyone who tries this luscious cake loves it, even those who aren't watching their weight. I have several cake recipes, but this is my favorite.
—Betty Kinser, Elizabethton, Tennessee

1 package (16 ounces) angel food cake mix
1 cup cold water
1/3 cup orange juice
2 teaspoons orange extract, *divided*
1-3/4 cups cold fat-free milk
1 package (1 ounce) sugar-free instant vanilla pudding mix
1 tablespoon grated orange peel
1-1/4 cups flaked coconut, *divided*
1 carton (8 ounces) frozen reduced-fat whipped topping, thawed, *divided*

In a large bowl, combine the cake mix, water, orange juice and 1 teaspoon orange extract. Beat on low speed for 30 seconds. Beat on medium for 2 minutes. Spoon into an ungreased 10-in. tube pan.

Bake at 375° for 30-35 minutes or until lightly browned and the entire top appears dry. Immediately invert the pan onto a wire rack; cool completely, about 1 hour. Run a knife around sides of cake and remove from the pan.

In a small bowl, whisk the cold milk and pudding mix for 2 minutes. Stir in the grated orange peel and remaining orange extract. Let stand for 2 minutes or until soft-set. Fold in 3/4 cup coconut and 3/4 cup whipped topping.

Split cake into three horizontal layers. Place bottom layer on a serving plate; top with half of the pudding mixture. Repeat layers. Top with remaining cake layer. Frost top and sides of cake with remaining whipped topping. Toast the remaining coconut; sprinkle over top and sides of cake. Store in the refrigerator. **Yield:** 14 servings.

Nutrition Facts: 1 slice equals 222 calories, 5 g fat (4 g saturated fat), 1 mg cholesterol, 361 mg sodium, 39 g carbohydrate, 1 g fiber, 4 g protein.

Sesame-Ginger Steak Salad

Prep/Total Time: 25 min.

This Asian-inspired salad makes a satisfying lunch. Cook the steak the night before, refrigerate, then simply toss with veggies and dressing when the lunch bell rings.
—Marla Clark, Moriarty, New Mexico

1 beef top sirloin steak (1 pound)
1/2 cup sesame ginger vinaigrette, *divided*
1/4 teaspoon salt
1/4 teaspoon coarsely ground pepper
1 package (10 ounces) hearts of romaine salad mix
4 radishes, thinly sliced
3 green onions, thinly sliced
1 cup sliced English cucumber
1 cup fresh snow *or* sugar snap peas
1 cup grape tomatoes
1/4 cup minced fresh cilantro

Brush steak with 2 tablespoons vinaigrette; sprinkle with salt and pepper. Cook steak in a large skillet coated with cooking spray over medium-high heat for 5-7 minutes on each side or until meat reaches desired doneness (for medium-rare, a meat thermometer should read 145°; medium, 160°; well-done, 170°). Let stand for 5 minutes before slicing.

Divide salad mix among four plates. Top with radishes, onions, cucumber, peas, tomatoes and cilantro. Arrange the sliced steak over salads; drizzle with remaining vinaigrette. **Yield:** 4 servings.

Nutrition Facts: 1 serving equals 300 calories, 14 g fat (3 g saturated fat), 46 mg cholesterol, 526 mg sodium, 15 g carbohydrate, 4 g fiber, 27 g protein. **Diabetic Exchanges:** 3 lean meat, 2 fat, 1 vegetable, 1/2 starch.

Grilled Salmon with Avocado Salsa

(Pictured below)

Prep/Total Time: 25 min.

I'm not usually a seafood fan, but I ordered a similar salmon dish at a restaurant, and I couldn't stop eating it. My recipe re-creation has become a favorite with family and friends. *—Renee McIlheran, Lockport, Illinois*

1 large tomato, seeded and chopped
1 medium ripe avocado, peeled and chopped
1 small onion, chopped
1/2 cup minced fresh cilantro
1-1/2 teaspoons olive oil
1 garlic clove, minced
2 tablespoons plus 2 teaspoons balsamic vinaigrette, *divided*
4 salmon fillets (4 ounces *each*)
1/4 teaspoon salt
1/4 teaspoon pepper

In a small bowl, combine the tomato, avocado, onion, cilantro, oil, garlic and 2 tablespoons vinaigrette. Chill until serving.

Moisten a paper towel with cooking oil; using long-handled tongs, lightly coat the grill rack. Sprinkle salmon with salt and pepper. Place the salmon skin side down on grill rack. Grill, covered, over medium heat for 7-9 minutes or until the salmon flakes easily with a fork. Brush with remaining vinaigrette. Serve with salsa. **Yield:** 4 servings.

Nutrition Facts: 1 fillet with 1/2 cup salsa equals 301 calories, 21 g fat (3 g saturated fat), 57 mg cholesterol, 295 mg sodium, 9 g carbohydrate, 4 g fiber, 21 g protein. **Diabetic Exchanges:** 3 lean meat, 2 fat.

CHAPTER 18

Appetizers & Beverages

This chapter features tasty quick bites, tantalizing finger food and warm beverages that are perfect for casual gatherings or holidays and special occasions.

French Quarter Cheese Spread and Ham and Broccoli Puffs are sure to be wildly successful at your next cocktail party. If you need a more laid-back snack for game day or a potluck, try the Marinated Antipasto Platter or Green Chili Beef Dip.

No need to go on a scavenger hunt at your supermarket for an impressive appetizer, because you'll be so inspired by these sensational starters that you'll definitely want to prepare them at home! ■

CALMING CUPS. Rich Hazelnut Coffee, Cider Wassail Punch and Butterscotch Mulled Cider (p. 282).

Chili Baked Brie

(Pictured above)

Prep: 15 min. **Bake:** 25 min.

Chili and garlic powder shine in this cheesy loaf that's best right out of the oven. It's my favorite when I entertain.
—Mary Spencer, Greendale, Wisconsin

1 round loaf sourdough bread (1 pound)
1 tablespoon butter, softened
1 teaspoon chili powder
1/2 teaspoon sugar
1/2 teaspoon garlic powder
1/2 teaspoon ground mustard
1 round (8 ounces) Brie cheese, rind removed

Cut top third off loaf of bread; hollow out enough bread from bottom to make room for cheese. Cube removed bread; set aside. Using a knife, make 2-in. cuts into loaf around edge of bread at 1-in. intervals. Spread inside of bread with butter.

Combine the chili powder, sugar, garlic powder and mustard; sprinkle 2 teaspoons into loaf. Top with cheese; sprinkle with the remaining spice mixture. Replace the bread top.

Transfer to an ungreased baking sheet. Bake at 350° for 25-30 minutes or until the cheese is melted. Let stand for 10 minutes. Serve with the bread cubes. **Yield:** 18 servings.

Chicken Skewers with Sweet & Spicy Marmalade

(Pictured below)

Prep: 25 min. + marinating **Broil:** 10 min.

These skewers are fantastic! My father-in-law said they reminded him of growing up in Southern California. They're a great way to bring sunshine to winter days!
—Laurel Dalzell, Manteca, California

1 pound boneless skinless chicken breasts
1/4 cup olive oil
1/4 cup soy sauce
2 garlic cloves, minced
1/8 teaspoon pepper

SAUCE:

2 tablespoons chopped seeded jalapeno pepper
1-1/2 teaspoons butter
1 teaspoon minced fresh gingerroot
3/4 cup orange marmalade
1 tablespoon lime juice
1 tablespoon thawed orange juice concentrate
1/4 teaspoon salt

Flatten the chicken to 1/4-in. thickness; cut lengthwise into 1-in.-wide strips. In a large resealable plastic bag, combine the oil, soy sauce, garlic and pepper; add the chicken. Seal the bag and turn to coat; refrigerate for 4 hours or overnight.

Drain and discard the marinade. Thread two chicken strips onto each of eight metal or soaked wooden skewers; place in a greased 15-in. x 10-in. x 1-in. baking pan. Broil 6 in. from the heat for 2-4 minutes on each side or until chicken is no longer pink.

Meanwhile, in a small saucepan, saute jalapeno in butter until tender. Add ginger; cook 1 minute longer. Reduce heat; stir in the marmalade, lime juice, orange juice concentrate and salt. Serve with chicken skewers. **Yield:** 8 servings (1 cup sauce).

Editor's Note: Wear disposable gloves when cutting hot peppers; the oils can burn your skin. Avoid touching your face.

French Quarter Cheese Spread

(Pictured above)

Prep/Total Time: 20 min.

Topped with toasty pecans, this sweet and savory cheese ball must be a hit because there's never any left over and everyone asks for the recipe. At home, make it ahead of time, then bring to room temp and serve.
—Heidi Blaine Hadburg, Safety Harbor, Florida

1 package (8 ounces) cream cheese, softened
1 tablespoon grated onion
1 garlic clove, minced
1/4 cup butter, cubed
1/4 cup packed dark brown sugar
1 teaspoon Worcestershire sauce
1/2 teaspoon prepared mustard
1 cup finely chopped pecans, toasted
Assorted crackers

In a small bowl, combine the cream cheese, onion and garlic. Transfer to a serving plate; shape into a 6-in. disk. Set aside.

In a small saucepan, combine butter, brown sugar, Worcestershire sauce and mustard. Cook and stir over medium heat for 4-5 minutes or until sugar is dissolved. Remove from the heat; stir in pecans.

Cool slightly. Spoon over cheese mixture. Serve with crackers. **Yield:** 8 servings.

APPETIZER ADVICE

For an appetizer buffet that serves as the meal, offer five or six different appetizers and plan on eight to nine pieces per guest. If you'll also be serving a meal, two to three pieces per person is sufficient.

Crispy Grilled Zucchini With Marinara

(Pictured below)

Prep: 15 min. **Cook:** 5 min./batch

You don't need a deep-fat fryer for the crispiest little snacks around—let the indoor grill do the work! Try this marinara over ziti or bow-tie pasta for a delicious side.
—Steve Foy, Kirkwood, Missouri

1 can (14-1/2 ounces) diced tomatoes with basil, oregano and garlic, undrained
1 can (6 ounces) tomato paste
1/2 cup water
2 teaspoons sugar
1/4 teaspoon salt
1/4 teaspoon dried basil
1/4 teaspoon dried oregano
1 egg
1/3 cup prepared Italian salad dressing
1 cup Italian-style panko (Japanese) bread crumbs
2 medium zucchini, cut diagonally into 1/4-inch slices

In a large saucepan, combine the first seven ingredients. Bring to a boil. Reduce heat; simmer, uncovered, for 5-10 minutes or until thickened, stirring occasionally.

Meanwhile, in a shallow bowl, whisk the egg and salad dressing. Place bread crumbs in another shallow bowl. Dip zucchini slices in egg mixture, then coat with bread crumbs. Cook on an indoor grill for 2-3 minutes or until golden brown. Serve with the marinara. **Yield:** 2 dozen (2-1/3 cups sauce).

Rich Hazelnut Coffee

(Pictured above)

Prep/Total Time: 15 min.

I love to try new recipes and entertain. This tasty beverage couldn't be more perfect for doing just that. Coffee lovers, your favorite drink just got better!
—Sharon Delaney-Chronis, South Milwaukee, Wisconsin

3 cups hot brewed coffee
1/2 cup packed brown sugar
2 tablespoons butter
3/4 cup half-and-half cream
1/4 cup hazelnut liqueur *or* 1/4 teaspoon almond extract
Whipped cream and instant espresso powder, optional

In a large saucepan, combine the coffee, brown sugar and butter. Cook and stir over medium heat until sugar is dissolved. Stir in cream; heat through.

Remove from heat; stir in liqueur. Ladle into mugs. Garnish with whipped cream and dust with espresso powder if desired. **Yield:** 4 servings.

Cider Wassail Punch

(Pictured above, top)

Prep/Total Time: 30 min.

Cinnamon, cloves, apple cider and cranberry juice blend together to create a delightful drink with an aroma to match. If you don't have a percolator, simmer this drink on the stove and strain well before serving.
—Sharon Tipton, Winter Garden, Florida

6 cups apple cider *or* juice
2 cups cranberry juice
1 cup orange juice
1/4 cup sugar
1 medium orange, quartered
2 cinnamon sticks (3 inches)
16 whole cloves
1 cup rum *or* 1 teaspoon rum extract
1/2 teaspoon bitters, optional
Orange peel strips, optional

In a percolator, combine the juices and sugar. Place the orange, cinnamon sticks and cloves in the percolator basket; cover and begin perking.

When cycle is complete, discard orange and spices. Stir in rum and bitters if desired. Garnish with orange peel strips if desired. **Yield:** 9 servings.

Butterscotch Mulled Cider

(Pictured above)

Prep: 5 min. **Cook:** 3 hours

Five minutes of preparation results in a dynamite slow-cooked drink. You'll love the sweet taste of butterscotch and apple in this warming cider.
—Karen Mack, Webster, New York

1 gallon apple cider *or* juice
2 cups butterscotch schnapps liqueur
8 cinnamon sticks (3 inches)

In a 6-qt. slow cooker, combine the apple cider, butterscotch liqueur and cinnamon sticks. Cover and cook on low for 3-4 hours or until heated through. **Yield:** 18 servings (4-1/2 quarts).

Roast Beef Spirals

Prep: 20 min. + chilling

This savory appetizer is simple, addictive and a nice change of pace from the usual tortilla pinwheels.
—Marcia Orlando, Boyertown, Pennsylvania

2 packages (8 ounces *each*) cream cheese, softened
2 garlic cloves, minced
1 teaspoon ground ginger
6 thin slices deli roast beef

In a small bowl, beat the cream cheese, garlic and ginger until blended. Spread over beef slices; roll up.

Wrap each roll-up in plastic wrap; refrigerate for at least 2 hours or until firm. Cut into 1-in. slices. **Yield:** 4 dozen.

Roasted Grape Tomatoes

(Pictured below)

Prep/Total Time: 25 min.

Everyone looks forward to this mouthwatering starter with just a few ingredients. We appreciate that it's a fast, simple way to use up extra homegrown tomatoes.
—Linda Green, Ardmore, Oklahoma

1/2 cup cider vinegar
1/4 cup packed brown sugar
2 tablespoons canola oil
4 garlic cloves, minced
1/2 teaspoon salt
1/2 teaspoon pepper
1 pound grape tomatoes
1 tablespoon minced fresh parsley
Assorted crackers and Gouda cheese slices

In a large bowl, whisk the first six ingredients. Add tomatoes; toss to coat. Transfer to a greased 15-in. x 10-in. x 1-in. baking pan. Sprinkle with parsley.

Bake, uncovered, at 375° for 12-14 minutes or until softened, stirring occasionally. Serve with crackers and cheese. **Yield:** 4 cups.

Peach-Glazed Meatballs

(Pictured above)

Prep: 25 min. **Cook:** 30 min.

When my daughter and her husband come to visit, we often play games together and snack in the evening. These meatballs are a delicious appetizer we all enjoy.
—Christine Martin, Durham, North Carolina

2 eggs, lightly beaten
1 can (8 ounces) water chestnuts, drained and chopped
3/4 cup dry bread crumbs
1 tablespoon beef bouillon granules
1-1/2 pounds ground beef
1 jar (16 ounces) peach preserves
1 bottle (12 ounces) chili sauce
1 envelope onion soup mix

In a large bowl, combine the eggs, water chestnuts, bread crumbs and bouillon. Crumble beef over mixture and mix well. Shape into 1-in. balls.

In a large skillet, cook meatballs in batches until no longer pink; drain. Return all to the skillet.

In a small saucepan, combine the preserves, chili sauce and soup mix. Cook over medium-low heat for 5 minutes. Pour over the meatballs. Simmer, uncovered, for 10 minutes or until heated through. **Yield:** about 4-1/2 dozen.

Fresh Tomato Bruschetta

(Pictured above)

Prep/Total Time: 25 min.

The topping for this simple appetizer can be put together ahead of time and refrigerated. We also love it on top of grilled chicken sandwiches, hamburgers and pizza.
—Samantha Cass, Swartz Creek, Michigan

4 plum tomatoes, seeded and chopped
1/2 cup shredded Parmesan cheese
1/4 cup minced fresh basil
3 tablespoons olive oil
2 tablespoons minced fresh parsley
3 garlic cloves, minced
2 teaspoons balsamic vinegar
1/8 teaspoon salt
1/8 teaspoon crushed red pepper flakes
1/8 teaspoon pepper
1 French bread baguette (10-1/2 ounces), cut into 1/2-inch slices
1/4 cup butter, softened
8 ounces fresh mozzarella cheese, sliced

In a small bowl, combine the first 10 ingredients.

Spread baguette slices with butter; top each with a cheese slice. Place on ungreased baking sheets. Broil 3-4 in. from heat for 3-5 minutes or until cheese is melted. With a slotted spoon, top each slice with about 1 tablespoon tomato mixture. **Yield:** 3 dozen.

Melon-Mango Salsa

(Pictured below)

Prep/Total Time: 20 min.

After tasting a similar salsa on top of fresh fish at a fishing tournament, I went home and tried to duplicate it. Here is my wonderful and surprising result! It tastes terrific with cinnamon pita chips.
—Sylvia Fincham, New Bern, North Carolina

1 cup finely chopped cantaloupe
1 cup finely chopped honeydew
1 cup finely chopped peeled mango
1/2 cup chopped cucumber
1/2 cup finely chopped sweet red pepper
1 green onion, thinly sliced
3 tablespoons lemon juice
1/4 teaspoon ground cinnamon
1/4 teaspoon cayenne pepper
Cinnamon sugar baked pita chips

In a large bowl, combine first six ingredients. Combine the lemon juice, cinnamon and cayenne. Pour over fruit mixture; toss to coat. Chill until serving. Serve with pita chips. **Yield:** 4 cups.

Tropical Guacamole

(Pictured above)

Prep/Total Time: 20 min.

Fresh pineapple stars in this fruity guacamole that sure hits the spot! Both kids and adults have enjoyed it as a poolside snack or as a satisfying summer appetizer.
—Sarah White, Salt Lake Cty, Utah

3 medium ripe avocados, peeled
2 cups finely chopped fresh pineapple
1 medium tomato, seeded and chopped
2 jalapeno peppers, seeded and chopped
1/3 cup minced fresh cilantro
2 tablespoons lime juice
3 garlic cloves, minced
1 teaspoon salt
1/2 teaspoon pepper
Tortilla chips

In a small bowl, mash two avocados. Stir in the pineapple, tomato, jalapenos, cilantro, lime juice, garlic, salt and pepper. Coarsely chop remaining avocado; gently stir into guacamole. Serve with chips. **Yield:** 3-1/2 cups.

Editor's Note: Wear disposable gloves when cutting hot peppers; the oils can burn your skin. Avoid touching your face.

HOW TO RIPEN AN AVOCADO

To quickly ripen an avocado, place it in a paper bag along with an apple. Poke the bag with a toothpick in several spots and leave the bag with its contents at room temperature. The avocado should be ripe in one to three days.

Chili-Cheese Egg Rolls

(Pictured below)

Prep: 15 min. **Cook:** 5 min./batch

More than an inventive way to use leftover or store-bought chili, this is the No. 1 request in our household. Try them with different dipping sauces, such as salsa and even barbecue sauce. —Jennifer Bender, Baldwin, Georgia

1 can (15 ounces) chili without beans
1 cup (4 ounces) shredded cheddar cheese
2 tablespoons finely chopped onion
2 tablespoons finely chopped seeded jalapeno pepper
8 egg roll wrappers
Oil for deep-fat frying
Sour cream and guacamole, optional

In a small bowl, combine the chili, cheese, onion and jalapeno. Place 1/4 cup chili mixture in the center of one egg roll wrapper. (Keep remaining wrappers covered with a damp paper towel until ready to use.) Fold the bottom corner over filling. Fold sides toward center over filling. Moisten the remaining corner with water; roll up tightly to seal. Repeat.

In an electric skillet, heat 1 in. of oil to 375°. Fry egg rolls for 1-2 minutes on each side or until golden brown. Drain on paper towels. Serve with the sour cream and guacamole if desired. **Yield:** 8 egg rolls.

Editor's Note: Wear disposable gloves when cutting hot peppers; the oils can burn your skin. Avoid touching your face.

Reuben Spread

(Pictured above)

Prep: 10 min. **Cook:** 4 hours

I love anything with Reuben flavors, and this is a favorite appetizer. It's also a warm and yummy crowd-pleaser and a stress-free way to rally spirits while watching football!
—June Herke, Watertown, South Dakota

- **2 packages (8 ounces *each*) cream cheese, cubed**
- **3-3/4 cups shredded Swiss cheese**
- **1 can (14 ounces) sauerkraut, rinsed and well drained**
- **4 packages (2 ounces *each*) thinly sliced deli corned beef, chopped**
- **1/2 cup Thousand Island salad dressing**
- **Snack rye bread**

In a 1-1/2-qt. slow cooker, combine the first five ingredients. Cover and cook on low for 4 hours; stir to blend. Serve with snack rye bread. **Yield:** 3-3/4 cups.

Hot Spiced Wine

Prep: 15 min. **Cook:** 4 hours

My friends, family and I enjoy this spiced wine during cold winter gatherings. This warm drink will be especially pleasing to people who enjoy dry red wines.
—Noel Lickenfelt, Bolivar, Pennsylvania

- **2 cinnamon sticks (3 inches)**
- **3 whole cloves**
- **2 bottles (750 milliliters *each*) dry red wine**
- **3 medium tart apples, peeled and sliced**
- **1/2 cup sugar**
- **1 teaspoon lemon juice**

Place cinnamon sticks and cloves on a double thickness of cheesecloth; bring up corners of cloth and tie with string to form a bag.

In a 3-qt. slow cooker, combine the wine, apples, sugar and lemon juice. Add spice bag. Cover and cook on low for 4-5 hours or until heated through. Discard spice bag. Serve warm. **Yield:** 8 servings.

Green Chili Beef Dip

(Pictured below)

Prep/Total Time: 30 min.

I love the crunch and flavor of pecans, so I decided to use them as a topping for a tangy cream cheese dip. I made it for a family reunion, and everyone liked it so much they asked for the recipe. It's so easy to prepare.

—Terry Maly, Olathe, Kansas

1/2 cup chopped pecans
2 tablespoons butter
1 package (8 ounces) cream cheese, softened
1 cup (8 ounces) sour cream
1 tablespoon 2% milk
1 can (4 ounces) chopped green chilies
1 package (2-1/2 ounces) thinly sliced dried beef, finely chopped
1 tablespoon prepared horseradish
1/2 teaspoon garlic salt
Assorted crackers

In a small skillet, saute the chopped pecans in butter until toasted; set aside.

In a small bowl, beat the cream cheese, sour cream and milk until smooth. Stir in the chilies, beef, horseradish and garlic salt; mix well. Transfer to a greased 8-in. square baking dish. Sprinkle with the pecans.

Bake, uncovered, in a toaster oven at 350° for 15-20 minutes or until heated through. Serve with crackers. **Yield:** 2-2/3 cups.

Hawaiian Cheese Bread

(Pictured above)

Prep: 15 min. **Bake:** 25 min.

This bread is absolutely delicious. My mother's friend brought it to a party at work, and after one bite, Mom knew she had to have the recipe. Simple and fast, this mouthwatering loaf is a hit with everybody and at every kind of function.

—Amy McIlvain, Wilmington, Delaware

1 loaf (1 pound) Hawaiian sweet bread
1 block (8 ounces) Swiss cheese
3 slices red onion, chopped
1/2 cup butter, melted
3 garlic cloves, minced
1 teaspoon salt

Cut bread diagonally into 1-in. slices to within 1 in. of bottom. Repeat cuts in opposite direction. Cut Swiss cheese into 1/4-in. slices; cut slices into small pieces. Insert into bread. Combine the onion, butter, garlic and salt; spoon over bread.

Wrap loaf in foil. Bake at 350° for 25-30 minutes or until cheese is melted. Serve warm. **Yield:** 16 servings.

HAWAIIAN SWEET BREAD

Hawaiian sweet bread, popular on the Hawaiian islands, is a slightly sweet and soft yeast bread that is made with eggs. It's similar to challah. One major manufacturer and brand of Hawaiian sweet bread is King's Hawaiian. To see if it's sold near you, check out their website: *www.kingshawaiian.com*.

Bacon-Wrapped Apricot Bites

(Pictured above)

Prep: 20 min. **Bake:** 20 min.

These sweet and slightly smoky snacks are easy to eat, so be prepared with an extra batch. For a change, sprinkle them with a bit of blue cheese or toasted almonds.
—Tammie Floyd, Plano, Texas

- **8 maple-flavored bacon strips**
- **1 package (6 ounces) dried apricots**
- **1/2 cup honey barbecue sauce**
- **1 tablespoon honey**
- **1-1/2 teaspoons prepared mustard**

Cut bacon strips widthwise into thirds. In a large skillet, cook bacon over medium heat until partially cooked but not crisp. Remove to paper towels to drain.

Wrap a bacon piece around each apricot; secure with a toothpick. Place in an ungreased 15-in. x 10-in. x 1-in. baking pan.

Bake at 350° for 18-22 minutes or until bacon is crisp. Meanwhile, in a small bowl, combine the barbecue sauce, honey and mustard. Serve with warm apricot bites. **Yield:** about 2 dozen (2/3 cup sauce).

Ham and Broccoli Puffs

(Pictured above)

Prep: 30 min. **Bake:** 15 min./batch

These starters look complex, but they're easy to make and still very elegant. I like to serve them for special occasions or during the holiday season.
—Lynda McCulloch, San Antonio, Texas

- **4 cups frozen broccoli florets, thawed and finely chopped**
- **1 carton (8 ounces) spreadable chive and onion cream cheese**
- **1 cup (4 ounces) shredded Swiss cheese**
- **1/4 pound thinly sliced deli ham, finely chopped**
- **1/2 cup finely chopped fresh mushrooms**
- **1/4 teaspoon salt**
- **1 package (17.3 ounces) frozen puff pastry, thawed**
- **2 eggs, beaten**

In a large bowl, combine the first six ingredients. On a lightly floured surface, unfold puff pastry. Roll each sheet into a 12-in. square. Cut each into 16 squares. Place a heaping tablespoonful of broccoli mixture in center of each square. Brush edges of pastry with eggs. Bring opposite corners over filling; pinch seams to seal.

Place on ungreased baking sheets. Bake at 425° for 12-15 minutes or until golden brown. Serve warm. **Yield:** 32 appetizers.

Marinated Antipasto Platter

(Pictured below)

Prep: 25 min. + marinating

Guests will find it difficult to stop eating the tidbits on this pretty platter. These tangy appetizers are addicting!
—Shirley Foltz, Dexter, Kansas

1/4 cup olive oil
1/4 cup red wine vinegar
2 tablespoons orange juice
1 teaspoon grated orange peel
1 teaspoon dried rosemary, crushed
1 teaspoon dried tarragon
1/2 pound part-skim mozzarella cheese, cubed
2/3 cup pimiento-stuffed olives
2/3 cup pitted Greek olives
2/3 cup pitted ripe olives
1 jar (4-1/2 ounces) whole mushrooms, drained
1/2 pound thinly sliced hard salami

In a large resealable plastic bag, combine the first six ingredients. Add the cheese, olives and mushrooms; seal bag and turn to coat. Refrigerate overnight.

Drain the marinade; reserving 2 tablespoons. Thread salami onto toothpicks. Arrange on a large platter; drizzle with reserved marinade. Arrange cheese mixture around salami. **Yield:** 16 servings.

Layered Artichoke Cheese Spread

(Pictured above)

Prep: 15 min. + chilling

My sister-in-law brought this to a family party, and it went fast. It feeds a lot, plus it's so colorful and pretty. And it takes just 15 minutes to prep!
—Gina Artrip, Mount Pleasant, South Carolina

1 jar (6-1/2 ounces) marinated quartered artichoke hearts, drained and chopped
1/3 cup roasted sweet red peppers, drained and chopped
2 packages (8 ounces *each*) reduced-fat cream cheese
1 envelope ranch salad dressing mix
3 tablespoons minced fresh parsley
Assorted crackers

Pat the artichokes and peppers dry; set aside. Line a 3-cup bowl with plastic wrap. In a large bowl, beat cream cheese and dressing mix until smooth. In another bowl, combine the artichokes, peppers and parsley.

Spread a third of the cream cheese mixture into prepared bowl; top with half of the artichoke mixture. Repeat layers. Top with remaining cream cheese mixture. Cover and refrigerate for at least 4 hours. Unmold onto a serving plate. Serve with crackers. **Yield:** 3 cups.

CHAPTER 19

Test Kitchen Secrets

Practical matters are always important, so food for your family not only needs to taste great, but also be affordable and easy to prepare. The recipes in this chapter are a lot like good advice, because they will teach you new ways of cooking that combine everyday ingredients to create fantastic food.

On the following pages, you'll find amazing omelets, budget dinners and easy-to-fix meals from leftovers. But don't let the humble subject matter fool you, because with recipes such as Potato & Bacon Frittata, Stuffing-Stuffed Pork Chops and yummy Pork Fried Rice, your family will feel as if they're being treated to an extra-special meal! ■

FIVE-STAR FLAVOR. Parmesan Baked Chicken and Tortellini with Tomato-Cream Sauce (p. 297).

EFFORTLESS OMELETS

Omelets aren't just for breakfast. Serve up one of our savory variations for a quick lunch or supper, too. Each of these omelets is ready in 20 minutes, serves one and costs $1 on average.

Making omelets is no big deal once you get the hang of it. Even your failures, if any, can be served as scrambled eggs. Whip up a skillet sensation any time with this foolproof recipe and tasty variations. ■

Basic Omelet

If you ask me, an omelet is truly nothing more than a scrambled egg pancake with a filling. You can use this basic, no-hassle recipe to form the base for the other omelets that appear here and on the following pages.
— Agnes Ward, Stratford, Ontario

1 tablespoon butter
3 eggs
3 tablespoons water
1/8 teaspoon salt
1/8 teaspoon pepper

In a small nonstick skillet, melt the butter over medium-high heat. Whisk the eggs, water, salt and pepper. Add the egg mixture to the skillet (the mixture should set immediately at edges).

As eggs set, push cooked edges toward the center, letting uncooked portion flow underneath. When the eggs are set, add filling as indicated on each recipe.

Fried Rice Omelet

(Pictured above right)

Prep/Total Time: 25 min.

Here's a fun way to use up leftover chicken and cooked rice. This delightful omelet made in our Test Kitchen, is perfect for dinner.

1/4 cup cooked rice
1/4 cup cubed cooked chicken
1/4 cup frozen stir-fry vegetable blend, thawed
1 tablespoon reduced-sodium teriyaki sauce
1 tablespoon butter
3 eggs
3 tablespoons water
1/8 teaspoon salt
1/8 teaspoon pepper

In a small nonstick skillet coated with cooking spray, saute the rice, cooked chicken, vegetable blend and teriyaki sauce until heated through. Remove from skillet and set aside.

In the same skillet, melt butter over medium-high heat. Whisk the eggs, water, salt and pepper. Add the egg mixture to the skillet (the mixture should set immediately at edges).

As eggs set, push the cooked edges toward the center, letting uncooked portion flow underneath. When the eggs are set, spoon rice mixture on one side; fold other side over filling. Slide omelet onto a plate. **Yield:** 1 serving.

Ham and Swiss Omelet

Prep/Total Time: 20 min.

This easy omelet is a snap to fix for breakfast or even for a fast supper. —Agnes Ward, Stratford, Ontario

1 tablespoon butter
3 eggs
3 tablespoons water
1/8 teaspoon salt
1/8 teaspoon pepper
1/2 cup cubed fully cooked ham
1/4 cup shredded Swiss cheese

In a small nonstick skillet, melt the butter over medium-high heat. Whisk the eggs, water, salt and pepper. Add the egg mixture to skillet (mixture should set immediately at edges).

As eggs set, push cooked edges toward the center, letting uncooked portion flow underneath. When the eggs are set, place ham on one side and sprinkle with cheese; fold other side over filling. Slide omelet onto a plate. **Yield:** 1 serving.

Apple Cinnamon Omelet

(Pictured below)

Prep/Total Time: 20 min.

This sweet and savory omelet is a cinch to whip up!
—Agnes Ward, Stratford, Ontario

1/2 cup thinly sliced peeled tart apple
2 teaspoons sugar
1/4 teaspoon ground cinnamon
2 tablespoons butter, *divided*
3 eggs
3 tablespoons water
1/8 teaspoon salt
1/8 teaspoon pepper
Sweetened whipped cream

In a small nonstick skillet, saute the apple, sugar and cinnamon in 1 tablespoon butter. Remove from skillet and set aside.

In the same skillet, melt the remaining butter over medium-high heat. Whisk the eggs, water, salt and pepper. Add egg mixture to skillet (mixture should set immediately at edges).

As eggs set, push cooked edges toward the center, letting uncooked portion flow underneath. When the eggs are set, spoon apple mixture on one side; fold other side over filling. Slide omelet onto a plate. Serve with whipped cream. **Yield:** 1 serving.

Chorizo Salsa Omelet

(Pictured above)

Prep/Total Time: 20 min.

A few ingredients jazz up an omelet to make it delish!
—Taste of Home Test Kitchen

1 tablespoon butter
3 eggs
3 tablespoons water
1/8 teaspoon salt
1/8 teaspoon pepper
1/4 cup cooked chorizo *or* sausage
2 tablespoons chunky salsa

In a small nonstick skillet, melt the butter over medium-high heat. Whisk the eggs, water, salt and pepper. Add egg mixture to skillet (the mixture should set immediately at edges).

As eggs set, push cooked edges toward the center, letting uncooked portion flow underneath. When the eggs are set, spoon chorizo and salsa on one side; fold other side over filling. Slide omelet onto a plate. **Yield:** 1 serving.

WHAT IS CHORIZO?

Chorizo is a coarsely ground fresh or smoked pork sausage that has Mexican, Spanish and Portuguese origins. Traditionally flavored with paprika or chili powder, chorizo is often used in egg dishes, soups, casseroles and a variety of Mexican dishes.

Italian Omelet

(Pictured below)

Prep/Total Time: 20 min.

Savory and special, this tasty omelet with classic pizza flavors will be a hit with all who taste it.
—Agnes Ward, Stratford, Ontario

3/4 cup sliced fresh mushrooms
2 tablespoons chopped onion
2 teaspoons olive oil
1 tablespoon butter
3 eggs
3 tablespoons water
1/8 teaspoon salt
1/8 teaspoon pepper
1/4 cup shredded part-skim mozzarella cheese
1/4 cup marinara sauce *or* spaghetti sauce, warmed

In a small nonstick skillet, saute mushrooms and onion in oil until tender. Remove from skillet and set aside.

In the same skillet, melt the butter over medium-high heat. Whisk the eggs, water, salt and pepper. Add the egg mixture to the skillet (mixture should set immediately at edges).

As eggs set, push cooked edges toward the center, letting uncooked portion flow underneath. When the eggs are set, spoon mushroom mixture on one side and sprinkle with cheese; fold other side over filling. Slide omelet onto a plate. Serve with marinara sauce. **Yield:** 1 serving.

Tomato and Green Pepper Omelet

(Pictured above)

Prep/Total Time: 20 min

Fresh green pepper, onion and tomato give this savory omelet garden-fresh flavor. You can easily vary it based on the fresh ingredients you have on hand.
—Agnes Ward, Stratford, Ontario

1/3 cup chopped green pepper
2 tablespoons chopped onion
2 teaspoons olive oil
1 tablespoon butter
3 eggs
3 tablespoons water
1/8 teaspoon salt
1/8 teaspoon pepper
1/3 cup chopped tomato

In a small nonstick skillet, saute green pepper and onion in oil until tender. Remove from skillet and set aside.

In the same skillet, melt the butter over medium-high heat. Whisk the eggs, water, salt and pepper. Add the egg mixture to the skillet (the mixture should set immediately at edges).

As eggs set, push cooked edges toward the center, letting uncooked portion flow underneath. When the eggs are set, spoon green pepper mixture and tomato on one side; fold other side over filling. Slide omelet onto a plate. **Yield:** 1 serving.

Potato Bacon Omelet

(Pictured above)

Prep/Total Time: 20 min.

Here's a great way to use up leftover potato and bacon. This yummy, Test Kitchen-created omelet will quickly become a favorite!

2 bacon strips, chopped
2 tablespoons chopped onion
1/2 cup cubed cooked potato
1 tablespoon butter
3 eggs
3 tablespoons water
1/8 teaspoon salt
1/8 teaspoon pepper
1/4 cup shredded sharp cheddar cheese

In a small nonstick skillet, cook bacon and onion over medium heat until bacon is crisp. Add the potato; heat through. Drain. Remove from skillet and set aside. Remove to paper towels to drain.

In the same skillet, melt the butter over medium-high heat. Whisk the eggs, water, salt and pepper. Add the egg mixture to the skillet (mixture should set immediately at edges).

As eggs set, push cooked edges toward the center, letting uncooked portion flow underneath. When the eggs are set, spoon bacon mixture and potato on one side and sprinkle with cheese; fold other side over filling. Slide omelet onto a plate. **Yield:** 1 serving.

Peanut Butter and Jelly Omelet

(Pictured below)

Prep/Total Time: 20 min.

Kids will devour this scrumptious omelet with peanut butter and jelly. Serving several for dinner? Fill each omelet with a different type of jelly. Our Test Kitchen knows your family will love it!

1 tablespoon butter
3 eggs
3 tablespoons water
1/8 teaspoon salt
1/8 teaspoon pepper
1/4 cup sliced ripe banana
2 tablespoons strawberry jelly
2 tablespoons peanut butter
Confectioners' sugar

In a small nonstick skillet, melt butter over medium-high heat. Whisk the eggs, water, salt and pepper. Add egg mixture to the skillet (mixture should set immediately at edges).

As eggs set, push cooked edges toward the center, letting uncooked portion flow underneath. When the eggs are set, place the banana, jelly and peanut butter on one side; fold other side over filling. Slide omelet onto a plate. Dust with the confectioners' sugar. **Yield:** 1 serving.

BUDGET COOKING

Creamy Veggie Meatballs is a soothing dish that takes advantage of low-cost ground beef. We combine it with vegetables and oats for meatballs, and serve over potatoes for a stick-to-the-ribs meal.

The eggs in the Potato & Bacon Frittata are an economical protein source. Here, we stretch them by adding inexpensive potatoes to create this quick-to-fix, hearty meal.

Kitchen staples shine in Parmesan Baked Chicken. Save even more by buying whole or cut-up chicken on sale and freezing it for later. Be sure to thaw the chicken in the fridge before using in this recipe.

And using a meat alternative, such as cheese-filled tortellini for the Tortellini with Tomato-Cream Sauce, can help decrease your grocery bill.

Creamy Veggie Meatballs

(Pictured below)

Prep: 30 min. **Bake:** 35 min.

My gang has enjoyed this comfort food for years. The kids don't even know they're getting veggies. The meatballs are also delicious over rice or egg noodles.

—Kathy Hinton, Gilbert, Arizona

1 egg
1/3 cup shredded carrot
2/3 cup shredded potato
1/3 cup shredded zucchini
1/4 cup finely chopped onion
1/2 cup quick-cooking oats
1/4 teaspoon salt

1/4 teaspoon pepper
1 pound ground beef
1 can (10-3/4 ounces) condensed cream of mushroom soup, undiluted
1 can (10-3/4 ounces) condensed cream of chicken soup, undiluted
1-1/4 cups 2% milk
Mashed potatoes
Minced fresh parsley, optional

In a large bowl, combine the first eight ingredients. Crumble the beef over mixture and mix well. Shape into 1-1/2-in. balls.

In a large skillet, brown meatballs in oil in small batches; drain. Transfer to a greased 13-in. x 9-in. baking dish. In a large bowl, combine the soups and milk; pour over the meatballs.

Cover and bake at 350° for 35-40 minutes or until bubbly. Serve with mashed potatoes; garnish with parsley if desired. **Yield:** 6 servings.

Potato & Bacon Frittata

(Pictured above)

Prep: 30 min. **Bake:** 20 min. + standing

This filling frittata is so versatile. You can serve it with pesto, fresh salsa or with almost any type of cheese.

—Mariela Petroski, Helena, Montana

10 eggs
1/4 cup minced fresh parsley
3 tablespoons 2% milk
1/4 teaspoon salt
1/8 teaspoon pepper
8 bacon strips, chopped
2 medium potatoes, peeled and thinly sliced
2 green onions, finely chopped
4 fresh sage leaves, thinly sliced
1 cup (4 ounces) shredded pepper Jack cheese
2 plum tomatoes, sliced

In a large bowl, whisk the eggs, minced parsley, milk, salt and pepper; set aside. In a 10-in. ovenproof skillet, cook the bacon over medium heat until partially cooked but not crisp.

Add potatoes, onions and sage; cook until potatoes are tender. Reduce heat; sprinkle with cheese. Top with egg mixture and tomato slices.

Bake, uncovered, at 400° for 20-25 minutes or until eggs are completely set. Let stand for 15 minutes. Cut into wedges. **Yield:** 8 servings.

Parmesan Baked Chicken

(Pictured above)

Prep: 10 min. **Bake:** 30 min.

This no-fuss recipe has been a longtime hit with my family. After a few minutes of prep, the oven does the rest.
—Janet Faldowski-McFarlan, Gahanna, Ohio

1 cup biscuit/baking mix
1/4 cup grated Parmesan cheese
1 teaspoon paprika
1/2 teaspoon salt
1/2 teaspoon pepper
1/8 teaspoon garlic powder
1 broiler/fryer chicken (3 to 4 pounds), cut up
1/4 cup butter, melted

In a large resealable plastic bag, combine the baking mix, cheese, paprika, salt, pepper and garlic powder. Add chicken, a few pieces at a time, and shake to coat.

Drizzle the butter into a 15-in. x 10-in. x 1-in. baking pan. Place the chicken, skin side down, in pan.

Bake, uncovered, at 425° for 20 minutes. Turn chicken over; bake 10-15 minutes longer or until juices run clear. **Yield:** 6 servings.

Tortellini with Tomato-Cream Sauce

(Pictured above)

Prep/Total Time: 25 min.

Put frozen food and pantry staples to mouthwatering use in this warm and satisfying meatless meal. It's so rich, meat eaters won't miss the meat.
—Barbra Stanger, West Jordan, Utah

1 package (16 ounces) frozen cheese tortellini
1 small onion, chopped
2 tablespoons olive oil
3 garlic cloves, minced
1 can (14-1/2 ounces) diced tomatoes, undrained
1 package (10 ounces) frozen chopped spinach, thawed and squeezed dry
1-1/2 teaspoons dried basil
1 teaspoon salt
1/2 teaspoon pepper
1-1/2 cups heavy whipping cream
1/2 cup grated Parmesan cheese
Additional grated Parmesan cheese, optional

Cook tortellini according to package directions. Meanwhile, in a large skillet, saute onion in oil until tender. Add garlic; cook 1 minute longer. Add the tomatoes, spinach, basil, salt and pepper. Cook and stir over medium heat until liquid is absorbed, about 3 minutes.

Stir in the heavy cream and cheese. Bring to a boil. Reduce heat; simmer, uncovered, for 8-10 minutes or until thickened.

Drain the tortellini and toss with the sauce. Sprinkle with additional grated Parmesan cheese if desired. **Yield:** 6 servings.

HOLIDAY LEFTOVERS

Need to find a creative way of using leftovers from the holidays? Here are four recipes that are exactly what you're looking for, because they use cooked turkey, cooked stuffing and cooked ham.

Don't let the word "leftovers" fool you, because these dishes have all the flavor and pizzazz of any restaurant-quality meal. Even better, each dish comes together quickly, so you have more time to rest! ■

Broccoli Turkey Pie

(Pictured below)

Prep: 10 min. **Bake:** 25 min.

Leftover turkey becomes a delicious weeknight meal with just 10 minutes of prep. The whole family will love this comforting casserole and its golden Parmesan topping.
—Pippa Milburn, Dover, Ohio

2 cups cubed cooked turkey
2 cups frozen chopped broccoli, thawed and drained
1-1/2 cups (6 ounces) shredded cheddar cheese
2 eggs
1 cup 2% milk
1/2 cup biscuit/baking mix
1/4 teaspoon salt
1/4 teaspoon pepper
1/8 teaspoon dried thyme
1/4 cup grated Parmesan cheese
1/2 teaspoon garlic powder

In a greased 9-in. deep-dish pie plate, layer the turkey, broccoli and cheddar cheese. In a large bowl, whisk the eggs, milk, biscuit mix, salt, pepper and thyme. Pour over filling. In a small bowl, combine Parmesan cheese and garlic powder; sprinkle over top.

Bake at 400° for 25-30 minutes or until a knife inserted near the center comes out clean. Let stand for 5 minutes before cutting. **Yield:** 6 servings.

Stuffing-Stuffed Pork Chops

(Pictured above)

Prep: 30 min. **Bake:** 25 min.

You'll want to make stuffing more often once you try these savory, elegant chops created in our Test Kitchen. They have fabulous flavor!

4 bone-in pork loin chops (8 ounces *each*)
2 cups cooked stuffing
1/4 teaspoon pepper
1 tablespoon canola oil
2 garlic cloves, minced
1/4 teaspoon dried thyme
1/2 cup white wine *or* chicken broth
2 tablespoons all-purpose flour
3/4 cup chicken broth

Cut a pocket in each chop by slicing almost to the bone. Fill each chop with 1/2 cup of the stuffing; secure with toothpicks if necessary. Sprinkle with pepper.

In a large ovenproof skillet, brown chops in oil. Bake, uncovered, at 350° for 25-30 minutes or until a meat thermometer reads 160°. Remove pork chops and set aside. Keep warm.

In the same skillet, cook the garlic and thyme in pan drippings over medium heat for 1 minute. Add wine, stirring to loosen browned bits from pan. In a small bowl, combine flour and broth until smooth. Gradually add to pan. Bring to a boil; cook and stir for 2 minutes or until thickened.

Remove toothpicks from the pork chops; serve with gravy. **Yield:** 4 servings.

Thai Turkey Salad Pitas

(Pictured below)

Prep/Total Time: 20 min.

Here's a quick and easy way to use up leftover turkey. My son likes to try foods from different nationalities, and he really enjoys these tasty pitas.

—Renee Dent, Conrad, Montana

2 cups cubed cooked turkey breast
2 cups coleslaw mix
1/2 cup golden raisins
1/3 cup chopped unsalted peanuts
1 green onion, chopped
1/4 cup lime juice
1/4 cup honey
3 tablespoons soy sauce
1 tablespoon sesame oil
2 teaspoons chili sauce
1/2 teaspoon garlic powder
8 pita pocket halves

In a large bowl, combine the first five ingredients. In another bowl, combine the lime juice, honey, soy sauce, oil, chili sauce and garlic powder; pour over the turkey mixture and toss to coat.

Fill each pita half with 1/2 cup turkey mixture. **Yield:** 4 servings.

Ham & Cheese Ziti

(Pictured above)

Prep: 25 min. **Bake:** 20 min.

This versatile dish is a crowd-pleaser. You can easily take the recipe and make it your own by changing up the cheeses or veggie. My family loves it!

—Donna Bailey, Oreland, Pennsylvania

1 package (16 ounces) ziti
1/4 cup butter, cubed
1/4 cup all-purpose flour
2 cups 2% milk
2 cups (8 ounces) shredded white cheddar cheese
1/4 cup grated Parmesan cheese
1 teaspoon garlic powder
1/2 teaspoon pepper
3 cups cubed fully cooked ham
1 package (10 ounces) frozen chopped spinach, thawed and squeezed dry

Prepare ziti according to package directions. Meanwhile, in a Dutch oven, melt butter. Stir in flour until smooth; gradually add milk. Bring to a boil; cook and stir for 2 minutes or until thickened. Reduce heat; stir in the cheeses, garlic powder and pepper; cook and stir until cheese is melted.

Drain ziti; add to sauce mixture. Stir in the ham and spinach. Transfer to a greased 13-in. x 9-in. baking dish. Bake, uncovered, at 375° for 20-25 minutes or until heated through. **Yield:** 6 servings.

SAY CHEESE!

Select sharp cheddar when using packaged shredded cheese for recipes that you'd like to have a bolder flavor. If you will be shredding cheese at home from bulk cheddar, you can choose from mild, medium, sharp and extra sharp.

PLANNED LEFTOVERS

The beauty of the Florentine Meatballs and Chipotle-Orange Pork Chops recipes is that they set you up for super-easy meal preparation the next day. The Italian Stroganoff uses a few pantry ingredients along with already-made meatballs for a wholesome, filling meal. And Pork Fried Rice uses last night's leftover pork chops to create a popular dish that is amazingly simple and flavorful. ■

Italian Stroganoff

(Pictured below)

Prep/Total Time: 20 min.

Mix the sauce in this creamy, comforting dish with the noodles or pour it on top; either way, it's excellent. Serve the hearty dish with a slice of warm buttered bread.
—Christina Nabert, Poplar Bluff, Missouri

1/2 pound sliced fresh mushrooms
1/4 cup finely chopped onion
1 garlic clove, minced
1 tablespoon butter
1 can (10-3/4 ounces) condensed golden mushroom soup, undiluted
3/4 cup sour cream
1/4 cup water
1/8 teaspoon salt
1/8 teaspoon pepper
16 Florentine Meatballs
Hot cooked egg noodles

In a large skillet, saute the mushrooms, onion and garlic in butter until tender. Stir in soup, sour cream, water, salt and pepper. Add meatballs; heat through (do not boil). Serve with noodles. **Yield:** 4 servings.

Florentine Meatballs

(Pictured above)

Prep: 20 min. **Bake:** 25 min.

These meatballs freeze and reheat well, so we use them as an addition to spaghetti, on subs or as an appetizer.
—Louise Graybiel, Toronto, Ontario

2 packages (10 ounces *each*) frozen chopped spinach, thawed and squeezed dry
1/2 cup seasoned bread crumbs
1/4 cup grated Parmesan cheese
4 garlic cloves, minced
2 teaspoons dried oregano
2 eggs, lightly beaten
2 pounds lean ground beef (90% lean)
1 jar (26 ounces) spaghetti sauce
Hot cooked spaghetti

In a large bowl, combine the first six ingredients. Crumble the beef over mixture and mix well. Shape into 32 balls.

Place meatballs on a greased rack in a shallow baking pan. Bake, uncovered, at 400° for 24-28 minutes or until no longer pink. Drain on paper towels.

Save half of the meatballs for Italian Stroganoff or for another use. In a large saucepan, heat spaghetti sauce; add the remaining meatballs. Serve with spaghetti. **Yield:** 4 servings plus 16 cooked meatballs.

Pork Fried Rice

(Pictured below)

Prep/Total Time: 15 min.

Making use of leftover pork and cooked rice, this delicious take on takeout comes together faster than you can order No. 5 on the value menu.

—Judy Lammers, Columbia, Missouri

- **1 teaspoon canola oil**
- **2 eggs, beaten**
- **3 cups cooked rice**
- **2 cups cubed cooked pork**
- **1/2 cup frozen peas, thawed**
- **1/4 cup reduced-sodium soy sauce**
- **1/2 teaspoon garlic powder**
- **2 cups shredded lettuce**
- **2 green onions, thinly sliced**

In a large skillet, heat oil over medium-high heat. Pour eggs into skillet. As eggs set, lift edges, letting uncooked portion flow underneath. When the eggs are completely cooked, remove to plate. Set aside.

In the same skillet, combine the rice, pork, peas, soy sauce and garlic powder; heat through. Meanwhile, chop egg into small pieces; add to skillet. Remove from the heat; stir in lettuce and onions. Serve immediately. **Yield:** 4 servings.

Chipotle-Orange Pork Chops

(Pictured above)

Prep/Total Time: 30 min.

Orange juice concentrate and maple syrup add a one-two punch of sweetness to smokin' flavors. With a method this easy, you'd be crazy not to fix extras.

—Billy Hensley, Mount Carmel, Tennessee

- **1/2 cup maple syrup**
- **1/2 cup thawed orange juice concentrate**
- **3 tablespoons chopped chipotle peppers in adobo sauce**
- **1 teaspoon salt**
- **1 teaspoon pepper**
- **8 bone-in pork loin chops (8 ounces *each* and 3/4 inch thick)**

In a small bowl, combine the first five ingredients. Set aside 1/3 cup for serving.

Moisten a paper towel with cooking oil; using long-handled tongs, lightly coat the grill rack. Grill the pork chops, covered, over medium heat or broil 4 in. from the heat for 6-8 minutes on each side or until a meat thermometer reads 160°, basting frequently with orange mixture. Serve with reserved sauce. **Yield:** 8 servings.

WHAT ARE CHIPOTLES?

Chipotles are smoked and dried jalapeno peppers originating in the region surrounding Mexico City. Often found canned in a chili sauce in the U.S., chipotles are medium to hot in heat and are used in a variety of spicy Mexican and American dishes.

CHAPTER 20

Easy Odds & Ends

This chapter features three handy sections: easy-to-make stovetop suppers, delicious grilled main courses and tasty homemade condiments.

The stovetop dishes come together in a jiffy for those days when you need something quick—they can be prepared in 30 minutes or less, and some in only 15 minutes.

You may want to make extras of the recipes featured in the grilling section, because the dishes have so much flavor, they are going to go fast!

And when the weather is beautiful and your garden is bountiful, take advantage of the recipes for condiments. It's like putting summer in a jar! ■

FROM THE GRILL. Chipotle-Honey Grilled T-Bones (p. 309).

STOVETOP SENSATIONS

Busy cooks need a cache of stovetop dishes for those days when time is short, and these recipes are just the ticket! From scrumptious pasta dishes, such as Summer Carbonara, to Asian-inspired noodle dishes, such as the Sweet & Sour Pineapple Chicken, each yummy meal has a short prep and cook time to make your life easier! ■

Teriyaki Pork

(Pictured below)

Prep: 10 min. + marinating **Cook:** 20 min.

I season tender pork loin and an assortment of crisp-tender vegetables with a garlicky soy sauce marinade for this savory stir-fry. Everyone will love it!

—Molly Gee, Plainwell, Michigan

3/4 cup reduced-sodium chicken broth, *divided*
1/3 cup reduced-sodium soy sauce
2 tablespoons red wine vinegar
2 teaspoons honey
2 teaspoons garlic powder
1 pound boneless pork loin chops, cut into thin strips
1 tablespoon canola oil
2 cups fresh broccoli florets
3 medium carrots, sliced
3 celery ribs, sliced
4 cups shredded cabbage
6 green onions, sliced
1 tablespoon cornstarch
Hot cooked brown rice, optional

In a small bowl, combine 1/4 cup broth, soy sauce, vinegar, honey and garlic powder. Pour 1/3 cup marinade into a large resealable plastic bag; add the pork. Seal bag and turn to coat; refrigerate for 1 hour. Cover and refrigerate remaining marinade.

Drain and discard marinade. In large nonstick skillet or wok, stir-fry pork in oil for 2-3 minutes or until no longer pink. Remove and keep warm.

In the same pan, stir-fry broccoli and carrots in reserved marinade for 2 minutes. Add celery; stir-fry for 2 minutes. Add cabbage and green onions; stir-fry 2-3 minutes longer or until vegetables are crisp-tender.

Combine the cornstarch and remaining broth until smooth; stir into vegetable mixture. Bring to a boil; cook and stir until thickened. Return pork to the pan; heat through. Serve with rice if desired. **Yield:** 4 servings.

Portobello & Basil Cheese Tortellini

(Pictured above)

Prep: 15 min. **Cook:** 20 min.

With portobello mushrooms and satisfying cheese tortellini, this earthy, elegant dish is perfect for either a quick, casual dinner or a more formal meal. I often use the fresh basil from my garden.

—Mary Shivers, Ada, Oklahoma

1 package (19 ounces) frozen cheese tortellini
1 pound sliced baby portobello mushrooms
1 small onion, chopped
1/3 cup butter, cubed
2 garlic cloves, minced
1 cup reduced-sodium chicken broth
1 cup heavy whipping cream
1/2 teaspoon salt
1/2 teaspoon pepper
1/3 cup grated Parmesan cheese
2 tablespoons minced fresh basil *or* 2 teaspoons dried basil

Cook tortellini according to package directions.

Meanwhile, in a large skillet, saute mushrooms and onion in butter until tender. Add garlic; cook 1 minute longer. Stir in the broth. Bring to a boil. Reduce heat; simmer, uncovered, for 12-15 minutes or until liquid is reduced by half.

Add the cream, salt and pepper. Cook 4-5 minutes longer or until slightly thickened. Drain tortellini; add to skillet. Stir in cheese and basil. **Yield:** 4 servings.

Summer Carbonara

(Pictured below)

Prep: 25 min. **Cook:** 10 min.

Basil and bacon make best pals in this smoky-sweet pasta. I pair it with a simple spring mix salad with balsamic dressing and a good white wine or a glass of iced tea.

—Cathy Dudderar, Lexington, Kentucky

- **1 package (16 ounces) spaghetti**
- **1 large sweet onion, finely chopped**
- **1 medium yellow summer squash, finely chopped**
- **1 medium zucchini, finely chopped**
- **2 garlic cloves, minced**
- **2 tablespoons olive oil**
- **4 plum tomatoes, seeded and chopped**
- **2 eggs, beaten**
- **1 cup grated Parmesan cheese**
- **12 bacon strips, cooked and crumbled**
- **1/4 cup fresh basil leaves, thinly sliced**
- **1 teaspoon minced fresh oregano *or* 1/2 teaspoon dried oregano**
- **1/2 teaspoon salt**
- **1/4 teaspoon pepper**

Cook the spaghetti according to package directions. Meanwhile, in a large skillet, saute the onion, squash, zucchini and garlic in oil until tender. Add tomatoes; heat through. Remove and keep warm.

Reduce heat to low; add eggs to the skillet. Cook and stir until egg mixture coats a metal spoon and reaches 160° (mixture will look like a soft frothy egg). Drain spaghetti and place in a bowl. Add eggs; toss to coat. Add the vegetable mixture, cheese, bacon, basil, oregano, salt and pepper; toss gently to coat. **Yield:** 6 servings.

Creole Chicken

(Pictured above)

Prep: 15 min. **Cook:** 25 min.

Chili powder lends just a hint of heat to this full-flavored, quick-prep chicken entree.

—Susan Shields, Englewood, Florida

- **2 boneless skinless chicken breast halves (4 ounces *each*)**
- **1 teaspoon canola oil**
- **1 can (14-1/2 ounces) stewed tomatoes, cut up**
- **1/3 cup julienned green pepper**
- **1/4 cup chopped celery**
- **1/4 cup sliced onion**
- **1/2 to 1 teaspoon chili powder**
- **1/2 teaspoon dried thyme**
- **1/8 teaspoon pepper**
- **1 cup hot cooked rice**

In a small nonstick skillet coated with cooking spray, cook chicken in oil over medium heat for 5-6 minutes on each side or a meat thermometer reads 170°. Remove and keep warm.

In the same skillet, combine the tomatoes, green pepper, celery, onion, chili powder, thyme and pepper. Bring to a boil. Reduce heat; cover and simmer for 10 minutes or until vegetables are crisp-tender. Return chicken to pan; heat through. Serve with the rice. **Yield:** 2 servings.

Sweet & Sour Pineapple Chicken

(Pictured above)

Prep: 15 min. **Cook:** 25 min.

Bamboo shoots, sweet red pepper and sugar snap peas give this weeknight dish a lovely look and pleasant crunch.
—Lorraine Caland, Thunder Bay, Ontario

6 bone-in chicken thighs (about 2-1/4 pounds)
1 teaspoon olive oil
1/2 cup chicken broth
2 jars (4-1/2 ounces *each*) sliced mushrooms, drained
1-1/2 cups frozen sugar snap peas, thawed
1 medium sweet red pepper, cut into strips
1/2 cup canned bamboo shoots
1/3 cup thinly sliced green onions
1 can (20 ounces) pineapple tidbits
7-1/2 teaspoons cornstarch
1/4 cup cider vinegar
3 tablespoons soy sauce
2 tablespoons sugar
Hot cooked rice noodles

In a large skillet, brown chicken in oil; drain. Add the broth. Bring to a boil. Reduce heat; cover and cook for 10 minutes.

Add the mushrooms, peas, red pepper, bamboo shoots and onions. Cover and cook 5-10 minutes longer or until a meat thermometer reads 180° and vegetables are tender.

Meanwhile, drain the pineapple, reserving juice; set pineapple aside. In a small bowl, combine the cornstarch, reserved juice, vinegar, soy sauce and sugar. Pour into the skillet. Bring to a boil; cook and stir for 2 minutes or until thickened.

Stir in pineapple; heat through. Serve with noodles. **Yield:** 6 servings.

Beef and Wild Rice Medley

(Pictured below)

Prep: 5 min. **Cook:** 40 min.

A packaged rice mix speeds up preparation of this meal-in-one entree. Cayenne pepper gives the beef a little kick, and an assortment of veggies add color and crunch.
—Janelle Christensen, Big Lake, Minnesota

1/2 teaspoon garlic powder
1/2 teaspoon dried thyme
1/8 teaspoon cayenne pepper
1 pound beef top sirloin steak, cut into 3/4-inch cubes
1 tablespoon canola oil
1/4 cup sliced celery
1/4 cup julienned green pepper
2-1/4 cups water
1 package (6 ounces) long grain and wild rice mix
1 small tomato, chopped
2 tablespoons chopped green onion

In a small bowl, combine the garlic powder, thyme and cayenne. Sprinkle over beef.

In a large saucepan coated with cooking spray, cook beef in oil until no longer pink; drain. Stir in celery and green pepper; cook 2 minutes longer or until vegetables are crisp-tender. Stir in the water and rice mix with contents of seasoning packet.

Bring to a boil. Reduce heat; cover and simmer for 23-28 minutes or until rice is tender. Stir in tomato; heat through. Sprinkle with onion. **Yield:** 4 servings.

READING MEAT LABELS

The label states the type of meat, the wholesale cut (loin, rib, leg, etc.) and the retail cut (steak, chops, roast, etc.). The label also states the sell-by date, the weight of the meat, cost per pound and total price. The wholesale cut is an indication of tenderness.

Chinese Pork 'n' Noodles

(Pictured above)

Prep: 20 min. **Cook:** 15 min.

I based the recipe for these noodles on a similar dish I found in a magazine. I changed a few things around, and my husband and I loved it. It's just as good when the pork is replaced with seafood.
—Jennifer Enzer, Manchester, Michigan

6 ounces uncooked angel hair pasta
3 tablespoons hoisin sauce
2 tablespoons reduced-sodium soy sauce
2 teaspoons sesame oil
1 pork tenderloin (1 pound), thinly sliced and halved
3 teaspoons canola oil, *divided*
3/4 cup julienned sweet red pepper
3/4 cup halved fresh snow peas
1/2 cup sliced onion
1 cup sliced cabbage
1/4 cup minced fresh cilantro

Cook pasta according to package directions. Meanwhile, in a small bowl, combine the hoisin sauce, soy sauce and sesame oil; set aside.

In a large nonstick skillet or wok, stir-fry the pork in 2 teaspoons canola oil for 3 minutes or until no longer pink. Remove and keep warm. In the same skillet, stir-fry the red pepper, peas and onion in remaining oil for 3 minutes. Add cabbage; stir-fry 2 minutes longer or until vegetables are crisp-tender.

Stir reserved hoisin sauce mixture and stir into skillet. Return pork to the pan; heat through. Drain pasta and add to the skillet; toss to coat. Sprinkle each serving with 1 tablespoon cilantro. **Yield:** 4 servings.

BBQ Shrimp Quesadillas

(Pictured below)

Prep: 30 min. + marinating **Cook:** 5 min.

My husband loves corn, shrimp and barbecue sauce. One night, when I was low on groceries, I went to the garden and this recipe was born. It was a hit!
—Christine Parsons, Bountiful, Utah

2 tablespoons lime juice
2 teaspoons olive oil
1-1/2 teaspoons grated lime peel
1/4 teaspoon salt
1/4 teaspoon pepper
3/4 pound uncooked medium shrimp, peeled and deveined
2 medium ears sweet corn, husks removed
2 medium zucchini, chopped
4 green onions, thinly sliced
2 tablespoons barbecue sauce
2 cups (8 ounces) shredded Monterey Jack cheese
8 flour tortillas (8 inches)
Salsa and additional barbecue sauce

In a large resealable plastic bag, combine the lime juice, oil, lime peel, salt and pepper. Add the shrimp; seal bag and turn to coat. Refrigerate for 15 minutes.

Meanwhile, remove the corn from cobs. Drain and discard marinade from shrimp. Chop shrimp and set aside. In a large nonstick skillet coated with cooking spray, saute the zucchini, corn and onions until crisp-tender. Add shrimp; saute 2-3 minutes longer or until shrimp turn pink. Remove from the heat; stir in barbecue sauce.

Sprinkle cheese over half of the tortillas. Spoon shrimp mixture over cheese. Top with remaining tortillas. Cook on a griddle coated with cooking spray over low heat for 1-2 minutes on each side or until cheese is melted. Serve with salsa and additional barbecue sauce. **Yield:** 4 servings.

THE THRILL OF THE GRILL

Let's face it, grilling simply makes meat taste better, especially after it's been soaking in a zippy marinade. These easy-to-make recipes range from classics, such as Can-Can Chicken, to new and zesty twists, like Grilled Sirloin with Chili-Beer Barbecue Sauce. For the outdoor cooking enthusiast, these recipes will be a welcome addition to your backyard menu. ■

Bourbon Brat Skewers

(Pictured below)

Prep: 20 min. + marinating **Grill:** 15 min.

When the executive decision was made to marinate veggies in a tasty bourbon sauce and serve with grilled bratwurst, this recipe made our VIP tailgate party list.
—Mary Marlowe Leverette, Columbia, South Carolina

1/2 cup reduced-sodium soy sauce
1/2 cup bourbon
3 tablespoons brown sugar
1 teaspoon seasoned salt
1/4 teaspoon cayenne pepper
2 cups whole mushrooms
2 medium sweet red peppers, cut into 1-inch pieces
1 medium green pepper, cut into 1-inch pieces
1 medium onion, cut into wedges
1 package (16 ounces) uncooked bratwurst links, cut into 1-inch slices

In a large resealable plastic bag, combine the first five ingredients. Add the vegetables; seal bag and turn to coat. Refrigerate for at least 1 hour.

Drain and reserve marinade. On six metal or soaked wooden skewers, alternately thread the vegetables and bratwurst. Brush with reserved marinade. Grill, covered, over medium heat for 15-20 minutes or until bratwurst is no longer pink and vegetables are tender, turning and basting frequently with the reserved marinade. **Yield:** 6 skewers.

Can-Can Chicken

(Pictured above)

Prep: 30 min. + chillng **Grill:** 1-1/4 hours + standing

To add color and flavor to my chicken, I spray it with a mixture of 2 cups apple cider and 1 tablespoon balsamic vinegar as it cooks. If you're frequently opening up the grill, you may need to increase the cooking time a bit.
—Steve Bath, Lincoln, Nebraska

1 tablespoon kosher salt
1 teaspoon sugar
1 teaspoon onion powder
1 teaspoon garlic powder
1 teaspoon cayenne pepper
1 teaspoon paprika
1 teaspoon ground mustard
1 broiler/fryer chicken (3-1/2 to 4 pounds)
1 can (12 ounces) beer

In a small bowl, combine the first seven ingredients. Loosen skin from around the chicken breast, thighs and legs. Rub the spice mixture onto and under skin. Tuck wing tips behind the back. Refrigerate for 1 hour.

Prepare grill for indirect grilling, using a drip pan. Pour out half of the beer, reserving for another use. Poke additional holes in top of the can with a can opener. Holding the chicken with legs pointed down, lower chicken over the can so it fills the body cavity.

Place the chicken over drip pan; grill, covered, over indirect medium heat for 1-1/4 to 1-1/2 hours or until meat juices run clear. Remove chicken from grill; cover and let stand for 10 minutes. Remove chicken from can. **Yield:** 6 servings.

Chipotle-Honey Grilled T-Bones

(Pictured below)

Prep: 20 min. + marinating **Grill:** 10 min.

If you like to kick things up on the grill, this is the steak for you (or your man). My husband even makes this in a Dutch oven, and the meat just sizzles.
—Donna Goutermont, Juneau, Alaska

1/2 cup minced fresh cilantro
1/2 cup lime juice
1/2 cup honey
2 tablespoons adobo sauce
3 garlic cloves, minced
1 tablespoon chopped chipotle pepper in adobo sauce
1 teaspoon salt
1 teaspoon ground cumin
1/2 teaspoon ground allspice
1/2 teaspoon pepper
1/4 teaspoon Dijon mustard
4 beef T-bone steaks (12 ounces *each*)

In a small bowl, combine the first 11 ingredients. Pour 1/2 cup marinade into a large resealable plastic bag. Add the steaks; seal the bag and turn to coat. Refrigerate for up to 1 hour. Cover and refrigerate the remaining marinade.

Drain and discard marinade. Grill steaks, covered, over medium heat or broil 4 in. from the heat for 5-6 minutes on each side or until the meat reaches desired doneness (for medium-rare, a meat thermometer should read 145°; medium, 160°; well-done, 170°), basting occasionally with 1/2 cup reserved marinade. Serve with remaining marinade. **Yield:** 4 servings.

Mexican-Seasoned Grilled Chicken

(Pictured above)

Prep: 15 min. **Grill:** 1-1/4 hours + standing

It's bright, spicy and prepared with beer. This recipe has all my favorites. I like to grill it with Tecate beer.
—Daniel Balderas, Milwaukee, Wisconsin

3 tablespoons Goya sazon with coriander and annatto
1 teaspoon adobo seasoning
1 teaspoon ground cumin
1 teaspoon pepper
1/2 teaspoon kosher salt
1 broiler/fryer chicken (3 to 4 pounds)
2 tablespoons butter, softened
1 can (12 ounces) beer *or* nonalcoholic beer

Combine the first five ingredients. Gently loosen skin from chicken breasts; rub butter and 1 tablespoon spice mixture under the skin. Rub remaining spice mixture over skin.

Prepare grill for indirect heat, using a drip pan. Pour out a third of the beer. Carefully poke additional holes in top of the can with a can opener. Holding the chicken with legs pointed down, lower chicken over the can so it fills the body cavity.

Place the chicken over drip pan; grill, covered, over indirect medium heat for 1-1/4 to 1-1/2 hours or until a meat thermometer reads 180°. Remove chicken from grill; cover and let stand for 10 minutes. Remove chicken from can. **Yield:** 6 servings.

Editor's Note: Look for Sazon Goya, a seasoning blend, in the international foods section.

GRILLING TIPS

Bring cold foods to a cool room temperature before grilling. Cold foods may burn on the outside before the interior is cooked. Use a meat thermometer to check the internal temperature of meat and poultry before the recommended cooking time is up.

Grilled Honey-Lime Chicken

(Pictured above)

Prep: 10 min. + marinating **Grill:** 10 min.

Make-ahead marinade is your best friend when feeding a crowd. Here's one that is very easy to memorize.
—Marybeth Wright, Maitland, Florida

3/4 cup oil and vinegar salad dressing
1/2 cup honey
3 tablespoons lime juice
1/2 teaspoon salt
1/2 teaspoon pepper
8 boneless skinless chicken breast halves (6 ounces *each*)

In a small bowl, combine the first five ingredients. Pour 1 cup marinade into a large resealable plastic bag; add the chicken. Seal bag and turn to coat; refrigerate for 2 hours. Cover and refrigerate remaining marinade.

Drain and discard marinade. Moisten a paper towel with cooking oil; using long-handled tongs, lightly coat the grill rack. Grill the chicken, covered, over medium heat or broil 4 in. from the heat for 4-5 minutes on each side, or until a meat thermometer reads 170°, basting occasionally with reserved marinade. **Yield:** 8 servings.

Grilled Asian Steak

Prep: 10 min. + marinating **Grill:** 15 min.

This is the first recipe I requested from my mother-in-law after I was married. My mouth waters just thinking about the juicy steaks.
—Lory Greathouse, Camano Island, Washington

1/4 cup lemon juice
1/4 cup soy sauce
2 garlic cloves, minced
1-1/2 teaspoons aniseed
1-1/2 teaspoons pepper
1 beef flank steak (1-1/2 pounds)

In a small bowl, combine the first five ingredients. Pour 1/4 cup marinade into a large resealable plastic bag. Add the beef; seal bag and turn to coat. Refrigerate for at least 4 hours or overnight. Cover and refrigerate remaining marinade.

Drain and discard marinade. Grill steak, covered, over medium heat or broil 4 in. from the heat for 6-8 minutes on each side or until meat reaches desired doneness (for medium-rare, a meat thermometer should read 145°; medium, 160°; well-done, 170°), basting occasionally with reserved marinade.

Let stand for 5 minutes; thinly slice across the grain. **Yield:** 6 servings.

Grilled Sirloin with Chili-Beer Barbecue Sauce

(Pictured below)

Prep: 40 min. **Grill:** 20 min.

Tender steak is treated to a tangy barbecue sauce that's so tasty. Our Test Kitchen added cayenne pepper and chili powder to add a hint of heat that gives it extra pizzazz.

1-1/2 cups beer *or* nonalcoholic beer
1 small onion, chopped
3/4 cup chili sauce

2 tablespoons soy sauce
1 tablespoon brown sugar
2 teaspoons chili powder
2 garlic cloves, minced
1/4 teaspoon cayenne pepper
1/4 teaspoon ground mustard
1/8 teaspoon ground cumin
2 beef top sirloin steaks (1-1/2 pounds *each*)
1/2 teaspoon salt
1/2 teaspoon pepper

In a small saucepan, combine the first ten ingredients. Bring to a boil. Reduce heat; simmer, uncovered, for 25-30 minutes or until thickened. Set aside 3/4 cup and keep warm.

Sprinkle the steaks with salt and pepper. Grill the steaks, covered, over medium heat or broil 4 in. from the heat for 9-13 minutes on each side or until the meat reaches desired doneness (for medium-rare, a meat thermometer should read 145°; medium 160°; well-done 170°), basting occasionally with the remaining sauce. Slice the meat and serve with reserved sauce. **Yield:** 8 servings.

INDIRECT HEAT GRILLING

To prepare a charcoal grill for indirect heat, bank half of the coals on one side of the grill and the other half on the other side. Place a foil drip pan in the center of the grill, replace the cooking grate and place the meat over the drip pan. Cover and grill according to recipe directions.

Grilled Stuffed Peppers

(Pictured above)

Prep: 20 min. **Grill:** 30 min.

I always tell my husband that he doesn't have to cook to impress; it's only me. But this classic was fabulous!
—Kathy Roth, Lansing, Illinois

1 *each* large sweet yellow, orange, red and green pepper
1 egg, beaten
1 small onion, chopped
1/2 cup seasoned bread crumbs
1 tablespoon garlic powder
1 tablespoon *each* minced fresh thyme, oregano and basil
1-1/2 teaspoons onion powder
1/2 teaspoon salt
1/4 teaspoon pepper
2 pounds ground beef
1 tablespoon olive oil
Marinara sauce, warmed

Cut peppers in half lengthwise; remove stems and seeds. Set aside. In a large bowl, combine the egg, onion, bread crumbs, garlic powder, herbs, onion powder, salt and pepper. Crumble beef over mixture and mix well. Spoon into pepper halves; brush with oil.

Prepare grill for indirect heat, using a drip pan. Place peppers over drip pan. Grill, covered, over indirect medium heat for 30-35 minutes or until beef is no longer pink and peppers are tender. Serve with marinara sauce. **Yield:** 8 servings.

CREATIVE CONDIMENTS

When the weather is warm and beautiful, and your garden has brought you plenty of produce and herbs, it's a shame to let any of it go to waste. These recipes are a great way to preserve the flavors of summer so that you and your family can continue to enjoy delicious pesto, jams and pickles in the autumn, winter and beyond! ■

Cilantro-Pepita Pesto

(Pictured below)

Prep/Total Time: 20 min.

This flavorful recipe is one of the ways I devised to use all the cilantro in my garden. Serve it with pasta, tortilla chips for dipping or in any dish that needs perking up.
—Ami Okasinski, Memphis, Tennessee

1 package (6 ounces) fresh baby spinach
2 cups fresh cilantro leaves
1/3 cup grated Romano cheese
1/3 cup salted pumpkin seeds *or* pepitas, toasted
3 to 4 garlic cloves
2 tablespoons lime juice
1 tablespoon lemon juice
1/8 teaspoon salt
3 tablespoons olive oil

Place first five ingredients in a food processor; cover and pulse just until chopped. Add lime and lemon juices and salt; cover and process until blended. While processing, gradually add oil in a steady stream. Store in an airtight container in the refrigerator. **Yield:** 1-1/2 cups.

Easy Refrigerator Pickles

(Pictured above)

Prep: 45 min. + chilling

When cucumbers are at their peak, I take advantage of garden extras by whipping up a few jars of pickles. My husband grows cucumbers, garlic and dill and eagerly waits for me to make these. The recipe originally came from my grandmother.
—Angela Lienhard, Blossburg, Pennsylvania

14 pickling cucumbers
40 fresh dill sprigs
4 garlic cloves, sliced
2 quarts water
1 cup cider vinegar
1/2 cup sugar
1/3 cup salt
1 teaspoon mixed pickling spices

Cut each cucumber lengthwise into six spears. In a large bowl, combine the cucumbers, fresh dill sprigs and garlic; set aside.

In a Dutch oven, combine the remaining ingredients. Bring to a boil; cook and stir just until sugar is dissolved. Pour over cucumber mixture; cool.

Transfer to jars if desired and cover tightly. Refrigerate for at least 24 hours. Store in the refrigerator for up to 2 weeks. **Yield:** 4-1/2 quarts.

Pina Colada Jam

(Pictured above right)

Prep: 15 min. **Cook:** 20 min. + cooling

If you like pina coladas, you'll love this! And here's the kicker: The secret ingredient is fresh zucchini. Because this jam is so unexpectedly delicious, our Test Kitchen challenges you to try it in a radical new way. Tell us what you think!

6 cups sugar
6 cups shredded peeled zucchini
1 can (8 ounces) crushed pineapple, undrained
1/4 cup lime juice
2 packages (3 ounces *each*) pineapple gelatin
1 teaspoon rum extract

In a Dutch oven, combine the sugar, zucchini, pineapple and lime juice. Bring to a boil. Boil for 10 minutes, stirring constantly. Remove from the heat; stir in gelatin and extract until gelatin is dissolved.

Pour into jars or freezer containers, leaving 1/2-in. headspace. Cool completely before covering with lids. Refrigerate for up to 3 weeks or freeze for up to 1 year. **Yield:** 3-1/2 pints.

Three-Berry Freezer Jam

(Pictured above)

Prep: 20 min. + standing **Cook:** 10 min.

Give in to temptation and buy fresh berries in bulk. You'll be glad you did when you transform those ripe little gems into a sweet spread that also makes a great gift.
—Shannon Becker, Burton, Ohio

2 cups fresh strawberries
2 cups fresh raspberries
2 cups fresh blackberries
5-1/4 cups sugar
2 tablespoons lemon juice
1 package (1-3/4 ounces) powdered fruit pectin
3/4 cup water

In a food processor, process the berries in batches until finely chopped. Transfer to a large bowl. Stir in the sugar and lemon juice. Let berry mixture stand for 10 minutes, stirring occasionally.

In a small saucepan, combine fruit pectin and water. Bring to a boil; cook and stir for 1 minute. Add to fruit mixture; stirring constantly for 4-5 minutes or until sugar is dissolved.

Pour into jars or freezer containers, leaving 1/2-in. headspace. Cover and let stand overnight or until set, but not longer than 24 hours. Refrigerate for up to 3 weeks or freeze for up to 1 year. **Yield:** 3 pints.

BERRY KNOW-HOW

To wash, place berries a few at a time in a colander in the sink. Gently spray, then spread out on paper towels to pat dry. One pint of blackberries yields 1-1/2 to 2 cups; one pint of raspberries is 2 cups; one pint of strawberries yields 1-1/2 to 2 cups, sliced.

General Recipe Index

This handy index lists every recipe by food category, major ingredient and/or cooking method, so you can easily locate recipes to suit your needs.

APPETIZERS & SNACKS *(also see Breads & Rolls)*

Cold Appetizers

Fresh Tomato Bruschetta, 284
Marinated Antipasto Platter, 289
Melon-Mango Salsa, 284
Roast Beef Spirals, 283

Dips & Spreads

Cranberry-Chili Cheese Spread, 102
Easy Hummus, 87
Fire-Roasted Salsa, 99
French Quarter Cheese Spread, 281
Green Chili Beef Dip, 287
Green Olive Dip, 156
Layered Artichoke Cheese Spread, 289
Party Vegetable Dip, 22
Pecan Cheese Logs, 23
Pesto Dip with Parmesan Toast, 90
Red Pepper & Feta Dip, 150
Reuben Spread, 286
Salsa Roja, 106
Seafood Cheese Dip, 152
Tomatillo Salsa, 146
Tropical Guacamole, 285

Hot Appetizers

Bacon-Wrapped Apricot Bites, 288
Brie Phyllo Cups, 95
Caribbean Shrimp Spring Rolls, 122
Chicken Skewers with Sweet & Spicy Marmalade, 280
Chili Baked Brie, 280
Chili-Cheese Egg Rolls, 285
Crispy Grilled Zucchini with Marinara, 281
Foolproof Mushrooms, 92
Ham and Broccoli Puffs, 288
Hawaiian Cheese Bread, 287
Mozzarella Sticks, 91
Parmesan-Coated Brie, 102
Peach-Glazed Meatballs, 283
Roasted Grape Tomatoes, 283
Sensational Stuffed Mushrooms, 23
Simmered Smoked Links, 151
Slow Cooker Cheese Dip, 95
Teriyaki Egg Rolls, 10

Snacks

Candied Pumpkin Spice Pecans, 151
Caribbean Chips with Apricot Salsa, 67
Chesapeake Snack Mix, 107
Italian Snack Mix, 100

APPLES

Apple-Almond Stuffing, 36
Apple Cinnamon Omelet, 293
Apple-Sage Roasted Turkey, 35
Apple-Stuffed Pork Tenderloins, 260
Autumn Harvest Cobbler, 220
Broccoli-Apple Salad, 63
Glazed Cinnamon Apples, 168
Sausage-Apple Puff Pancake, 181
Sausage Sliders with Cran-Apple Slaw, 69
Tipsy Apple Pie, 235

APRICOTS

Apricot & White Chocolate Coffee Cake, 29
Apricot Baked Ham, 261
Apricot Thumbprints, 43
Autumn Harvest Cobbler, 210
Bacon-Wrapped Apricot Bites, 288
Caribbean Chips with Apricot Salsa, 67
✓Chili-Apricot Pork Chops, 273
Fruit & Nut Cereal Bars, 148

ARTICHOKES

Artichoke Tuna Melt, 113
Greek Chicken Penne, 208
Layered Artichoke Cheese Spread, 289

ASPARAGUS

Champagne Salmon & Fettuccine, 206
Herbed Asparagus, 50
Prosciutto-Wrapped Asparagus with Raspberry Sauce, 86
Spring Morning Casserole, 241

AVOCADO

Avocado Chicken Salad, 62
Avocado-Tomato Salad, 12
✓Grilled Salmon with Avocado Salsa, 277
Ham and Avocado Scramble, 16
Shrimp & Avocado Salads, 213
Tropical Guacamole, 285

BACON

Bacon & Egg Potato Salad, 31

✓ Recipe Includes Nutrition Facts (and Diabetic Exchanges when applicable)

Bacon & Tomato-Topped Haddock, 255
Bacon-Beef Barley Soup, 159
Bacon-Wrapped Apricot Bites, 288
Breaded Brunch Bacon, 28
Brussels Sprouts with Bacon, 138
Cheddar & Bacon Burgers, 152
Hash Brown Pancetta Casserole, 184
Meat-atarian Sub, 189
Potato & Bacon Frittata, 296
Potato Bacon Omelet, 295
Summer Carbonara, 305
Touchdown Brat Sliders, 195

BANANAS
Banana Macadamia Muffins, 180
✓Banana-Pineapple Ice, 276
Rocky Road Grilled Banana Splits, 232
Whipped Banana Latte, 145

BARLEY
Bacon-Beef Barley Soup, 159
Hearty Barley Bake, 264
Mediterranean Chicken Stir-Fry, 127

BARS & BROWNIES
Caramel-Pecan Dream Bars, 225
Chocolate-Peanut Cheesecake Bars, 231
Coconut Citrus Bars, 233
Creamy Lemon Cake Bars, 89
Fruit & Nut Cereal Bars, 148
German Chocolate Bars, 224
Hugs 'n' Kisses Brownie, 229
Peanut Butter Blondies, 78
Pumpkin Walnut Squares, 233
Salted Peanut Bars, 78
Spooktacular Brownies, 33
Toffee Triangles, 42

BEANS
Black Bean-Chicken Quesadillas, 55
Burrito Pie, 245
Chili-Cheese Egg Rolls, 285
Chipotle-Black Bean Chili, 190
Easy Hummus, 87
Game-Night Nacho Pizza, 75
Green Olive Dip, 156
Italian Bean Soup, 194
Jamaican Ham and Bean Soup, 67
Pepperoni Pizza Chili, 195
Provencal Bean Salad, 138
✓Salsa Black Bean Burgers, 268
Spicy Turkey Bean Soup, 169
Tex-Mex Chicken with Black Beans & Rice, 171
Tex-Mex Chili with a Cincinnati Twist, 164
Turkey Chili with Pasta, 32
White Chili with a Kick, 196

BEEF *(also see Ground Beef)*
Appetizers
Green Chili Beef Dip, 287
Reuben Spread, 286
Roast Beef Spirals, 283
Main Dishes
Asian Beef with Noodles, 54
Basil-Butter Steaks with Roasted Potatoes, 119
Beef & Tortellini Marinara with Green Beans, 161
Beef and Wild Rice Medley, 306
Beef Tip Stew over Fusilli, 120
Broiled Steaks with Parmesan-Sage Potatoes, 110
Chipotle-Honey Grilled T-Bones, 309
Family-Favorite Beef Roast, 166
French Onion Portobello Brisket, 166
Game-Night Nacho Pizza, 75
Gingered Short Ribs with Green Rice, 165
Grilled Asian Steak, 310
Grilled Sirloin with Chili-Beer Barbecue Sauce, 310
Italian Roast Beef Sandwiches, 56
Marmalade-Glazed Steaks, 87
Mini Reuben Casseroles, 117
Mom's Celery Seed Brisket, 173
Old-World Corned Beef and Vegetables, 168
✓Sesame-Ginger Steak Salad, 277
Spinach-Stuffed Beef Tenderloin, 252
Steaks with Molasses-Glazed Onions, 51
Stout & Honey Beef Roast, 118
Sweet-and-Sour Beef Stew, 162
Salad
Citrus Steak Salad, 132
Sandwich
Very Best Barbecue Beef Sandwiches, 191
Soups & Stew
Bacon-Beef Barley Soup, 159
Hearty Vegetable Beef Soup, 197
Satisfying Beef Stew, 196

BEVERAGES
Berry Breakfast Smoothies, 16
Butterscotch Mulled Cider, 282
Caramel Macchiato Floats, 144
Chai Tea, 184
Cider Wassail Punch, 282

✓ Recipe Includes Nutrition Facts (and Diabetic Exchanges when applicable)

BEVERAGES *(continued)*
Cinnamon Berry Cider, 73
French Vanilla Mocha, 144
Fresh Peach Lemonade, 84
Heavenly Hot Chocolate Mix, 38
Hot Fruit Punch, 152
Hot Spiced Wine, 286
Iced Skinny Hazelnut Latte, 144
Lemon Spiced Tea, 10
Mulled Dr. Pepper, 158
Orange-Peach Thirst Quencher, 73
Raspberry Pomegranate Smoothies, 99
Rich Hazelnut Coffee, 282
Spanish Coffee, 145
Watermelon Spritzer, 243
Whipped Banana Latte, 145

BLUEBERRIES
Berry Breakfast Smoothies, 16
Berry-Topped Puff Pancake, 183
Blueberry Cheesecake Parfait, 103
Blueberry Cobbler, 95
Blueberry Fizz Pops, 76
Over-the-Top Blueberry Bread Pudding, 218
Summer Fruit Pizza, 31
Summer Turkey Salads, 123
Very Berry Bruschetta, 226
✓Whole Wheat Blueberry Muffins, 270

BREADS & ROLLS *(also see Coffee Cake; Cornmeal; Muffins & Scones)*
Chive and Cheese Breadsticks, 81
Garlic-Cheese Flat Bread, 62
Hawaiian Cheese Bread, 287
Monterey Ranch Bread, 84
Pesto Dip with Parmesan Toast, 90

BREAKFAST & BRUNCH *(also see Coffee Cake; Crepes; Doughnuts; Eggs; Muffins & Scones; Quiche & Tarts; Pancakes & Waffles)*
Baked Fruit Compote, 182
Berry Breakfast Smoothies, 16
Breaded Brunch Bacon, 28
Breakfast Biscuit Cups, 183
Breakfast Tortas, 182
Brie and Sausage Brunch Bake, 176
Chicken and Egg Hash, 179
Ham and Avocado Scramble, 16
Hash Brown Egg Breakfast, 180
Hash Brown Pancetta Casserole, 184
Italian Brunch Bake, 246
Raspberry Pomegranate Smoothies, 99
Scrambled Eggs with the Works, 29
Strawberry Breakfast Shortcakes, 79

BROCCOLI
Broccoli-Apple Salad, 63
Broccoli Turkey Pie, 298
Cheddar Broccoli Soup, 56
Ham and Broccoli Puffs, 288
Italian Dressed Broccoli, 68
Lemon-Pepper Broccoli, 8
Nutty Broccoli, 57
Skillet Ziti with Chicken and Broccoli, 272
Slow-Cooked Broccoli, 132
Slow-Cooked Ham 'n' Broccoli, 167
Zesty Lemon Broccoli, 107

BRUSSELS SPROUTS
Brussels Sprouts with Bacon, 138
Maple-Dijon Sprout Medley, 36

BUTTER
Butter Almond Cookies, 43
Butter & Herb Turkey, 167
Carrots with Lemon Butter, 47
Chicken in Lime Butter, 211
Garlic Butter Shrimp, 86
Garlic Butter Topping, 104
Quick Cookie Mix, 42
Tarragon Butter, 37

CABBAGE & COLESLAW MIX
Caribbean Shrimp Spring Rolls, 122
Catfish Po'boys, 203
Orange Chicken Wraps, 197
Poppy Seed Slaw, 135
Sausage Sliders with Cran-Apple Slaw, 69
Slow-Cooked Cabbage Rolls, 165
Southwest Fish Tacos, 12
Teriyaki Egg Rolls, 10
✓Tilapia Tostadas, 274
✓Turkey Stir-Fry with Cabbage, 274

CAKES, CHEESECAKES & CUPCAKES
Almond Chocolate Torte, 227
Cherry Cordial Cake Balls, 144
Chocolate Cannoli Cake Roll, 224
Chocolate Chip Cheesecake, 220
Chocolate Cookie Cheesecake, 226
Chocolate Frosted Peanut Butter Cupcakes, 80
Cinnamon & Sugar Cake, 219
Citrus Pound Cake, 231
Cranberry Orange Cake, 234
Creamy Lemon Cake Bars, 89

✓ Recipe Includes Nutrition Facts (and Diabetic Exchanges when applicable)

Fluted Tiramisu Cake, 219
Fruit-Filled Cupcakes, 74
Lemon Cream Cake, 230
Mardi Gras Cupcakes, 24
Minty Hot Fudge Sundae Cake, 171
✓Orange-Coconut Angel Food Cake, 276
Orange Marmalade Cake Sauce, 54
Pistachio Cake, 236
Pumpkin Streusel Cupcakes, 232
Triple-Chocolate Cake with Raspberry Sauce, 228

CANDY & CONFECTIONS
Cherry Cordial Cake Balls, 144
Deep-Fried Candy Bars on a Stick, 225
Double Chocolate Truffles, 222
Kahlua Fudge, 224
Onion Rings, 73
Peanut Butter Clusters, 92
S'more-Dipped Cherries, 222
Snickers Cookies, 91
Toffee Triangles, 42

CARAMEL
Caramel-Pecan Dream Bars, 225
Chocolate Caramel Cookies, 86
Pull-Apart Caramel Coffee Cake, 179
Spooktacular Brownies, 33

CARROTS
Carrots with Lemon Butter, 47
Cider-Glazed Pork Chops with Carrots, 112
Classy Carrots, 60
Garlic Carrots, 132
Squash & Carrot Saute, 136

CASSEROLES *(also see Breakfast & Brunch; Oven Entrees; Quiche & Tarts)*
Blend of the Bayou, 258
Broccoli Turkey Pie, 298
Burrito Pie, 245
Cajun Shrimp Lasagna Roll-Ups, 255
Chicken & Cheese Noodle Bake, 242
Chicken Club Casseroles, 246
Chicken Mole Casserole, 114
Company Lasagna, 242
Country Chicken Casserole, 244
Creamy Chicken Enchiladas, 240
Easy Beef-Stuffed Shells, 247
Elegant Smoked Salmon Strata, 241
Ground Beef Macaroni Casserole, 74
Harvest Vegetable Bake, 252
Hash Brown Pancetta Casserole, 184
Hearty Alfredo Potatoes, 253
Hearty Barley Bake, 264
Jazzed-Up Green Bean Casserole, 37
Lattice Chicken Potpie, 257
Make-Ahead Lasagna, 245
Mexican Chicken Alfredo, 249
Mexican Lasagna, 257
Mini Reuben Casseroles, 117
Reunion Casserole, 256
Sausage Fettuccine Bake, 248
Sausage Lasagna Rolls, 248
Southwest Enchilada Bake, 246
Spring Morning Casserole, 241
Tarragon Mashed Potato Casserole, 34
Tater Tot Casseroles, 242
Three-Cheese & Pepper Penne, 249
Wagon Wheel Casserole, 80

CHEESE *(also see Cream Cheese)*
Appetizers
Brie Phyllo Cups, 95
Chili Baked Brie, 280
Foolproof Mushrooms, 92
French Quarter Cheese Spread, 281
Green Olive Dip, 156
Mozzarella Sticks, 91
Parmesan-Coated Brie, 102
Pecan Cheese Logs, 23
Pesto Dip with Parmesan Toast, 90
Red Pepper & Feta Dip, 150
Seafood Cheese Dip, 152
Slow Cooker Cheese Dip, 95
Breads
Chive and Cheese Breadsticks, 81
Monterey Ranch Bread, 84
Main Dishes
Blue Cheese Walnut Tart, 247
Brie and Sausage Brunch Bake, 176
Chicken & Cheese Noodle Bake, 242
Chicken Cheese Strata, 114
Hearty Mac & Cheese, 79
Parmesan Baked Chicken, 297
Pepper Jack Mac, 49
Pepperoni Pizza, 72
Sloppy Joe Pizza, 205
Squash Fajitas with Goat Cheese, 215
Three-Cheese & Pepper Penne, 249
Sandwiches
Cheddar & Bacon Burgers, 152
Ham & Jack Pudgy Pie, 149

✓ Recipe Includes Nutrition Facts (and Diabetic Exchanges when applicable)

CHEESE *(continued)*
Mexican Grilled Cheese Sandwiches, 116
Three-Cheese Florentine Burgers, 189
Side Dishes
Broiled Parmesan Tomatoes, 98
Lemon-Feta Angel Hair, 52
Spinach & Feta Saute, 99
Sweet Corn with Parmesan and Cilantro, 31
Soups
Cheddar Broccoli Soup, 56
Cheddar Seafood Chowder, 188

CHERRIES
Cherry-Barbecue Pork Ribs, 30
Cherry-Chocolate Pudgy Pie, 148
Cherry Cordial Cake Balls, 144
Cherry Nut Cookies, 237
Italian Spumoni Cookies, 41
Roast Pork with Cherry-Almond Glaze, 258
Sensational Stuffed Mushrooms, 23
S'more-Dipped Cherries, 222

CHICKEN
Appetizer
Chicken Skewers with Sweet & Spicy Marmalade, 280
Main Dishes
Asian Chicken Skillet, 209
Baja Chicken Taco Pizza, 259
Barbecue Chicken Tacos, 100
Black Bean-Chicken Quesadillas, 55
Can-Can Chicken, 308
"Candy Corn" Quesadillas, 33
Cashew Chicken with Noodles, 18
Chicken & Pear Bundles, 111
Chicken & Vegetables with Mustard-Herb Sauce, 170
Chicken Cheese Strata, 114
Chicken Club Casseroles, 246
Chicken in Lime Butter, 211
Chicken Loaf with Mushroom Gravy, 261
Chicken Marsala, 50
Chicken Mole Casserole, 114
Chicken Tetrazzini, 81
Country Chicken Casserole, 244
Creamy Chicken Enchiladas, 240
Creole Chicken, 305
Family-Favorite Italian Chicken, 212
Fiesta-Twisted Brunswick Stew, 162
Garlic Chicken Breasts, 87
✓Greek Chicken Dinner, 271
Greek Chicken Penne, 208
Grilled Honey-Lime Chicken, 310
Harvest Vegetable Bake, 252
Italian Chicken Cordon Bleu, 208
Lattice Chicken Potpie, 257
Mediterranean Chicken Stir-Fry, 127
Mexican Chicken Alfredo, 249
Mexican Lasagna, 257
Mexican-Seasoned Grilled Chicken, 309
Mexican Smothered Chicken Thighs, 254
Mimosa Roasted Chicken, 252
Moroccan Chicken, 160
New Orleans Gumbo, 24
Orange-Spiced Chicken, 146
Parmesan Baked Chicken, 297
Pumpkin-Curry Chicken Over Cashew Rice, 204
Quick Sweet-and-Sour Chicken, 84
Quicker Chicken and Dumplings, 200
Roasted Chicken with Lemon Sauce, 265
Roasted Chicken with Veggies, 262
Roasted Pepper Chicken Penne, 212
Santa Fe Chicken, 207
✓Saucy Peach-Balsamic Chicken, 268
Simply Seasoned Chicken, 59
Skillet Ziti with Chicken and Broccoli, 272
Slow Cooker Chicken Curry, 172
Smoky Chicken Enchilada Skillet, 213
Smothered Italian Chicken, 121
Sweet & Sour Pineapple Chicken, 306
Tex-Mex Chicken with Black Beans & Rice, 171
Thai Fried Chicken, 118
Whole Wheat Pasta Bake, 126
Salads
Avocado Chicken Salad, 62
Curried Chicken Salad, 92
Sandwiches
Greek Grilled Chicken Pitas, 243
Orange Chicken Wraps, 197
Soups & Chili
Au Gratin Chicken Chowder, 190
Creamy Chicken Rice Soup, 192
Lemon-Chicken Velvet Soup, 192
White Chili with a Kick, 196

CHOCOLATE
Almond Chocolate Torte, 227
Cherry-Chocolate Pudgy Pie, 148
Cherry Cordial Cake Balls, 144
Chocolate Cannoli Cake Roll, 224
Chocolate Caramel Cookies, 86
Chocolate Chip Cheesecake, 220

✓ Recipe Includes Nutrition Facts (and Diabetic Exchanges when applicable)

Chocolate Cookie Cheesecake, 226
Chocolate Frosted Peanut Butter Cupcakes, 80
Chocolate-Peanut Cheesecake Bars, 231
Double Chip Cookies, 148
Double-Chocolate Holiday Pie, 234
Double Chocolate Truffles, 222
French Vanilla Mocha, 144
German Chocolate Bars, 224
German Chocolate Thumbprint Cookies, 230
Heavenly Hot Chocolate Mix, 38
Hot Fudge Sauce, 103
Hugs 'n' Kisses Brownie, 229
Kahlua Fudge, 224
Makeover Chocolate Truffle Dessert, 27
Mocha Dessert Fondue, 23
Rocky Road Cookie Pizza, 151
S'more-Dipped Cherries, 222
Spooktacular Brownies, 33
Toffee Triangles, 42
Triple-Chocolate Cake with Raspberry Sauce, 228
White Chocolate-Macadamia Snowball Cookies, 40

COCONUT
Coconut Citrus Bars, 233
German Chocolate Bars, 224
German Chocolate Thumbprint Cookies, 230
✓Orange-Coconut Angel Food Cake, 276
White Chocolate-Macadamia Snowball Cookies, 40

COFFEE CAKE
Apricot & White Chocolate Coffee Cake, 29
Cinnamon Roll Coffee Cake, 185
Coffee Cake Muffins, 143
Cranberry-Pecan Coffee Cake, 178
Pull-Apart Caramel Coffee Cake, 179

CONDIMENTS
Cilantro-Pepita Pesto, 312
Cranberry BBQ Sauce, 39
Easy Refrigerator Pickles, 312
Lemon Cranberry Sauce, 36
Pina Colada Jam, 313
Tarragon Butter, 37
Three-Berry Freezer Jam, 313
Tomatillo Salsa, 146

COOKIES
Apricot Thumbprints, 43
Butter Almond Cookies, 43
Butter Pecan Biscotti, 142
Cherry Nut Cookies, 237
Chocolate Caramel Cookies, 86
Double Chip Cookies, 148
Drizzled Peppermint Cookies, 39
German Chocolate Thumbprint Cookies, 230
Glazed Ornament Cookies, 40
Holiday Pinwheel Cookies, 40
Italian Spumoni Cookies, 41
Joyful Cutout Cookies, 42
Key Lime Bites, 236
Lemon & Rosemary Shortbread Cookies, 223
Lemon Shortbreads, 229
Peanut Butter Blossoms, 43
Quick Cookie Mix, 42
Raisin Sweet Potato Cookies, 223
Rocky Road Cookie Pizza, 151
Snickers Cookies, 91
Waffle Cookies, 220
White Chocolate-Macadamia Snowball Cookies, 40

CORN *(also see Cornmeal)*
"Candy Corn" Quesadillas, 33
Creamy Sweet Corn with Okra, 66
Green Bean & Corn Medley, 48
Red Pepper Corn, 55
Sweet Corn with Parmesan and Cilantro, 31
Zucchini & Corn with Cilantro, 53

CORNMEAL
Confetti Cornmeal Muffins, 32
Cornmeal-Wheat Pancakes, 16

CRANBERRIES & CRANBERRY JUICE
Berry Breakfast Smoothies, 16
Cranberry BBQ Sauce, 39
Cranberry-Chili Cheese Spread, 102
Cranberry-Dijon Pork Roast, 159
Cranberry-Ginger Pork Ribs, 168
Cranberry Orange Cake, 234
Cranberry Orange Pancakes, 177
Cranberry-Pear Crisp, 221
Cranberry-Pecan Coffee Cake, 178
Double-Chocolate Holiday Pie, 234
Lemon Cranberry Sauce, 36
Sausage Sliders with Cran-Apple Slaw, 69

CREAM CHEESE
(also see Cakes, Cheesecakes & Cupcakes)
Butter Almond Cookies, 43
Cherry Nut Cookies, 237
Cranberry-Chili Cheese Spread, 102

✓ Recipe Includes Nutrition Facts (and Diabetic Exchanges when applicable)

CREAM CHEESE *(continued)*
French Quarter Cheese Spread, 281
Layered Artichoke Cheese Spread, 289
Pecan Cheese Logs, 23
Red Pepper & Feta Dip, 150
Reuben Spread, 286
Tiramisu, 240

CREPES
Tiramisu Crepes, 178

CUCUMBERS
Easy Refrigerator Pickles, 312
Fresh Tomato & Cucumber Salad, 134

DESSERTS *(also see Bars & Brownies; Cakes, Cheesecakes & Cupcakes; Candy & Confections; Chocolate; Cookies; Frozen Pops; Ice Cream, Sherbet & Granita; Pies & Tarts)*
Asti & Strawberries Dessert, 227
Autumn Harvest Cobbler, 220
Blueberry Cheesecake Parfait, 103
Blueberry Cobbler, 95
Cranberry-Pear Crisp, 221
Dunked Strawberries, 12
Fluffy Lemon Squares, 218
Frozen Macaroon Dessert, 89
Glazed Cinnamon Apples, 168
Makeover Chocolate Truffle Dessert, 27
Marshmallow Snowmen, 38
Over-the-Top Blueberry Bread Pudding, 218
Pumpkin Walnut Squares, 233
Slow-Cooker Bread Pudding, 172
Summer Fruit Pizza, 31
Sunshine Cobbler, 237
Tiramisu, 240
Very Berry Bruschetta, 226

DOUGHNUTS
Brunch Beignets, 25
Coffee & Cream Doughnuts, 144

EGGS *(also see Breakfast & Brunch; Casseroles)*
Apple Cinnamon Omelet, 293
Bacon & Egg Potato Salad, 31
Chicken and Egg Hash, 179
Chorizo Salsa Omelet, 293
Elegant Smoked Salmon Strata, 241
Fried Rice Omelet, 292
Ham and Avocado Scramble, 16
Ham and Swiss Omelet, 292
Hash Brown Egg Breakfast, 180
Italian Brunch Bake, 246
Italian Omelet, 294
Peanut Butter and Jelly Omelet, 295
Potato & Bacon Frittata, 296
Potato Bacon Omelet, 295
Scrambled Eggs with the Works, 29
Smoked Salmon Egg Salad, 98
Spring Morning Casserole, 241

FISH & SEAFOOD
Appetizers
Caribbean Shrimp Spring Rolls, 122
Seafood Cheese Dip, 152
Main Dishes
Bacon & Tomato-Topped Haddock, 255
BBQ Shrimp Quesadillas, 307
Blend of the Bayou, 258
Caesar Shrimp and Pasta, 92
Cajun Pecan Catfish, 66
Cajun Shrimp Lasagna Roll-Ups, 255
Captain Russell's Jambalaya, 25
Champagne Salmon & Fettuccine, 206
Cheddar Seafood Chowder, 188
Chimichurri Shrimp Skillet, 210
Coquille St. Jacques, 201
Crab Quiche, 176
Crab-Stuffed Tilapia, 253
Creole Shrimp & Sausage, 125
Crumb-Coated Cod Fillets, 205
✓Crumb-Coated Red Snapper, 269
Curry Scallops and Rice, 120
Elegant Smoked Salmon Strata, 241
Garlic Butter Shrimp, 86
✓Grilled Salmon with Avocado Salsa, 277
Halibut with Orange Salsa, 263
Honey-Pecan Baked Cod, 201
Lemon-Caper Baked Cod, 61
Maple-Glazed Salmon, 8
Mediterranean Roasted Salmon, 52
New Orleans Gumbo, 24
Orange Roughy Italiano, 207
Pesto Halibut, 89
Scalloped Shrimp and Potatoes, 91
Scallops with Thai Sauce, 202
✓Shrimp & Tomato Linguine Toss, 272
Shrimp Linguine with Parmesan Cream Sauce, 65
Shrimp Risotto, 115
Shrimp Skewers with Asian Quinoa, 127
Southern Shrimp & Grits, 200
Southwest Fish Tacos, 12
✓Tilapia Tostadas, 274

✓ Recipe Includes Nutrition Facts (and Diabetic Exchanges when applicable)

Tilapia with Green Beans Amandine, 112
Tomato and Onion Salmon, 211
Tuna Zucchini Cakes, 206
Salads & Sandwiches
Artichoke Tuna Melt, 113
Catfish Po'boys, 203
✓Garden Tuna Pita Sandwiches, 276
Shrimp & Avocado Salads, 213
Smoked Salmon Egg Salad, 98
✓Warm Szechuan Shrimp and Spinach Salad, 269

FROZEN POPS
Berry Blue Pops, 76
Blueberry Fizz Pops, 76
Cool Watermelon Pops, 76
Crazy-Colored Fruit Pops, 76
Tropical Strawberry Pops, 73

FRUIT *(also see specific kinds)*
Baked Fruit Compote, 182
Fruit & Nut Cereal Bars, 148
Lemonade Fruit Salad, 133
Summer Fruit Pizza, 31
Tequila-Lime Fruit Salad, 130

GARLIC
Garlic Butter Shrimp, 86
Garlic Butter Topping, 104
Garlic Carrots, 132
Garlic-Cheese Flat Bread, 62
Garlic Chicken Breasts, 87
✓Garlic Green Bean Medley, 275

GREEN BEANS
Beef & Tortellini Marinara with Green Beans, 161
✓Garlic Green Bean Medley, 275
Greek Green Bean Medley, 61
Green Bean & Corn Medley, 48
Green Beans with Tomatoes & Basil, 26
Jazzed-Up Green Bean Casserole, 37
Maple-Glazed Green Beans, 134
Peachy Green Beans, 136
Provencal Bean Salad, 138
Tilapia with Green Beans Amandine, 112

GRILLED RECIPES
Appetizer
Crispy Grilled Zucchini with Marinara, 281
Desserts
Grilled Pineapple Sundaes, 18
Rocky Road Grilled Banana Splits, 232
Main Dishes
Bourbon Brat Skewers, 308
Can-Can Chicken, 308
Cherry-Barbecue Pork Ribs, 30
Chipotle-Honey Grilled T-Bones, 309
Chipotle-Orange Pork Chops, 301
Grilled Asian Steak, 310
Grilled Honey-Lime Chicken, 310
Grilled Jerk Chops, 121
✓Grilled Salmon with Avocado Salsa, 277
Grilled Sirloin with Chili-Beer Barbecue Sauce, 310
Grilled Stuffed Peppers, 311
Mexican-Seasoned Grilled Chicken, 309
Orange-Glazed Ham Steaks, 46
Orange-Spiced Chicken, 146
Shrimp Skewers with Asian Quinoa, 127
Vegetable-Stuffed Grilled Portobellos, 124
Sandwiches & Side Dishes
Cheddar & Bacon Burgers, 152
Greek Grilled Chicken Pitas, 243
Grilled Potato Packets, 135
Lemon-Sesame Veggie Kabobs, 147
Prosciutto-Wrapped Asparagus with Raspberry Sauce, 86
Steak House Burgers, 194
Three-Cheese Florentine Burgers, 189
Unstuffed Jalapeno Popper Burgers, 124

GROUND BEEF
Appetizers
Green Olive Dip, 156
Peach-Glazed Meatballs, 283
Hamburgers
Cheddar & Bacon Burgers, 152
Three-Cheese Florentine Burgers, 189
Steak House Burgers, 194
Unstuffed Jalapeno Popper Burgers, 124
Main Dishes
Beef 'n' Turkey Meat Loaf, 263
Beef Chow Mein, 214
Burrito Pie, 245
Chipotle Chili Dogs, 58
Creamy Veggie Meatballs, 296
Easy Beef-Stuffed Shells, 247
Florentine Meatballs, 300
Grilled Stuffed Peppers, 311
Ground Beef Macaroni Casserole, 74
Hamburger Steaks with Mushroom Gravy, 47
Hearty Mac & Cheese, 79
Italian Stroganoff, 300

✓ Recipe Includes Nutrition Facts (and Diabetic Exchanges when applicable)

GROUND BEEF *(continued)*
Make-Ahead Lasagna, 245
Skillet Lasagna, 115
Sloppy Joe Pizza, 205
Slow-Cooked Cabbage Rolls, 165
Southwest Enchilada Bake, 246
Stovetop Italian Macaroni, 68
Stuffed Burger Bundles, 254
Wagon Wheel Casserole, 80

Salad, Sandwiches & Chili
✓Fiesta Taco Salads, 271
Hearty Italian Sandwiches, 192
Pepperoni Pizza Chili, 195
Sloppy Pizza Joes, 63
Tex-Mex Chili with a Cincinnati Twist, 164

HAM & PROSCIUTTO
Apricot Baked Ham, 261
Baked Ham with Honey-Chipotle Glaze, 26
Ham and Avocado Scramble, 16
Ham and Broccoli Puffs, 288
Ham & Cheese Ziti, 299
Ham & Jack Pudgy Pie, 149
Ham and Swiss Omelet, 292
Hot Ham Sandwiches, 194
Italian Chicken Cordon Bleu, 208
Jamaican Ham and Bean Soup, 67
Jim's Honey-Glazed Ham, 262
Meat-atarian Sub, 189
Mom's Scalloped Potatoes and Ham, 158
Orange-Glazed Ham Steaks, 46
Prosciutto-Wrapped Asparagus with Raspberry Sauce, 86
Slow-Cooked Ham 'n' Broccoli, 167
Zesty Grilled Sandwiches, 200

HOT DOGS
Chipotle Chili Dogs, 58

ICE CREAM, SHERBET & GRANITA
(also see Frozen Pops)
✓Banana-Pineapple Ice, 276
Butter Brickle Ice Cream Pie, 147
Caramel Macchiato Floats, 144
Frozen Macaroon Dessert, 89
Green Sherbet Froggie, 79
Grilled Pineapple Sundaes, 18
Hot Fudge Sauce, 103
Meatball Sub, 75
Minty Hot Fudge Sundae Cake, 171
Pistachio Meringue Sundaes, 14
Rhubarb Strawberry Granita, 95
Rocky Road Grilled Banana Splits, 232

LEMONS
Carrots with Lemon Butter, 47
Citrus Pound Cake, 231
Coconut Citrus Bars, 233
Creamy Lemon Cake Bars, 89
Fluffy Lemon Squares, 218
Fresh Peach Lemonade, 84
Gingerbread Scones with Lemon Butter, 181
Lemon & Rosemary Shortbread Cookies, 223
Lemon-Caper Baked Cod, 61
Lemon-Chicken Velvet Soup, 192
Lemon Cranberry Sauce, 36
Lemon Cream Cake, 230
Lemon-Dill Couscous, 99
Lemon-Feta Angel Hair, 52
✓Lemon Pasta with Spinach, 273
Lemon-Pepper Broccoli, 8
Lemon-Sesame Veggie Kabobs, 147
Lemon Shortbreads, 229
Lemon Spiced Tea, 10
Lemonade Fruit Salad, 133
Roasted Chicken with Lemon Sauce, 265
Turkey Penne with Lemon Cream Sauce, 123
Zesty Lemon Broccoli, 107

LIMES
Best Lime Tart, 222
Chicken in Lime Butter, 211
Cool Watermelon Pops, 76
Grilled Honey-Lime Chicken, 310
Key Lime Bites, 236
Tequila-Lime Fruit Salad, 130
Watermelon Spritzer, 243

MAPLE
Butter Pecan Biscotti, 142
Maple Balsamic Dressing, 102
Maple-Dijon Sprout Medley, 36
Maple-Glazed Green Beans, 134
Maple Glazed Salmon, 8

MELONS
Melon-Mango Salsa, 284
Watermelon Spritzer, 243

MUFFINS & SCONES
Banana Macadamia Muffins, 180
Coffee Cake Muffins, 143
Confetti Cornmeal Muffins, 32
Gingerbread Scones with Lemon Butter, 181
✓Whole Wheat Blueberry Muffins, 270

✓ *Recipe Includes Nutrition Facts (and Diabetic Exchanges when applicable)*

MUSHROOMS
Chicken Loaf with Mushroom Gravy, 261
Chicken Marsala, 50
Foolproof Mushrooms, 92
French Onion Portobello Brisket, 166
Hamburger Steaks with Mushroom Gravy, 47
Italian Mushrooms, 138
Orzo Pilaf with Mushrooms, 64
Porcini-Crusted Pork with Polenta, 262
Portobello & Basil Cheese Tortellini, 304
Potato and Mushroom Gratin, 26
Sausage & Mushroom Stuffed Squash, 256
Savory Mushroom & Herb Pork Roast, 173
Sensational Stuffed Mushrooms, 23
Tangy Turkey Saute, 57
Vegetable-Stuffed Grilled Portobellos, 124
Wagon Wheel Casserole, 80

NUTS *(also see Peanut Butter)*
Almond & Mandarin Orange Salad, 18
Almond Chocolate Torte, 227
Almond Rice Pilaf, 130
Banana Macadamia Muffins, 180
Blue Cheese Walnut Tart, 247
Butter Almond Cookies, 43
Butter Pecan Biscotti, 142
Cajun Pecan Catfish, 66
Candied Pumpkin Spice Pecans, 151
Caramel-Pecan Dream Bars, 225
Cashew Chicken with Noodles, 18
Cherry Nut Cookies, 237
Chocolate-Peanut Cheesecake Bars, 231
Cranberry-Pecan Coffee Cake, 178
Honey-Pecan Baked Cod, 201
Nutty Broccoli, 57
Pecan Cheese Logs, 23
Pecan-Crusted Turkey Cutlets, 48
Pistachio Cake, 236
Pistachio Meringue Sundaes, 14
Pumpkin-Curry Chicken Over Cashew Rice, 204
Pumpkin Walnut Squares, 233
Romaine and Walnut Salad, 49
Salted Peanut Bars, 78
Tilapia with Green Beans Amandine, 112
White Chocolate-Macadamia Snowball Cookies, 40

ONIONS
Maple-Dijon Sprout Medley, 36
Steaks with Molasses-Glazed Onions, 51
Tomato and Onion Salmon, 211

ORANGES
Almond & Mandarin Orange Salad, 18
Chipotle-Orange Pork Chops, 301
Citrus Pound Cake, 231
Coconut Citrus Bars, 233
Cranberry Orange Cake, 234
Cranberry Orange Pancakes, 177
Halibut with Orange Salsa, 263
Mimosa Roasted Chicken, 252
Orange Chicken Wraps, 197
✓Orange-Coconut Angel Food Cake, 276
Orange-Glazed Ham Steaks, 46
Orange Marmalade Cake Sauce, 54
Orange-Peach Thirst Quencher, 73
Orange-Spiced Chicken, 146
Orange Turkey Croissants, 100

OVEN ENTREES
(also see Breakfast & Brunch; Casseroles)
Beef & Ground Beef
Basil-Butter Steaks with Roasted Potatoes, 119
Beef 'n' Turkey Meat Loaf, 263
Broiled Steaks with Parmesan-Sage Potatoes, 110
Creamy Veggie Meatballs, 296
Game-Night Nacho Pizza, 75
Marmalade-Glazed Steaks, 87
Sloppy Joe Pizza, 205
Spinach-Stuffed Beef Tenderloin, 252
Stuffed Burger Bundles, 254
Chicken
Baja Chicken Taco Pizza, 259
Chicken & Pear Bundles, 111
Chicken Cheese Strata, 114
Chicken Loaf with Mushroom Gravy, 261
Chicken Tetrazzini, 81
Garlic Chicken Breasts, 87
✓Greek Chicken Dinner, 271
Mexican Smothered Chicken Thighs, 254
Mimosa Roasted Chicken, 252
Parmesan Baked Chicken, 297
Roasted Chicken with Lemon Sauce, 265
Roasted Chicken with Veggies, 262
✓Saucy Peach-Balsamic Chicken, 268
Smothered Italian Chicken, 121
Whole Wheat Pasta Bake, 126
Fish & Seafood
Bacon & Tomato-Topped Haddock, 255
Cajun Pecan Catfish, 66

✓ *Recipe Includes Nutrition Facts (and Diabetic Exchanges when applicable)*

OVEN ENTREES *(continued)*
Crab-Stuffed Tilapia, 253
Crumb-Coated Cod Fillets, 205
✓Crumb-Coated Red Snapper, 269
Halibut with Orange Salsa, 263
Lemon-Caper Baked Cod, 61
Mediterranean Roasted Salmon, 52
Pesto Halibut, 89
Tomato and Onion Salmon, 211

Meatless
Veggie Calzones, 244

Pork
Apple-Stuffed Pork Tenderloins, 260
Apricot Baked Ham, 261
Baked Ham with Honey-Chipotle Glaze, 26
Big Daddy's BBQ Ribs, 260
✓Chili-Apricot Pork Chops, 273
Cider-Glazed Pork Chops with Carrots, 112
Ham & Cheese Ziti, 299
Jim's Honey-Glazed Ham, 262
✓Just Peachy Pork Tenderloin, 270
Peachy Pork Chops, 264
Pepperoni Pizza, 72
Porcini-Crusted Pork with Polenta, 262
Pork Tenderloins with Wild Rice, 126
Potato & Bacon Frittata, 296
Roast Pork with Cherry-Almond Glaze, 258
Sausage & Mushroom Stuffed Squash, 256
✓Spiced Pork Medallions with Bourbon Sauce, 275
Zesty Calzone, 197

Turkey
Apple-Sage Roasted Turkey, 35
Smoked Turkey Sausage Pizza, 259

PANCAKES & WAFFLES
Berry-Topped Puff Pancake, 183
Cinnamon Flapjacks, 29
Cornmeal-Wheat Pancakes, 16
Cranberry Orange Pancakes, 177
Sausage-Apple Puff Pancake, 181
Strawberry Breakfast Shortcakes, 79
Waffle Cookies, 220

PASTA & NOODLES
Main Dishes
Asian Beef with Noodles, 54
Barbecue Pork and Penne Skillet, 214
Beef & Tortellini Marinara with Green Beans, 161
Beef Tip Stew over Fusilli, 120
Caesar Shrimp and Pasta, 92
Cashew Chicken with Noodles, 18
Champagne Salmon & Fettuccine, 206
Chicken & Cheese Noodle Bake, 242
Chicken Tetrazzini, 81
Chinese Pork 'n' Noodles, 307
Company Lasagna, 242
Creamy Sausage & Bow Ties, 209
Easy Beef-Stuffed Shells, 247
Family-Favorite Italian Chicken, 212
Greek Chicken Penne, 208
Ground Beef Macaroni Casserole, 74
Ham & Cheese Ziti, 299
Hearty Mac & Cheese, 79
✓Lemon Pasta with Spinach, 273
Make-Ahead Lasagna, 245
Mexican Chicken Alfredo, 249
Mexican Lasagna, 257
Pepper Jack Mac, 49
Pork & Tomato Pasta Sauce, 90
Portobello & Basil Cheese Tortellini, 304
Ravioli with Creamy Squash Sauce, 214
Reunion Casserole, 256
Rigatoni with Roasted Sweet Potatoes, 111
Roasted Pepper Chicken Penne, 212
Sausage Fettuccine Bake, 248
Sausage Lasagna Rolls, 248
✓Shrimp & Tomato Linguine Toss, 272
Shrimp Linguine with Parmesan Cream Sauce, 65
Skillet Lasagna, 115
Skillet Ziti with Chicken and Broccoli, 272
Stovetop Italian Macaroni, 68
Summer Carbonara, 305
Tex-Mex Chili with a Cincinnati Twist, 164
Three-Cheese & Pepper Penne, 249
Tortellini with Tomato-Cream Sauce, 297
Turkey Chili with Pasta, 32
Turkey Penne with Lemon Cream Sauce, 123
Wagon Wheel Casserole, 80
Whole Wheat Pasta Bake, 126

Salads
Caesar Tortellini Salad, 137
Colorful Spiral Pasta Salad, 152

Side Dishes
Lemon-Feta Angel Hair, 52
Orzo Pilaf with Mushrooms, 64

PEACHES
Fresh Peach Lemonade, 84
✓Just Peachy Pork Tenderloin, 270
Orange-Peach Thirst Quencher, 73

✓ Recipe Includes Nutrition Facts (and Diabetic Exchanges when applicable)

Peach-Glazed Meatballs, 283
Peachy Green Beans, 136
Peachy Pork Chops, 264
✓Saucy Peach-Balsamic Chicken, 268

PEANUT BUTTER
Chocolate Frosted Peanut Butter Cupcakes, 80
Chocolate-Peanut Cheesecake Bars, 231
Peanut Butter and Jelly Omelet, 295
Peanut Butter Blondies, 78
Peanut Butter Blossoms, 43
Peanut Butter Clusters, 92
Salted Peanut Bars, 78

PEARS
Autumn Tossed Salad, 34
Chicken & Pear Bundles, 111
Cranberry-Pear Crisp, 221

PEPPERONI
Meat-atarian Sub, 189
Pepperoni Pizza, 72
Pepperoni Pizza Chili, 195
Sicilian Salad, 104

PEPPERS
Grilled Stuffed Peppers, 311
Red Pepper & Feta Dip, 150
Red Pepper Corn, 55
Roasted Pepper Chicken Penne, 212
Three-Cheese & Pepper Penne, 249
Three-Chili Turkey Tacos, 53
Tomato and Green Pepper Omelet, 294
Vegetarian Stuffed Peppers, 157

PHYLLO & PUFF PASTRY
Brie Phyllo Cups, 95
Chicken & Pear Bundles, 111
Ham and Broccoli Puffs, 288

PIES & TARTS *(for savory pies and tarts, see Breakfast & Brunch; Casseroles; Quiche & Tarts)*
Best Lime Tart, 222
Butter Brickle Ice Cream Pie, 147
Cherry-Chocolate Pudgy Pie, 148
Double-Chocolate Holiday Pie, 234
Eggnog Pie, 236
Elegant Pumpkin Pie, 235
S'more Pudgy Pie, 149
Strawberry Ginger Tart, 228
Strawberry Pies, 89
Tipsy Apple Pie, 235

PINEAPPLE
✓Banana-Pineapple Ice, 276
Grilled Pineapple Sundaes, 18
Sweet & Sour Pineapple Chicken, 306

POLENTA
Polenta Rounds with Sausage Ragout, 14
Porcini-Crusted Pork with Polenta, 262

PORK *(also see Bacon; Ham & Prosciutto; Hot Dogs; Pepperoni; Sausage)*
Apple-Stuffed Pork Tenderloins, 260
Apricot Baked Ham, 261
Barbecue Pork and Penne Skillet, 214
Big Daddy's BBQ Ribs, 260
Cherry-Barbecue Pork Ribs, 30
✓Chili-Apricot Pork Chops, 273
Chinese Pork 'n' Noodles, 307
Chipotle-Orange Pork Chops, 301
Cider-Glazed Pork Chops with Carrots, 112
Cranberry-Dijon Pork Roast, 159
Cranberry-Ginger Pork Ribs, 168
Flavorful Pork Chops, 60
Ginger Pork Stir-Fry, 10
Grilled Jerk Chops, 121
Harvest Butternut & Pork Stew, 162
Herb Stuffed Chops, 161
Hoisin Pork Wraps, 191
Jim's Honey-Glazed Ham, 262
✓Just Peachy Pork Tenderloin, 270
Peachy Pork Chops, 264
Porcini-Crusted Pork with Polenta, 262
Pork & Tomato Pasta Sauce, 90
Pork Chops Normandy, 210
Pork Chops with Mustard Sauce, 204
Pork Fried Rice, 301
Pork Tenderloins with Wild Rice, 126
Pulled Pork Taters, 170
Roast Pork with Cherry-Almond Glaze, 258
Savory Mushroom & Herb Pork Roast, 173
Slow-Cooked Pork Tacos, 164
Soda Pop Chops with Smashed Potatoes, 117
Southern Pulled Pork, 156
✓Spiced Pork Medallions with Bourbon Sauce, 275
Spicy Tomato Pork Chops, 64
Stuffing-Stuffed Pork Chops, 298
Sweet Potato Pork Stew, 193
Tangy Tomato Pork Chops, 160
Teriyaki Pork, 304
Zesty Calzone, 197

✓ Recipe Includes Nutrition Facts (and Diabetic Exchanges when applicable)

POTATOES
- Bacon & Egg Potato Salad, 31
- Basil-Butter Steaks with Roasted Potatoes, 119
- Broiled Steaks with Parmesan-Sage Potatoes, 110
- Chicken and Egg Hash, 179
- Crispy Ranch Fries, 58
- Dill Potato Wedges, 8
- ✓Greek Chicken Dinner, 271
- Grilled Potato Packets, 135
- Hash Brown Egg Breakfast, 180
- Hash Brown Pancetta Casserole, 184
- Hearty Alfredo Potatoes, 253
- Herbed Potato Fans, 51
- Mom's Scalloped Potatoes and Ham, 158
- Potato & Bacon Frittata, 296
- Potato and Mushroom Gratin, 26
- Potato Bacon Omelet, 295
- Pulled Pork Taters, 170
- Roasted Rosemary Potatoes, 134
- Scalloped Shrimp and Potatoes, 91
- Soda Pop Chops with Smashed Potatoes, 117
- Tarragon Mashed Potato Casserole, 34
- Tater Tot Casseroles, 242

PUMPKIN
- Candied Pumpkin Spice Pecans, 151
- Elegant Pumpkin Pie, 235
- Pumpkin-Curry Chicken Over Cashew Rice, 204
- Pumpkin Streusel Cupcakes, 232
- Pumpkin Walnut Squares, 233

QUICHE & TARTS
- Blue Cheese Walnut Tart, 247
- Crab Quiche, 176
- Crescent Zucchini Pie, 177
- Crustless Quiche Bake, 179
- Southwest Breakfast Tart, 180
- Tomato Olive Quiche, 185

RASPBERRIES
- Berry Breakfast Smoothies, 16
- Berry-Topped Puff Pancake, 183
- Prosciutto-Wrapped Asparagus with Raspberry Sauce, 86
- Raspberry Pomegranate Smoothies, 99
- Summer Fruit Pizza, 31
- Three-Berry Freezer Jam, 313
- Triple-Chocolate Cake with Raspberry Sauce, 228

RICE
- Almond Rice Pilaf, 130
- Beef and Wild Rice Medley, 306
- Beef Chow Mein, 214
- Brown Rice Pilaf, 46
- Chimichurri Shrimp Skillet, 210
- Creamy Chicken Rice Soup, 192
- Curry Scallops and Rice, 120
- Fried Rice Omelet, 292
- Gingered Short Ribs with Green Rice, 165
- Pork Fried Rice, 301
- Pork Tenderloins with Wild Rice, 126
- Pumpkin-Curry Chicken Over Cashew Rice, 204
- Shrimp Risotto, 115
- Southwestern Vegetables & Rice, 215
- Tex-Mex Chicken with Black Beans & Rice, 171

SALADS & SALAD DRESSING

Coleslaw
- Poppy Seed Slaw, 135

Dressing
- Creamy Taco Dressing, 102
- Maple Balsamic Dressing, 102

Fruit Salads
- Lemonade Fruit Salad, 133
- Tequila-Lime Fruit Salad, 130

Green Salads
- Almond & Mandarin Orange Salad, 18
- Autumn Tossed Salad, 34
- Balsamic Arugula Salad, 14
- Crunchy Romaine Strawberry Salad, 130
- Italian Spinach Salad, 104
- Romaine and Walnut Salad, 49
- Sicilian Salad, 104

Main-Dish Salads
- Avocado Chicken Salad, 62
- Citrus Steak Salad, 132
- Curried Chicken Salad, 92
- ✓Fiesta Taco Salads, 271
- ✓Sesame-Ginger Steak Salad, 277
- Shrimp & Avocado Salads, 213
- Summer Turkey Salads, 123
- ✓Warm Szechuan Shrimp and Spinach Salad, 269

Pasta & Potato Salads
- Bacon & Egg Potato Salad, 31
- Caesar Tortellini Salad, 137
- Colorful Spiral Pasta Salad, 152

Vegetable Salads
- Avocado-Tomato Salad, 12
- Broccoli-Apple Salad, 63

✓ Recipe Includes Nutrition Facts (and Diabetic Exchanges when applicable)

Caramelized Grapefruit Salad, 137
Fresh Tomato & Cucumber Salad, 134
Provencal Bean Salad, 138

SANDWICHES
Cold Sandwiches
✓Garden Tuna Pita Sandwiches, 276
Greek Grilled Chicken Pitas, 243
Italian Roast Beef Sandwiches, 56
Orange Chicken Wraps, 197
Orange Turkey Croissants, 100
Smoked Salmon Egg Salad, 98
Thai Turkey Salad Pitas, 299
Hot Sandwiches
Artichoke Tuna Melt, 113
Catfish Po'boys, 203
Cheddar & Bacon Burgers, 152
Chipotle Chili Dogs, 58
Ham & Jack Pudgy Pie, 149
Hawaiian Kielbasa Sandwiches, 156
Hearty Italian Sandwiches, 192
Hoisin Pork Wraps, 191
Hot Ham Sandwiches, 194
Meat-atarian Sub, 189
Mexican Grilled Cheese Sandwiches, 116
✓Salsa Black Bean Burgers, 268
Sloppy Pizza Joes, 63
Steak House Burgers, 194
Three-Cheese Florentine Burgers, 189
Touchdown Brat Sliders, 195
Unstuffed Jalapeno Popper Burgers, 124
Veggie Calzones, 244
Very Best Barbecue Beef Sandwiches, 191
Zesty Grilled Sandwiches, 200

SAUSAGE *(also see Hot Dogs; Pepperoni)*
Appetizer
Sensational Stuffed Mushrooms, 23
Simmered Smoked Links, 151
Breakfast & Brunch
Breakfast Biscuit Cups, 183
Brie and Sausage Brunch Bake, 176
Chorizo Salsa Omelet, 293
Italian Brunch Bake, 246
Sausage-Apple Puff Pancake, 181
Southwest Breakfast Tart, 180
Main Dishes
Bourbon Brat Skewers, 308
Cajun-Shrimp Lasagna Roll-Ups, 255
Captain Russell's Jambalaya, 25
Company Lasagna, 242
Creamy Sausage & Bow Ties, 209
Creole Shrimp & Sausage, 125
Fiesta-Twisted Brunswick Stew, 162
Hearty Barley Bake, 264
Home-Style Sausage Gravy and Biscuits, 202
Italian Sausages with Provolone, 158
Make-Ahead Lasagna, 245
New Orleans Gumbo, 24
Polenta Rounds with Sausage Ragout, 14
Pork & Tomato Pasta Sauce, 90
Sausage & Mushroom Stuffed Squash, 256
Sausage Fettuccine Bake, 248
Sausage Lasagna Rolls, 248
Smoked Turkey Sausage Pizza, 259
Side Dish
Apple-Almond Stuffing, 36
Soups, Chili & Sandwiches
Hawaiian Kielbasa Sandwiches, 156
Hearty Italian Sandwiches, 192
Italian Sausage Soup, 188
Pepperoni Pizza Chili, 195
Sausage Sliders with Cran-Apple Slaw, 69
Simple Italian Sausage Soup, 188
Touchdown Brat Sliders, 195

SIDE DISHES *(also see Condiments; Salads & Salad Dressing)*
Almond Rice Pilaf, 130
Apple-Almond Stuffing, 36
Broiled Parmesan Tomatoes, 98
Brown Rice Pilaf, 46
Brussels Sprouts with Bacon, 138
Carrots with Lemon Butter, 47
Classy Carrots, 60
Creamy Sweet Corn with Okra, 66
Crispy Ranch Fries, 58
Dill Potato Wedges, 8
Farmer's Market Squash Saute, 59
Garlic Butter Topping, 104
Garlic Carrots, 132
✓Garlic Green Bean Medley, 275
Greek Green Bean Medley, 61
Green Bean & Corn Medley, 48
Green Beans with Tomatoes & Basil, 26
Grilled Potato Packets, 135
Herbed Asparagus, 50
Herbed Potato Fans, 51
Italian Dressed Broccoli, 68
Italian Mushrooms, 138
Jazzed-Up Green Bean Casserole, 37
Lemon-Dill Couscous, 99

✓ Recipe Includes Nutrition Facts (and Diabetic Exchanges when applicable)

SIDE DISHES *(continued)*
Lemon-Feta Angel Hair, 52
✓Lemon Pasta with Spinach, 273
Lemon-Pepper Broccoli, 8
Lemon-Sesame Veggie Kabobs, 147
Maple-Dijon Sprout Medley, 36
Maple-Glazed Green Beans, 134
Minted Sugar Snap Peas, 107
Nutty Broccoli, 57
Orzo Pilaf with Mushrooms, 64
Peachy Green Beans, 136
Potato and Mushroom Gratin, 26
Prosciutto-Wrapped Asparagus with Raspberry Sauce, 86
Red Pepper Corn, 55
Roasted Rosemary Potatoes, 134
Roasted Winter Vegetables, 133
Sauteed Spinach, 65
Slow-Cooked Broccoli, 132
Spiced Sweet Potato Fries, 69
Spinach & Feta Saute, 99
Squash & Carrot Saute, 136
Sweet Corn with Parmesan and Cilantro, 31
Tangerine Tabbouleh, 136
Tarragon Mashed Potato Casserole, 34
Zesty Lemon Broccoli, 107
Zucchini & Corn with Cilantro, 53

SLOW COOKER RECIPES
Appetizers & Beverages
Butterscotch Mulled Cider, 282
Chai Tea, 184
Green Olive Dip, 156
Hot Spiced Wine, 286
Mulled Dr. Pepper, 158
Reuben Spread, 286
Seafood Cheese Dip, 152
Simmered Smoked Links, 151
Slow Cooker Cheese Dip, 95
Desserts
Blueberry Cobbler, 95
Glazed Cinnamon Apples, 168
Minty Hot Fudge Sundae Cake, 171
Slow-Cooker Bread Pudding, 172
Main Dishes
Beef & Tortellini Marinara with Green Beans, 161
Butter & Herb Turkey, 167
Chicken & Vegetables with Mustard-Herb Sauce, 170
Cranberry-Dijon Pork Roast, 159
Cranberry-Ginger Pork Ribs, 168
Family-Favorite Beef Roast, 166
Fiesta-Twisted Brunswick Stew, 162
French Onion Portobello Brisket, 166
Gingered Short Ribs with Green Rice, 165
Harvest Butternut & Pork Stew, 162
Hash Brown Egg Breakfast, 180
Herb Stuffed Chops, 161
Italian Sausages with Provolone, 158
Moist Turkey Breast with White Wine Gravy, 169
Mom's Celery Seed Brisket, 173
Mom's Scalloped Potatoes and Ham, 158
Moroccan Chicken, 160
Old-World Corned Beef and Vegetables, 168
Pulled Pork Taters, 170
Satisfying Beef Stew, 196
Savory Mushroom & Herb Pork Roast, 173
Slow-Cooked Cabbage Rolls, 165
Slow-Cooked Ham 'n' Broccoli, 167
Slow-Cooked Pork Tacos, 164
Slow Cooker Chicken Curry, 172
Southern Pulled Pork, 156
Stout & Honey Beef Roast, 118
Sweet-and-Sour Beef Stew, 162
Tangy Tomato Pork Chops, 160
Tex-Mex Chicken with Black Beans & Rice, 171
Vegetarian Stuffed Peppers, 157
Sandwiches
Hawaiian Kielbasa Sandwiches, 156
Hearty Italian Sandwiches, 192
Hoisin Pork Wraps, 191
Hot Ham Sandwiches, 194
Very Best Barbecue Beef Sandwiches, 191
Side Dishes
Italian Mushrooms, 138
Jazzed-Up Green Bean Casserole, 37
Slow-Cooked Broccoli, 132
Soups, Stews & Chili
Bacon-Beef Barley Soup, 159
Butternut Squash Soup, 166
Chipotle-Black Bean Chili, 190
Fiesta-Twisted Brunswick Stew, 162
Harvest Butternut & Pork Stew, 162
Satisfying Beef Stew, 196
Spicy Turkey Bean Soup, 169
Tex-Mex Chili with a Cincinnati Twist, 164

SOUPS, STEWS & CHILI
Au Gratin Chicken Chowder, 190
Bacon-Beef Barley Soup, 159
Beef Tip Stew over Fussili, 120
Butternut Squash Soup, 166

✓ Recipe Includes Nutrition Facts (and Diabetic Exchanges when applicable)

Cheddar Broccoli Soup, 56
Cheddar Seafood Chowder, 188
Chipotle-Black Bean Chili, 190
Creamy Chicken Rice Soup, 192
Fiesta-Twisted Brunswick Stew, 162
Harvest Butternut & Pork Stew, 162
Hearty Vegetable Beef Soup, 197
Italian Bean Soup, 194
Italian Sausage Soup, 188
Jamaican Ham and Bean Soup, 67
Lemon-Chicken Velvet Soup, 192
Pepperoni Pizza Chili, 195
Satisfying Beef Stew, 196
Spicy Turkey Bean Soup, 169
Sweet-and-Sour Beef Stew, 162
Sweet Potato Chili Bake, 265
Sweet Potato Pork Stew, 193
Tex-Mex Chili with a Cincinnati Twist, 164
Turkey Chili with Pasta, 32
White Chili with a Kick, 196

SPINACH
Autumn Tossed Salad, 34
Florentine Meatballs, 300
Italian Spinach Salad, 104
✓Lemon Pasta with Spinach, 273
Ravioli with Creamy Squash Sauce, 214
Sauteed Spinach, 65
Scalloped Shrimp and Potatoes, 91
Shrimp Risotto, 115
Spinach & Feta Saute, 99
Spinach-Stuffed Beef Tenderloin, 252
Three-Cheese Florentine Burgers, 189
✓Warm Szechuan Shrimp and Spinach Salad, 269

STOVETOP ENTREES
(also see Sandwiches; Soups, Stews & Chili)
Beef & Ground Beef
Asian Beef with Noodles, 54
Beef and Wild Rice Medley, 306
Beef Chow Mein, 214
Beef Tip Stew over Fusilli, 120
Ground Beef Macaroni Casserole, 74
Hamburger Steaks with Mushroom Gravy, 47
Hearty Mac & Cheese, 79
Italian Stroganoff, 300
Skillet Lasagna, 115
Sloppy Pizza Joes, 63
Smothered Italian Chicken, 121
Steaks with Molasses-Glazed Onions, 51
Stovetop Italian Macaroni, 68

Chicken
Asian Chicken Skillet, 209
Black Bean-Chicken Quesadillas, 55
Cashew Chicken with Noodles, 18
Chicken in Lime Butter, 211
Chicken Marsala, 50
Creole Chicken, 305
Family-Favorite Italian Chicken, 212
Greek Chicken Penne, 208
Italian Chicken Cordon Bleu, 208
Mediterranean Chicken Stir-Fry, 127
New Orleans Gumbo, 24
Pumpkin-Curry Chicken Over Cashew Rice, 204
Quick Sweet-and-Sour Chicken, 84
Quicker Chicken and Dumplings, 200
Roasted Pepper Chicken Penne, 212
Santa Fe Chicken, 207
Simply Seasoned Chicken, 59
Skillet Ziti with Chicken and Broccoli, 272
Smoky Chicken Enchilada Skillet, 213
Sweet & Sour Pineapple Chicken, 306

Fish & Seafood
BBQ Shrimp Quesadillas, 307
Caesar Shrimp and Pasta, 92
Captain Russell's Jambalaya, 25
Catfish Po'boys, 203
Champagne Salmon & Fettuccine, 206
Chimichurri Shrimp Skillet, 210
Coquille St. Jacques, 201
Creole Shrimp & Sausage, 125
Curry Scallops and Rice, 120
Garlic Butter Shrimp, 86
Honey-Pecan Baked Cod, 201
Orange Roughy Italiano, 207
Scalloped Shrimp and Potatoes, 91
Scallops with Thai Sauce, 202
✓Shrimp & Tomato Linguine Toss, 272
Shrimp Linguine with Parmesan Cream Sauce, 65
Shrimp Risotto, 115
Southern Shrimp & Grits, 200
Tilapia with Green Beans Amandine, 112
Tuna Zucchini Cakes, 206

Meatless
Pepper Jack Mac, 49
Portobello & Basil Cheese Tortellini, 304
Ravioli with Creamy Squash Sauce, 214
Southwestern Vegetables & Rice, 215
Squash Fajitas with Goat Cheese, 215
Tortellini with Tomato-Cream Sauce, 297

✓ Recipe Includes Nutrition Facts (and Diabetic Exchanges when applicable)

STOVETOP ENTREES *(continued)*

Pork

Barbecue Pork and Penne Skillet, 214
Chinese Pork 'n' Noodles, 307
Chipotle Chili Dogs, 58
Flavorful Pork Chops, 60
Ginger Pork Stir-Fry, 10
Pork Chops Normandy, 210
Pork Chops with Mustard Sauce, 204
Pork Fried Rice, 301
Soda Pop Chops with Smashed Potatoes, 117
Spicy Tomato Pork Chops, 64
Stuffing-Stuffed Pork Chops, 298
Summer Carbonara, 305
Teriyaki Pork, 304

Sausage

Creamy Sausage & Bow Ties, 209
Home-Style Sausage Gravy and Biscuits, 202
Polenta Rounds with Sausage Ragout, 14

Turkey

Pecan-Crusted Turkey Cutlets, 48
Tangy Turkey Saute, 57
Three-Chili Turkey Tacos, 53
Turkey Penne with Lemon Cream Sauce, 123
✓Turkey Stir-Fry with Cabbage, 274

STRAWBERRIES

Asti & Strawberries Dessert, 227
Berry-Topped Puff Pancake, 183
Crunchy Romaine Strawberry Salad, 130
Dunked Strawberries, 12
Fruit-Filled Cupcakes, 74
Rhubarb Strawberry Granita, 95
Strawberry Breakfast Shortcakes, 79
Strawberry Ginger Tart, 228
Strawberry Pies, 89
Summer Fruit Pizza, 31
Three-Berry Freezer Jam, 313
Tropical Strawberry Pops, 73
Very Berry Bruschetta, 226

SUMMER SQUASH *(also see Zucchini)*

Farmer's Market Squash Saute, 59
Squash & Carrot Saute, 136
Squash Fajitas with Goat Cheese, 215
Summer Carbonara, 305

SWEET POTATOES

Raisin Sweet Potato Cookies, 223
Rigatoni with Roasted Sweet Potatoes, 111
Spiced Sweet Potato Fries, 69
Sweet Potato Chili Bake, 265
Sweet Potato Pork Stew, 193

TOMATOES & TOMATILLOS

Avocado-Tomato Salad, 12
Bacon & Tomato-Topped Haddock, 255
Broiled Parmesan Tomatoes, 98
Fire-Roasted Salsa, 99
Fresh Tomato & Cucumber Salad, 134
Fresh Tomato Bruschetta, 284
Green Beans with Tomatoes & Basil, 26
Pork & Tomato Pasta Sauce, 90
Roasted Grape Tomatoes, 283
Salsa Roja, 106
✓Shrimp & Tomato Linguine Toss, 272
Spicy Tomato Pork Chops, 64
Tangy Tomato Pork Chops, 160
Tomatillo Salsa, 146
Tomato and Green Pepper Omelet, 294
Tomato and Onion Salmon, 211
Tomato Olive Quiche, 185

TURKEY

Main Dishes

Apple-Sage Roasted Turkey, 35
Beef 'n' Turkey Meat Loaf, 263
Broccoli Turkey Pie, 298
Butter & Herb Turkey, 167
Hearty Alfredo Potatoes, 253
Moist Turkey Breast with White Wine Gravy, 169
Pecan-Crusted Turkey Cutlets, 48
Smoked Turkey Sausage Pizza, 259
Tangy Turkey Saute, 57
Three-Chili Turkey Tacos, 53
Turkey Penne with Lemon Cream Sauce, 123
✓Turkey Stir-Fry with Cabbage, 274

Salad & Sandwiches

Orange Turkey Croissants, 100
Summer Turkey Salads, 123
Thai Turkey Salad Pitas, 299

Soup & Chili

Spicy Turkey Bean Soup, 169
Turkey Chili with Pasta, 32

VEGETABLES *(also see specific kinds)*

Chicken & Vegetables with Mustard-Herb Sauce, 170
Creamy Veggie Meatballs, 296
Garlic Butter Topping, 104
Harvest Vegetable Bake, 252
Hearty Vegetable Beef Soup, 197
Lemon-Sesame Veggie Kabobs, 147

✓ Recipe Includes Nutrition Facts (and Diabetic Exchanges when applicable)

Old-World Corned Beef and Vegetables, 168
Party Vegetable Dip, 22
Roasted Chicken with Veggies, 262
Roasted Winter Vegetables, 133
Southwestern Vegetables & Rice, 215
Vegetable-Stuffed Grilled Portobellos, 124
Vegetarian Stuffed Peppers, 157
Veggie Calzones, 244

WINTER SQUASH *(also see Pumpkin)*
Butternut Squash Soup, 166
Harvest Butternut & Pork Stew, 162
Moroccan Chicken, 160
Ravioli with Creamy Squash Sauce, 214
Roasted Winter Vegetables, 133
Sausage & Mushroom Stuffed Squash, 256

YOGURT
Berry Breakfast Smoothies, 16
Citrus Pound Cake, 231
Greek Grilled Chicken Pitas, 243
Raspberry Pomegranate Smoothies, 99
Strawberry Breakfast Shortcakes, 79

ZUCCHINI *(also see Summer Squash)*
Crescent Zucchini Pie, 177
Crispy Grilled Zucchini with Marinara, 281
Farmer's Market Squash Saute, 59
Mediterranean Chicken Stir-Fry, 127
Orange Roughy Italiano, 207
Pina Colada Jam, 313
Summer Carbonara, 305
Tuna Zucchini Cakes, 206
Zucchini & Corn with Cilantro, 53

Alphabetical Index

This handy index lists every recipe in alphabetical order, so you can easily locate the dishes you enjoy most.

A
Almond & Mandarin Orange Salad, 18
Almond Chocolate Torte, 227
Almond Rice Pilaf, 130
Apple-Almond Stuffing, 36
Apple Cinnamon Omelet, 293
Apple-Sage Roasted Turkey, 35
Apple-Stuffed Pork Tenderloins, 260
Apricot & White Chocolate Coffee Cake, 29
Apricot Baked Ham, 261
Apricot Thumbprints, 43
Artichoke Tuna Melt, 113
Asian Beef with Noodles, 54
Asian Chicken Skillet, 209
Asti & Strawberries Dessert, 227
Au Gratin Chicken Chowder, 190
Autumn Harvest Cobbler, 220
Autumn Tossed Salad, 34
Avocado Chicken Salad, 62
Avocado-Tomato Salad, 12

B
Bacon & Egg Potato Salad, 31
Bacon & Tomato-Topped Haddock, 255
Bacon-Beef Barley Soup, 159
Bacon-Wrapped Apricot Bites, 288
Baja Chicken Taco Pizza, 259
Baked Fruit Compote, 182
Baked Ham with Honey-Chipotle Glaze, 26
Balsamic Arugula Salad, 14
Banana Macadamia Muffins, 180
✓Banana-Pineapple Ice, 276
Barbecue Chicken Tacos, 100
Barbecue Pork and Penne Skillet, 214
Basil-Butter Steaks with Roasted Potatoes, 119
BBQ Shrimp Quesadillas, 307
Beef & Tortellini Marinara with Green Beans, 161
Beef 'n' Turkey Meat Loaf, 263
Beef and Wild Rice Medley, 306
Beef Chow Mein, 214
Beef Tip Stew over Fusilli, 120
Berry Blue Pops, 76
Berry Breakfast Smoothies, 16
Berry-Topped Puff Pancake, 183
Best Lime Tart, 222
Big Daddy's BBQ Ribs, 260
Black Bean-Chicken Quesadillas, 55
Blend of the Bayou, 258
Blue Cheese Walnut Tart, 247
Blueberry Cheesecake Parfait, 103
Blueberry Cobbler, 95
Blueberry Fizz Pops, 76
Bourbon Brat Skewers, 308
Breaded Brunch Bacon, 28
Breakfast Biscuit Cups, 183
Breakfast Tortas, 182
Brie and Sausage Brunch Bake, 176
Brie Phyllo Cups, 95
Broccoli-Apple Salad, 63

✓ Recipe Includes Nutrition Facts (and Diabetic Exchanges when applicable)

Broccoli Turkey Pie, 298
Broiled Parmesan Tomatoes, 98
Broiled Steaks with Parmesan-Sage Potatoes, 110
Brown Rice Pilaf, 46
Brunch Beignets, 25
Brussels Sprouts with Bacon, 138
Burrito Pie, 245
Butter Almond Cookies, 43
Butter & Herb Turkey, 167
Butter Brickle Ice Cream Pie, 147
Butter Pecan Biscotti, 142
Butternut Squash Soup, 166
Butterscotch Mulled Cider, 282

C

Caesar Shrimp and Pasta, 92
Caesar Tortellini Salad, 137
Cajun Pecan Catfish, 66
Cajun Shrimp Lasagna Roll-Ups, 255
Can-Can Chicken, 308
Candied Pumpkin Spice Pecans, 151
Candy Corn Quesadillas, 33
Captain Russell's Jambalaya, 25
Caramel Macchiato Floats, 144
Caramel-Pecan Dream Bars, 225
Caramelized Grapefruit Salad, 137
Caribbean Chips with Apricot Salsa, 67
Caribbean Shrimp Spring Rolls, 122
Carrots with Lemon Butter, 47
Cashew Chicken with Noodles, 18
Catfish Po'boys, 203
Chai Tea, 184
Champagne Salmon & Fettuccine, 206
Cheddar & Bacon Burgers, 152
Cheddar Broccoli Soup, 56
Cheddar Seafood Chowder, 188
Cherry-Barbecue Pork Ribs, 30
Cherry-Chocolate Pudgy Pie, 148
Cherry Cordial Cake Balls, 144
Cherry Nut Cookies, 237
Chesapeake Snack Mix, 107
Chicken & Cheese Noodle Bake, 242
Chicken and Egg Hash, 179
Chicken & Pear Bundles, 111
Chicken & Vegetables with Mustard-Herb Sauce, 170
Chicken Cheese Strata, 114
Chicken Club Casseroles, 246
Chicken in Lime Butter, 211
Chicken Loaf with Mushroom Gravy, 261
Chicken Marsala, 50
Chicken Mole Casserole, 114
Chicken Skewers with Sweet & Spicy Marmalade, 280
Chicken Tetrazzini, 81
✓Chili-Apricot Pork Chops, 273
Chili Baked Brie, 280
Chili-Cheese Egg Rolls, 285
Chimichurri Shrimp Skillet, 210
Chinese Pork 'n' Noodles, 307
Chipotle-Black Bean Chili, 190
Chipotle Chili Dogs, 58
Chipotle-Honey Grilled T-Bones, 309
Chipotle-Orange Pork Chops, 301
Chive and Cheese Breadsticks, 81
Chocolate Cannoli Cake Roll, 224
Chocolate Caramel Cookies, 86
Chocolate Chip Cheesecake, 220
Chocolate Cookie Cheesecake, 226
Chocolate Frosted Peanut Butter Cupcakes, 80
Chocolate-Peanut Cheesecake Bars, 231
Chorizo Salsa Omelet, 293
Cider-Glazed Pork Chops with Carrots, 112
Cider Wassail Punch, 282
Cilantro-Pepita Pesto, 312
Cinnamon & Sugar Cake, 219
Cinnamon Berry Cider, 73
Cinnamon Flapjacks, 29
Cinnamon Roll Coffee Cake, 185
Citrus Pound Cake, 231
Citrus Steak Salad, 132
Classy Carrots, 60
Coconut Citrus Bars, 233
Coffee & Cream Doughnuts, 144
Coffee Cake Muffins, 143
Colorful Spiral Pasta Salad, 152
Company Lasagna, 242
Confetti Cornmeal Muffins, 32
Cool Watermelon Pops, 76
Coquille St. Jacques, 201
Cornmeal-Wheat Pancakes, 16
Country Chicken Casserole, 244
Crab Quiche, 176
Crab-Stuffed Tilapia, 253
Cranberry BBQ Sauce, 39
Cranberry-Chili Cheese Spread, 102
Cranberry-Dijon Pork Roast, 159
Cranberry-Ginger Pork Ribs, 168
Cranberry Orange Cake, 234
Cranberry Orange Pancakes, 177
Cranberry-Pear Crisp, 221
Cranberry-Pecan Coffee Cake, 178
Crazy-Colored Fruit Pops, 76
Creamy Chicken Enchiladas, 240
Creamy Chicken Rice Soup, 192
Creamy Lemon Cake Bars, 89
Creamy Sausage & Bow Ties, 209
Creamy Sweet Corn with Okra, 66
Creamy Taco Dressing, 102
Creamy Veggie Meatballs, 296
Creole Chicken, 305

✓ Recipe Includes Nutrition Facts (and Diabetic Exchanges when applicable)

Creole Shrimp & Sausage, 125
Crescent Zucchini Pie, 177
Crispy Grilled Zucchini with Marinara, 281
Crispy Ranch Fries, 58
Crumb-Coated Cod Fillets, 205
✓Crumb-Coated Red Snapper, 269
Crunchy Romaine Strawberry Salad, 130
Crustless Quiche Bake, 179
Curried Chicken Salad, 92
Curry Scallops and Rice, 120

D

Deep-Fried Candy Bars on a Stick, 225
Dill Potato Wedges, 8
Double Chip Cookies, 148
Double-Chocolate Holiday Pie, 234
Double Chocolate Truffles, 222
Drizzled Peppermint Cookies, 39
Dunked Strawberries, 12

E

Easy Beef-Stuffed Shells, 247
Easy Hummus, 87
Easy Refrigerator Pickles, 312
Eggnog Pie, 236
Elegant Pumpkin Pie, 235
Elegant Smoked Salmon Strata, 241

F

Family-Favorite Beef Roast, 166
Family-Favorite Italian Chicken, 212
Farmer's Market Squash Saute, 59
✓Fiesta Taco Salads, 271
Fiesta-Twisted Brunswick Stew, 162
Fire-Roasted Salsa, 99
Flavorful Pork Chops, 60
Florentine Meatballs, 300
Fluffy Lemon Squares, 218
Fluted Tiramisu Cake, 219
Foolproof Mushrooms, 92
French Onion Portobello Brisket, 166
French Quarter Cheese Spread, 281
French Vanilla Mocha, 144
Fresh Peach Lemonade, 84
Fresh Tomato & Cucumber Salad, 134
Fresh Tomato Bruschetta, 284
Fried Rice Omelet, 292
Frozen Macaroon Dessert, 89
Fruit & Nut Cereal Bars, 148
Fruit-Filled Cupcakes, 74

G

Game-Night Nacho Pizza, 75
✓Garden Tuna Pita Sandwiches, 276
Garlic Butter Shrimp, 86
Garlic Butter Topping, 104
Garlic Carrots, 132
Garlic-Cheese Flat Bread, 62
Garlic Chicken Breasts, 87
✓Garlic Green Bean Medley, 275
German Chocolate Bars, 224
German Chocolate Thumbprint Cookies, 230
Ginger Pork Stir-Fry, 10
Gingerbread Scones with Lemon Butter, 181
Gingered Short Ribs with Green Rice, 165
Glazed Cinnamon Apples, 168
Glazed Ornament Cookies, 40
✓Greek Chicken Dinner, 271
Greek Chicken Penne, 208
Greek Green Bean Medley, 61
Greek Grilled Chicken Pitas, 243
Green Bean & Corn Medley, 48
Green Beans with Tomatoes & Basil, 26
Green Chili Beef Dip, 287
Green Olive Dip, 156
Green Sherbet Froggie, 79
Grilled Asian Steak, 310
Grilled Honey-Lime Chicken, 310
Grilled Jerk Chops, 121
Grilled Pineapple Sundaes, 18
Grilled Potato Packets, 135
✓Grilled Salmon with Avocado Salsa, 277
Grilled Sirloin with Chili-Beer Barbecue Sauce, 310
Grilled Stuffed Peppers, 311
Ground Beef Macaroni Casserole, 74

H

Halibut with Orange Salsa, 263
Ham and Avocado Scramble, 16
Ham and Broccoli Puffs, 288
Ham & Cheese Ziti, 299
Ham & Jack Pudgy Pie, 149
Ham and Swiss Omelet, 292
Hamburger Steaks with Mushroom Gravy, 47
Harvest Butternut & Pork Stew, 162
Harvest Vegetable Bake, 252
Hash Brown Egg Breakfast, 180
Hash Brown Pancetta Casserole, 184
Hawaiian Cheese Bread, 287
Hawaiian Kielbasa Sandwiches, 156
Hearty Alfredo Potatoes, 253
Hearty Barley Bake, 264
Hearty Italian Sandwiches, 192
Hearty Mac & Cheese, 79
Hearty Vegetable Beef Soup, 197
Heavenly Hot Chocolate Mix, 38
Herb Stuffed Chops, 161
Herbed Asparagus, 50

✓ Recipe Includes Nutrition Facts (and Diabetic Exchanges when applicable)

Herbed Potato Fans, 51
Hoisin Pork Wraps, 191
Holiday Pinwheel Cookies, 40
Home-Style Sausage Gravy and Biscuits, 202
Honey-Pecan Baked Cod, 201
Hot Fruit Punch, 152
Hot Fudge Sauce, 103
Hot Ham Sandwiches, 194
Hot Spiced Wine, 286
Hugs 'n' Kisses Brownie, 229

I

Iced Skinny Hazelnut Latte, 144
Italian Bean Soup, 194
Italian Brunch Bake, 246
Italian Chicken Cordon Bleu, 208
Italian Dressed Broccoli, 68
Italian Mushrooms, 138
Italian Omelet, 294
Italian Roast Beef Sandwiches, 56
Italian Sausage Soup, 188
Italian Sausages with Provolone, 158
Italian Snack Mix, 100
Italian Spinach Salad, 104
Italian Spumoni Cookies, 41
Italian Stroganoff, 300

J

Jamaican Ham and Bean Soup, 67
Jazzed-Up Green Bean Casserole, 37
Jim's Honey-Glazed Ham, 262
Joyful Cutout Cookies, 42
✓Just Peachy Pork Tenderloin, 270

K

Kahlua Fudge, 224
Key Lime Bites, 236

L

Lattice Chicken Potpie, 257
Layered Artichoke Cheese Spread, 289
Lemon & Rosemary Shortbread Cookies, 223
Lemon-Caper Baked Cod, 61
Lemon-Chicken Velvet Soup, 192
Lemon Cranberry Sauce, 36
Lemon Cream Cake, 230
Lemon-Dill Couscous, 99
Lemon-Feta Angel Hair, 52
✓Lemon Pasta with Spinach, 273
Lemon-Pepper Broccoli, 8
Lemon-Sesame Veggie Kabobs, 147
Lemon Shortbreads, 229
Lemon Spiced Tea, 10
Lemonade Fruit Salad, 133

M

Make-Ahead Lasagna, 245
Makeover Chocolate Truffle Dessert, 27
Maple Balsamic Dressing, 102
Maple-Dijon Sprout Medley, 36
Maple-Glazed Green Beans, 134
Maple-Glazed Salmon, 8
Mardi Gras Cupcakes, 24
Marinated Antipasto Platter, 289
Marmalade-Glazed Steaks, 87
Marshmallow Snowmen, 38
Meat-atarian Sub, 189
Meatball Sub, 75
Mediterranean Chicken Stir-Fry, 127
Mediterranean Roasted Salmon, 52
Melon-Mango Salsa, 284
Mexican Chicken Alfredo, 249
Mexican Grilled Cheese Sandwiches, 116
Mexican Lasagna, 257
Mexican-Seasoned Grilled Chicken, 309
Mexican Smothered Chicken Thighs, 254
Mimosa Roasted Chicken, 252
Mini Reuben Casseroles, 117
Minted Sugar Snap Peas, 107
Minty Hot Fudge Sundae Cake, 171
Mocha Dessert Fondue, 23
Moist Turkey Breast with White Wine Gravy, 169
Mom's Celery Seed Brisket, 173
Mom's Scalloped Potatoes and Ham, 158
Monterey Ranch Bread, 84
Moroccan Chicken, 160
Mozzarella Sticks, 91
Mulled Dr. Pepper, 158

N

New Orleans Gumbo, 24
Nutty Broccoli, 57

O

Old-World Corned Beef and Vegetables, 168
Onion Rings, 73
Orange Chicken Wraps, 197
✓Orange-Coconut Angel Food Cake, 276
Orange-Glazed Ham Steaks, 46
Orange Marmalade Cake Sauce, 54
Orange-Peach Thirst Quencher, 73
Orange Roughy Italiano, 207
Orange-Spiced Chicken, 146
Orange Turkey Croissants, 100
Orzo Pilaf with Mushrooms, 64
Over-the-Top Blueberry Bread Pudding, 218

✓ Recipe Includes Nutrition Facts (and Diabetic Exchanges when applicable)

P

Parmesan Baked Chicken, 297
Parmesan-Coated Brie, 102
Party Vegetable Dip, 22
Peach-Glazed Meatballs, 283
Peachy Green Beans, 136
Peachy Pork Chops, 264
Peanut Butter and Jelly Omelet, 295
Peanut Butter Blondies, 78
Peanut Butter Blossoms, 43
Peanut Butter Clusters, 92
Pecan Cheese Logs, 23
Pecan-Crusted Turkey Cutlets, 48
Pepper Jack Mac, 49
Pepperoni Pizza, 72
Pepperoni Pizza Chili, 195
Pesto Dip with Parmesan Toast, 90
Pesto Halibut, 89
Pina Colada Jam, 313
Pistachio Cake, 236
Pistachio Meringue Sundaes, 14
Polenta Rounds with Sausage Ragout, 14
Poppy Seed Slaw, 135
Porcini-Crusted Pork with Polenta, 262
Pork & Tomato Pasta Sauce, 90
Pork Chops Normandy, 210
Pork Chops with Mustard Sauce, 204
Pork Fried Rice, 301
Pork Tenderloins with Wild Rice, 126
Portobello & Basil Cheese Tortellini, 304
Potato & Bacon Frittata, 296
Potato and Mushroom Gratin, 26
Potato Bacon Omelet, 295
Prosciutto-Wrapped Asparagus with Raspberry Sauce, 86
Provencal Bean Salad, 138
Pull-Apart Caramel Coffee Cake, 179
Pulled Pork Taters, 170
Pumpkin-Curry Chicken Over Cashew Rice, 204
Pumpkin Streusel Cupcakes, 232
Pumpkin Walnut Squares, 233

Q

Quick Cookie Mix, 42
Quick Sweet-and-Sour Chicken, 84
Quicker Chicken and Dumplings, 200

R

Raisin Sweet Potato Cookies, 223
Raspberry Pomegranate Smoothies, 99
Ravioli with Creamy Squash Sauce, 214
Red Pepper & Feta Dip, 150
Red Pepper Corn, 55
Reuben Spread, 286
Reunion Casserole, 256
Rhubarb Strawberry Granita, 95
Rich Hazelnut Coffee, 282
Rigatoni with Roasted Sweet Potatoes, 111
Roast Beef Spirals, 283
Roast Pork with Cherry-Almond Glaze, 258
Roasted Chicken with Lemon Sauce, 265
Roasted Chicken with Veggies, 262
Roasted Grape Tomatoes, 283
Roasted Pepper Chicken Penne, 212
Roasted Rosemary Potatoes, 134
Roasted Winter Vegetables, 133
Rocky Road Cookie Pizza, 151
Rocky Road Grilled Banana Splits, 232
Romaine and Walnut Salad, 49

S

✓Salsa Black Bean Burgers, 268
Salsa Roja, 106
Salted Peanut Bars, 78
Santa Fe Chicken, 207
Satisfying Beef Stew, 196
✓Saucy Peach-Balsamic Chicken, 268
Sausage & Mushroom Stuffed Squash, 256
Sausage-Apple Puff Pancake, 181
Sausage Fettuccine Bake, 248
Sausage Lasagna Rolls, 248
Sausage Sliders with Cran-Apple Slaw, 69
Sauteed Spinach, 65
Savory Mushroom & Herb Pork Roast, 173
Scalloped Shrimp and Potatoes, 91
Scallops with Thai Sauce, 202
Scrambled Eggs with the Works, 29
Seafood Cheese Dip, 152
Sensational Stuffed Mushrooms, 23
✓Sesame-Ginger Steak Salad, 277
Shrimp & Avocado Salads, 213
✓Shrimp & Tomato Linguine Toss, 272
Shrimp Linguine with Parmesan Cream Sauce, 65
Shrimp Risotto, 115
Shrimp Skewers with Asian Quinoa, 127
Sicilian Salad, 104
Simmered Smoked Links, 151
Simply Seasoned Chicken, 59
Skillet Lasagna, 115
✓Skillet Ziti with Chicken and Broccoli, 272
Sloppy Joe Pizza, 205
Sloppy Pizza Joes, 63
Slow-Cooked Broccoli, 132
Slow-Cooked Cabbage Rolls, 165
Slow-Cooked Ham 'n' Broccoli, 167
Slow-Cooked Pork Tacos, 164
Slow-Cooker Bread Pudding, 172
Slow Cooker Cheese Dip, 95
Slow Cooker Chicken Curry, 172

✓ *Recipe Includes Nutrition Facts (and Diabetic Exchanges when applicable)*

Smoked Salmon Egg Salad, 98
Smoked Turkey Sausage Pizza, 259
Smoky Chicken Enchilada Skillet, 213
S'more-Dipped Cherries, 222
S'more Pudgy Pie, 149
Smothered Italian Chicken, 121
Snickers Cookies, 91
Soda Pop Chops with Smashed Potatoes, 117
Southern Pulled Pork, 156
Southern Shrimp & Grits, 200
Southwest Breakfast Tart, 180
Southwest Enchilada Bake, 246
Southwest Fish Tacos, 12
Southwestern Vegetables & Rice, 215
Spanish Coffee, 145
✓Spiced Pork Medallions with Bourbon Sauce, 275
Spiced Sweet Potato Fries, 69
Spicy Tomato Pork Chops, 64
Spicy Turkey Bean Soup, 169
Spinach & Feta Saute, 99
Spinach-Stuffed Beef Tenderloin, 252
Spooktacular Brownies, 33
Spring Morning Casserole, 241
Squash & Carrot Saute, 136
Squash Fajitas with Goat Cheese, 215
Steak House Burgers, 194
Steaks with Molasses-Glazed Onions, 51
Stout & Honey Beef Roast, 118
Stovetop Italian Macaroni, 68
Strawberry Breakfast Shortcakes, 79
Strawberry Ginger Tart, 228
Strawberry Pies, 89
Stuffed Burger Bundles, 254
Stuffing-Stuffed Pork Chops, 298
Summer Carbonara, 305
Summer Fruit Pizza, 31
Summer Turkey Salads, 123
Sunshine Cobbler, 237
Sweet-and-Sour Beef Stew, 162
Sweet & Sour Pineapple Chicken, 306
Sweet Corn with Parmesan and Cilantro, 31
Sweet Potato Chili Bake, 265
Sweet Potato Pork Stew, 193

T

Tangerine Tabbouleh, 136
Tangy Tomato Pork Chops, 160
Tangy Turkey Saute, 57
Tarragon Butter, 37
Tarragon Mashed Potato Casserole, 34
Tater Tot Casseroles, 242
Tequila-Lime Fruit Salad, 130
Teriyaki Egg Rolls, 10
Teriyaki Pork, 304
Tex-Mex Chicken with Black Beans & Rice, 171
Tex-Mex Chili with a Cincinnati Twist, 164
Thai Fried Chicken, 118
Thai Turkey Salad Pitas, 299
Three-Berry Freezer Jam, 313
Three-Cheese & Pepper Penne, 249
Three-Cheese Florentine Burgers, 189
Three-Chili Turkey Tacos, 53
✓Tilapia Tostadas, 274
Tilapia with Green Beans Amandine, 112
Tipsy Apple Pie, 235
Tiramisu, 240
Tiramisu Crepes, 178
Toffee Triangles, 42
Tomatillo Salsa, 146
Tomato and Green Pepper Omelet, 294
Tomato and Onion Salmon, 211
Tomato Olive Quiche, 185
Tortellini with Tomato-Cream Sauce, 297
Touchdown Brat Sliders, 195
Triple-Chocolate Cake with Raspberry Sauce, 228
Tropical Guacamole, 285
Tropical Strawberry Pops, 73
Tuna Zucchini Cakes, 206
Turkey Chili with Pasta, 32
Turkey Penne with Lemon Cream Sauce, 123
✓Turkey Stir-Fry with Cabbage, 274

U

Unstuffed Jalapeno Popper Burgers, 124

V

Vegetable-Stuffed Grilled Portobellos, 124
Vegetarian Stuffed Peppers, 157
Veggie Calzones, 244
Very Berry Bruschetta, 226
Very Best Barbecue Beef Sandwiches, 191

W

Waffle Cookies, 220
Wagon Wheel Casserole, 80
✓Warm Szechuan Shrimp and Spinach Salad, 269
Watermelon Spritzer, 243
Whipped Banana Latte, 145
White Chili with a Kick, 196
White Chocolate-Macadamia Snowball Cookies, 40
✓Whole Wheat Blueberry Muffins, 270
Whole Wheat Pasta Bake, 126

Z

Zesty Calzone, 197
Zesty Grilled Sandwiches, 200
Zesty Lemon Broccoli, 107
Zucchini & Corn with Cilantro, 53

✓ Recipe Includes Nutrition Facts (and Diabetic Exchanges when applicable)